Bowled Over

The bowling greens of Britain

Bowled Over
© Historic England 2015

Historic England is the
government's statutory advisor
on all aspects of the historic
environment

Fire Fly Avenue
Swindon SN2 2EH
www.historicengland.org.uk

Series designer Doug Cheeseman
Imaging Jörn Kröger

Series editor Simon Inglis

Production and additional research
Jackie Spreckley

Maps and diagrams Mark Fenton

For image credits see page 226

Malavan Media is a creative
consultancy responsible
for the Played in Britain series

www.playedinbritain.co.uk

Printed by Zrinski, Croatia

ISBN: 978 1 905624 98 0

Bowled Over

The bowling greens of Britain

Hugh Hornby

Editor Simon Inglis

A finely attired woman opens the season at an unidentified bowling green in London in 1910 (*right*), at a time when women's clubs were first starting to be formed in Britain. A century later and mixed clubs are now the norm. Of just over 111,000 players registered in 2015 with Bowls England – the governing body for flat green bowling – 32 per cent were female.

Page Two Keswick, Cumbria, in August 2014 – an early evening game in the Eden Valley League, as Fitz Park Bowling Club, in the red and yellow shirts, host their visitors from Shap in Penrith. Tracing their roots back to 1876, the Fitz Park club has around 75 playing members, including half a dozen juniors and 30 ladies. A second green in the park was known in the 20th century as the 'penny' or 'clog' green, as it was mainly used on a 'pay and play' basis by working men.

Page One A mixed game of flat green bowls at the Sunderland Bowling Club, Ashbrooke, in 2010. Ashbrooke is a rare example of a surviving Victorian multi-sport club where six different sports are still played. The bowling green was opened in 1889, two years after the main grounds, with the bowls pavilion following in 1906. A view of its interior follows on page 33.

Contents

Gentlemen play bowls and take drinks on the green in front of Hartwell House, Buckinghamshire – one of eight views of the estate painted by Balthasar Nebot in 1738. The individual in the brown, seen pointing, is believed to have been Frederick, Prince of Wales, who was known to have visited nearby Stowe in 1737. Bowling greens, usually laid out as part of formal terraces or parterres, were a common feature of English country gardens in the 17th and early 18th centuries. Many, being narrow, were referred to also as bowling 'alleys', a usage that has confused many a historian (an 'alley' being usually equated with an indoor facility designed for skittles). Twenty years after this scene was captured the green and formal gardens were swept away, followed by the octagonal pond and canal, to make way for a more naturalistic landscape, as was the new fashion. However a model of the original gardens can be seen at Hartwell House, now a hotel and spa owned by the National Trust, while Nebot's paintings are exhibited at the Buckinghamshire County Museum in Aylesbury.

Introduction

by Hugh Hornby

Whenever there is a debate as to which is Britain's 'national sport', invariably football is the winner, closely followed by cricket. Rarely does bowls even rate a mention. Yet taking a long term historical view, bowls has arguably a stronger claim to the title than any other sport.

People of all social classes and both sexes, from childhood to their dotage, have played bowls in Britain for at least 500 years.

They have played on common land and at royal palaces, behind pubs and in the gardens of stately homes, at company sports grounds and in public parks.

For sure the game's popularity has ebbed and flowed over the centuries. But bowls has never gone away. It has always been stitched into the fabric of our sporting landscape, and as such, forms an integral part of our national heritage.

Not that the general public is aware of this. Bowlers today are, on the whole, a modest bunch.

Bowls, in general, suffers from a low profile. It appears rarely on television and hardly at all in the pages of national newspapers.

Most people think of it as a tame, harmless sport, the province only of the older generation. Which in some respects it is, and is by no means the worse for it.

But this perception reflects only a smidgeon of the reality of modern bowls. Furthermore the game can claim a lively past in which large crowds, gambling and showmanship were to the fore.

And it has long been enjoyed by a wider range of the population than most people would imagine.

My own experience of the game began as a schoolboy in the early 1980s, using my late grandfather's 'woods' at the local club in St Michael's on Wyre in Lancashire.

Despite being in a small village, the club has won numerous league titles and remained unbeaten at home in its first 75 years.

My early memories are of President's Day teas, of marking scorecards and of playing doubles on Saturday nights with characters who had been members since the 1930s and knew every inch of the club's crown green. Always they were generous with their advice.

Boarding school and university took me away for a while, but on my return, hours of practice were eventually rewarded with promotion to the first team and then, in 1995, to the North Lancashire & Fylde county team.

Like many enthusiasts, playing has turned out to be only one part of my life in bowling. Apart from captaining three teams, I have served as club secretary for 24 years (and counting), as county secretary and as a county selector.

As seen on the right, I also bear another, weighty responsibility.

Such devotion is hardly uncommon. When politicians talk about the values of volunteering, they need look no further than bowls. There are volunteers such as myself at every club, if not taking on official duties then coaching or refereeing, tending

the bar or the flower beds, making sandwiches or maintaining a website. It is my fervent hope that, as a result of this book, more will also take on the much needed role of club historian and archivist.

History and heritage are, after all, the core themes of this book.

But they cannot be studied only in libraries. Rather, in the spirit of *Played in Britain*, myself and the team, led by editor Simon Inglis, have been out and about in the field since 2005, with notebooks and cameras.

Bowls presents a challenge unlike every other sport in this respect, for there are over 7,400 clubs spread around England, Scotland and Wales, plus dozens more locations where greens once lay. I alone have visited some 500 clubs since research began in 2005.

But it is thanks to this approach that a picture of bowls in Britain, with all its subtle local variations, has been able to emerge, one that has never before been recorded, not least in photographs.

My thanks go to English Heritage and NFU Mutual for their financial support for the book.

Inevitably there will be clubs whose members will feel they should have been included. In certain areas readers may wish to consult other *Played in Britain* titles which have chapters of their own on bowls. Even then, what we present can only be a summary.

Bowls is, after all, a truly national game, and one which richly deserves the attention that I hope this book will attract.

In addition to playing the game and acting as club secretary at St Michael's Bowling Club, near Preston, Hugh Hornby also tends the green, which lies next to the parish church. When the club formed in 1886 it hired a contractor to clear the site (then an orchard), for the sum of £10. But he went a shilling over budget and had to appear before the committee to plead his case. Fortunately for him, they relented.

Chapter One

Bowls in Britain

Most people, even those with no interest in sport, have at least some basic understanding of the likes of football, rugby, cricket, tennis and golf. Exposure through school or university, through friends or relatives, or through television, lends them all a certain familiarity. Bowls, on the other hand, tends to be more of a mystery. Is it a game played by old men in flat caps in the industrial north, or by old ladies in starched white skirts in the Home Counties? Is it a pub game, or a genuine sport? In this first chapter we set out the basics, for until we understand bowls as it is played today, we cannot begin to appreciate just how deeply rooted it is in our nation's heritage.

Several of the sports that are played in Britain are divided into different types or codes. In horse racing there is flat racing and National Hunt racing. In tennis there is lawn tennis and real tennis. Cycling is split between road racing and track racing.

But only two major sports are split into categories that can be defined by geography.

Most famously there is rugby, split since 1896 into rugby union, which covers most of Britain, and rugby league, concentrated in, although no longer exclusive to, Lancashire, Yorkshire and Cheshire. Then there is bowls, whose geographical divisions are rather more complex.

As this study will show, there have always been different forms of bowling, going back to the time of Shakespeare. But only during the 19th and early 20th centuries did those differences start to polarise along distinctly geographical lines.

Later in this chapter we will briefly mention various forms of indoor bowling. There will also crop up occasional references to the game of skittles, which has often been described in historical accounts as taking place in 'bowling alleys'.

But skittles and bowls are quite different games. In bowling, the aim is to bowl as close as possible to a small target known as a jack.

In skittles the aim is to knock over pins. Hence the modern game known as ten pin bowling is in truth a form of skittles.

Similarly the reason that we describe the action of delivering a ball in cricket as 'bowling' is because in the sport's early years balls were delivered underarm.

Our primary concern however is outdoor bowling in its various forms, and the greens on which they are played. All these variants are detailed in later chapters, but for now our first point of reference is the map opposite.

Flat green bowls

As its name suggests, this type of bowls is played on level greens. Because each green is divided into strips known as rinks (explained later), it is also known as 'rink bowling', and also as 'lawn bowls'.

The flat green game is to be found in every region of Britain, from the Shetlands down to the Scilly Isles. Its clubs are governed by **Bowls England** (formed in 2008 by the merger of the English Bowling Association and English Women's Bowling Association), **Bowls Scotland** (formed in 2011 by the merger of the Scottish Bowling Association and its women's equivalent), the **Welsh Bowling Association** and the **Welsh Women's Bowling Association**.

Some older bowlers still refer to flat green as 'Association rules'.

Flat green is the only form of bowling found in large swathes of southern England and is the sole form of outdoor bowls played in Scotland. This is no coincidence. Flat green bowls played in rinks is in essence a Scottish invention, codified in the 19th century.

It is also the only form of bowls played overseas, in countries such as Canada, Australia and South Africa, under the auspices of the World Bowls organisation.

When you see bowls at the Commonwealth Game, flat green is the version being contested.

'Severall places for Bowling: First, Bowling greens are open wide places made smooth and even, these are generally palled or walled about. Secondly, Bares are open wide places on mores or commons. Thirdly, Bowling-alleys are close places, set apart and made more for privett persons than publick uses. Fourthly, Table Bowling, this is tables of a good length in halls or dineing roomes, on which for exercise and divertisement gentlemen and their associates bowle with little round balls or bullets.'

from **The Academy of Armory** by **Randle Holme**
Server to the Chamber in Extraordinary for Charles II, 1683

Crown green bowls

Crown green bowls, in theory, is played on greens that rise up in the centre to form a crown. In practice, most are simply not flat.

Were it not for the Scots, most bowling in Britain would now be classed as crown green.

But perhaps not under that name. For the main reason why this once mainstream form of bowls came to be known as 'crown green', as occurred in the early 20th century, was to distinguish it from the newly emerging flat, or rink game – much as the old original form of tennis renamed itself 'real tennis' in response to the emergence of lawn tennis in the 1870s. In this respect crown green might have more accurately been renamed 'real bowls' instead.

Overseen by the **British Crown Green Bowling Association** (BCGBA), crown green today is played in a region of England extending from the Lake District down to the West Midlands, and from Shropshire across to South Yorkshire.

It is also played in North Wales and Anglesey, on the Isle of Man, and by a handful of clubs on the east Yorkshire coast, between Bridlington and Whitby.

In fact Whitby is one of crown green's most northerly clubs, along with Elterwater in Cumbria.

Its most southerly is Dorstone, out on a limb in Herefordshire, 25 miles south of its nearest counterpart, in Ludlow.

Crown green is most dominant in Cheshire (where there is only one flat green club), Lancashire, (where there are only five), and in South and West Yorkshire.

Crown green clubs otherwise co-exist with flat green clubs in several towns and cities. In Birmingham and Wetherby there are even clubs with one flat green and one crown green.

The English Bowling Federation

The EBF oversees another form of flat green rink bowling, differing slightly from the World Bowls rules. It covers mainly the east of England, from Northumberland down to Essex, extending to Nottinghamshire and Derbyshire.

Derby itself is unique in hosting clubs belonging to the EBF, to the BCGBA and to Bowls England.

Among several anomalies within the EBF, clubs in the vicinity of Peterborough and Stamford, in Cambridgeshire, affiliate to the EBF county organisation of Northamptonshire. Similarly, the EBF's North Essex county takes in clubs based around Sudbury and Haverhill in Suffolk.

Some clubs affiliate to both the EBF and to Bowls England, since the distinction between the two forms of bowls is relatively fine.

Roving cot

Within EBF territory are clubs centred on Norwich which play a game called 'roving cot', in which the 'cot' (or jack), may be sent to any part of the green, as is the norm in crown green. Yet 'roving cot' clubs also play in rinks at other times, and may even be affiliated to the EBF.

'Roving cot' is also played in the Kidderminster area, but is known there confusingly as 'Federation Bowls', even though there is no connection with the EBF.

Old English Bowls

There is no evidence that this particular form of the game is especially old, but it is certainly a distinctive form of rink bowling, as our later case study will show, and is played by just six clubs in and around the Portsmouth area.

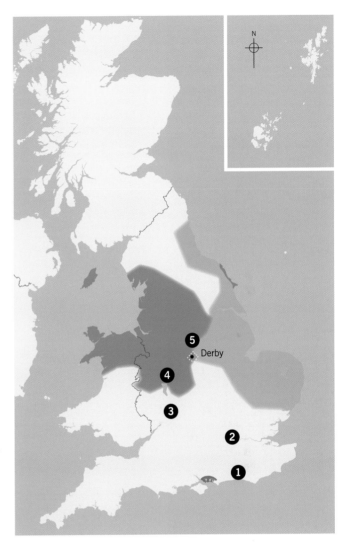

Unaffiliated clubs

Finally around 330 clubs dotted around England, Scotland and Wales remain unaffiliated to any national or regional body. Five are especially interesting from an historical perspective and are the subject of case studies. They are at Lewes (labelled 1 on map), Barnes (2), Hadley (3), Cannock (4) and Chesterfield (5).

Key to map

- flat green bowling areas
- crown green bowling areas
- English Bowling Federation area
- Norwich 'roving cot' and Kidderminster 'Federation' area
- Old English bowls area

▲ The essence of bowls, the one factor that sets it apart from all other games, is its use of balls that possess an in-built 'bias'.

Although numerous ball games exist in which the imparting of 'spin' is integral – games such as cricket, golf, snooker and baseball – only in bowls does the ball, by design, travel along the ground in a curved trajectory.

It does this because its shape has, to a greater or lesser extent, been flattened on one side, traditionally by a skilled craftsman, hand turning the bowl on a lathe.

As Robert Recorde wrote in *The Castle of Knowledge* in 1556, 'A little altering of the one side maketh the bowl to run biasse waies.'

This 'little altering' can clearly be seen on the bowl shown here.

Dating possibly from the 19th century and still in use at **Framlingham Castle Bowling Club** in **Suffolk** (*page 78*), it was made from oak grown locally for use in building ships for the Royal Navy.

Bowls of this vintage generally have a bias stronger than is usual with modern bowls. That is, they travel in a more pronounced curve.

The use of oak and other native timbers by British bowls makers all but ended by the 19th century thanks to the availabilty of a hardwood called **lignum vitae**.

First imported from the Caribbean in the 16th century, lignum vitae ('the wood of life') was ideally suited to bowls making. Dense and durable, its strong cross-grain prevents splitting and its high resin content resists rot. Other uses have included bearings for ship's propellers, tool handles, truncheons and even in Mosquito aircraft during World War Two.

But in common with other hardwoods, supplies became difficult to source, leading to a number of experiments to find an alternative. Finally a breakthrough occurred in 1931 when William Hensell in Australia came up with a 'composite' made from phenol-formaldehyde (the polymer from which Bakelite was produced).

Even so, tradition is so ingrained that even today, at a time when the vast majority of players use composite bowls, many still refer to them as **'woods'** and call out 'good wood' in response to another player's delivery.

That is not to say that lignum vitae woods have disappeared.

As will be noted, they are still in use at some clubs and in certain conditions. **'Fram woods'** however, once common in Suffolk and usually fashioned by a gunsmiths called Norman's, are now a rarity.

▶ An ideal place to demonstrate how bias works is the **Barnes Bowling Club** in **London**, hidden behind the Sun Inn, a Grade II listed building dating from the mid 18th century. Not only is Barnes the last remaining pub green in London, it is also a rare, and probably unique green which, neither flat nor crown, is more typical of how greens were in the London area before the late 19th century (*see page 134*).

That is, it slopes down from the edges to form a relatively flat basin and, crucially, is bowled only from **corner to corner**, rather than in any direction (as in crown green) or in rinks (as in flat green).

This form of bowls is sometimes referred to as Elizabethan by club members, but in truth no-one knows its exact provenance.

Reflecting this heritage, Barnes members still use lignum vitae bowls which, as shown in this multiple exposure photograph, have an unusually strong bias.

Notice in particular how in its final phase the 'wood' approaches the jack (the white ball) from behind. While it is true that the curl of any bowl increases in proportion to its bias as it slows towards the end of its journey, what we see here is a trajectory similar to that of a 'half-bowl,' a medieval form of skittles, explained on page 46.

Before the late 19th century there was no way to quantify the

strength of a bowl's bias. Bowlers instead became familiar with each bowl through trial and error. Often, bowls sold in sets would be numbered 1,2,3 and 4 to help players choose which bowl to use when circumstances required.

Then in the 1870s, the Glasgow bowl makers, Thomas Taylor, who pioneered the art of manufacturing lignum vitae bowls with a consistent bias (of which more later) drew up a scale that is still in use today. As the number on the scale increases,

so does the 'strength' of the bias. Thus the Barnes woods have a bias of 12–13. To put this into context, the current standard used in crown green bowling is 2, and in flat green it is 3.

As noted opposite, bias is created by skilled craftsmen turning the woods on a lathe. However a number of old woods have been identified where metal discs or coins have been inserted into one side, or where molten lead has been poured into holes, for example

at Milton Regis (*page 81*). Thus, bias was created by adding weight rather than changing the shape.

There is one way to counteract bias and bowl in a straight line.

That is to throw it hard, an act known as 'firing' or 'striking'.

Effective though this can be to displace an opponent's bowl – in which context it is known as 'skittling' – it has always been frowned upon by purists as a display of brute force rather than skill.

Modern composite bowls are manufactured to a high degree of accuracy. On the left (made by Thomas Taylor in Glasgow) is a typical flat green bowl. According to the regulations, these can range in size from 116–134mm across their widest point, and weigh up to a maximum of 1.59kg (3lb 8oz). Crown green bowls, as shown on the right (made by Drakes Pride

in Liverpool) are smaller, ranging in weight from 2lbs to 2lbs 12 ozs (0.90–1.25kg). The side with the bias can either be placed next to the little finger, known in flat green circles as 'forehand' and in crown green as 'finger peg' ('peg' meaning curl or bend), or next to the thumb, known in flat green as 'backhand' and in crown green as 'thumb peg'.

▲ The object of bowls, as noted earlier, is to deliver a bowl closer to the 'jack' than one's opponents.

This Taylor-Rolph **flat green jack**, 65mm (2½ inches) in diameter and 290g (10¼ oz) in weight, is from the collection of Geoff Barnett, and was made in c.1900.

Surprisingly it is ceramic.

Ceramic jacks were heavier than wooden ones and so moved less when hit. Nowadays however, like bowls, they are made from plastic.

Note that the jack is spherical and therefore non-biased, whereas crown green jacks are in effect a smaller version of a biased bowl.

In flat green, jacks are sent to the centre of the 'rink', to rest at least 23m from the point of delivery (a rectangular mat, placed at least 2m from the green's edge, or 'ditch'). In crown green a player can send the jack to any point on the green, as long as it stops at least 19m from the point of delivery (a round mat, placed at least 1m from the ditch).

◀ Flat green bowling, as noted earlier, is often referred to as '**rink**' bowling. This is because, as shown here at **Hyndland Bowling Club, Glasgow**, in 2009, each game is played on a 'rink', a rectangular strip running the length of the green.

Rink bowling may be seen as a natural progression from the narrow 'alleys' that were common in the 16th and 17th centuries, particularly in country house gardens (see page 56). But rink bowling as we know it today was introduced in Scotland in the mid 19th century, almost certainly influenced by the game of curling (as noted in Chapter Seven).

Dividing a green into rinks allows more people to play at any one time (up to a maximum of 48 on a standard six rink green).

But it also requires each rink to be as uniform as possible, so that players on the green's edges are not disadvantaged. This explains why Victorian Scots were at the forefront of attempts to create level greens.

As can be seen at Hyndland, the passage of woods and feet, up and down, does lead to wear and tear. To alleviate this, clubs regularly switch directions, playing east-west on one day, north-south the next.

Discreet white markers along the edge of the green show bowlers the limits of each rink.

The word 'rink' is also used to describe a team of four players.

At **Titwood BC**, also in **Glasgow** in 2009 (left), two members of a rink are indicating to their team-mates at the other end either how far away a particular bowl is from the jack, or how much weight might be needed for the next delivery.

Tactics play a huge part as bowls are positioned in anticipation of what the opposition might attempt. But it is always the 'skip' who bowls last, and who has the final say.

▲ Whichever the form of bowls, the aim is the same, to make sure that your bowl (or that of one of your team-mates) ends up the closest to the jack – a judgement that, if not obvious, must be made by the players calling for **'measures'**.

The most common method is a string measure, as seen above at Rastrick in Yorkshire.

Other methods include tape measures, calipers, a straight rule (*see page 74*) and the oldest of all, first cited in 1628, a straw, cut to length (*page 158*).

The act of measuring can often provide tense moments for players and spectators. In crown green there is the added complication that as the jack is not spherical the nearest point of the jack being measured varies in terms of its height above the green.

▲ In contrast with flat green, **crown green bowls** appears a much less orderly affair, as can be seen here, with jacks, woods and bowlers all over the green at **Owley Wood** in **Weaverham, Cheshire** in 2012.

This is because crown green players are free to send the jack wherever they wish, provided that, as noted opposite, the jack ends up a minimum of 19m from their mat, and that they do not block the route to a jack already set by other players on the green.

An additional challenge is that crown greens vary enormously.

True, some will rise up in the centre, forming a crown, but most undulate in different directions.

Players must therefore develop the ability to read each green and find lines that suit them best, or which exploit any weaknesses their opponents might display.

That, in essence, is why the jack in crown green is biased. It is so that players, as they deliver the jack (known as 'setting a mark')

can watch its path closely and thereby gain a reading of the green's surface before going on to deliver their bowls.

Some choose to play from corner to corner, which on larger greens can entail sending a bowl 50 yards or more (whereas in flat green the maximum is around 37 yards).

Others may play along an edge, while a few will play to the centre, known as playing 'up to the knob'.

And because several games often take place simultaneously, players must avoid being distracted, yet be patient whilst others proceed.

Combined with all the other strategies and ploys that a player may adopt, 'greencraft', as it is called, forms a vital part of a crown green player's armoury.

A final factor is that while rain rarely stops play, as is true in all other forms of bowls, conditions on crown greens can vary more, for the simple reason that the season runs longer, from March to October (as opposed to April-September in flat green). In fact some crown green bowlers play all year round, even in the snow, as in Westhoughton (*see page 159*).

Crown green jacks old and new (*left*), lignum vitae and composite. Apart from being biased rather than spherical, crown green jacks are larger than their flat green counterparts, measuring 90-91mm wide at their widest and between 97.5-98.5mm high, and weighing c.666g. By comparison flat green jacks are 63-64mm in diameter and 225-285g in weight.

▶ In the context of Britain's bowling heritage, the **indoor game** is seldom considered, even though, as will be shown in Chapter Ten, it emerged in the late 19th century (in Scotland) and has bequeathed several purpose-built indoor clubhouses dating from the 1930s.

One reason for this oversight is that the majority of indoor facilities, such as the **West of Scotland Indoor Bowling Club** in **Glasgow** (*top right*) – built in 1964 with twelve rinks – are relatively modern, purely functional in design and of little architectural interest. Certainly they lack the character and even romance of many of the outdoor clubs featured in this book.

Nevertheless it should be noted that, from the 1970s onwards, an increasing number of outdoor clubs have expanded their clubhouses to include indoor rinks, and that these facilities allow thousands of bowlers to continue playing all year round, whatever the weather.

For technical reasons it has proved difficult to reproduce indoors the conditions necessary for crown green bowling (although there have been several attempts since the mid 1950s). As such, all indoor clubs nowadays offer the equivalent of flat green bowls, but with slightly heavier jacks and bowls being used to counteract the quicker speeds encountered on modern artificial surfaces.

All other forms of indoor bowling are smaller in scale and can therefore be played in a range of buildings, such as clubhouses, village halls, leisure centres and community centres.

The most common form is called **short mat bowling**. This is played on a mat measuring 45 feet by six feet, as seen in the clubhouse of the **Royal Leamington Spa Bowling Club** (*below right*).

Note the white block of wood placed in the centre of the mat, towards the far wall. This is to prevent players 'firing' shots.

Short mat bowling is thought to have been developed in Northern Ireland during the 1940s, arriving in England in 1967. It is strongest in Cheshire (including amongst crown green bowlers), the West Midlands, Kent and the South West, and is overseen by the **English Short Mat Bowling Association**, formed in 1984.

A smaller version still, known simply as **carpet bowling**, governed by the **English Carpet Bowls Association**, uses mats of just 30 feet long and is found mostly in north east England, East Anglia, Bedfordshire and Hertfordshire.

Meanwhile, sets of small-scale **carpet bowls**, designed for use in the home, have been on sale since William Gaunt, a maker of china figures and ornaments, launched 'parlour bowling' in 1846.

Other potteries were quick to spot the potential, resulting in a range of patterned ceramic bowls such as those seen here at **York Castle Museum** (*right*) from the late 19th century. Some examples, from potteries in Kirkcaldy, Glasgow, Portobello, Sunderland and Staffordshire, are highly collectable.

Not so their modern equivalents, merely smaller versions of full size composite bowls.

▲ Back in Scotland, in an area stretching from the Borders to Dumfries and Galloway, another version of **carpet bowling** holds sway. In this, as seen here at the **Jedforest Rugby Club** in **Jedburgh**, the action takes place on individual rinks measuring 24 feet x 3 feet, formed by wooden boards covered by underlay and carpet.

This form of the game, formalised in 1896 by the establishment of the **Scottish Carpet Bowling Association** (now based in Castle Douglas), originated from a Victorian parlour game played with ceramic bowls known as 'piggies' (*as illustrated opposite*).

Its rules, rink markings and vocabulary are based clearly on the Scottish ice sport of curling, albeit with all measurements reduced in size to a third of those used in curling. No jack is used. Instead, a target area of concentric rings, known as the 'house', is marked out at the end of each rink.

The bowls themselves, made from wood or composite, are unbiased and, unusually, are delivered on hands and knees through a metal 'guard', usually with the bowl held between thumb and forefinger (*above right*).

As in curling, maintaining a 'clean head' by removing previously delivered blocking bowls is part of the tactics, and so unlike in short mat and the other versions of indoor bowls, 'firing' shots are allowed.

(Unlike curling on ice, however, there is, patently, no need for one of the players to brush the rink surface in advance.)

Thanks to a group of drapers from Dumfries, this distinctly Scottish version of carpet bowling soon spread to the Wirral peninsula, where the Birkenhead Carpet Bowling Society was formed in 1896. Still going strong, it is today based in a church hall in Noctorum.

Another club exists in Wrexham, formed also by men from Dumfries in 1903.

Finally, **table bowls**, we know from the writings of Randle Holme (*see page 8*) was played as early as 1683.

Today, two varieties are known, both played on snooker tables. At the **Knott End Working Men's Club**

on the Lancashire coast (*above*) the jack is biased and the bowls released from a wooden ramp placed inside the 'D'. Four pairs of bowls are used, with the number 1s having the weakest bias and the 4s the strongest.

In other clubs, for example in Carlisle, the jack is unbiased and the ramp is placed up to the baulk cushion.

Chapter Two

Bowling greens

In Preston Park, Brighton, as in so many of Britain's parks, the message is the same. For bowlers, the quality of their home turf is of paramount importance. Poor quality greens, whether caused by neglect, poor maintenance or, increasingly in public parks, by anti-social behaviour, are a cause of deep frustration. Matches are ruined. Fixtures against other clubs become harder to arrange. More motivated players move on, literally seeking pastures new. To understand bowls, therefore, it is imperative to understand greens.

Be it during the commentary on a Wembley final or when judging a competition for the Best Kept Village, no higher praise can be heaped upon turf than to liken it to 'a bowling green'.

There is much in our temperate, maritime climate to favour the cultivation of grass, not least regular rainfall. In western parts of this 'green and pleasant land', especially, where dairy farming thrives, grass will grow for much of the year, without added irrigation. Though it may turn brown during periods of drought, its lustre will soon return.

Bowling on grass, as opposed to bowling on earth or gravel (as in France) is, in this respect, as much a product of our environment as ice skating in Holland or surfing in California.

But the quality of Britain's bowling greens reflects also centuries of accumulated knowledge and experience.

No doubt Charles II, one of whose greens was likened to 'a billiard table' (see below), had access to the finest greenkeepers that money could buy.

Until the 20th century however, the majority of greens were rather more 'natural', formed mostly from grassland that had been mown as low as the scythe could go, then perhaps rolled to create a faster surface.

Photographs in this book from the Victorian era clearly show the grass to have been longer than is the norm today. Nor were greens necessarily shaped into neat rectangles, and rarely were they level. A reminder of this is the barely changed green at Lewes (see page 58), with its sward of many species and its undulating surface.

More extreme was a green at a house in the New Forest, recalled by a correspondent to the *Caledonian Mercury* in 1766. This, it was said, was 'long but narrow, and full of high ridges, it being never levelled since it was plowed'.

Bowlers then worked *with* nature rather than *against* it.

At the same time they were entreated not to make matters worse. Among the 'Orders Agreed Upon by Gentleman Bowlers' cited by Randle Holme in *The Academy of Armory*, published in 1683, is this:

'Noe high heeles enter for spoiling the green, they forfeit 6d.'

Furthermore, 'all stamping or smoothing is barred.' Stamping, by which a player attempts to make a bowl run further by bringing his foot down heavily on the ground just in front of it, remains a contentious issue in crown green bowls to this day.

In Chapter One we outlined the differences between crown green and flat green bowling, differences that emerged in the 19th century largely thanks to advances in the art and science of greenkeeping.

The first of these advances was the invention of the lawn mower.

The story of how, in 1830, Edwin Beard Budding, an engineer in Gloucestershire, adapted a helical cutter developed in the woollen cloth industry for the cutting of grass is well told in numerous other sources (see Links).

In the context of sport it was, quite literally, a game changer.

The lawnmower smoothed the way for two new sporting crazes: croquet in the 1850s, then lawn tennis in the 1870s. It also changed forever the game of bowls.

'The game requires both art and address. It is only in use during the fair and dry part of the season, and the places where it is practised are charming, delicious walks called bowling greens, which are little square grass plots where the turf is almost as smooth and level as the cloth of a billiard table... a turf more soft and smooth than the finest carpet in the world.'

from **Memoirs of the Count de Grammont: containing the amorous history of the English Court under the reign of Charles II** (1713)

▶ In 1832 Budding granted a licence to manufacture his patented grass cutter to the agricultural engineering firm of **Ransome's** in **Ipswich**, following which articles and advertisements started to feature regularly in the press. This one, dated c.1840 and reproduced in the Sports Turf Research Institute's manual on bowling greens (*see Links)* declared, 'This machine is so easy to manage that persons unpractised in the Art of Mowing may cut the Grass on Lawns, Pleasure Grounds and Bowling Greens, with ease. It is easily adjusted to cut any length, and the beauty of its operation is that it leaves no seam, nor any of the cut grass upon the Lawn.

'Other advantages of this machine are that the grass may be cut when dry, and consequently it may be used at such hours as most convenient to the Gardener or Workman, while the expense of Mowing is considerably lessened, as more than double the work may be done with the same labour that is requisite with the scythe.'

The groundsman at London's Regent's Park Zoo reckoned that Budding's invention did the work of six to eight men and produced a better surface. Later Ransome adverts went further by showing young women pushing their mowers with consummate ease.

Budding died in 1846, by which time Shanks of Arbroath had started to manufacture their own lawnmowers, followed by Thomas Green of Leeds in 1856.

But not everyone was converted. As seen in this early photograph of **Wellcroft Bowling Club, Glasgow**, at its Eglinton Street headquarters in 1859 (*right*), much to the fore stands the greenkeeper wielding his scythe, alongside two boys, pulling the heavy roller.

That he persisted with a scythe despite lawn mowers becoming available is on one hand an indication of the conservatism that has long characterised the world of bowls. But it also says much about the quality of surface that he and generations of greenkeepers were able to achieve using this most ancient of tools. In the 1890s *The Field* noted that a scythesman 'who had established a reputation for this kind of work was always in demand, and in many cases he could command his own price'.

Even as late as 1912, JA Manson (*see Links*) reported that most Scottish greens were still being mown with a scythe, which 'in the opinion of many, is the only instrument which should be used on a first class green.'

Manson nevertheless conceded that a lawnmower offered 'a capital substitute', and by the 1920s use of the scythe had all but ended.

BUDDING'S PATENT GRASS-CUTTING MACHINE.

SOLD BY APPOINTMENT, BY
J. R. & A. RANSOME, IPSWICH.

▲ Hard at work on the shores of **Morecambe Bay,** between **Arnside** and **Storth,** this is **David Brailsford,** the last man engaged in the ancient enterprise of cutting and gathering **sea-washed Cumberland turf** – for years the ultimate choice of surface for the bowling greens of Britain, not to mention golf courses and Wembley Stadium.

Celebrated for the fineness of its grass and the strength of its roots, Cumberland turf copes well in hot, dry weather and can easily withstand close mowing.

So it was that from around 1800 until the 1950s, any club that had the means, no matter how far they were based from the Cumberland coast, or indeed from alternative sources in the Solway Firth or Ayrshire, insisted on sea-washed turf as an essential mark of quality.

In their listings in association handbooks, in their advertisements in newspapers and brochures, 'sea-washed turf' would be highlighted as a badge of pride. Even as recently as 2001, in the *Bowls Club Directory,* of 158 clubs listed in Kent, to take just one county, 76 specified having 'sea-washed turf', 71 described it as being of the Cumberland variety, and a further five cited theirs as having come from Lancashire.

The first recorded use of sea-washed turf for bowling greens was in 1738, at Cowane's Hospital in Stirling (*see page 105*): 'The patrons considering a petition given in by several of the merchants, trades and other inhabitants showing the badness of the Bowling Green, and craving the same might be laid with salt faill, they therefore appoint the masters to cause William Dawson, gardener, and keeper of the said Green, to lay the same with salt faill as soon as possible, the expense thereof not exceeding the sum of £10 sterling.'

'Faill' is the Gaelic word for turf.

By the mid 19th century, the arrival of the railways allowed the market to grow, fed in the world of bowls by the new benchmarks for greens being set in Scotland.

Today, that market is quite different. High quality turf can be cultivated almost anywhere in Britain, using seed from carefully selected species, usually bents and fescues. Hence Brailsford, who followed his father into the business, now supplies not bowls clubs or sports grounds but local authorities and the Environment Agency (who use the turf to counter coastal erosion).

The work is tough. Harvesting selected areas each autumn and winter, when the dangerous tides allow, Brailsford uses a machine to cut rectangular turves, one inch deep. He must then stack each one – twice as heavy as inland turf owing to the sand and moisture content – by hand onto pallets.

Once stripped, the bare areas are left to regenerate naturally for around seven years. But whereas in the past weed killers were used to remove unwanted species, thereby making it more attractive to would-be users, the turf is nowadays managed organically.

It is striking nevertheless how such a wild environment gave birth to turf that, once transplanted and tamed, could appear so perfect.

And ironic too that once it had been transplanted to a bowling green in some distant suburb or town, sea-washed turf had a tendency to deteriorate relatively quickly, being prone to compaction and infiltration by unwanted species such as annual meadow grass.

But try telling bowlers that.

◄ Often spotted nestling in the bushes, as here at **Lewes** in **East Sussex**, the **heavy roller** no longer plays a vital role in green-keeping.

Until at least the 1950s, when most clubs were still using hand-pushed mowers, rolling was as important a task as grass cutting.

It was a long established practice too. A 'rowling stone' is mentioned in the records of Milton Regis bowling green from 1680 (*see page 80*). The Lewes example, with its wrought iron handle and limestone roller, may well date from that period. Certainly it resembles a sketch drawn in c.1660 by John Evelyn for his unpublished encyclopaedia *Elysium Britannicum*, and also one seen in a painting of 1738 by Balthasar Nebot, depicting gardeners at Hartwell House.

Stone rollers were eventually superceded by cast iron models in the early 19th century.

Samuel Sorbière's 1709 travelogue *A Voyage to England* remarked of Kent that 'the grass here seemed... finer and of a better colour than in other places and therefore 'tis fitter to make those parterres, some of which are so even that they bowl upon them as easily as on a great billiard table.

'And as this is the usual Diversion of Gentlemen in the Country, they have thick Rowling Stones to keep the Green smooth.'

Pulling a roller was heavy work, especially for those 'bowls lads' otherwise employed at clubs (such as at Wellcroft on page 17) to look after the members' woods.

Or if not lads, then donkeys.

In 1714, John Macky noted how at Lord Hereford's Park in Ipswich, the green 'is rolled by Asses in Boots, that their Feet may make no Impression on the Green.'

In 1869, Blackburn Subscription BGC bought a donkey for £3 to cover its keep for five years, plus a set of shoes at 8s. Even at that time however it was known that heavy rollers could cause problems.

In his *Manual of Bowl-Playing*, William Mitchell advised in 1864: 'Never roll the Green till the afternoon, and then only when it is dry. The reason for doing so is to avoid caking the surface, and rendering it impervious to wet.'

'Rolling the Green in the morning, when the dew is on the grass,' Mitchell added, 'injures its texture and destroys its elasticity, as may be seen as soon as it is dried in the sun, when it resembles a newly-dressed shirt, and becomes brown in the colour.'

Nowadays, petrol mowers are in themselves considered heavy enough to smooth a green. Still, many clubs appear unwilling to part with their rollers, in some cases turning them into decorative items, as at **Queen's Park Bowling Club** in **Glasgow** (*below left*). Note that both their cast-iron rollers are in two sections. This system was invented in 1851 to enable rollers to negotiate corners more easily.

Is it sentimentality to preserve these now redundant implements? Or a desire to preserve an important part of bowling's heritage?

Or is it simply because the clubs cannot find anyone willing to haul the beasts away?

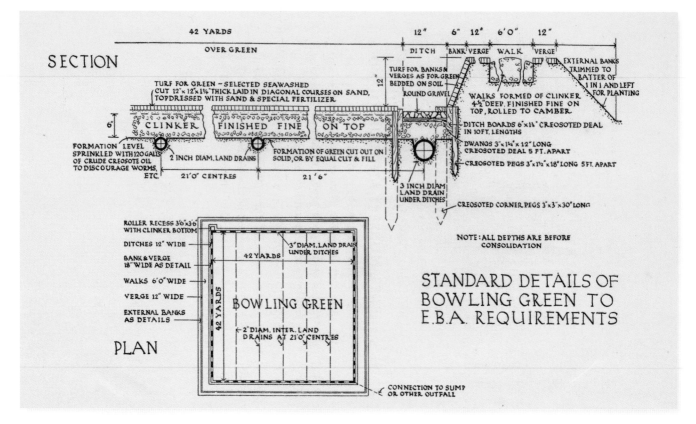

SECTION

STANDARD DETAILS OF BOWLING GREEN TO E.B.A. REQUIREMENTS

NOTE: ALL DEPTHS ARE BEFORE CONSOLIDATION

PLAN

BOWLING GREEN

▲ It is appropriate that this oft reproduced diagram of a **flat green's construction** – first seen in a 1950s booklet, *Notes on the Maintenance of Bowling Greens* – should have originated from a Glasgow-based company, Maxwell M Hart Ltd. For flat greens were in essence made possible by research initiated by the Scots in the 19th century. Moreover it was the improvements rendered by their research that allowed for the formulation of revised rules by Scottish bowlers. As such, flat green bowls became known to many as 'Scottish rules'.

Central to the construction of a flat green was and remains efficient drainage. Hence the recommendation here for a six inch layer of clinker (a by-product of coal burning) under a top surface, inevitably, of sea-washed turf.

Ditches, meanwhile, almost unknown at English greens before 1870, now became an essential element of 'Scottish rules' (which the English Bowling Association adopted in 1903, and which are now governed by the World Bowls organisation.) This is because in flat green bowls, the jack remains 'live' in the ditch, provided that it has exited through the end rather than the side of the rink. So too does any bowl which has struck the jack

when first played and then follows it off the green and into the ditch.

The design of flat greens offered a real challenge to clubs thinking of joining the EBA in its early years. Most had to rebuild their greens completely, while some, such as Cheltenham in 1917, had to move to a new site with more space.

As shown on the left, at **Milton Regis** in **Kent**, modern ditches, all of which must meet standard dimensions, tend to be lined with rubber to prevent the bowls from rolling away. Note also the height of the bank. For years flat green banks were made from wooden boards. Nowadays they are mostly formed from pre-fabricated concrete blocks covered by artificial turf.

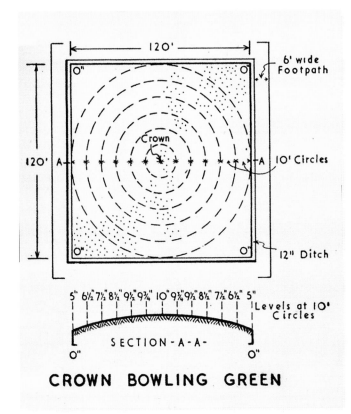

CROWN BOWLING GREEN

120'

6' wide Footpath

120'

A — — A

10' Circles

Crown

12" Ditch

5" 6½" 7½" 8½" 9½" 9¾" 10" 9¾" 9½" 8½" 7½" 6½" 5"

Levels at 10' Circles

SECTION - A - A -

0"   0"

▲ This diagram, reproduced from a Batsford guide to *Sports Buildings and Playing Fields*, published in 1957 (*see Links*), shows an idealised version of a **crown green**.

In reality, however, few crown greens have such uniform contours, and nor has this, nor any other 'standard' form of design, ever been specified by the British Crown Green Bowling Association.

Indeed, as explained in Chapter One, the very name 'crown green' seems only to have crept into use after 1900, purely as a means of distinguishing the old game of bowls from the newly emerging flat green game from Scotland.

That said, many crown greens, particularly those laid to order in recent decades, do rise up towards the centre by 6–12 inches. But the crown may be offset towards one side or a corner. Or there may even be two crowns.

In fact it is not even essential for a crown green to have a crown at all. Many are more or less flat

from edge to edge but have various ridges, humps and hollows in between. This is especially true of older greens, laid without the benefit of heavy machinery.

As such, the different weights of delivery required to play either up or down a slope, or across any uneven surface, forms a fundamental part of the challenge of crown green bowling.

Furthermore, although most crown greens are nowadays square, as we see overleaf, almost any shape is permissible.

Two consequences arise from this more laissez-faire approach.

Firstly, it allows for crown greens to be accommodated on a much wider variety of sites than is the case in flat green.

Secondly, because home players are better acquainted with their own green's idiosyncracies, visitors have a more testing time in crown green bowls. Some clubs, such as Cannock and Newark, even make it their boast not to have lost at home for a century or more.

Another is the author's home club, St. Michael's in Lancashire.

Formed in 1886, when finally it lost a home game in 1961, the result card was sent off to the league secretary edged in black.

(Incidentally, uneven greens are also tolerated by the English Bowling Federation, albeit flat greens are preferred.)

Another difference with crown greens, as seen at Hoghton in Lancashire (*left*), is that there is no need for a prescribed design for ditches or banks, since any jack or bowl that runs off the green is 'dead'. All that is required is a gutter, plus boards or a raised kerb to prevent bowls leaving the playing area, particularly those travelling at speed after a firing shot.

▲ Widely considered the most difficult crown green to play is the number 1 green at **Bedworth**, near **Nuneaton**. Using the same multiple exposure technique employed at Barnes (*see page 11*), again the position of the bowl is plotted as it travels on a long, corner-to-corner mark of around 60 yards.

The bowl was sent 'finger peg' (or forehand in flat green parlance), so note how it begins by moving slightly towards the biased side, as expected, but then falls back dramatically towards the camera, overcome by the effect of the slope. This is known as a 'dropping mark'.

Sadly, 2015 will be the green's final year, as the club is being relocated to make way for housing.

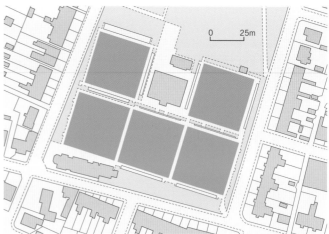

▲ Few clubs need or can afford to maintain more than two greens. However regional, national and international tournaments, which can involve hundreds of players in the early rounds, require more.

For many years the Scottish Bowling Association (SBA), renamed **Bowls Scotland** in 2011, staged their major tournaments at the Queen's Park Bowling Club in Glasgow, which has three greens.

But in 1989 they relocated to the **Northfield Bowling Centre** in **Ayr** (*above*), where funding from South Ayrshire Council, World Bowls, Bowls Scotland and the National Lottery has helped fund a five green complex, plus a School of Excellence and offices.

Ayr Northfield is the home club.

A similar collaboration between the English Bowling Association (now **Bowls England**), Warwick District Council and the **Royal Leamington Spa BC** has resulted in a five green complex in **Victoria Park**, **Leamington** (*below*).

Here the greens lie side by side and are maintained by Warwick District Council.

Leamington took over from another five green public complex in Worthing, on the south coast, which for many bowlers in the north and Midlands required long journeys and more overnights.

Currently Britain's largest concentration of greens, six in total, is at Kelvingrove Park, Glasgow, venue for the 2014 Commonwealth Games (*see page 205*).

Flat greens have to be square or rectangular, the common pre-metric standard being 42 x 42 yards (38.4 x 38.4m). Otherwise, modern rules require a minimum length of 31m and a maximum of 40m. Most greens are to be found in singles, as at Valentines Park, Redbridge (*above*), or doubles, usually side by side, as at Mount Florida, Glasgow (*top*).

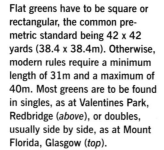

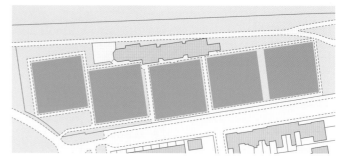

▲ Although, as stated, the **British Crown Green Bowling Association** places no restrictions on the shape or size of greens, there must be room on the green to achieve a mark of at least 19m. Any other idiosyncracies may be worked around by applying 'local rules'.

This relaxed approach has given rise to a variety of green designs.

Darwen in **Lancashire**, for example, has four circular greens, including **Whitehall Park** (*above*), while the largest single green in Britain is the public crown green at **West Park**, **Macclesfield (1)**.

Shaped like an elongated clover leaf, this measures a daunting 90m or so from end to end (more than twice the norm), and although some bowlers do occasionally manage to bowl its whole length, in competition matches a player has the right to object if a mark is too long.

Despite this rule, in recent years two tenant clubs have nevertheless opted to move to smaller greens in Macclesfield. The sheer size of the West Park green, combined with the quality of its surface, also makes it an obvious target for impromptu kickabouts.

At **Bishop's Castle**, **Shropshire (2)**, the green is roughly octagonal, echoing the shape of its 18th century bowls house (*page 101*).

At the **Bowling Green Hotel** in **Chorlton**, **Manchester (3)** the green is pentagonal, while five miles south east in **Stockport**, the green at the **Railway Club** in **Edgeley (4)** is triangular, its long edge being cut off, predictably, by a railway line.

Elsewhere neighbouring developments have given rise to a number of L-shaped greens, such as at the Bell Inn in Harborne, Birmingham, and unusually, at two flat greens. These are at Banwell in Somerset, where uniquely the green occupies the site of the former village pond, and at the Mitre in Norwich (*page 179*).

Another rarity **(5)** is the crown green at the **Stile Inn**, **Wolverhampton** (*see page 135*), where one corner is cut into by the pub and another by the bowls pavilion, housed in a former stable.

Finally Britain's smallest green is also behind a pub, the canal side **Bird in Hand** in **Stourport**, **Worcestershire (6)**.

One of several undersized greens hosting 'Federation' bowls in the Kidderminster area (*page 180*), the green is trapezium shaped, its longest edge being 18m, its shortest just 13m. In terms of its total area it is less than half that of a standard square green – yet another reminder that before the 20th century, few greens were alike, and all had their quirks.

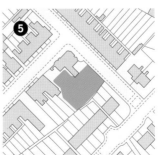

▲ Bowling greens appear in a variety of settings, in private clubs, in parks, garden estates, pubs and a range of institutions.

But nowhere seems more appropriate than the grounds of a castle. This is **Dirleton Castle** near **North Berwick**. Built in the 13th century and a ruin since the Civil War, its green was laid on a raised knot garden in around 1830. An 1834 report describes how Dirleton bowlers had for 'several years' played a team from Haddington (*see page 105*). That year's match was followed by supper at Craven's Inn and dancing on the green accompanied by a local band.

'Their sweet and plaintive notes among the ruins of the romantic castle, and the surrounding woods and dells,' reported the *Caledonian Mercury,* 'had a fine effect.'

▲ It is often said there is nothing more quintessentially English than the sight of cricketers on a village green. Yet bowls is common to all parts of Britain, found even in the smallest of villages.

In the 19th and early 20th centuries at least, laying a green was hardly a major enterprise, and a club might easily thrive with no more than 20–30 members. **Northwick Bowling Club** in the Gloucestershire village of **Blockley** – population 2,041 according to the 2011 Census – is one of many such clubs in rural Britain. In one sense its green presents a contrast of man-made order amidst the rolling hills of the Cotswolds.

On the other, it appears a modest intervention, a gentle oasis.

For many bowlers, here is the perfect setting. Match results apart, old newspapers report a familiar cycle of social occasions, of annual suppers and whist drives.

As at many village clubs, the same surnames crop up from generation to generation. One such family in Blockley is the Cothers.

Common also are the links between bowling clubs and local landowners who, in many cases,

provided sites and funding for the green, and whose representatives preside over the ceremonies that traditionally accompany the opening of the green every season.

Northwick Bowling Club takes its name from nearby Northwick Park. In July 1911, we learn from a cutting, Lady Northwick gave visiting bowlers from Cheltenham a tour of the house and gardens, and then after the match entertained the ladies in their party for tea.

The church, like the aristocracy, appears also at ease with bowling, as suggested at **Clevedon**, **Somerset** (*left*), where the current green, laid in 1911, sits on Chapel Hill, cheek by jowl with the Grade II* listed early Victorian Christ Church.

As later chapters will show, such a juxtaposition is relatively common. Whether found in the shadows of spires or castles, or nestled between hills and cottages, bowling greens rarely jar, or appear out of place.

◀ Sheltered behind a privet hedge, the green at **Parliament Hill Fields** in **London** may appear to be private. There is a club based there, formed in 1938, and a pair of well kept timber-framed pavilions. But it is in fact a park green, one of over 2,000 in Britain, second in number only to private club greens.

After public parks started to appear during the 1830s and '40s – Moor Park in Preston and Birkenhead Park being the pioneers – park greens were aimed at working men who lived too far from, or could not afford to join their nearest club. It was also hoped that they might lure bowlers away from greens at public houses.

Leith in Scotland is believed to have been the earliest, in 1857, followed by Adderley Park, Birmingham (1859), Alexandra Park, Manchester (1871), and Sophia Gardens, Cardiff (1878).

Although intended for use on a 'pay and play' basis, by the early 20th century it was common for park greens to have their own resident clubs, often renting a portion of the adjoining pavilion.

But in recent years as income from greens has fallen and green keeping costs have risen, a number have been turned into gardens or play areas (*see Chapter 12*). Or, in the case of Parliament Hill Fields, the bowlers have been obliged to share with a croquet club.

This handsomely situated crown green is at Crowgill Park, Shipley. When it opened in 1914 bowlers were charged a penny to rent a pair of woods for half an hour. So strong is parks bowling in West Yorkshire that nearly half the total number of clubs in the area are parks-based, while of 62 greens in the Bradford Metropolitan District, 52 are publicly funded.

▶ This the green at **The Wheatsheaf** in **Sutton Leach**, just south of **St Helens**, another contender for the most challenging crown green in the country.

Apart from the fact that the whole area has been affected by mining subsidence – so that walking through the pub can feel like lurching across the deck of a ship – the green has an unusually high crown in its centre, plus a slope down from the pub. Thus when the green is 'wick' (or running fast), the difference between sending a bowl racing into the gutter at the lower end, or leaving it stranded twenty yards short of the jack on top of the crown, is so small as to be barely perceptible to the player on the mat.

Enough to drive anyone to drink.

After private clubs and parks, **pub greens** form the third largest category, currently totalling around 350. Like park greens their numbers have dropped, because the pubs have closed or the greens have been turned into beer gardens or sold for development.

Even taking this decline into consideration, however, pub greens have never been as widespread as might be imagined. For many years now both London and Cornwall have only had one each. In all of Wales there is also only one, the Gate Hangs High in Wrexham.

This leaves the greatest concentration of pub greens in Lancashire, Cheshire, the West Midlands and Norfolk.

Just four remain in Scotland, including the **Polmaise Bowling Club**, near **Stirling** (*right*).

Formed in 1911, this is based at the **Fallin Public House Society Ltd**, part of the Gothenburg Movement, which sought to bring co-operative ownership to pubs in coal mining villages.

▲ To complete our round up of greens, on this page is but a sample of the other, surprisingly diverse settings in which bowls is played.

One of many hospitals around Britain to offer the game as a benefit to both patients and staff is **Whitchurch Psychiatric Hospital** in **Cardiff** (*top left*), where a bowling club was founded in 1927.

Other former asylums with greens, no longer in use, include Woodilee in Dunbartonshire and Moor Hospital, Lancaster.

Meanwhile, as will become apparent in later chapters, bowling greens forming part of larger sports clubs are relatively common.

But only **Thirsk Athletic Bowling Club** (*centre left*) is located within a racecourse.

Finally, Britain's only green where players arrive by boat. Founded in 1909 on Fry's Island, in the middle of the Thames in Reading, the Island Bohemian BC (*left*) **lives up to its romantic name. By necessity a number of its members must train as ferrymen. A lucky few may rent wooden chalets placed around the green. Not surprisingly, the waiting list is long.**

Formed in c.1920, the club cannot play on race days, of which there are sixteen a year. The same applies to the cricket, rugby and hockey facilities also on the site.

Still in Yorkshire, Dringhouses BC plays on a green located in the centre of one of York Racecourse's stable blocks. It was formed by a Clerk of the Course in 1929.

Finally, we tend to think of bowling greens in scenic or leafy surrounds. But as seen above in **Edinburgh**, they pop up in all kinds of urban settings. Laid originally for workers at J & G Cox, a local glue works, in 1905, this is the **Gorgie Mills Bowling Club**, an independent club since 1971, offering a green oasis in the heart of a working class district of the city.

Chapter Three

Bowling clubs

Whether announcing their presence via weathervanes, as at Reading Bowling Club (*above*), by ironwork, as at Merton Park in London (*below right*), by flagpoles or by signs, the bowling clubs of Britain are by nature welcoming, harbouring within their hedged and walled surrounds a rich and rewarding social universe all of their own.

The club forms the heart and soul of the game of bowls.

Found in all quarters of the British Isles, in hamlets and big cities, in leafy suburbs and amid council estates, bowling clubs may be based in fine pavilions or modest sheds, play in strict uniforms or everyday garb, have 150 members or just 20. (In fact the average is around 50-75.)

But wherever they are located, whichever type of bowls they play, and whichever area, social group or class they represent, bowling clubs are bound by the same goals: to foster club spirit and goodwill, to offer hospitality and, above all, increasingly alas, to survive. For if there is one facet of bowling heritage that is most precious of all to bowlers in Britain, it is the game itself.

A bowling club, in this respect, is not merely a local association.

It is for its members a way of life, and perhaps even a cause.

As will be explored in Chapter Six, Britain's first properly constituted clubs and societies were formed during the 18th century. Among those still functioning today is the Lewes Bowling Green Society, in existence since at least 1745.

It was around that time that the great lexicographer Samuel Johnson defined a club as 'an assembly of good fellows meeting under certain conditions'.

Nowadays we associate clubs with premises, with a fixed abode.

But in Johnson's day clubs were more likely to meet on a fixed day, once a week, at a public house with an adjoining green. Post match suppers, drinks and toasts were central to this fellowship, arguably more than the game itself.

As the concept matured and memberships grew, gradually clubs sought out their own properties where they might become self-sufficient. Or they sought to escape the pub in order to appear more respectable. Thus in the 19th century, as detailed in Chapter Eight, came the rise of the private members' club.

Often backed by the issue of shares, the title 'Subscription' or 'Proprietary' might be added to a club's name, to denote its status, as in the Blackburn Subscription Bowling Green Club, formed c.1753, or the Nottingham Proprietary Bowling Club, formed in 1849. But whatever the business model, a pattern emerged throughout the bowling world.

Committees were formed, officers appointed, pavilions built, greens laid and, in time, traditions established. Each club, a little history in the making.

Needless to add, until the early 20th century this was almost exclusively a male world. It was also largely introspective.

That is, despite Britain's ever improving transport links, club members mostly played amongst themselves, with only occasional forays to neighbouring clubs.

For example a Wolverhampton League was established in 1891 but lasted only four years. It turned out that most clubs preferred to play for fun. Even in 1959, when Godfrey Bolsover compiled his *Who's Who and Encyclopedia of Bowls*, in counties such as Essex and Kent it remained common for clubs to specify 'friendly games only'.

'Friendly' is a word that one hears often at bowling clubs.

▲ Ensconsed atop a prominent earthwork, once the eastern bailey of **Clun Castle** – whose 13th century ruins overlook the green from a neighbouring hill – the 30 or so members of **Clun Bowling Club** in **Shropshire** enjoy one of the most idyllic locations in British bowls.

After the Fitzalan family vacated the castle and it fell into ruins, the eastern bailey served as the site of a manorial court, until this was demolished in c.1780. The bowls club, formed in the town in the 1880s, then took on the hilltop site in 1909, laboriously laying a crown green – with six crowns, so it was said – until finally the surface was deemed playable in 1922.

There is a price for occupying such exalted ground. Under the terms of their tenancy from the castle's guardians, English Heritage, the club cannot impose itself upon the landscape. Hence the small pavilion and the plain palisade to mark the boundary of their green. A mere 90 feet in length it is too, not large enough for the South Shropshire League, but perfectly acceptable for the Borders Friendly League, which in such a location seems appropriate.

Where better than to gather on a summer's evening, high above the town, watched over by the ancient stones of a Scheduled Monument, with the leaves rustling and the awning rippling in the breeze?

Small wonder that other clubs love to play here, even if there are few amenities and little space.

For the bigger picture at Clun, see page 232.

▲ Lovers of sheds will find rich pickings at bowling clubs, as at the **Severnside BC** in **Shrewsbury**, formed in 1896. It should be noted however that in many instances the sheds that clubs now use for storage started out life as their pavilions, an example being at the aforementioned **Island Bohemian BC** in **Reading** (*above right*).

In each case, as the club became established and its numbers grew, larger pavilions became a priority. This was especially so in flat green circles, where strict dress codes created a need for changing rooms, and at clubs where ladies' sections started to be formed from the 1920s onwards.

In other locations pavilions were simply extended, as at **Duns Park BC** in **Berwickshire**, where the original section, built in 1896 is clearly distinguishable (*right*).

This process continues into the present day. **Mitcham BC** in **London** moved to their present site in 1960, formed a ladies section in 1961, but for 30 years had to make do with a basic shed. The nearest toilets were 300 yards away and the only tap was by the side of the green. But, as seen below, in 1990 wings were added to allow for a kitchen, lounge and changing rooms, thereby helping to pave the way for the mens' and ladies' sections to amalgamate in 2003.

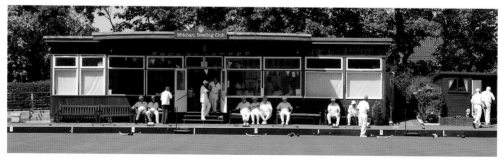

▲ Three more clubs in Scotland illustrate the different styles to be found in clubhouse architecture.

In **Stirling** (*above*), where the town's bowlers moved to their current home in 1858 from an 18th century green at Cowane's Hospital (*see page 105*), members opted for the Baronial Gothic style then very much in vogue.

Opened in 1886 the pavilion was designed by William Simpson (better known for designing the Albert Hall in Stirling). For his services he was presented with a pair of bowls. The building itself cost £108, of which members and friends contributed £86, in addition to their annual subs of 30s.

In other words, here was a club for men of means and status.

Regrettably Simpson's original polychromatic brickwork and stone dressings have since been overpainted, and two utilitarian, flat-roofed extensions added.

But Stirling BC are not alone in putting function before form. Few Victorian pavilions anticipated the wider social role and financial challenges that bowling clubs would increasingly face during the 20th century.

A similar process can be seen at **Girvan Bowling Club** in **South Ayrshire** (*above*), formed in 1841.

In the centre, with the slate roof, is an earlier pavilion, built in 1898. To its left is an extension added in the 1950s, and on the right, a flat roofed function room built in 1961. Not visible is a kitchen added at the rear in the 1960s and a cellar created in the 1970s, to replace a railway wagon where the club had until then stored its drinks.

With four greens, Girvan is one of Britain's largest clubs.

The piecemeal development of pavilions has resulted in few being listed, anywhere in Britain (*see Chapter 13*). An exception is that of **Burntisland** in **Fife** (*top right*).

Listed Category B, this fine, little altered clubhouse was opened in 1893 at a cost of £300 by the Burntisland Recreation Company, to serve three tennis courts and the bowling green, which itself had opened the year before – hence the date of 1892 on the distinctive jerkin-head gable, seen here in 2014 on the opening day of the season.

▲ To belong to a bowling club is to respect rules and not to cross any lines, as shown at **Temple Bowling Club** in **Herne Hill**, **London** (*above*), at **Ellesmere**, **Ludlow**, **Lyme Regis** and **Banbury** (*left, top to bottom*), and at **Milton Regis**, **Patons & Baldwin Recreation & Welfare Assocation** in **Alloa**, **Gloucester** and the **Rolls Royce Crown Green BC**, **Derby** (*right, top to bottom*).

It might be assumed that this emphasis on orderliness and conformity derives from the Victorians. Certainly until recent years it was common for applicants to more exclusive clubs to be black-balled by members if it was felt they lacked social standing or might turn out to be troublesome.

But in truth bowlers have been bound by convention for much

longer. In 1683 Randle Holme warned that anyone wearing block heels on a green would be fined 6d, while in the 18th century, Rugeley Bowling Green in Staffordshire had no fewer than 45 rules, covering admission charges, how to play the game and the behaviour of those 'abetting' (or gambling) at the green. Rule Two stated, 'Any that swear or Blaspheme shall be outed ye Green.'

In the early days of the English Bowling Association, as is still largely the case in crown green bowls, most players played in their everyday clothes (albeit often quite formally on special occasions). But as the years went by and both the EBA and local associations started to draw up **dress codes** – typically white shirts, ties and grey trousers for men – clubs had to adapt or extend their pavilions to provide changing rooms.

This included, as seen here at **Portland Bowling Club** in **Jesmond, Newcastle** (founded in 1874), the provision of private lockers, and in many cases of showers also.

Nowadays Bowls England issues a 'Clothing Protocol' to make sure that not only players but officials and referees are all attired in the correct blazers and ties, shirts and blouses, trousers and skirts, waterproofs and fleeces, and so on.

The arrival of women at bowls clubs in the 20th century, starting in the 1920s, required further extensions to be built, as at the **Sunderland Bowling Club** (*left, and page 1*). As many men would concede, the involvement of women led also to pavilions becoming homelier and more welcoming.

Note the honours boards, the club shields, the bell, and that vital element of club life, the noticeboard. As for the box labelled 'Jumbles' all will explained overleaf.

◄ When someone at a bowls club, most likely one in Scotland, calls for a **'promiscuous game'**, there need be no cause for alarm.

What is meant is that all club members present enter a draw to see who plays in which rink and in which order, thereby mixing players of differing abilities, and, in the process, helping to raise standards and promote club spirit.

At the **Lewes Bowling Green Society** in **East Sussex** (*left*), coloured balls are drawn from a bag to determine who plays who.

At **Hadley** in **Worcestershire** (*below left*), homemade tiles do the same job, while at the **Abercorn Bowling Club** in **Paisley** (*right*) a well organised corner of the pavilion has been set aside for the purpose.

The four lines per rink denote who plays lead (that is, bowls first), second, third and 'skip' (or fourth).

At some clubs everyone pays a small entry fee, half going to the club and half to the winners.

In Scotland another term used to describe such matches is 'wappenshaw'. This was a 16th or 17th century Scots word for a muster called by the local laird to check whether his men were properly armed. It was, literally, a 'show of weapons'.

Other terms for this mixing up of members at bowls clubs include 'bounce', 'bunnets' and 'scrambles'.

At Sunderland (*see previous page*) the term used is 'jumbles'.

Whichever team wins on the day has a card with their names on put into the jumbles box. At the end of the season the player whose name appears most often on a winning team, and it could as well be a novice as an old hand, wins the jumbles trophy.

From club records from the 18th and 19th centuries it would appear that this philosophy – of giving

everyone a chance, and of ensuring that everyone mixes on the green – is deeply rooted in bowls culture. That way the banker might play the baker and the solicitor face the publican, and in doing so, ease social barriers on and off the green.

In recent years an increase in league and competition play, particularly in crown green bowls, has tended to undermine this approach. One tradition, that of Saturday night foursomes, has all but disappeared. But at flat green clubs social bowling continues, especially at midweek 'roll-ups' where rinks are made up as members arrive.

Above all, bowlers abhor nothing more at their clubs than a clique.

Promiscuity is in this sense, therefore, a virtue.

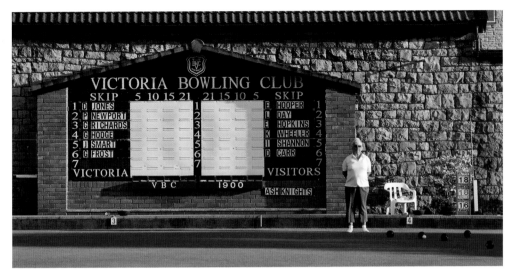

▲ Purpose-built **scoreboards** were once considered a standard feature of bowling greens, a good example being at **Victoria Bowling Club** in **Weston-super-Mare**, **Somerset**.

Nowadays, if they survive, often they stand unused, the preference being for portable scoreframes such as the one seen at **Hampden Bowling Club**, Glasgow (*top right*).

At other clubs old-fashioned blackboards and chalk still suffice.

From the surnames listed in the example shown on the left, we may guess the general location.

A further clue? GHH stands for the **Gate Hangs High**, this being the only pub green left in **Wales**, more specifically in a suburb of Wrexham.

Today most bowls matches, whether played between singles, pairs, threes or fours, are contested to '21 up'. That is, a score of 21 is needed to win. However from our old friend Randall Holme, writing in *The Academy of Armory* in 1683, we learn that 'A Game is at Bowles 5' and that 'very rearly among gamesters doth exceed that number, except agreed upon to make 7 or 9 up'.

By limiting the points required, games would have been shorter, at no more than 30 minutes or so each. Also, as specified in rules set down at the behest of Charles II in 1670 (*see page 53*), matches then consisted of the best of three, a convention known as 'rubbers' (common in card games too).

At the green in Rugeley, Staffordshire, in the 18th century, the rules required that any player failing to score a single point, known as a 'lurch', had to pay a fine to the alley or greenkeeper.

At the other end of the scale, in the late 19th century, in the north of England particularly, there were frequent 'money matches', played by the top professionals of the day, to scores of up to '101 up'.

Such matches would inevitably take hours to complete, sometimes split over two days and even different venues, thereby providing ample time for spectators to drink and gamble as the scores ebbed and flowed, and the odds changed accordingly.

Plenty of chalk needed on those occasions, no doubt.

▲ The welcome mat goes out at the **Brentham Bowling Club** in **Ealing, west London**, formed for residents of the Brentham Garden Estate in 1911. Hospitality is deeply ingrained within the culture of bowling, a tradition that goes back to the summer houses of the aristocracy and the public houses of the rank and file. To host a visiting club is to put on a spread.

In the main picture, tea is being prepared at the **Northern Bowling Club** in **Edinburgh**, while at the **Newlands Bowling Club** in **Glasgow** (*right*) there is time for a chat after the tables have been cleared.

But patently the real heart of most clubs, and indeed their main source of revenue, as at the **North London Bowling Club** (*far right*), is the bar.

▲ One of the great traditions of bowling, as demonstrated at **Bush Hill Park Bowls Club** in **Enfield, North London**, is the **after-match meal**, particularly at weekends when there is less pressure on people's time.

Hours of unpaid work are undertaken by club members to honour this tradition, with great pride taken to maintain reputations and to repay the hospitality of visiting clubs, who in many cases have been regular opponents over the generations. Toasts and speeches form an integral part of this time-honoured ritual.

Newspaper reports of bowls in the 18th and 19th centuries suggest that the post-match celebrations were in fact of much greater interest to readers than the actual matches. Often there is just a perfunctory mention of the score, followed by a detailed account of what was eaten at a nearby inn afterwards, the speeches, toasts, songs and all. The records of the Cheetham Hill Bowling Society in Manchester from 1812-32 reflect this. Bowls is barely mentioned, yet there is an account of the wine bill on almost every page.

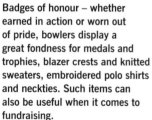

Badges of honour – whether earned in action or worn out of pride, bowlers display a great fondness for medals and trophies, blazer crests and knitted sweaters, embroidered polo shirts and neckties. Such items can also be useful when it comes to fundraising.

▲ Most bowls pavilions, amongst the honours boards and photos, have on display a few artefacts and trophies. But few are as impressive as those of **Clevedon Bowling Club** in **Somerset** (*top*). Built in 1973, the pavilion houses the collection of its most eminent member, **David Bryant**, holder of 20 World and Commonwealth titles and an England regular for over 35 years.

Many of the badges reproduced on this book's insider covers are also on display at Clevedon, in a collection created by Eric Cook.

It is actually common for clubs to display badges in glass front display cases. Above is one such example, at **Titwood Bowling Club** in **Glasgow**. Every badge represents a club that Titwood have played at one time or another.

▶ Compared with their modern day equivalents, bowlers in the 18th and early 19th centuries competed for rather more practical rewards.

On Whit Monday 1734, at The Salutation Inn in Ipswich, 20 men paid five shillings each to enter a bowls match for which the prize was a dark chestnut mare valued at seven guineas. The second prize was a new bridle worth half a crown. The next day a hat was up for grabs, worth 10s 6d.

According to the *Blackburn Standard*, in July 1836 at the annual match on the green at Snig Brook, next to a brewery, sixteen bowlers contested a match of '13 up' for a silver snuff box.

The same newspaper reported in October 1840 that 32 subscribers at the Waterloo Bowling Green in Little Bolton played for 'a good fat pig', while in July 1860 the first prize at the Bowling Green Inn at Denton, near Manchester, was 'a good fat sheep'.

As more private clubs and societies were formed however, and as middle class Victorian bowlers increasingly embraced the tenets of amateurism – albeit hardly with the degree of moral vehemence exhibited by their counterparts in such sports as cricket, rowing and athletics – cash and other prizes were gradually superceded by ceremonial baubles instead.

In Chapter Five we will see how since 1776 the winner of the Knight's Competition, contested annually at the Old Bowling Green in Southampton, has been awarded a silver medal, bearing the motto 'Win it and Wear It'.

Another early surviving example of this trend, seen below, is this white metal medal, presented by the **Newbury and Speenhamland Bowling Club** in **Berkshire** (now known simply as the Newbury Bowling Club), to the winner of their singles championship in 1858.

Measuring 38mm in diameter, the medal's inscription *Palmam qui meruit ferat* (which had also been the motto of Lord Nelson) may be

translated as 'Let he who merits the palm bear it.'

From a photograph held by Newbury Museum showing club members in the 1880s – by which time the favoured attire, in contrast with the dapper young bowler portrayed on the medal, appears to have been tailcoats, waistcoats and top hats – we are able to gain a clear idea of the class of men who formed and sustained such clubs in the Victorian era.

They included at Newbury a bank manager, a draper, a retailer of pianos, a school master, an ironmonger, a wine and spirits merchant, a veterinary surgeon and a professor of music.

▲ Members of **Pollokshaws Bowling Club** in **Glasgow**, formed in 1854, sit beneath their trophy cabinet, the focal point of many a clubroom. Often donated by patrons or in memory of a club stalwart, mass produced cups and trophies from silversmiths in the likes of Bradford and Birmingham became a part of the bowls scene in the mid 19th century. A number of clubs also run 'spoons' tournaments, for which the prize is, of course, a silver spoon.

Tradition originally dictated that once won, a trophy would be filled with something suitably alcoholic by its new holder and then passed around for all to take a sip, thereby strengthening the bond between club members and allowing all to share a taste of success.

▶ Members of the **Bedale Bowling Club** in North Yorkshire (since renamed the Bedale Bowling Green Society), pose for their annual photograph in 1861. Amongst them are three doctors and either two sets of brothers, or two sets of father and sons.

Group photographs such as this, one of many found hanging on the walls of clubhouses and pavilions across the country, provide us with a fascinating insight into the social make-up of Victorian bowling clubs.

They also form an important part of local history. As such, it is to be commended that the records of the Bedale club, which date back to 1794 – two years after its formation – have been placed in the safe hands of the North Yorkshire County Record Office in Northallerton, where they remain available for public access. They include minute books, account books, visitor books, lists of rules, sundy correspondence and photograph albums, a rich store of information for anyone interested in bowls, in Bedale, and in the workings of Victorian clubs and societies. From these records and those of other bowling clubs there are so many strands that can be pursued, for example in relation to the history of local families, businesses and Masonic groups.

From the first minutes at Bedale we learn that one James Lunn was

paid 8s 3d for preparing a piece of wasteground for the new green, at a rate of 1s 6d a day. Marmaduke Gill, the local publican, was paid a further 6s 4d for supplying ale to Lunn's workmen.

The two largest subscribers to the new green, each giving five guineas, were Henry Peirse of Bedale Hall (the local MP and lord of the manor), and another prominent local resident, William Milbank, of Thorp Perrow.

They were among 20 members in the early months, three of whom were men of the cloth.

As will be noted, group photos in the 19th and early 20th centuries often included the 'bowls lad', in the case of Bedale in 1861 named only as '(Boy) Smith'.

Notice that around his neck is a board on a string. This was used to record the scores during matches. At some clubs a simple slate would

suffice. But this method was hardly foolproof, especially when money was at stake. This might explain why at the **Lewes Bowling Green Society** in East Sussex (the subject of our first case study on page 58), a rather more sophisticated **clock scorer** was in use (*above*). Still kept by the club, albeit now only as a curiosity, and thought to date from the 18th or 19th centuries, it is a

foot long and features two dials, one for those bowlers drawn to play together by choosing a white ball (hence the W), the other for those who had drawn the black. Each brass pointer is connected to a ratchet on the back to prevent it from being turned back one notch.

Such a simple, handcrafted device, worn by the bowls lad on a string around his neck.

▲ Aside from the walls of the pavilion, one does not have to look far at a bowls club to find a plaque or memorial of one sort or another.

Top left is a typical example of a member honoured at **Cardiff Athletic Club**. Top right is a gate, gifted by a member at **Kilmarnock Bowling Club** in **Ayrshire**.

Above, a brass plate records the erection of the pavilion at the **Shewsbury Severnside BC** in 1897, on the occasion of Queen Victoria's diamond jubilee. At the neighbouring **Shrewsbury Crescent BC**, on the right, **Dick Meyrick**, was one of the great crown green bowlers of all time, a winner of the 'All England' Merit four times, in 1948, 1961, 1962 and 1966.

Meyrick's longevity as a player, and these plaques and memorials, remind us that whereas in most sports, such as football or cricket, members typically stay active for only a decade or two before having to revert to social membership, a bowler can play on... Indeed it is not uncommon for bowlers to die on the green.

What better way to go, many a bowler will say. Unless one point from victory at the time, obviously.

▲ Ninety two year old farmer, businessman and racehorse owner **Dennis Allington**, in action in 2014 at **Hadley Heath** in **Worcestershire**, itself one of the oldest greens still in use in British bowling.

One of the barbs often thrown at bowls is that it is a game for elderly 'trundlers'. 'Old men's marbles' is another typical jibe, as if sport were the sole province of the young.

But with average life expectancy across the nation reaching 79 for men and 83 for women in 2015, and with some 17 per cent of the total population now being 65 or over, bowling clubs would appear to have much to offer the Britain of tomorrow.

▶ Bowls 'is a very quiet game and calculated rather for the steady old gentleman than for his rackety son.'

So said the *Manual of British Rural Sports* in 1861, a publication whose author, under the pen name of 'Stonehenge', had clearly never been to a pub green such as the **Gate Hangs High** in **Wrexham**.

For there are plenty of league teams in which the age gap between the oldest and youngest bowlers might be 50 years or more.

In addition to which, clubs hold special events where grandparents and grandchildren are paired in order to introduce the youngster to the basics.

Of course like any physical skill, bowls is best learnt young, when limbs are supple and the eye is keen. But it takes years to learn the tactical subtleties of line and length. As a result, except perhaps on a very slow green in poor weather, many a young whippersnapper has been taken down by a wily old hand who knows just how to spot a weakness in his opponent.

This aspect of bowls culture is unlikely to change. But another is dying out, and that is the 20th century phenomenon of standalone single-sex clubs.

Formed in Blackpool in 1928, **Highfield Ladies** is a now a relatively rare example of this kind, especially since most governing bodies have become mixed, and mixed leagues have become routine. Even on very large crown greens, women can now 'outreach' men by using small-sized bowls.

But while the older generation lives on, a certain conservatism is inevitable. At **Tamworth Castle** (*right*), and elsewhere, there are bowlers whose competitive careers began in the 1950s. Their knowledge, and not least their fund of tales, can never be discounted.

"THE HEALTH OF NATIONS."

"The Old English Game of Bowls ought to be revived in every Village in the Kingdom, as it 'brings every muscle into play, and does not suddenly exhaust by single and violent paroxysms of effort.'"

A Review of the Works of EDWIN CHADWICK.   By B. W. RICHARDSON, M.D., F.R.S.

▲ Framed on the pavilion walls of one of Britain's oldest clubs, **Great Torrington** in **Devon**, this quote by **Benjamin Ward Richardson** is taken from *The Commonhealth*, a series of essays on health and wellbeing (*see Links*). Published in 1887, the essays were inspired by the works of Sir Edwin Chadwick, a staunch advocate of Poor Law reform and public sanitation.

Richardson was by no means the first to see bowls in the context of health. As early as 1572, John Jones, whilst extolling the virtues of Buxton Spa, recommended 'bowling in allayes' or, should the weather be 'convenient, and the bowles fitte to such a game, as eyther in playne or longe allayes, or in suche as have crankes with halfe bowles, whiche is the fyner and gentler exercise.'

Today, it is for that same reason that Sport England funds the game, via an organisation called the Bowls Development Alliance. For people of advanced years, bowls has numerous health benefits.

But to understand what Jones meant by 'allayes' and 'halfe bowles' our focus is now the past, and the very roots of bowling's place in the heritage of Britain.

Chapter Four

Medieval bowls, romance and bias

'Formed' not in 1299, but 'prior to 1299'. That is the claim of the Southampton Old Bowling Green Club, a claim first aired in 1894. In 1913 bowlers in Chesterfield then published a history of their green, tracing its use back to 1294. In this chapter we begin our overview of Britain's bowling history by establishing the context of these and other claims, and examining what evidence exists of the game during the Medieval period. Can modern bowls genuinely trace its origins to the 13th century, or have the facts fallen victim to romance?

Such is the competitive nature of sport that it is tempting to fall into a debate as to which is the oldest in Britain.

Without revisiting that debate in detail, many writers have made a strong case for bowls.

Indeed if there is one theme that characterises the heritage of bowls in this country, and has done since the 19th century, it is the deep-seated desire of bowlers to connect their game to the Medieval period, and in doing so assert both its longevity and its age-old place, particularly, in English culture.

Certainly it is true that a form of bowling that would be recognisable today, played on grass, with biased bowls and a jack, had become established in England by the Elizabethan era, as will be confirmed in Chapter Five.

It is undeniable too that the first rules of the game were published in 1670, some 74 years before both cricket and golf followed suit.

It could also be argued that archery only started to evolve as a sport in its own right after bowmen ceased to be recruited to military service in 1595.

But what of bowls prior to the Tudors and Stuarts?

Most accounts of bowling history start with references to games involving the throwing of balls or stones in ancient Egypt, Greece and Rome. Attention has also been drawn to a well known account of life in London penned in c.1174 by William Fitzstephen.

Among various sports he describes in Latin – ball games on Shrove Tuesday, horse racing and skating – is *jactus lapidum*.

From this, some bowls historians have surmised that the word 'jack' – a key element of bowls – might derive from *jactus*.

But *jactus* means 'putting' or 'casting', while *lapidum* means a stone. Fitzstephen was therefore almost certainly referring to an activity closer to modern day shot putting than to bowls.

Another two centuries pass before further references survive relating to popular sports. Both are in royal ordinances aimed at forcing Englishmen to practice archery – in order to be militarily prepared – rather than engage in 'useless' or 'dishonest' games.

The first appears in a letter from Edward III in 1363, and in addition to *jactus lapidum* prohibits ball games played with the hand, foot or a stick. The second is in an Act of Richard II in 1388 in which the Norman term for casting a stone is *gettre de peer*. This act applied to servants, artificers and labourers, and specifically mentions tennis, football, quoits, dice and 'kailes' (a form of skittles). But not bowls.

Our search then leaps forward another century to 1477, when an Act of Edward IV made it unlawful to play certain games in 'Houses, Tenements, Gardens and other Places', not only because they were a distraction from archery but because they encouraged gambling and riotous behaviour.

Anyone caught hosting such activities could expect a swingeing fine of £20 and three years' imprisonment.

The Act's list of 'unlawful plays' included dice, quoits, tennis, football, and three forms of what we would now call skittles (that is games in which pins or targets are knocked down): these were 'closhe', 'keyles' and 'half bowl'.

90. BOWLING.—XIII. CENTURY.

Half bowl, as noted overleaf, has been shown to have existed in England in the late 13th century, coeval with the claims made for bowls in Southampton and Chesterfield. It shares in common with modern bowls the use of a biased ball. But half bowl was, nevertheless, still a form of what we would now call skittles (a term that first appears in the 1630s) and was not a game suited to grass.

Not that the distinction between bowls and skittles has always been clear in history. Nor is it today, given that, for example, 'bowlers' can also be cricketers aiming at a wicket, while by far the best known form of modern skittles is 'ten-pin bowling'.

Our lack of understanding of bowls in the Middle Ages is further clouded by an image described in 1801 by Joseph Strutt (*see Links*), as dating from the 13th century.

Reproduced opposite, it shows two men bowling balls along the ground between two cones. Were these cones targets to be aimed at, as a jack would be in modern bowls? Or were they targets to be knocked over, as in skittles?

Other early references are similarly open to interpretation.

For example, in c.1440, an English-Latin dictionary, the *Promptorium Parvulorum*, written by Geoffrey the Grammarian, a friar in Norfolk, translates the Latin *bolo* as 'Bowlyn, or pley wythe bowlys'.

Note that this distinguishes bowls from 'balls', the Latin for which is *pilae*. But it does not explain what form 'bowlyn' took.

Another question is raised by the use of the term 'alley'.

An early instance appears in a romance poem, *The Squire of Low Degree*, written c.1475 but of which only later transcripts survive. In it, the King of Hungary tries to

distract his heartbroken daughter with diversions, among them 'An hundreth knightes truly tolde, Shall play with bowles in alayes colde, Your disease to drive awaie.'

But do these cold alleys consist of bare earth, or stone or wooden floors, as might be expected for games resembling skittles?

Or could they be outdoor alleys consisting of a narrow strip of turf, as would become common in the Tudor period?

As every attempt to analyse these fragmentary pieces of evidence must inevitably conclude, we simply cannot know for sure what form of bowls was being played in Medieval Britain. Only that by around 1500 the words 'bowls' and 'alley' were in use.

We next come to the sensitive matter of how to treat various claims, all made in later centuries, concerning when and where bowls – whatever is meant by the term – was played in the Medieval period.

Is it at all possible to identify Britain's oldest bowling green, and, in turn, Britain's oldest bowling club? »

▲ Visual evidence of early bowling in Britain is sparse, which is why this exquisite detail from a much celebrated illuminated manuscript, *The Romance of Alexander* – dated 1338–44 and held in the collection of Oxford University's **Bodleian Library** – will be familiar to many students of the game.

The text itself, written in French, the language of the ruling Norman elite, consists of verses recounting legends from the life of Alexander the Great. But it is the fanciful illustrations in the margins, some showing animals in subversive roles – for example giant hares chasing men – that are of concern in the present context.

It should be noted that the illustrations were the work of a Flemish illuminator, **Jehan de Grise**. It is therefore possible that what we see here is a game of bowls not as it was played in Britain at the time, but in Flanders.

More significant however is that instead of a cone, the bowlers appear to be aiming at a jack, perhaps one of the smaller bowls on the left.

As Joseph Strutt wrote in *The Sports and Pastimes of the People of England,* published in 1801, 'the action of the middle figure, whose bowl is supposed to be running towards the jack, will not appear by any means extravagant to such as are accustomed to visit the bowling-greens'.

Indeed not. He contorts in a manner that will appear equally familiar to a modern day bowler.

Similarly, in time honoured fashion the bowler on the right places his left hand on his leg for balance (as may be seen several times in this book, for example on page 73). His body position further suggests that rather than throw the bowl, he intends to roll it.

So although this delightful illustration may not provide conclusive evidence that a form of modern bowls was being played on these shores at that time, it is certainly the closest we have to suggest that a game that was at least similar was being played in a part of northern Europe that lay within the compass of English readers.

▲ Measuring just 10cm or four inches in diameter, and weighing 400g, this oddly shaped lump of wood, in the collection of the **Hull and East Riding Museum**, has been described in earlier books in the *Played in Britain* series as the oldest sports-related ball known to have been purpose-made in Britain.

Excavated in Hull, from the site of a medieval hall on the corner of High Street and Blackfriargate, amid materials reliably dated between 1280–1300, it was at first believed to be a spherical ball that had split on one side. But after examination by *Played in Britain* experts it was confirmed that far from being damaged, the ball had been intentionally fashioned in this shape, for use in a well known game known as **'half bowl'**.

This was one of several 'plays' banned by Edward IV in 1477 and was later called **'rolly polly'**.

As illustrated below, half bowl was strictly speaking a form of

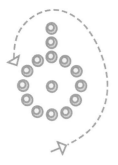

skittles. That is, the half bowl was aimed not at a jack but at a set of pins set up in a circle, with an extra pin in the centre and two outliers at the far end. The object was to roll the half-bowl around the back of the circle, past the outliers, and only then to knock down the pins.

How was this possible? Because the shape of the half-bowl gave it an extreme, in-built bias and therefore a curved trajectory over a short distance (for this was a game almost certainly played indoors or at least on smooth, hard floors).

Why is this discovery significant? Firstly because it confirms that the concept of bias was understood in 13th century Britain, some two centuries before Edward IV's ban.

The half bowl's existence also puts paid to a much repeated legend that bias was discovered accidentally in 1522 by Charles Brandon, the Duke of Suffolk. (The tale has it that after one of his bowls split in the middle of a game in Goole he entered a nearby house and sliced a timber ball off the top of the newel post on a staircase, only then to discover that it was not quite spherical and rolled in a curious fashion.)

The discovery of the Hull half bowl further confirms that long before Robert Recorde's comments in 1556 (see page 10), bowls makers knew how to create bias by shaping bowls rather than by inserting lead weights, a practice that would become commonplace in later centuries.

It remains impossible to state with any accuracy when biased bowls were first aimed at jacks, rather than at pins. But thanks to the Hull half bowl we can at least be confident that this important stage in the evolution of modern bowls did occur before the 16th century.

》 The answer is that we can come to a series of reasonably informed judgements, but none that pre-date the accession of Henry VII, the first Tudor monarch, in 1485.

This is why our first set of case studies, which include the greens at Southampton and Chesterfield, and a later claim made by Hereford for a formation date of 1484, are all dealt with in the next chapter, on the Tudor and Stuart periods.

In each case it is only in the 16th and 17th centuries that reliable evidence of bowling in specific locations can be found.

This is not to say that the Victorian and Edwardian bowlers who made certain claims about bowls' early history deliberately set out to falsify events.

Or that a marked vagueness in historical analysis is confined to the world of bowling.

Longstanding myths and legends, or what some historians have described as 'invented traditions', are common to most sports and indeed most branches of cultural life. (As a newspaper editor in the Hollywood classic of 1962, *The Man Who Shot Liberty Valance*, famously proclaimed, 'When the legend becomes fact, print the legend'.)

In bowls the two most significant impediments to precise historical judgement are these.

Firstly, because in the years between 1363 and 1660, for most sectors of society other than in royal circles and the aristocracy, bowling was a proscribed sport, inevitably when it did take place it did so in secret.

As noted earlier, the fines for hosting games and for playing in them were severe.

Nevertheless they did take place. We know this because the earlier Acts prohibiting unlawful sports

and games had to be re-enacted several times, the last occasion coming in 1541 during the reign of Henry VIII (despite his own great love of all things sporting).

In addition, as certain historians have suggested, the huge social and economic changes wrought by the Black Death in around 1350 – when an estimated five million people in England died, some 70 per cent of the total – ripened the opportunities for ordinary men to indulge in games and gambling.

With labour scarce and wages rising, with feudalism in retreat and the merchant class growing in the nation's burgeoning towns and cities, the conditions for a sport such as bowls to take root were surely ideal.

Yet because of the repeated prohibitions, what little written evidence there is of the game is inevitably confined to instances where cuplrits were caught and their punishments recorded.

So bowls may well have been established in one form or another before 1500. But if it was, it was an essentially clandestine activity.

The second reason why the early history of bowls has become hard to pin down is that in the Victorian and Edwardian eras, as happened in many sports, enthusiasts latched onto any references they could find to establish the game's historical credentials.

Why so? Because then, as now, heritage mattered.

And also because at a time when sport was under continual attack from moralists – whether it be for encouraging gambling, drinking or jollity on the Sabbath – by demonstrating that their sports were especially ancient, and deeply rooted, and part of the warp and weft of local life, they lent it respectability and provenance.

The evolving legend that grew from the tale of Sir Francis Drake playing bowls as the Armada approached in 1588 – a story we will return to often – was but one manifestation of this phenomenon.

No-one ever pointed out that Drake had committed a crime by playing bowls in a public place. Which technically he did. Rather, they celebrated him as a brave patriot and man of the people.

Swept along by a wave of nostalgia and imperial flag-waving in the late 19th and early 20th centuries, a number of assumptions were made by bowling enthusiasts, assumptions that have persisted to this very day.

In both Southampton and Chesterfield, for example, the assumption was made that the earliest known references to the land on which their greens stood, and indeed still stand, 1299 and 1294 respectively, meant that bowls was played on those sites in those years. As our case studies show, actual references to bowls in both places are in fact much later, in 1600 and 1664 respectively.

Now by any standards, in almost every other sport, verified instances of a sport having been played in either 1600 or 1664 would be celebrated. How much more provenance could a bowler desire? And yet in bowls it matters to be as old as possible, to go back even to the age of knights and longbows, castles and Crusaders.

A further assumption made in bowling history, again largely by the Victorians and Edwardians, is that the earliest known reference to bowls in any one area must equate also with the foundation of the local bowls club.

Thus 'formed prior to 1299' started to appear as a fact in

Southampton when no records of a club can be found prior to 1776. And yet once again, in most sports for any club to be able to trace its history to 1776 would in itself be a great badge of honour.

Similarly in Chesterfield the earliest records pertaining to the present club start in 1828, still well before the majority of clubs in most other sports.

There are also claims in bowls that may well be based on false readings of historical documents.

In Hereford, for example, the claim for bowls having been played in the town in 1484 may have emanated from a mis-reading of a document actually dated 1684.

None of this need detract at all from the hallowed place that bowls occupies in the canon of sport, both in Britain and globally.

All it means is that on the evidence available we cannot be certain that bowls, as we recognise it today, was played in Britain before c.1500, or that it was played in any form before that date on the sites which are claimed to house our oldest bowling greens.

Only in the Tudor period, to which we now turn, do the facts start to speak for themselves.

◀ Illusive juxtapositions are so commonplace within the context of sporting history that few people question them. They seem right, so they must be right.

Here amidst the ruins of **Knaresborough Castle**, dating from the 14th century, alongside a medieval courthouse (now a museum), lies a bowling green.

Surely it must have been there for centuries. Bowling is, after all, such an ancient sport. And yet the green was laid only in the early 20th century, and strictly speaking, in conservation terms, is entirely incongruous. At the very least, as a character appraisal of the Conservation Area in which it sits described it in 2008, the green 'represents something of a municipal intrusion'.

Yet lest this should seem rather mean spirited, it adds that the green must no doubt also be 'a much-enjoyed facility'.

Conversely **Raglan Castle** in Wales was built between 1430 and 1600 and did indeed have a bowling green in the early 17th century (*below left*). 'Much liked... for its situation' by Charles I, it fell into disuse after his demise.

So the signs are not always obvious, and the narratives not always straightforward. Such are the vagaries of heritage. If myths and fancy are what we crave, bowls is an ideal sport in which to revel.

Chapter Five

Tudors and Stuarts 1485–1688

If there is one story that everyone knows about bowls, it is Francis Drake, bowling on Plymouth Hoe (as seen on this pub sign near Chorley, Lancashire), cool as a cucumber, as the Spanish Armada approached in 1588. In common with most legends we cannot be sure this actually happened. But nor can we prove that it did not. What it does confirm, however, is that by the time the story emerged in print, in the 1620s, bowls had become a national pastime. To be a bowler was to be a regular guy. One of the chaps. A true Englishman.

As we progress into the Tudor and Stuart periods, the range and depth of evidence for bowling increases appreciably, even if the terms 'bowls' and 'bowling' continue to remain tantalisingly open to interpretation.

James IV of Scotland, who ruled from 1488-1513, is for example recorded as losing bets on two forms of 'bowls' played at Holyrood and Stirling, 'lang bowlis' and 'row bowlis'.

The former, 'long bowls', was probably a test of how many throws were needed to cover a set distance (known later as 'road bowls'). The word 'row', by contrast, would indicate a rolling ball in Scottish dialect. Yet this too could be a skittles game, possibly half-bowl. We cannot be sure.

One issue does become clear however. That is that by the early 17th century, when James VI of Scotland ascended the throne in England, the British were bowling in ways that would be immediately recognisable to modern bowlers.

This much we can confirm from the extract below, in which Gervase Markham summarises the three types of bowling enjoyed during James' reign.

The first clearly refers to yet another form of skittles, in which a 'flat bowle' – a heavy, disc-like wooden projectile we would call a 'cheese' – is thrown down a short alley at a set of pins. Such an alley could be indoors or outdoors.

Popular until the mid 20th century, this game, known also as Old English or London skittles, is now played in only one alley in Britain, at the Freemasons Arms in Hampstead, London. (More details can be found in *Played at the Pub, see Links*).

However Markham's two other types of bowls clearly equate with modern forms of the game.

His 'round biazed bowls for open grounds of advantage' describes the game that was the dominant form of outdoor bowls played until the 19th century.

Today it is found in its original form in only two locations, Lewes in East Sussex and Hadley Heath in Worcestershire (both case studies later in this chapter), although modern day crown green bowls is clearly its direct descendant.

Markham then states that for 'green swathes that are plain and level', a round, and therefore unbiased bowl is best.

Unbiased balls are of course not used in modern bowls at all. But Markham's comment confirms the visual evidence we have, from paintings and prints of the period, that for those wealthy enough to create and maintain them, 'plain and level' lawns were available, over 200 years before the Scots evolved the new form of 'flat green' or 'rink' bowling on them in the mid 19th century.

That by 1615, when Markham was writing, bowls culture appears to have become well established in England and Scotland, suggests that the hardline restrictions put in place during the Medieval period had eased.

But this was not the case. The Tudors maintained the stance initiated by their Plantaganet predecessors. Henry VIII in particular is remembered for the stark contrast between his own passion for sport, and his repeated attempts to suppress it amongst the lower orders.

'A man shall find great art in chusing out his ground, and preventing the winding, hanging and many turning advantages of the same, whether it be in open wilde places or close allies; and for his sport, the chusing of the bowle is the greatest cunning; your flat bowles being best for allies, your round biazed bowls for open grounds of advantage, and your round bowles like a ball for green swathes that are plain and level.'

from **Countrey Contentments, or The English Huswife** by Gervase Markham, first published in London in 1615

Thus in 1511 he issued another ban on popular games – one in which the word 'bowls' is used for the first time – and in 1515 ordered the keepers of a bowling alley and three tennis courts in London 'not to suffer common players to occupy their plays'.

Yet Henry was quite happy to raise money from bowls and other sports if practised by the upper classes. In 1535 – shortly after he had installed a bowling alley, a cockpit and four tennis courts at Whitehall Palace – the first recorded official licence to operate a bowling alley was issued in London, to one Hugh Foster. Four further licences were issued before Henry's death in 1547.

It may have been to reinforce this licensing system, which of course brought in useful revenue, as well as to clamp down on alleys of ill-repute, that in 1541 Henry sanctioned one of the most draconian bans yet enacted.

This required that no-one 'by himself, factor, deputy, servant, or other person, shall, for his or their gain, lucre, or living, keep, have, hold, occupy, or maintain any common house, alley or place of bowling.'

Moreover, only if a man were worth £100 a year would he be allowed to bowl on his own land.

As for lowly artificers and servants, they were allowed to play on Christmas Day, but only in their masters' houses, and not in any open space or orchard.

This restriction again suggests that 'bowling' referred as much to skittles (as an indoor pursuit) as it did to the outdoor game.

Indeed the bowling, or skittle alley, was to become the bête-noir of the era. 'Common bowling alleys,' wrote Stephen Gosson in *The School of Abuse* in 1579, »

▲ Whether or not **Sir Francis Drake** did bowl as the Armada approached in July 1588, there can be no doubt that the **Hoe** at **Plymouth** – 'hoe' being an Old English word for a promontory – was typical of the sort of open, natural terrain where bowling took place.

Seen here is a siege map of the area and its fortifications, drawn in 1643 during the Civil War, 55 years after the Armada. The Hoe is the expanse south of the walled town of Plymouth, featuring just a fort in its south east corner and a windmill facing out onto Plymouth Sound and St Nicholas' Island (now better known, predictably, as Drake's Island). Most likely its turf would have been of the finer fescue and bent varieties which, being the main species found in sea-washed turf, were deemed 300 years later to be ideal for bowling greens.

There is no point speculating where Drake and his companions might have played on the Hoe. It could have been anywhere, for this was a wild space before it was tamed and reduced by encroaching development in the 19th century.

The effects of this are clear in the modern aerial photograph (*below*). In the foreground lies **Tinside Lido** and beyond it the red and white banded **Smeaton's Tower** (close to where the windmill had stood in 1643). But notice in the upper left an enclosed green, flanked by trees.

Located on Lockyer Street, this is a public green, home to three clubs: the **City of Plymouth Bowling Club**, **Plymouth Hoe Ladies Club** and **Plymouth Visually Impaired Club**.

The sign for the green is the one reproduced on the opposite page.

Plymouth was, ironically, rather late in acknowledging its bowling past. For when, on the 300th anniversary of the Armada in 1888, it was decided to stage a bowls match, no bowlers were to be found locally. Instead, players from Great Torrington, 50 miles away, and Leeds, contested the match.

Not until 1907 was the current Hoe green laid, and the **Plymouth (Sir Francis Drake) Bowling Club** formed. Even then they decided to quit the green in 1922 for a more sheltered inland spot in Mannamead, a suburb of Plymouth, where they remain to this day.

▲ From the collection of the **National Maritime Museum** at **Greenwich**, this is perhaps the best known depiction of **Sir Francis Drake** on **Plymouth Hoe**.

It was painted in 1880 by **John Seymour Lucas**, a specialist in stirring, patriotic scenes. Drake is seen holding a bowl and waving away the urgings of **Lord Howard of Effingham**, the Lord High Admiral, to prepare for battle. (So not only was Drake a cool customer, as a Vice Admiral he was also behaving in an insubordinate fashion.)

But even if this rendition is a Victorian fiction (almost certainly based on Charles Kingsley's 1855 novel *Westward Ho!*), again we cannot discount the possibility that bowls was played that day on the Hoe. After all there are many references to bowls being popular amongst military men of all ranks during this period.

Also in the late 16th century, an elongated trough at **Peel Castle** on the **Isle of Man** (*below*) is known to have served as a bowling green when the garrison was beefed up to meet the threat from Spain.

In 1642, during the Civil War, it is recorded that Parliamentary troops seized Upnor Castle in Kent 'whilst the soldiers were at bowls'.

Meanwhile Oliver Cromwell was known to enjoy the game, and in 1647, Adam Eyre, a Roundhead captain near Sheffield, recorded several days at bowls in his diary. Having lost money repeatedly, his entry for July 30 notes: 'This day I stayed at home all day, by reason my wife was not willing to let me goe to bowles at Bolstertone.'

Charles I, whose love of bowls is well known, would no doubt have sympathised. In the 1640s, just as in 1588, bowls was what Englishmen did. Like football today, it was rooted in their everyday life.

'are privy moths that eat up the credit of many idle citizens; whose gains at home are not able to weigh down their losses abroad; whose shops are so far from maintaining their play, that their wives and children cry out for bread, and go to bed supperless often in the year.'

The mention of shops, meaning not only retail stores but workshops and other places of business, is interesting, for here we have neither the social elite nor the lower orders, but the emergent, if not yet respectable, middle class.

Gosson's writings equally reflect concerns that alleys and sports in general were, if no longer luring men from archery practice – the last time English archers played a decisive role in battle was at Flodden Field in 1513 – then they were at least distracting people from Sunday observance.

Typical of this is a report in 1571 of bowls being played whilst church services took place in Newbury. More examples will be cited in later pages, for they were to increase in the 17th century as the Puritans sought to clamp down further on sports and games.

But before turning to the Stuart era, another of Henry VIII's actions merits mention. By the Dissolution of the Monasteries, begun in 1536, the Crown seized thousands of acres of land, the largest land grab in England ever recorded. Yet within a few years, two thirds of this land had been sold on to finance Henry's military campaigns. These sales in turn released vast swathes of land for all kinds of new uses, one of which – albeit only in small plots – was the laying out of bowling greens to serve the growing number of urban dwellers.

An example of this is in Tewkesbury, where the town's green at the Bell Inn lay originally within the Abbey grounds, hence being described in the 19th century as the 'monks' green'.

Finally the most persuasive evidence we have that bowls had become mainstream by the end of the Tudor period are the numerous references made to the game in the works of Shakespeare, written during the period 1590-1613.

All suggest that he expected his audiences to pick up on, and enjoy the nuances intended.

To give but one example, in *Cymbeline*, Cloten exclaims:

'Was there ever man had such luck! When I kissed the jack, upon an up-cast to be hit away! I had a hundred pound on't.'

According to the Oxford English Dictionary, this reference, written in at least 1611, is the earliest to use 'jack' in the context of bowls.

Most likely it had been coined in a diminutive sense, the jack being smaller than the other bowls.

The same applies to other terms for jack in use around Britain, even today, such as 'kitty', 'monkey' and 'cot'. But another word used for a jack that does not fit in with this pattern is 'block', still commonly heard in crown green circles.

John Taylor, the Water Poet – he was a Thames waterman – showed an intimate knowledge of bowls when he wrote on the subject of the jack, or block, in 1630.

'This wise game doth make the fathers surpasse their children in apish toyes and most delicate dog tricks... The mark that which they argue at hath sundry names and epithites, as a 'blocke', a 'jacke' and a 'mistresse'... but I hold 'mistresse' to be the fittest name for it, for there are some that are commonly termed mistresses

which are not much better than mine aunts, and a mistresse is oftentimes a marke for every knave to have a fling at. Everyone strives to come so neere her that he would kisse her, and yet some are short, some wide and some over, and to whoso doth kisse it may perhaps sweeten his lips but I assure him it shall never fill his belly but rather empty his purse.'

As for the bowls themselves, we have already noted from the words of Robert Recorde in 1556 (*see page 10*), that bowlmakers knew how to create bias by shaping them on a lathe. Various native woods were used, including ash, yew and oak.

However all these would be superceded by the new wonder material of the age, lignum vitae.

A dense, heavy and oily wood first imported to England from the Caribbean and South America in the 16th century, its use to make bowls that did not split easily and held their shape, and therefore their bias, would constitute a crucial advance to the game.

But there is also evidence that 17th century tricksters knew well how to drill holes into woods and fill them, undetectably, with molten lead, thereby distorting their bias. Many an innocent was apparently caught out by such chicanery, especially in the less seemly alleys of London.

On which note, perhaps the most significant development of all concerning the social aspect of bowls in this period was that in the modern vernacular, it went 'upmarket'. That is to say, it became fashionable.

To give but one example. In 1618 Nicholas Breton wrote in *The Court and Country* that the essential qualities of a gentleman were that he was able to 'speake well, ride well, shoote well and bowle well.'

For his part, Charles I, who succeeded James I in 1625, enjoyed bowls throughout his life, in good times and bad.

Early in his reign he opened up to the public – or at least those able to pay the admission charges – the royal green at Spring Gardens, near Charing Cross. Its licensee went under the name of the Keeper of the King's Garden and Bowling Green. In 1631 this position was taken by Simon Osbaldeston.

Four years later Osbaldeston opened new premises at Shaver's Hall (in the vicinity of Leicester Square), which had both a bowling alley and a green.

Among other greens Charles I is known to have frequented were those at Raglan Castle in Wales (*see page 47*), at Collins End (near Goring Heath in Oxfordshire), Althorp and Great Harrowden (both Northamptonshire) and, most famously of all, Barking Hall in Essex, the home of Richard Shute MP, a 'turkey merchant', where Charles was famously said to have lost the vast sum of £1,000 before deciding to quit playing, he said, in the interests of his wife and children.

»

▲ Fellows of **Pembroke College, Cambridge**, exercise their exclusive right to bowl on the College green, overlooked by the Old Master's Lodge (rebuilt in the 19th century).

One characteristic of the green is that a ridge runs across its centre. Another is that the Fellows still use lignum vitae woods. One report described early woods in use there as 'sliced'. That is, similar in profile to those at Framlingham (*see page 10*), a site owned by Pembroke from 1636-1948 (*page 78*). But no examples have been found to compare them with 'Fram woods'.

Other early bowling greens in Cambridge have included those at St John's (laid in 1625), Trinity and Emmanuel Colleges, and in Oxford at New and Magdalen Colleges.

Viriufq; crepundia Merces.
Will: *Marshall Sculpsit:*

▲ In *Emblems, Divine and Moral,*
written in 1635 by **Francis Quarles**
and illustrated by **William Marshall**,
we find the **Devil's Bowling Green.**

Quarles' theme is a familiar one.
'The world's the Jack; the gamesters
that contend are Cupid, Mammon;
that judicious fiend that gives the
ground is Satan.'

John Earle, a York clergyman,
issued a similar warning in 1628
in *Microcosmographie.* 'A bowling
green or bowling alley is a place
where three things are thrown away
besides the bowls: time, money and
curses, and the last ten for one...

'Never did Mimmicke screw
his body into half the forms these
men to theirs; and it is an article of
their creed that the bending back
of their body or screwing in of their
shoulders is sufficient to hinder
the over-speed of the bowl, and
that the running after it adds to the
speed.. How senseless these men
appear when they are speaking
sense to these bowls, putting
confidence in their intreaties for a
good cast.'

Satanic or not, here are
behavioural traits that every bowler
today will recognise all too readily.

» One of those children inherited
his passion. After the Restoration
Charles II created new greens at
Windsor Castle (costing £20 7s
11d) and Whitehall, and in 1670
gave his name to a set of rules.

Reproduced opposite, these
are the earliest known rules of any
British sport that is still played
today in essentially the same form.

Most of the 1670 rules will be
understood by modern bowlers,
especially the last one, concerning
the need for players to keep their
temper. The final clause adds that
bowlers 'must take rubbers'. This
had nothing to do with equipment.

A rubber, in bowls as in card
games, meant simply that all
games had to be the 'best of three'.

Restoration England's love of
bowls was reflected in the works
of dramatists and polemicists. As
in Shakespeare's work the game
was used as a metaphor for life, or
as a study in evil. It pops up in the
entries of diarists, such as Samuel
Pepys and John Evelyn, and in
the jottings of John Aubrey, who
was particularly caustic about the
hypocrisy of Puritans at Emmanuel
College, Cambridge,

'They carried themselves
outwardly with great sanctity and
strictnesse... They preached up
very strict keeping and observing
the Lord's day; made, upon the
matter, damnation to breake it,
and that 'twas lesse sin to kill a
man than break the sabbath.

'Yet these hypocrites did bowle
in a private green at their colledge
every Sunday after sermon; and
one of the colledge... to satisfie
him one time lent him the key of
a private back dore to the bowling
green, on a Sunday evening, which
he opening, discovered these
zealous preachers, with their
gownes off, earnest at play. But
they were strangely surprized to

see the entrey of one that was not
of the brotherhood.'

Emmanuel's green, we can be
reasonably sure, was fairly level
and well maintained.

But from other sources we
read that for most bowlers before
the advent of heavy rollers, lawn
mowers and weedkillers, in most
towns and villages, away from the
colleges, palaces, great houses and
big cities, bowling took place on
much less groomed surfaces.

Several accounts, for example,
locate games in orchards and on
public commons (like the Hoe),
where grass mingled with weeds
and wildflowers, and must have
been an inch long or more.

Randle Holme, we recall (*see
page* 8), also referred to bowling
on 'bares', meaning 'open wide
places' found on moors and
commons. From the very name we
must assume that he also meant
bare surfaces, formed either by
compacted earth or gravel.

Then there is this description
of a green at Foyhaven (Fowey)
in Cornwall, penned by Richard
Carew in 1602. 'It is cut out in the
side of a steepe hill, whose foote
the salt water washeth, evenly
levelled, to serve for bowling,
floored with sand, for soaking up
the rayne, closed with two thorne
hedges, and banked with sweete
senting flowers. It wideneth
to a sufficient breadth, for the
march of five or six in front, and
extendeth, to not much lesse, than
halfe a London mile: neyther doth
it lead wearisomely forthright, but
yeeldeth varied, & yet, not over-
busie turnings, as the grounds
opportunity affoordeth.'

Readers who bowl may easily
imagine the challenges presented
by such a naturalistic terrain.

The first known public green in
Scotland, at Haddington, east of

Edinburgh, was similarly located, on the floodbank of the River Tyne, (known as 'the Sands') from 1662.

In the 1680s, meanwhile, Thomas Baskerville, in his *Notes on Journeys in England*, listed public greens in Bedford, Bury St Edmunds, Gloucester, Great Yarmouth ('a place to bowl in on the greens of the shore'), Norwich, Pontefract, Romford (where 'adjoining to the churchyard they have a fair bowling green, frequented by the gentry'), Saffron Walden and Warwick.

In Bath, where bowling is first recorded in 1637, Edward Ward described the gentry at play in 1700. 'About five in the Evening, we went to see a great Match at Bowling; there was Quality, and Reverend Doctors of both Professions, Topping Merchants, Broken Bankers, Noted Mercers, Inns of Court Rakes, City Beaus, Stray'd Prentice, and Dancing Masters in abundance.

'Fly, fly, fly: said one: Rub, rub, rub, cry'd another. Ten Guinies to five, I uncovered the Jack, says a Third. Damn these nice fingers of mine, cry'd my Lord, I slipt my bowl, and mistock the Bias.

'Another Swering he knew the Ground to an Inch, and, would have hold five Pound his Bowl came in.

'But in Short, the Citizens won the Courtiers Money, and the Courtiers Swore to be Reveng'd on their Wives, and Daughters.'

To work out where exactly this vivid scene might have taken place in Bath, turn the page.

For another facet of the game that must also be noted in the 17th century is that, along with cockpits and tennis courts, bowling greens were among the first purpose-built sports facilities to appear on maps in Britain.

Rules for Game of Bowls, as settled by His Most Excellent Majesty King Charles II, His Royal Highness James, Duke of York, and His Grace George, Duke of Buckingham, in the year 1670: the game to consist of five or more points as may be agreed upon by the party engaged. Four or six bowlers constitute a set.

1. The party who hath the highest die shall lead the jack, keeping his foot on the trig, which must be placed at least one yard from the verge of the green. No cast shall be less than thirty yards.

2. Whoever shall once throw the jack off the green shall lose the leading of the jack to their opponents, and shall be obliged to follow the jack so led by their opponents or adverse party.

3. At the commencement of every end the trig shall be placed where the jack was taken up, or three strides wide of it in any direction before the jack be thrown; provided that by so doing the cast be not less than thirty yards.

4. If the jack be bowled off the green, there shall be a fresh cast, and the same party again lead.

5. If a bowl whilst running be stopped by the adverse party, it shall be laid closely behind the jack.

6. If any bowler do take up the jack before the cast or casts won be granted, he shall lose the cast to the adverse party.

7. If any bowler who lieth all, ie, who is nearest the jack, do take the jack up, or cause the same to be taken up, before his opponent has thrown the last bowl, his side shall lose the cast and the lead shall begin again.

8. If any bowler who lieth all do take up the jack or cause the same to be taken up, before his own partner hath thrown his last bowl, he shall lose the benefit of that bowl.

9. If any bowl do lie between the jack, and the bowl that is to be measured, or the jack leaneth upon the bowl, or the bowl upon the jack, it shall be lawful to bolster up the bowl or jack, and to take away that which hindered the measuring, provided it does not prejudice the adverse party in so doing. If it shall appear to the spectators (being no bettors) the adverse party was prejudiced thereby, although the bowl did win, yet the benefit thereof shall be lost.

10. If in measuring it shall appear that the bowl or jack was removed or made worse by the measure, the cast so measured shall be allowed to the adverse party.

11. If any bowler bowl out of turn, his bowl may be stopped by the adverse party, but not by him who delivered the same.

12. If any bowl be stopped whilst running or touched by its own party, it shall then be taken away.

13. If any bowler do deliver his bowl or bowls not touching the trig with his foot, it shall be lawful for the adverse party to stop same whilst running and make him bowl it again, but it shall not be lawful for him that bowls to stop it.

14. If any bowler who lieth all do take up a bowl or bowls before the adverse party hath granted them, the cast shall be lost and the jack shall be thrown away.

15. Bowlers nor bettors shall do nothing to prejudice or favour a bowl by wind, hat, foot or otherwise, and if done the cast shall be lost.

16. No cast shall be measured before all the bowls are bowled.

17. If he that is to throw the last bowl do take up the trig, or cause it to be taken up, supposing the game to be won, or that he may do some hurt, the same bowls shall not be bowled that cast or end, for the trig once taken up shall not be set again.

18. If any running bowl be stopped or touched by a spectator, not being a bettor, whether it be to the benefit or hindrance to the caster, the same bowl shall take its chance and lie.

19. If a bowl be moved out of its place by the party that bowled the same at any time before the cast be ended, the same may be cleared away by the adverse party.

20. Keep your temper and remember that he who plays at bowls must take rubbers.

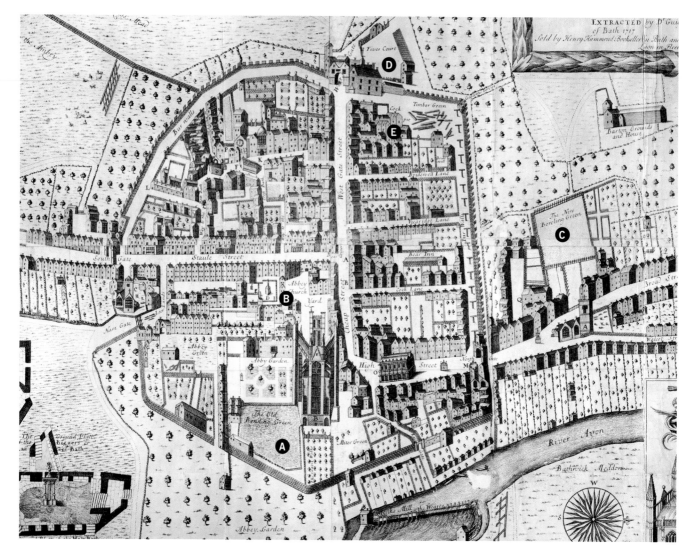

▲ First published in 1694 and seen here in its 1717 edition, **Gilmore's Map of Bath** was intended as a guide to would-be visitors, offering details of 29 lodging houses and 23 inns. But in the present context it illustrates the typical sporting attractions of the late Stuart era.

The 'old' bowling green **(A)** to the west of the Abbey was one of many examples of land released by the Dissolution and turned into recreational use. William Master leased the green from the corporation in 1637 for 10s and in 1638 for £1. It was still in use in 1725, by which time there was a building at its side, possibly offering refreshments. Today, York Street runs through the site.

To the north, as shown on an earlier map of 1600, there used to be an **open air tennis court**, where the Pump Room now stands **(B)**.

As Bath expanded, by 1694 a second bowling green appeared to the east of the walls **(C)**. This site is now bound appropriately by Green Street and Milsom Street.

Also shown is a **Fives Court (D)**, where Sainsbury's now stands on Monmouth Street and a **Cockpit (E)**, where Saw Close is now.

▼ Rare was the country house of the 17th century that did not have its own bowling green, or, if only a narrow strip of turf was set aside, a 'bowling alley'. And although none is still bowled upon, at least not formally, many remain as lawns.

One such example, still with slightly raised banks on three sides, is the former bowling green on the north west side of **Norton Conyers Hall**, near Ripon in North Yorkshire.

Both the house and its extensive gardens are listed, Grade II* and Grade II respectively.

Laid out in c.1630, the bowling green was still in use when this photograph appeared in *Country Life* in May 1900. Indeed, Ripon Bowling Club had played Bedale BC on it in the 1890s.

Both Charles I, in 1633, and the future James II, in 1679, stayed at Norton Conyers. It is therefore not unreasonable to assume that both might have played there too.

Certainly its owners were loyal. The estate had been acquired in 1624 by Sir Richard Graham, who was later to die of wounds sustained whilst fighting for the Royalist cause at Marston Moor in 1644. Since then the Graham family has remained in residence.

During the political ferment of the Civil War, bowling greens were mentioned often in despatches. Anthony Ashley Cooper wrote of Hanley in East Dorset as a major meeting place. 'Though neither the green nor the accommodation was inviting yet it was well-placed for to contrive the correspondence of the gentry in those parts.'

▲ Before the Civil War, one of the Isle of Wight MPs, Sir John Oglander, was among a group of gentlemen who met twice a week for bowls and socialising at a nearby inn. So when Charles I was sent to **Carisbrooke Castle** under house arrest in 1647, the island's governor, Robert Hammond, knew just what to do. He laid down a bowling green within the ramparts – seen above as the oval-shaped patch on the left – and had a pavilion built alongside.

Charles bowled almost every evening, but still tried to escape, before he was returned to London and executed in 1648.

Rather poignantly two years later his 14 year old daughter Elizabeth also met her end, having caught a chill, it is said, whilst bowling on the same green at Carisbrooke.

In the 19th century the green was used as a parade ground. But like Norton Conyers it has not been used for serious bowling for a century or more.

TERRACE. BRAMSHILL. HANTS.

▲ In **Gloucestershire**, **Berkeley Castle** has a good example of what was often called in the 17th century a 'bowling alley' but which to modern eyes is simply a long, narrow lawn. Charles I may not have bowled here, but Elizabeth I did. Or so it is said.

Alleys of this type fitted neatly into terraced gardens, and offered a discreet, sheltered place for walks and perhaps illicit liaisons.

Narrower still is the alley at the Grade I listed **Cranborne Manor** in **Wimborne**, **Dorset**.

Featured in *Country Life* in July 1901 (*right*), this 'alley' was and remains flanked by yew hedges, and is part of gardens, now also listed, laid out in 1608–12 by John Tradescant and Mounten Jennings.

▲ Reproduced in a four volume series *Mansions of England in the Olden Time*, published in 1839, this is how lithographer Joseph Nash imagined a 17th century game of bowls might have looked on the terrace at **Bramshill House** in **Hampshire**. By Nash's day this part of the Jacobean house was called the **Troco Terrace**, 'troco' or 'trucks' being a game of lawn billiards, similar to croquet.

Nash drew another version of this view but with fencing taking place instead of bowling.

Today Bramshill House is Grade I listed, and is best known as the Police Staff College, a role it served from 1960–2014.

▶ A number of buildings from the Tudor and Stuart periods have been described as bowling green pavilions, yet have equally been billed as 'summer' or 'banqueting' houses. This is because they were designed for a range of social gatherings at which, in addition to bowling, there would be eating, drinking, card games and even candlelit dancing on the green.

One of the earliest surviving examples (*right*) is the Grade II* **Bowling Green House** (or Summer House) at **Melford Hall** in **Long Melford, Suffolk**, dating from the 16th century, but with 18th century windows. An octagonal red brick building, this looked out over a narrow, tree-lined walk between the hall's main garden and its moat, a walkway traditionally referred to as the 'bowling green', even though it was narrow enough to have genuinely merited the name 'alley'.

Another instance of how the terminology of bowls in this period can lead to confusion.

Even grander is the Grade I listed **Bowling Green House** at **Swarkestone**, in **Derbyshire** (*right*).

Built in 1631-32 at the time of the marriage between Sir John Harpur and Catherine Howard, it was originally referred to in the family accounts as the 'Bowle Alley house'. Richard Shepperd, a mason, was paid £111 12s 4d for its construction. The architect may have been John Smythson.

Swarkestone forms part of a network of Derbyshire estates with historical connections to bowling.

This includes Chatsworth (*see page 87*), where Smythson's father Robert also worked, and Haddon Hall, which has a Bowling Green terrace in its Upper Garden.

Yet in Swarkestone's case it is only the pavilion, and not the original house that survives.

Swarkestone Hall was largely demolished during the 1740s, leaving the pavilion to deteriorate gradually, not least after it was struck by lightning in 1844.

By the 20th century it was hardly more than a shell, until it was granted an unlikely spot in the limelight by featuring in promotional material for the Rolling Stones' album *Beggar's Banquet* in 1968.

It was photographed again on the back cover of the band's *Hot Rocks* compilation in 1971.

Fortunately in 1985 the ruins were taken over by the **Landmark Trust**, as a result of which the Bowling Green House, as seen here in all its restored glory, is now available as a holiday let.

Visitors, we are informed, should bring their own set of bowls.

Notes on case studies
On the pages that follow are case studies relating to bowling greens and clubs whose roots lie in the Tudor and Stuart periods.

As stated in Chapter Four, three of these clubs claim to be older; specifically Chesterfield (who date their green back to 1294), Southampton ('prior to 1299'), and Hereford (1484).

These and the claims at several other clubs are based on narratives compiled in the late Victorian and Edwardian years.

In the same way that the legend of Sir Francis Drake may not be true, but is certainly not beyond the bounds of historical feasibility, it is possible that bowling at these locations did predate the Tudors.

But research carried out for *Bowled Over* has so far failed to find evidence to support this.

As such, the case studies are ordered not in a *chronological sequence* that mirrors the various claims, but in an order that reflects the *heritage assets* found in each location. The two main criteria are the *survival of original elements of the greens*, and of *the form of bowls* that is now played on them.

Clearly such an approach is open to debate. However we at *Played in Britain* welcome this, helping as it should all parties to arrive at a more faithful understanding of bowling history.

Case study

Lewes Bowling Green Society

Traced from John Deward's map of Lewes in 1620, here is a simplified, but charming rendition of one of Britain's most important sites of sporting heritage, the castleyard or bailey at Lewes, at around the time it was turned into a bowling green. The identity of the three gabled building in the lower left has not been determined. One of the two smaller buildings may well have served as a pavilion. The central place of the green in the town itself, to the east of the castle keep, is illustrated in a later map, published in 1799 (*right*).

There are bowling greens which have claims to be older than the one at Lewes, and bowling clubs whose roots may predate the formation of the Lewes Bowling Green Society in 1753.

But let there be no doubt. For anyone interested in the history of bowls, as a game, Lewes must be their starting point.

For two reasons. Firstly the green itself – that is, its setting, its undulating profile and its surface – has changed remarkably little since the 17th and 18th centuries.

Or to put it another way, unlike the majority of historic greens in southern England, for example Southampton and Milton Regis, it has never been modernised.

Secondly, the type of bowls played at Lewes is closer to the form of the game as it was played during the Tudor and Stuart periods than anywhere in Britain. This includes not only the rules in force, but also the size, shape and bias of the woods and jacks in use.

Add to this the age of the club, the unusual character of the pavilion, plus the various artefacts connected with the green – such

as its aged limestone roller (*see page 19*) and antique clock scorer (*page 40*) – and what emerges is one of the most important sites of sporting heritage in Britain.

To set this in context, beyond the world of bowls, only a trio of enclosed sports grounds or sports-related buildings are older and still functioning. These are the real tennis courts at Falkland Palace in Fife (built in 1539) and Hampton Court (with elements from 1625), and the Roodee Racecourse in Chester (in use also since 1539).

Yet such is the historic provenance of bowling that Lewes, for all its significance, is only one of a dozen or so greens whose origins can, with reason, be traced back to the 17th century or earlier.

By comparison cricket's oldest grounds date back to c.1700-30.

But that is not all. For what makes Lewes even more remarkable is that within the town there lies a second historic sportscape, the wonderfully named Dripping Pan. Seen at the foot of the 1799 map below,

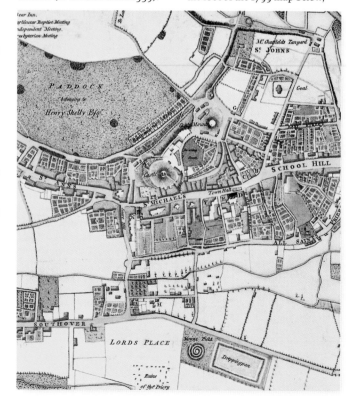

this sunken rectangular site has staged, since 1600, bull baiting, firework displays – Lewes is famous for its bonfire societies – cricket and athletics and, since 1885, has been the home of Lewes Football Club.

Overlooking the Dripping Pan is the Mount, a curious mound with a spiral path, created, as was the fashion in the late 16th century, by Lord Buckhurst, in the grounds of Lord's Place (shown on the 1799 map), a mansion he built on part of the dissolved Lewes Priory. The earth and chalk that formed its heights may have been excavated from the adjoining field, hence the sunken profile of, and its name, the Dripping Pan. (The mounds at Northala Fields in London are the modern equivalent.)

On the west side of the Mount lies the other Lewes bowling club, formed in 1922. Its standard square shaped flat green lies just north of the ruins of Lewes Priory, also shown on the 1799 map.

On the north side of Lewes, meanwhile, is the Pells Pool, one of the oldest operational public outdoor pools in Britain, opened in 1861, and to the west, the Paddock (in the top left corner of the 1799 map), which in the summer hosts nine local clubs playing stoolball, a game widely regarded as the precursor of modern day cricket.

Added to which Lewes has a string of pubs where historic pub games are contested, as featured in *Played at the Pub* (see Links).

So no question, sporting heritage ranks highly in this enchanting corner of East Sussex.

But the jewel in the crown, for sure, is the bowling green.

Lewes Castle itself was built from soon after 1066 by one of the conquering Norman families, the

Warennes. As can be seen on the map of 1799 it comprises a bailey or castle yard, now the bowling green, flanked by two mottes.

The one to the east is called Brack Mount. The one to the west has a fortified keep (see above).

By the mid 15th century the castle had fallen into ruins, and when a tenancy of the bailey, or castle green, was on offer in 1567, there were no takers.

By 1620, as recorded on the map by John Deward, (see opposite), there was a building on one side of the green, with two storeys and three gables. This may have been an ale house. Extraordinarily, a second map was drawn in 1620 by George Randoll. This shows a similar building and a smaller edifice in almost exactly the same position as the present day pavilion.

Perhaps its precursor.

Whatever, confirmation that the green was now in use for bowls comes from a document dated January 1639. Discovered by Lewes historian Colin Brent (see Links), it is a petition to the Justices of the Peace signed by 20 gentlemen. It states, 'Wee whose names are heer underwritten doe conceive John Standinge of Lewes to be a very fitt man to keepe the bowling greene and sell drinke in the house wheer he now dwelleth...'

Located as it was, close to the Market Hall, the green was often used for gatherings. Until 1595 it staged elections to the town's governing body before these were moved to the Sessions House 'for the avoidance of further disorder'.

In 1658 a Quaker prayer meeting was reported to have been held on 'the old Castle Green (now made a bowling green) at Lewis'. »

A typical Saturday morning on the green at Lewes, in May 2011, as Society members gather to play amongst themselves (*above*). This insularity was for centuries the norm in bowling, but is rare nowadays, at a time when leagues and friendlies are common. But in any case, who would play on this green? Certainly not flat green players from other parts of East Sussex, with no experience of such undulating turf, or of lignum vitae bowls with such a pronounced bias. In the background stands the Society's unusual pavilion, with the Castle keep on the motte behind. Oddly, the most modern structure in view is the wall surrounding the green. Built in 1976, in advance of the Queen's Silver Jubilee celebrations, it is made from the flint that so characterises the urban scene in Lewes.

▲ It might be expected that a green which has no straight lines or level areas should have a pavilion that appears equally eccentric.

Listed Grade II and thought to date back to the mid or late 18th century, the building consists of a timber frame with timber cladding, raised on a red brick plinth and with a slate roof sloping at the rear.

But why such an unusual shape?

The answer is that this was built not as a pavilion but as a display stand, or more strictly an **'auricula theatre'**, with canted sides and an open front, allowing flowers to be displayed on shelves at the back.

Although such structures were fashionable in 18th and 19th century horticultural circles, only one survivor is known to serve its original purpose, at Calke Abbey in Ticknall, Derbyshire (coincidentally close to the Bowling Green House at Swarkestone, seen on page 57).

The Lewes example is believed to have been donated to the Society,

one theory being that it was either moved from the garden of a house adjoining the green, or left as compensation for damage caused in July 1852 by a horticultural show.

During the show a glass pavilion from the 1851 Great Exhibition in Hyde Park was erected in the centre of the green, while several thousand visitors attended over three, exceptionally hot days. The effect on the turf can be imagined.

Being such a basic structure the pavilion has needed much love and care over the years. It was given a major overhaul in the 1980s, since when the Society has added detachable panels at the front so that the contents can be locked up at the end of play and protected from the elements.

Seated on the far bench is the Society's longest serving member, **John Chaplin**, 22 times winner of the Singles Competition and, before retiring in 2014, honorary greenkeeper for 52 years.

>> There is however no record of any tilting (or jousting) having taken place on the green, as claimed on a modern plaque by the entrance (*see page 63*).

This story, it is believed, was hatched by a local publican in the 20th century in order to boost visitor numbers.

From the late 17th century the character of the area around the green started to change. For many years the manorial rights had been held by successive Earls of Abergavenny, who were only too happy to grant leases to members of the gentry wishing to build houses in the vicinity. Among them, Samuel and Robert Chester took on several leases, one being of the bowling green, in 1745. Their businesses included a brewery and, from *c*.1750, the Castle Inn.

In fact it was the Castle Inn's publican, Charles Boore, who on May 4 1753 published a notice aimed at bowlers:

'... all Gentlemen who are lovers of that diversion are entreated to subscribe their names to a CLUB, the condition being to pay Five Shillings for the season and to spend Sixpence when present. No penalty for being absent.'

Thus was born the Lewes Castle Bowling Green Society.

Despite the claims of other clubs such as Kilmarnock (whose formation date is given as 1740 but whose records have been lost), this 1753 notice confirms Lewes as the joint oldest bowls club in Britain, alongside Blackburn Subscription Bowling Green Club (*see page 140*), which, coincidentally, was also formed in 1753.

One of the early subscribers at Lewes was Tom Paine, who from 1768-74 lived nearby. According to an early biographer, James Cheetham, it was a remark

made after a game of bowls that prompted Paine to pen *The Rights of Man*.

After the Chesters, from the 1790s onwards the Society was beholden to a succession of leaseholders, all gentlemen resident in the castle precincts.

But in 1853 the Society decided to take on the tenancy of the green directly. As noted on the left, this was as a result of damage caused by the staging of a horticultural show in July 1852.

So it was that on April 15 1853 the Society reformed itself under the new name of the Lewes Bowling Green Society, with its forerunner's perpetual lease at a peppercorn rent of £8 a year being reconfirmed by the Earl of Abergavenny (whose successor remains the Society's landlord to this day).

During the 20th century, like the green itself, the Society has experienced many ups and downs.

Membership fell during the First World War, and in 1936 the green's viability came under discussion by Lewes Council.

More problems arose during the Second World War when an air raid shelter and water tank were positioned in opposite corners of the green, causing dips that can still be seen. Membership at one point sank to just twelve.

Then in the early 1960s, tragically, some of the Society's records were destroyed during a house clearance, while the green itself required extensive treatment.

But at no time, it appears, was it ever considered that the Society should follow the lead of other long established clubs and convert the green to a standard flat green.

Which, in the wider context of bowling heritage, is perhaps the most salient fact of all in the Lewes story.

▲ Viewed from the south west, the bowling green's origins as the bailey of **Lewes Castle** are self evident. In the foreground, the ruined keep, Barbican and gateway, all owned by the Sussex Archaeological Society, span the entrance from the **High Street**. Not visible is a railway tunnel which, cut in the 1840s and heading north towards Plumpton and the racecourse, runs directly under the nearside of the bowling green and pavilion. On the far side of the green the long building is the Grade II listed **Maltings** (formerly the East Sussex Record Office).

Beyond the Maltings is **Brack Mount**, a turfed mound once part of the Castle's defences and, from the 1840s to the 1920s, the site of a pleasure garden. Together, the Mount, Castle and green are designated as a Scheduled Ancient Monument. Added to the fact that most of the historic buildings are also individually listed, the bowls pavilion included, and that the whole forms part of a Conservation Area, here, surely, is the most protected bowling green in England.

And that is before we even consider its importance in sporting terms...

▲ First and foremost, what makes the game in **Lewes** so different from any other played in Britain is the type of **jack** that is used.

Because the green is so uneven, the jack, as would be expected, is biased (as explained on page 13).

But note that, compared with a standard biased crown green jack (held on the right), the Lewes jack is smaller and with flatter sides, like a cheese, thereby giving it extra bias. It is also lighter, weighing 10 oz, compared with 24 oz for its modern counterpart.

It will be noticed too that the jack, in common with the Lewes **woods** (*right*), is made from lignum vitae. Lewes is one of only two British clubs yet to allow composites onto its premises, Barnes being the other (*page 102*).

Each wood weighs around 1 lb 12 oz (again lighter than the crown green minimum of 2 lb), and measures about 4½ inches in diameter (also smaller). This means that when replacements are needed, it is possible to use old crown green woods, turned down on a lathe and shaped accordingly.

Note how flat they appear on one side, and also how all are matched in pairs. Since the late 19th century all commercially produced bowls have come with a measured and tested bias, making it simple to create a set. The Lewes woods, by contrast, have all been matched by hand and eye, and all differ subtly. Hence each player learns from experience and chooses which is his lead wood, and which his second.

Quite how old the Lewes jacks and woods are is difficult to state without dendrochronological testing, but some have Georgian pennies screwed on as mounts and almost certainly date back to the 18th century. So too may those with lead weights inserted, a once common method of adjusting a wood's bias.

In total the Society owns 55 pairs, and six jacks – this being the maximum number that can be comfortably used on the green at any one time. For the same reason membership is limited to 55.

When a member dies, his bowls are allocated to the next man joining. And yes it will be a man. For although the Society rules do not spell it out, membership is by invitation only, and to date no member has proposed a woman.

Maybe in another century or so...

One of the many quirks at Lewes is that one bowler in each of the games taking place on the green carries with him a hinged, two yard wooden rule in order to be able to measure when the need arises. Again, at a time when most bowlers use modern tape measures or strings, this harks back to what was once standard practice on bowling greens.

▲ Viewed from the Castle keep on a Saturday morning – the best time to catch some action – we see that, as in crown green bowls, members of the **Lewes Bowling Green Society** play in any direction, using the full extent of the green. However at Lewes the green covers just over three quarters of an acre.

Before incursions by neighbouring properties started in the 18th century it was even larger. As it is, it still measures more than twice the area of a typical flat, or crown green. Casts can therefore vary in length between 20–60 yards.

'The latter distance, when uphill', wrote Society Secretary and proprietor of the White Horse Hotel, Herbert Walton, in 1945, 'requires a vigorous, long, steady pendulum swing, sometimes accomplishable only by the lusty player, of whom there are a few.' That said, given the age range amongst members, it remains a convention that no-one sends the jack so far that the other players are unable to reach it.

A further challenge is presented by the green's profile. It falls away to the south by at least six feet, with countless depressions, ridges and channels for the bowlers to negotiate at every turn. Hardest of all is when both the slope and the bias act in the same direction.

Because of this, experienced players tend to play with the bias fighting against the gradient.

Then there is the surface itself.

Described as 'indigenous Southdown turf', it was recently found to consist of a mixture of at least 30 types of grass. In effect, just as most greens were in the days of scythes and heavy rollers.

As is only to be expected, the Society has its own set of rules and conventions. Each player pays a fee of £1 per session, with the losers stumping up a further 50p.

Each game is played to '11 up'. To decide who plays whom, coloured balls are drawn from a bag (*see page 34*). Marks may be set in any direction, but it is an unwritten rule that players do not bowl across the line being played in another game. Unusually, the order of play is determined by the position of the first woods sent by each player, with the man closest to the jack going next with his second wood.

Finally, tradition has it that at the end of a session it is off to the White Hart, on the High Street, the gathering point for Society members since records began.

Case study

Bowling Green Inn, Hadley Heath

As of 2015 there are 34 English pubs that have the words 'Bowling Green' in their names. But only five still have functioning greens, the oldest of which is the picture-perfect Grade II listed Bowling Green Inn at Hadley Heath, near Ombersley, Worcestershire. The others are at Stoke Prior, also in Worcestershire, Lichfield, Chorlton (Manchester) and Lancaster. Many a Bowling Green Inn, predictably, features Elizabethans on its sign. But at Hadley (*above*) it is with good reason.

Whether rural or urban, pub greens are, as already noted, a dying breed. For this reason alone the green at the Bowling Green Inn, Hadley Heath, is a precious survivor.

Located between Ombersley and Droitwich Spa, the pub stands alone on a winding lane in the midst of open farmland. In other words, less likely to attract passing trade, more a destination in its own right.

And a delightful one at that.

That, however, is not why its green merits inclusion as a case study. Rather, Hadley shares with Lewes several outstanding heritage assets. These are an unmodernised green, two historic shelters, a form of play barely changed since the 17th century (including the use of lignum vitae biased jacks and woods), and a club with a distinguished history.

In fact two clubs play on the green. The Monday Club formed in the 1970s, is less rooted in the past. Some of its members, for example, use composite bowls. The Hadley Bowling Club, which meets on Thursdays, is the old original.

Whereas modern bowlers must bowl with one foot on a rubber mat, Hadley members continue to use metal rings, or 'trigs' instead. One of the club's rules from 1808 requires that 'the trig be placed not less than one yard from the trench'. This is echoed in today's rules concerning mats. In crown green bowls the specified distance is a minimum of 1m from the ditch.

Quite how old is difficult to say. What is certain is that the Bowling Green Inn is Elizabethan in origin. English Heritage's listing description places it in the late 16th century. However it also believes that the building was originally a house. So did this house have its own bowling green? Or was the green only laid when the house became an inn? And if so, when did that occur?

Alas these questions must remain unanswered for now.

One other intriguing piece of evidence is that the bowling club owns a panel bearing the arms of 73 peers of the realm, a panel which, as pointed out in the journal *Archaeologia*, in 1920 (*see Links*), bears a remarkably close resemblance to a set of heraldic roundels held by the British Museum and dated 1587.

One theory is that the Hadley panel might have been linked to a visit made by Queen Elizabeth to Worcester in 1575.

Coincidentally, one of the peers named on it is Lord Howard of Effingham, supposedly present on Plymouth Hoe in 1588 (*see page 50*).

Another is Baron Abergavenny, whose family would, a few decades later, purchase the site of the bowling green in Lewes.

How wonderful to discover if either of these men, or any of the other peers for that matter, actually bowled.

As for the Hadley Bowling Club, it has minutes and notes of subscriptions that go back to 1775 (now held at the Worcestershire County Record Office).

But it may be older. Another source, unattributed, has it that one Albert Beck, a Hadley member from 1859 to 1907, once stated that the club had existed long before 1775, but that its early records had been destroyed (an all too common occurence).

Writing in the journal of the Worcestershire Archaeological Society in 1924 (*see Links*), Mildred Berkeley went further. She reported that in the 19th century the innkeeper's wife had used pages from old minute books to cover her jam pots.

Berkeley found a wealth of other colourful entries relating to the club in the 18th century, so typical of clubs and societies from this period. For Hadley was not just a bowling club.

She writes how the club had 30 members in 1775, and that any who failed to attend paid a forfeit. Dinner was called at three o'clock, with each member getting through one bottle. By 1831 consumption was down to two bottles between three members. In 1911 it dropped back to half a bottle each.

So much for the Edwardians.

One member, a clergyman known as 'The Lion', celebrated 60 years in the club with a jubilee dinner in 1849. Another was the Rev Thomas Newport, 'The Tiger', described in 1851 as 'another good fellow and good player, who often won enough to pay his score, his luncheon and his horse'.

But it is the green and the form of bowls played at Hadley which provide the strongest links with bowling in the pre-modern era.

In particular the club still pays great heed to a set of 48 rules, also lodged in the Record Office, which date from May 1808.

In these rules, as was common in the 17th century, jacks are referred to as 'blocks' (as they still are on the green today). The rules mention 'rubbers', as did those published in 1670 (*see page 53*), and again, as was common, there were strict rules about betting.

One stated, 'If any breaker-in shall not pay his debts, the servant of the green shall draw him on his breech across the green.'

Despite being in a relatively isolated spot the pub and green clearly acted as important focal points for the surrounding rural community.

In April 1791, a 'main of cocks' (that is, a cock-fighting match) was held there between the gentlemen of Worcestershire and Shropshire.

In 1857 the *Worcester Herald* records the following: in January pigeon-shooting, in February hare coursing, in June (in the Inn presumably) an inquest into a drowned boy, and in December an annual sale of Fat-Stock.

This tradition appears to have been revived in 2013 when the green hosted a production of Noel Coward's *Private Lives*.

▲ Members of the **Monday Club** in action in front of one of the historic shelters at **Hadley Heath**. The other, smaller of the pair is shown below.

Both are open to the elements and have brick sides, timber facings and bench seating. Both almost certainly date from the late 18th or early 19th centuries. Note how similar they are to the shelter in Robert Cruikshank's drawing of bowlers at the Hand and Glove in Worcester in 1825 (*see page 90*).

There about 45 members in the Monday Club, mostly retired, one of whom is over 90 (*page 42*). In lieu of paying rent to the Hadley Bowling Club – which leases the green from the pub and is limited to just 18 members – it is the responsibility of the Monday Club to maintain the green.

Compared with Lewes it is modest in size, measuring about 35 yards x 45 yards, roughly the same as a standard modern green. But its surface is similar to Lewes,

being a mixtures of grasses and full of undulations. Where it falls away under a line of ancient yews lies a spot the bowlers call 'Peggy's Corner' (for reasons unknown).

The Monday Club play with standard crown green jacks and bowls. Some members use woods, some composites. The Hadley Club, as noted earlier, play with biased lignum vitae jacks, one of which is similar to the jacks in use at Lewes.

As at Lewes the type of game differs subtly from modern forms, being neither flat green, nor exactly

crown green. Instead it mixes elements from both, rather as is the custom in the Kidderminster area, as detailed on page 180.

Indeed one of the clubs playing in the Kidderminster League is based in Ombersley, a mile up the road.

Patently the best time to see play at Hadley is on Monday or Thursday evenings (though not every week).

Patently the best way to enjoy the scene is by calling into the pub. Look out for some interesting bowling artefacts and archive images on display when you do.

Case study

Chesterfield Bowling Club

By a narrow gate on Beetwell Street, a few hundred yards from Chesterfield's famous Crooked Spire and a world away from the bustle of the town centre, a plaque (*above*) informs passersby of what lies hidden behind a long, tall stone wall. Below right is an etching of the green from an 1839 history of the town. Although the surroundings have changed beyond recognition, the gateway to the green, in the top right of the etching, is in the same place as today. The key question is, when did bowling start here? Could it have been 'possibly 13th century' as the plaque suggests?

There can no doubt that the bowling green at Chesterfield is one of the oldest in Britain.

Even if the club itself may date back only to 1828 (and its earliest minutes to 1852), the green, in common with those at Lewes and Hadley, is essentially unmodernised. Only two concessions to modernity have been made. Some members now bowl with composites, and the jacks in use are standard flat green non-biased jacks (even though the green is a classic crown green).

For its part the club is suffused in tradition and plays to its own, unique set of rules. But writing in a locally published history in 1913 (*see Links*), George Lee made the claim that the Beetwell Street green dates back to 1294 and was therefore the oldest in the world.

This would appear to trump, perhaps intentionally, or at least match the claim made in 1894 that the green at Southampton (the subject of our next case study), dates back to 1299 or even earlier.

Unfortunately neither claim can be substantiated by evidence.

Instead, the earliest evidence for bowling in Chesterfield dates, as in Lewes, from documents relating to the 17th century. This, we need hardly repeat, is still exceptional in terms of English sporting history.

But why choose the date 1294?

To understand we have to go back to the 1830s, and a review that took place in Chesterfield (and other towns) under the auspices of the Municipal Reform Act. This review sought to confirm which properties were actually owned by the Corporation. Among them was the bowling green and adjoining Guild Hall, depicted shortly afterwards, in 1839, in a *History of Chesterfield* (*see Links*), as reproduced below.

Chesterfield Corporation was able to prove that it had purchased the site between 1594 and 1604, from Sir Thomas Foljambe.

Most likely it was nearer 1594 because that was the year in which Elizabeth I granted a charter charging the Mayor, Aldermen and Brethren with the provision of a Guild Hall 'wherein they might assemble in council together'.

Now it is possible that in or around 1594 bowling was taking place on the site. As we have established, bowls was relatively commonplace by this time.

But Lee went much further.

Presumably using as his source *The History of Chesterfield*, he noted that a Guild of Merchants had been established in the town... in 1294. He then noted that a new Guild had been established in 1392, and that the land on which the green stood had formed part of this Guild's holdings after being endowed by Thomas Dur.

It was this land which, some time after 1547 and the Dissolution of the Monasteries, had come into the possession of Sir Godfrey Foljambe – one of Henry VIII's favourites – before being sold to the Corporation by his nephew, Sir Thomas Foljambe, some time

GUILD HALL,
CHESTERFIELD.

after 1594. In other words, Lee erroneously took the formation of the guild in 1294 to represent also the origins of the bowling green.

In fact a more accurate estimate would have been some time between 1594 and 1664.

Why the latter date? Because that is when the first reference to bowling in Chesterfield appears.

It comes in the letters of George Sitwell, a Derbyshire ironmaster, landowner and builder of Renishaw Hall. Whilst in town attending the Quarter Sessions Sitwell recorded how he would retire to the Angel Inn to dine with his friends, after which they went to the green to play bowls.

Then, as now, the green was owned by the Corporation (now under the name of Chesterfield Borough Council), and there follows plenty of evidence that it took a close interest in the place. Indeed it is clear that since Sitwell's day the green has been very much the preserve of the great and good in the town. Not least its location immediately next to the Guild Hall gave it special status.

Thus we learn that in the 1780s the Corporation spent £37 19s 9d on erecting a building at the green, possibly an arbour in one corner that survived until the early 20th century. In 1790 the beadle, John Stringfellow, who doubled as town crier, was paid for 'the taking up of sods and replacing same with new grass on the bowling green'.

This was followed on March 8 1828 by an advert in the newly-established *Chesterfield Gazette* offering for let a plot of land 'heretofore used and known as a Bowling Green... together with the Bowl House, and productive garden ground attached thereto... 'Applications to be made at the Town Clerk's Office'.

Clearly the new lessee was happy to let bowling continue because on October 18 the *Gazette* reported: 'The Subscribers to the Bowling Green in this town had their first annual dinner... at Mr Pinder's, The King and Miller (on High Street). The evening was spent in toast and song, with all that hilarity which was to be expected from the lovers of the good old English game of bowls.'

That Mr Pinder also acted as secretary to the subscribers suggests that 1828 may be considered the birth of the present day club. Moreover in 1849 we learn that another office holder was Mr Henson, landlord of the Anchor Inn. He was titled 'Curator', an office that continues to this day.

▲ This, one of the earliest photographs of bowlers in Britain, shows members of the **Chesterfield Bowling Club** on August 24 1859.

Behind them is the **Municipal Hall**, built on the site of the Guild Hall ten years earlier.

Thanks to a club member who annotated the photograph in 1902, we know the identities of most of the individuals. Among them are JH Ramsden, governor of the Chesterfield Union Workhouse and George Shaw, Deputy Registrar of the County Court. There were also two drapers, two grocers, a printer, sadler, confectioner, farmer, coach builder, watchmaker, chemist and a flour and corn dealer. From their names we know that many a member in later generations came from the same families, and trades.

As noted earlier the earliest club minutes that survive are from 1852. By then the club was renting the green directly from the town council. In 1774 we know that a publican, John Dakin, had paid six guineas a year. By 1852 that had risen only to eight guineas. But now the council was seeking to raise it to £14.

Voicing their complaints, one club member, Mr Busley, argued that surely 'bowls of wood' were preferable to the alternative that members might seek out, namely 'bowls of beer'.

Point taken, the parties settled on a compromise of £10 a year, to include the green and club rooms on the ground floor of the Municipal Hall, accessed through the open arches seen above.

▲ Owing to its backstreet location and high walls, many people in **Chesterfield** are unaware of the historic green in their midst. But nor do the surrounds give any hints.

Municipal Hall apart, for much of the 20th century the green was bordered by small works, terraced houses and, to the south, a Corporation baths. In the corner by the gate there was a public urinal.

This has gone. But the biggest change occurred in the 1970s when the Municipal Hall, which had lately served as a courthouse, was demolished.

Having lost its magnificent headquarters, in return the club gained, courtesy of the council, a rather plain, single storey flat-roofed pavilion. Meanwhile on the opposite, north side of the

newly widened Beetwell Street, a modern red brick library went up, changing completely the outlook, and ambience of the green, as is apparent from the photograph above. Taken in 2004 from almost the same spot as the 1859 image, the occasion is the **opening of the green**, a ceremony held every year on the second Wednesday in April (Wednesday being traditionally half day closing in Chesterfield).

As is customary, the club President opens the season by

All the lignum vitae woods at Beetwell Street have a bias of around 8-10, compared with 2 in crown green bowling and 3 in flat green. Those members who do not have their own sets, and who prefer not to use composites, hire theirs from the club, paying £4 for life. To make sure woods are not mixed up, each set has its own markings or initials.

bowling a gilded jack. The Mayor of Chesterfield – who on taking office is automatically made an honorary member of the club, along with the local Chief Constable – then bowls the first wood.

Highly recommended footage of this same ceremony from April 1933 can be viewed on YouTube, footage in which the old hall at the rear is much in evidence.

Once the formalities are over a gentle game takes place amongst members to shake off the winter

cobwebs, followed by a grand tea in the nearby Market Hall.

Amongst the membership recently have been several former mayors. One had been a bowls lad in his youth (that is, hired to collect and clean woods for the members). He ended up dying on the green as an old man, after a match.

Another mayor attended a seasonal opening in the 1980s having never bowled before, but immediately caught the bug and became a regular.

Not so another mayor, or rather mayoress. During her year of office she became the first woman to bowl on the green. And so far, the last. As at Hadley and Lewes, Beetwell Street remains a male stronghold.

Meanwhile the council has proved tougher than its predecessors in the 1850s. After well over a century of charging £13 a year, in the 1990s the rent shot up and is now £1,300 a year.

▼ **Chesterfield** has a wealth of characters and a list of arcane rules to match. Membership is limited to 100, and there is always a waiting list. As of 2015 the oldest member was aged 89, the youngest 17.

Two of the members are designated as 'Curators'.

The Club Curator oversees all activities inside the clubhouse. This includes the provision of thirteen buffets a year (all part of the annual subscription of £120), plus carpet bowls and dominoes during the winter months.

Another tradition is that in order for any member to have a drink in the clubhouse, the Club Curator must invite him first to drink 'with the President' (whether or not Mr President is present). Also, no drinks are paid for directly. Instead, donations are placed discreetly in the President's Locker Fund.

For his part the President, who serves a one year term, has his own chair in the clubhouse and has the privilege of always choosing in which position he plays.

Because most games are played by three a side, that means he can choose between being 'lead' (that is, going first), 'pin' or 'back man'.

To ensure that members mix as fully as possible, short games of 'seven up' are generally played ('21 up' being the norm in crown green). Losing players pay a penny to the winners, as also happens at Hadley.

Similarly, in common with Lewes and Hadley, the club does not bowl in any leagues. In fact their only contact with other bowlers is when they play two friendlies a year; against Mansfield BC, another venerable institution with its roots in the early 18th century, and the Arboretum BC, from Derby.

Both are crown green clubs incidentally. But even if Chesterfield's green is in essence a crown green, the club rules are different. Indeed the members even compete amongst themselves in one competition in which they play with an unbiased jack and in rinks, just as in the flat green game.

Also compared with many crown green clubs, Chesterfield members have always been subject to strict codes of conduct.

Victorian members were required to wear dress coats, silk hats and patent shoes, or in hotter weather, white linen drill suits and straw hats. Today's rules require a collar and tie, and no shoes with heels on the green.

In 1854, the club rules included fines of 1s for an indecent act – 'proper places being provided' – and 6d for swearing or treading on

any of the flowerbeds. The same decorum is expected today. As well as a swearbox in the corner, no member is allowed to use a mobile telephone on the green.

On which subject, the second Curator at the club is the Green Curator. He is responsible for the grounds, but not the actual green, which is tended by a professional.

The green itself is some 40 yards wide and 46 yards long, similar to a standard modern green, but slopes down from the pavilion end by 40 inches and has a curved edge in one corner. Almost needless to add, it undulates all over.

'To the unwary bowler', as George Lee put it in 1913 it is, 'full of surprising uncertainties...'

Just like the green's history, it would seem.

Three wise men – enjoying the opening day at Chesterfield in April 2010, from their vantage point in front of the pavilion, are (*left to right*) Jim Wilkins, who was club president in 2006, Fred Rushton, president in 2000, and Paul Cooper, who would become president in 2014, having been a member since 1969.

Case study

Southampton (Old) Bowling Green Club

'Oh yea, oh yea, oh yea!' It is the third Thursday in August in the year 2002 and, as is customary on the Old Bowling Green at Southampton, the Town Crier – in this instance Jack Hibberd (*above*) – declares open the annual Knights Competition. This is the oldest bowls competition in the world, having first been staged in 1776. But the green itself is also claimed to be the world's oldest, established 'prior to 1299'. Once again we must ask, can this be so?

As the club name suggests, the bowling green at Southampton is indeed old. It is also a doughty survivor, having withstood centuries of urban development and, during the Second World War, owing to its proximity to the docks, near obliteration courtesy of the Luftwaffe.

Thus although no historic buildings or walls survive, and the green today is of the standard, modern flat variety, conforming to Bowls England's requirements, it is a site of great significance.

But, alas, as at Chesterfield, evidence that it was in use for bowling in the 1290s cannot be found. Instead, it would appear that at one point in the 19th century, probably 1894, a report on the green's history was misinterpreted, and that the first actual reference to bowls on the current site dates from 1600, and in the vicinity from 1550.

In response to such doubts, histories of the club written in the 20th century contend that records before 1550 did not exist because bowling was banned. For sure, this cannot be discounted. But nor can

'World's oldest bowling green' declares a banner on the wall of the green (*right*), facing Town Quay and a vast car park next to the docks across the road. On the left is God's House Tower. Taking its name from a 12th century hospital on the site, the tower was rebuilt in 1417, has been used as a gaol, as a museum, and is now to be an arts and heritage centre, opening in 2017.

doubts concerning other parts of the story. These concern the God's House Tower, which overlooks the south west corner of the green.

The God's House was a hospital, founded in c.1185 to look after pilgrims and the poor.

It had a Master, and a 'Master's Close', or garden, for his use.

It is this 'close' that later writers took to be a 'green', inferring that the Master must have organised a form of bowling on it. However, from Henry de Bluntesdon in 1293 and onwards, Masters of the God's House held the title as a sinecure and were rarely in residence.

Furthermore, the word 'close' in a medieval context indicates an enclosed place. Yet when depicted on a map in 1611 (*see opposite*), the bowling green appeared anything but enclosed.

More likely is that the Master's Close lay within a quadrangle of hospital buildings, rather as is the

case with other closes found next to cathedrals of the period.

The Master, or Warden's house lay on the west side of this quadrangle. We know from account rolls that c.1300 the hospital was occupied by two priests, a clerk, two or three monks, no more than nine nuns, a handful of paupers and a staff of indoor and outside servants, including ploughmen and herdsmen. Much of the work was devoted to rearing animals and growing crops to feed the community and provide income.

It is of course possible that games of some sort were played within the Master's Close. But this is pure speculation, for the earliest actual reference to bowling in Southampton does not appear until 1550. Appearing in the Court Leet records of that year is mention of a man caught keeping 'common playing with bowls,

tabylles, draughts or backgammon and other unlawfull games agaynst the King's statute'. The statute in question was that of Henry VIII in 1541 (*page 49*). However the location of this misdemeanour was not the Master's Close but the King's Orchard.

In 1581 the Court heard that the King's Orchard had a back door leading into the fields, 'made for the comoditie of those that kept those grounds for their pleasures, but now being turn'd & used for tipling houses & maintenaunce of unlawful games...'

In 1596 fourteen labourers and craftsmen were fined 6s 8d for bowling in the orchard, 'especially on Sundays'. In this and in other citations the names appear of individuals who were clearly running a lucrative business. So, in 1600, 'we present John Parker for the like comon bowlinge alley at the Kinges orcherde, wherefore we amerce him in 20/- in that he was a Burgesse and hath had sundry warnings for the same abuse'.

Not that this seemed to do Parker much harm. For the following two years he remained a juror for the Court.

Meanwhile the earliest reference to bowling on 'God's House Green' (the current site), again from Court Leet records, is also in 1600. That year 'artificers' were accused of playing there without any redress from the authorities.

Then in 1611 the green appeared on a map (*right*).

It is worth noting that in earlier court records, reference had been made to 'Common Bowlers espetially of mean qualitie'. Yet in 1635 (also given as 1637) the green was described as a ground 'where many gentlemen, with the gentile merchants of this town, take their recreation'. »

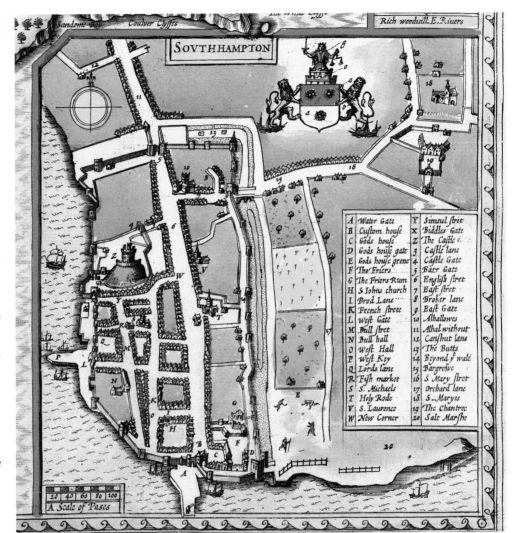

▲ Published in 1611, this map of **Southampton** is one of the earliest known to depict a bowling green.

Forming part of a larger map of the Isle of Wight, it was the work of **John Speed**, one of England's first great cartographers, known for doing much of his own surveying and therefore for his accuracy.

'God's Boule Grene' – featuring four bowlers, one of whom appears to be holding a measuring stick – is identified as item E on the map, an unenclosed area east of the town walls. God's House is at C, with God's House Gate (whose tower is extant) at D.

To the north of the bowling green, on Orchard Lane, is an enclosed orchard, perhaps King's Orchard. Beyond, to the east, lay the Saltmarsh (20).

Significantly in 1503 the site of the Saltmarsh had been declared common land after various claims were made to it, including by the Warden of the God's House. And when several complaints were made to the Court Leet between 1618-24, relating to bowling on God's Boule Grene, a recurrent theme was that this was illegal activity on 'town land'.

>> In short, bowling was becoming respectable.

Nevertheless, tenure of the green would come under renewed scrutiny after the bowlers formed a club –at least by 1776 (*see right*) – yet paid no rent to the Corporation.

Similar scrutiny occurred in Chesterfield and Cannock (a later case study). In Southampton it culminated in a report by the Town Clerk, GB Nalder, in 1894.

Nalder concluded that 'although the ground itself no doubt belongs to the town, the present Club or Association who occupy and manage the Green would appear to have obtained certain prescriptive rights thereon from length of usure for the purpose of playing the game of bowls.'

The club, he stated, had occupied the green 'for the past 100 years and upwards'.

But before the club? Before 1611, 1600 or even 1550? As the *Southampton and Hampshire Observer* concluded in August 1891, 'Its origin is concealed behind and beyond the mists between the present and a very remote past.'

But not as far as the late Victorian bowlers were concerned.

They read Nalder's account of a Master of the Green having been in place 'so far back as 1299' and considered the rest to be history.

Which it is, of a sort.

But what of Southampton's claim to be the oldest green in the world? Our research suggests that this may actually still be correct.

As will become apparent in our next case study, it all depends on whether an elusive reference to the existence of the green at Painswick in Gloucestershire, from the 1550s, can be tracked down.

If it cannot, then Southampton's claim holds good. But for 1600 rather than 1299.

▲ Members of the **Southampton Bowling Green Club** (the 'Old' is a 20th century addition) pose in the 1870s. Note how the pavilion, rebuilt in 1873, abutted onto the west side of the green, as also seen in 1923 (*below*). The proximity of the docks is apparent too. In the background looms the *Mauretania*.

Southampton was typical of clubs formed in the 18th century. Its subscribers were upstanding figures of the community. They enjoyed bibulous suppers at The

Half Moon, The George and The Dolphin. But one aspect of the club lent it a special character, and that is its **Knights Competition**.

This began in 1776 when the then 82 year old Samuel Miller – described as having been a patron of the green for '60 years or more', suggesting that the club might date from the 1720s – donated a silver medal to be played for on an annual basis. Soon after it was decided to strike a new medal every year, and by August 1815, winners were

being described in the *Hampshire Courier* as having been 'knighted' in 'the usual ceremony'.

Perhaps this ritual was a patriotic reaction to the Napoleonic Wars. Or a nod to the Arthurian myth.

Whatever, the tradition continues to this day, with every winner being referred to as 'Sir', and all other club members being known as 'Gentlemen Commoners'.

In the 1870s group above are 'Sir' John Child (far left, knighted in 1872), 'Sir' George Hussey (fourth from left, 1868), 'Sir' Jacob Bartlett (second from right, 1857) and 'Sir' George Pellatt (far right, 1870).

Note also the man standing to the rear. He was captioned on the photograph as 'Dymott, gardener' (meaning greenkeeper). Yet he was no mere retainer, for in 1850 John Dymott was awarded a special medal, and in 1857 his portrait was painted in recognition of his years of service (*see page 220*).

Little could this 'faithful servitor' (as once described) have realised how much his beloved old green was about to change.

▶ August 2011 and a contender in the **237th Knights Competition** at the **Old Green**, **Southampton,** bowls from the south end of the green (where the pavilion is now sited), towards a group of Knights, dressed in their black top coats, at the north end.

Prominent amidst the modern flats overlooking the green is the Grade II listed **Bowling Green House**, with its green tiled roof and cupola. Built by an Italian merchant in the mid 19th century, the house has no direct association with the green, other than by name, and is accessed separately from Orchard Place. In the early 20th century it provided lodgings for seafarers. Amongst them in April 1912 were two Italian waiters, staying in town before their next ship set sail from across the road. Neither made it back. The ship was the *Titanic*.

Today Bowling Green House is occupied by Wainwright Brothers, a shipping agency.

The process by which the 'Old Green' assumed the characteristics of a 'new' flat green took several years. It started with the creation of banks and ditches in 1887.

Then in 1895 the Southampton club became one of eleven clubs to form the London and Southern Counties Bowling Association.

Eight were based in the London area. One was Reading. The other two were Southampton and their recently formed neighbours, the County Bowling Club, whose green had opened in 1889 at the Hampshire County Cricket Ground on Northlands Road (*see page 137*). In reports this became known as the 'Upper Green', and its older counterpart the 'Lower Green'.

Some bowlers frequented both. For example a dinner staged at the Lower Green to mark the opening of the 1897 season was addressed by 'Sir' John Clarke. But equally he was known as 'Master of the Upper Green'.

Clarke's speech, reported in the *Southampton Observer*, offers a fascinating insight to the changes then taking place in bowls, as more English clubs were adopting the Scottish 'rink' game (as explained in Chapter Seven). When Clarke expressed the hope that one day this new game would be played on the Old Green he was greeted by cries of 'No, No!'

Despite this opposition, the rink game did soon take hold. It was first reported on the Old Green in 1902, a year before the formation of the English Bowling Association.

Then in 1929 the old pavilion was demolished so that the green could, once and for all, be reformed into an Association green. That is, flat and square.

But of course Southampton did not abandon the old ways altogether. Come August and rinks were forgotten as the old way of playing in any direction was temporarily restored for the duration of the Knights Competition.

Viewed from Bowling Green House during the Knights Competition in 2011, the Old Green finds itself very much in the modern world. More flats overlook the west side (where the old pavilion stood). Gods House Tower is behind the far corner. Today's clubhouse was built in 1929, bombed in 1940 and extended both in 1956-58 and 1988.

▲ In surreal contrast to the modernity of the nearby docks, the rules and rituals of the **Knights Competition** remain rooted in the past (although the woods and jacks used are of the modern variety).

The day begins with a procession of Knights onto the green, after which the Mayor of Southampton delivers a token wood to loud hurrahs. Next, the Senior Knight delivers an impassioned speech. When these images were taken in 2011, 'Sir' Fred Rolph finished with the words, 'No fighting, no punching, no kicking! Mine's a pint and may the best man win!'

To begin each 'end', the Knights, all past winners, all dressed in black, place the jack on a penny, in a position of their choosing. A Commoner then bowls two woods.

Next, forming a huddle, the Knights measure the distance between the woods and the jack (*above*) and make a record (*below*).

If a wood dislodges the jack, the jack is put back on the penny before measuring. If that is not possible because the penny is completely obscured by the wood, it is recorded as a 'lodger'. If some of the penny is visible, it is deemed a 'toucher'.

In scoring, a 'lodger' beats a 'toucher', or if neither is registered, the winner is the nearest wood. In

any event the winner gains a single point, or 'shot'. If a player's woods are both nearer the jack than any others, he scores two shots.

After everyone has bowled, one of the Knights announces the result of that end, using a splendid old megaphone (*below right*).

A new end is then played to a different corner of the green. The first to reach seven 'shots' wins.

Because the number of entrants varies each year – the record was 37 in 1945 – some years it can take days to find a winner. Once apparently it took ten days.

Inevitably some Commoners never achieve Knight status, despite years of trying. Yet one man won at his first attempt.

Knights apart, we should add that it is quite possible to achieve playing honours and high office at Southampton – the highest being that of Master of the Green, elected annually – without being a Knight.

And of course for the rest of the year the club competes as does any other flat green club, in rinks. It is, in this respect, a typical open membership club, including, since 1994, a dozen or so ladies. When it was suggested a few years ago that one might compete for a Knighthood it was the ladies who cried 'No, no!' the loudest. But as was shown in 1897, just as in the big wide world that beckons from the quayside, over the wall, one can never say never on a bowling green.

▲ In time honoured fashion **David Welch**, a retired engineer and winner of the **2011 Knights Competition**, is knighted on the green in the presence of the Mayor.

Later 'Sir' David would be presented with a **silver medal**. On one side, as always, are the words **'Win it and Wear it'**. On the other is an inscription relating to events of the year, in this case the wedding of Prince William and Kate Middleton.

Often when a Knight dies his medal is returned to the club.

The earliest (*above right*), from the ninth year of the competition, dates from **1784** and was won by **Thomas Waight**. Below right is the medal from **1815**, featuring a view of the green and God's House Tower. On the back is an inscription celebrating victory at Waterloo, which had occurred six weeks prior to the competition.

This pair, and a further 60 medals, mostly dating from the 19th century are displayed in a cabinet (*below*) made in 1930 for the club's new pavilion, by **William Frost**, who had himself been knighted the year before.

Twice, gold medals have been struck instead of silver; first, it is believed, to mark the 100th Knights Competition, and again in 1899 to celebrate the 600th anniversary of the green.

Faced with such fine artefacts, it seems churlish to quibble over dates. For the Southampton (Old) Bowling Green Club may or may not be playing on the world's oldest bowling green, but it certainly can claim a unique heritage.

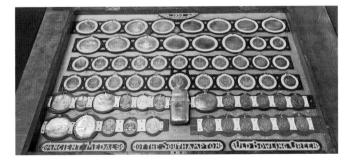

Case study

Painswick Falcon Bowling Club

After the high walls and urban surrounds of Chesterfield and Southampton, the green at the rear of the Falcon Inn brings us to the glorious Gloucestershire village of Painswick, 'the Queen of the Cotswolds'. In the background, the 17th century spire of St Mary's. But what is this we read in the club history? 'One of the oldest, if not the oldest green in the world'. And so another visit to the archives beckons...

For the legions of tourists passing through Painswick, the Falcon Inn is but one of many delights. In fact unless specifically going into the inn's car park at the rear, accessed off New Street – a 15th century thoroughfare lined with historic buildings all glowing in the distinct, yellowish limestone of the Cotswolds – it would be easy to miss the bowling green.

Surrounded by flower beds, clipped hedges and manicured shrubs, it has a thatched shelter, probably Victorian, in one corner, but is otherwise a thoroughly modern flat green. In another corner stands a tidy and functional pavilion built in 1996, with a tiled roof and a prominent gable.

But look again and on this gable is a clock (*below right*), and on the clock is a date.

Just to recap. The earliest confirmed reference to bowling on the green at Chesterfield dates back to 1664, at Lewes to 1639, at Southampton to 1600, and at Hadley, we know not when, possibly in the late 16th century.

So what is the evidence for bowling at Painswick in 1554?

Firstly, we know that the original building on the site of the Falcon Inn had been built by a prominent local family, the Kingstons, as a guest house for visitors, in either 1551 or 1554.

Secondly, we know that the Jerningham family, from Cossy (now Costessey) in Norfolk, acquired the manor of Painswick in 1557, via marriage to a member of the Kingston family.

When the guest house later became an inn, which from local records occurred by at least 1684, it took the name Falcon in honour of the Jerninghams, on whose family crest a falcon appeared.

But when was a bowling green laid next to the inn?

Was it around 1684? Was it after 1711, when the present day Falcon Inn was built? Or was it earlier?

If it was 1554, Painswick's green would be the oldest in Britain, older even than Southampton, where as we noted in the previous case study, the earliest record for bowling on the site is 1600.

So what is the evidence for 1554?

That is the question. The only reference to a date near to 1554 that our research has been able to uncover is from a secondary source, *World Bowls*, written by Dr John Fisher in 1956 (*see Links*).

A medical doctor and English international bowler, Fisher wrote, concerning the Falcon Inn, that 'In the original deeds the property is described as a "messuage with a bowling green and a cockpit".

'These were part of the amenities of a guest inn built in

1551 by the Jerningham family of Cossy, Norfolk.'

Frustratingly Fisher does not specify the source of this finding. He was a physician, not an historian.

Even more frustratingly, nor could our own research track down the source, or anything similar; not from the deeds attached to the Falcon, not from records held in Painswick, in the Gloucestershire County Archives or in the Jerningham family archives, held at the Staffordshire County Record Office.

And so, at least until further research can be undertaken, Southampton's claim to be the oldest green must stand.

Moreover, no further mention of bowling at the Falcon appears until nearly a century after the inn was rebuilt, when in 1808 it was put up for sale and described as having a 'stable yard, garden, bowling green and premises with the appurtenances thereto adjoining and belonging'.

Despite this gap it is nevertheless reasonable to suppose that between the 1550s and 1808 bowling did take place on the site, and certainly from the 1750s, bearing in mind what else is known about the Falcon.

Grown prosperous from wool, Painswick hosted a weekly market and staged an annual fair. In the 19th century daily coach services to Birmingham, Bath, Cheltenham and Gloucester made the Falcon a busy transport hub. At various times the inn also served as an

excise and posting house, held sessions of the manorial court, and in 1794 hosted the earliest known Masonic ceremony in Gloucestershire.

Members of the local gentry, farmers and merchants; all would have patronised the Falcon. In other words, here was exactly the sort of inn, in exactly the sort of location to have a bowling green.

In addition, there was indeed a cockpit at the inn.

We know this from reports of a great main (or cockfighting match) that took place there in June 1731. As recorded on a panel in the pavilion, this was between the Gentlemen of Painswick and Stroud and involved 24 cocks, ten of which were obliged to fight for 'two guineas a battle'.

After 1808, the next reference to bowling comes in the form of a photograph, dated 1870 (*above*). The thatched arbour, then the only form of shelter available, was sited to give a view across the green as it fell away towards the church (as seen on the right in 2014).

Among those portrayed are HT and HW Spring. Members of this family are said to have bowled on the green as early as the 1750s, and were still active in the 1950s. James Tidmarsh, third from the right, was the Falcon's landlord. On the far left sat the vicar. With his arms folded was the doctor. In short, stalwarts of the community.

And, as so often in Victorian photographs, standing apart was the greenkeeper, William Bridgeman, his face a blur, his stance humble. No doubt his besom was well used too, for judging by the proximity of trees – no ditches in those days – and the length of the grass, he would have been kept busy sweeping.

As at Southampton this would soon change. In 1908 the decision was taken to adopt the rink game. So the green was levelled and squared off, albeit with the old turf relaid, and ditches created, a process illustrated on page 126.

Formally constituted in 1912, Falcon Bowling Club soon became a leading light in Gloucestershire,

providing several internationals, notably Tom Goddard. In the process it was nicknamed 'the Paddington of the West' (Paddington then being the venue for the EBA's championships.)

After years of pressure, a proper pavilion was finally built in 1934, funded by the Stroud Brewery (owners of the Falcon).

This was then replaced by the current pavilion, as noted earlier, in 1996 (funded largely by the National Lottery). This much larger building offered improved accommodation for all, including ladies, who formed their own section in 1958.

Today the green is leased from the current owners of the Falcon, Enterprise Inns, and enjoys protection by virtue of falling within a Conservation Area.

As for the club, it has often claimed, albeit without a banner, to play on 'the oldest bowling green in the world'. If that elusive reference cited by Dr Fisher could be traced, that would indeed be the case. Until then, there is more than enough history in Painswick to compensate, and a rather lovely thatched shelter from which to survey the scene, and ponder how slender are the threads that bind us to the distant past.

Case study

Framlingham Castle Bowling Club

Before they were manufactured in bulk, each with a measured bias – a breakthrough achieved in the late 19th century – bowls were crafted by local woodworkers to meet local needs. At Framlingham before 1952, and at other Suffolk greens, including the Sun Hotel, Woodbridge, such were the slopes and undulations that a form of local wood with a strong bias became popular. 'Fram woods' as they were known in Suffolk, were made from oak by a gunsmith, whose stamp 'Norman – Framlingham' can just be read on this example. As illustrated on page 10, Fram woods were shaped like a cheese, though not as flat as those at Lewes.

Unlike most of the castles at which bowling greens have survived, the castle at Framlingham, a market town 15 miles north east of Ipswich, remains remarkably intact.

More so, ironically, it might be said, than the actual green.

Scheduled as an Ancient Monument, the castle as we see it today dates largely from the late 12th century, when Roger Bigod constructed thirteen square towers linked by a curtain wall.

Later owners, the Howard family, amongst them the 2nd Duke of Norfolk, added modern quarters, hence the presence of Tudor red brick chimney stacks.

It was at Framlingham where in 1553 Mary Tudor, whose Catholic cause the 3rd Duke of Norfolk had championed, gathered supporters before being proclaimed Queen.

One tale has it that the Duke bowled at the castle at this time. However the earliest record of bowling dates from a century later.

By that time the castle had been bequeathed by its last private owner, Sir Robert Hitcham, to his old Cambridge College, Pembroke (where a bowling green, possibly also dating from the 17th century, still exists, *see page 51*).

The first reference to the Framlingham green appears during the Civil War in parish records written by the Rector of St Michael's (whose tower is seen on the right, viewed from the castle, across the green). Describing land holdings in Framlingham, the Rev Richard Golty recorded,

'Castle yards, 4 acres, John Moore had them in 1649... and an acre of barley in the bowling aly.'

As already established, the term 'alley' often referred equally to a green. Certainly if the site could support an acre of barley – possibly planted as a wartime measure – then it can hardly have been long and narrow (an acre being nearly three times the area of a modern green).

Presumably the green was restored for bowling some time after the Restoration, because in 1747 the *Ipswich Journal* described it as 'pleasant and beautiful'.

Interestingly, the report also links the green to a nearby pub on Church Street, the Black Swan (where the Conservative Club now stands), suggesting that the lack of facilities at the castle meant that bowlers had to meet elsewhere to drink and dine after matches.

After this comes a lyrical description in *The History of Framlingham and Saxted* by R Green, published in 1833:

'In Summer there is a fine bowling green adjoining the Castle for recreation abroad.'

'There can be little doubt that the latter is a spot which has from time immemorial been used for the enjoyment of bowling, even among the once noble inmates of the Castle. In fact its very situation within the immediate precincts of the old walls where there were arbours, pleasant walks and trees planted for profit and delight, warrants such a conclusion, more particularly as bowling greens were generally a necessary appendage to baronial residences, affording an amusement best calculated, as the poet Green says, "to cure the mind's wrong bias-spleen".'

The description continues, 'The Green is open from the first week in May to the first week in October, and two clubs are held, viz., the Tradesmen's on Wednesday and the Gentleman's on Thursday every week during the season.'

Note, a similar arrangement with two distinct classes of clubs exists today at Hadley (*page 64*).

Another similarity with previous case studies is that the green was used for gatherings. In June 1832 an auction was held there of the public houses owned by bankrupt brewer, George Brooke Keer.

And in 1833, the Framlingham Horticultural Society held its inaugural show on the green.

When reporting on the event the *Ipswich Journal* again linked the green to a local pub, this time the Crown and Anchor.

Concerning the green itself, by the dawn of the 20th century a number of Suffolk clubs were starting to level their greens for rink play, while Framlingham's remained unchanged, on a slope, or 'on the huh', as Suffolk dialect would have it.

This was to have a serious effect on its regulars (who clearly had formed a club by this point), as reported in the *Framlingham Weekly News* on August 21 1909: 'Sad to relate, not one of the members of Framlingham Bowling Club who visited Saxmundham on Monday succeeded in achieving anything worth talking about.

'This result is due entirely to their biased bowls, which, though best adapted to the Framlingham green, are next to useless on level courts of the Scotch pattern.

'The Framlingham bowlers will probably play in tournaments next year and for years after that, but it would be well for them to recognize that only Scotch woods will be ever likely to triumph, and achieve the success which up to the present they have vainly been striving for, for they must lay their 'curlers' aside for those occasions in favour of the straighter pattern.'

This they did in 1919, when level lawns at Framlingham College were used for a rinks tournament.

So successful was this that the event continued until 1939.

Meanwhile although Pembroke College remained its owners, the castle's management was taken over by the government's Commissioners of Works.

For the next three decades the bowlers debated modernising the castle green, but it was only in 1948 that a member, Ken Freeman, was able to purchase the site from the College. He then sold it to an Ipswich solicitor, who promptly gifted it back to the club in memory of his father, John Martin, a member of the club.

Only then could levelling begin.

◀ Viewed from the south in 2007, with **St Michael's Church** in the lower left corner, the manicured square turf of the bowling green at **Framlingham Castle** stands out amid its medieval surrounds.

Having taken possession of the site in 1948 the club finally took the plunge in 1952.

At that time the green was described as sloping four feet down to the west, and also as being saucer-shaped, perhaps meaning that it had a dip in the centre.

As in 1948, Ken Freeman, himself a prominent flat green player, took the initiative. He paid for a team of castle workers to square off and level the green.

Futher advice came from a local farmer and expert on grass seed, Herman Kindred.

Despite this radical change, the club, which changed its name to **Framlingham Castle Bowling Club** in 1957, has since kept alive its use of traditional Fram woods, getting them out once a year for a special tournament.

Seen below left is action from the 2012 final, with a frequent winner, of the competition, John Carr, having just delivered his wood.

As in the rink game, an unbiased jack is used, but in this competition it is 'roving', that is with play going in any direction (as in the old days).

Players may set a mark down the edges as long as the jack is at least six feet from any of the ditches.

As at Lewes, a measuring stick (seen lying on the green) is always available during play.

The club's pavilion it has to be said, built in 1973, does not quite match the quality of either the green or the castle (which is now managed by English Heritage). But at a site that has hosted bowling since at least 1649, there is time yet for that to be addressed.

Case study

Milton Regis Bowling Club

Decked out perhaps for a Coronation in either 1902 or 1911, the old pavilion at Milton Regis in Kent originally bore the date 1900 on its pediment. Yet at some point between the wars, this was amended to 1540 (*below right*). No-one at the club today can explain why this date was chosen. But no matter. In 2015 the 475th anniversary celebrations took place in the club's much grander replacement pavilion, erected in 1994 on the north side of the green, which itself had been modernised in 1939, on the eve of the 400th anniversary. So 1540 may have been plucked out of the air. But it is well and truly part of the club's heritage now.

Milton Regis today is just one of several districts within the larger conurbation of Sittingbourne. But in the 16th century, where our trail begins, the town was a thriving port on the River Swale, perfectly placed to service trade passing through the Thames and Medway estuaries.

There were a number of early bowling greens in Kent. New Romney, Dover and Hythe, for example, all within 25-30 miles of Milton, were recorded as having greens in 1587, 1605 and 'before 1652' respectively.

There is also the intriguing, and oft raised notion that because Francis Drake's father, Edmund, was vicar of Upchurch, four miles from Milton, from 1553-66, it is just possible that young Francis might have bowled there. Alas this is unlikely. During those years he was growing up in Plymouth, before embarking on his seafaring career. But in any case, as noted, no evidence has been found of any green existing in Milton at this time, let alone in 1540.

By 1674, however, it definitely was in place. We know this from the accounts of the churchwarden in Milton. The reason these accounts mention the green is that it lay on church land, within an area that had formerly served as the town's archery butts.

(Another favourite tale at Milton is that the four ancient yew trees that still line one side of the green might have been planted at the butts because yew was the favoured material for longbows.)

In the church accounts, the first reference to the butts was in 1661, when Abraham Ames was paid a total of 13s for 300 stakes 'to enclose the Butts'. By then of course the butts would no longer have been needed for military training, but may well have been used for recreational archery.

Then in 1674 came the first of over 30 entries relating to the bowling green.

The first, dated July 14 1674, read: 'Paid to Stephen Baker for house in the bowling green, £1 11s 6d'. Could this have been the first pavilion? This was followed by payment of 16s 6d in 1675 for 'work done about the butts and Bowling green', also to Baker.

Some fascinating snippets lie amongst the later entries.

In 1680 'a Rowling stone for ye bowling green' was purchased for £1 12s 6d. But in 1685 'ye Rowle' had to be repaired by Careek at a cost of 1s 6d, and again in 1686, by John Herrington, who was paid 2s 'for mending the Role'.

Other payments in 1684-85 were to Goodman Jordan for 'makeing readie' the green (20s), to

Goodman Cheesman for 'scouring the dike about the green (1s 9d), and to Rob Turner for repairing the hedge (7s).

We then learn of a bonfire lit on the green, in honour of the birth of the Prince of Wales (the 'Old Pretender') in June 1688. On that occasion Nick Walter was paid 4s for supplying eight gallons of beer.

The following year John Martin was paid £1 10s 6d to erect a fence.

By the 1690s the going rate for one year's maintenance of the green was set at 10s. On top of this, extra payments were made for killing hedgehogs and 'pulle cats'.

In 1714 Mr Earle and Mr Watts received 2s 6d for surveying the 'bowling green house'. The last entry, again for the repair of the green and fence, was dated 1755.

No other bowling green of this period is as minutely recorded.

Thereafter, the story follows a now familiar pattern.

There is no indication of when Milton Bowling Club itself formed, although it definitely existed in the 1860s. There continued to be events on the green, including in 1862 a firework and hot air balloon display, followed by a party for children at the National School, which had just been built on the south side of the green.

To the north stood a large Union Workhouse, built in 1836.

This was at a time when the industrial growth of Sittingbourne – its brickfields and paper mills in particular – was starting to impinge upon Milton's boundaries. Indeed it partly explains why the suffix 'Regis' was adopted in 1907, to retain a measure of local identity.

For the bowling club changes were in the air too. Responding to the growth of Association bowling, in 1925 a three rink green was created on a vegetable garden on the north side of the main green. Opened with great ceremony by the manager of the Sittingbourne Paper Mill, the largest of its kind in the world, its turf came from Kemsley, where a second paper mill had just been opened to feed the ever growing appetite of Fleet Street.

Reporting on the event, the *East Kent Gazette* extolled the 'billiard-table like' surface, divided from the old 'crown green' by that row of yew trees, '1,000 years old'.

And so, unusually, flat and old style bowls continued side by side until in 1939, with Milton clearly out of step with its Kentish counterparts and losing members, the main green was levelled too.

As reported in the *East Kent Gazette*, this was close to the 400th anniversary of the green, 'founded in 1540'.

But there was still more to do before the future could be made secure. In 1960, having noted that the bowls club in Sittingbourne had closed after losing its green, two members at Milton stumped up £250 to buy the freehold.

Then in 1966 the green was finally squared off to create the one we see today. This was joined in 1994 by the new pavilion, funded by the members and Swale Borough Council, and in 1996 by changing rooms and a storage block on the south side.

Happily, throughout all this, as seen on the right in 2015, the yews have survived. As have some other artefacts from the club's past...

▲ To most visitors **Milton Regis Bowling Club** appears a typically spruce, exceptionally friendly, flat green club, secreted in the midst of an anonymous, late 20th century housing estate. But in a cupboard lies a precious haul... a selection of gnarled and battered **lignum vitae woods** left over from the 'crown green' games played in 1938.

Some are cheese shaped (*above right*), as at Lewes, as is the white painted jack (*top right*). Some are pudding shaped, as at Chesterfield.

Each bears its own markings and scars; rings created when the wood was originally turned on a lathe (*above right*), an owner's initial, plugs made from lead and pewter.

One is both patched up on its sole, and plugged (*above*).

In another part of the pavilion is a heritage corner (*see page 220*), created by one of the members.

In this is a cutting, thought to be from the *Daily Chronicle* in 1917 (a paper owned by Edward Lloyd Ltd, the company that also owned the local paper mills). In the article the reporter describes visiting Milton in the company of the vicar and two club members, and being shown charity records 'in musty old books, some in chests at the ancient church, and some preserved at the Vicarage,' written in 'quaint and crabbed handwriting'.

Most interesting of all, went the report, was an entry dated 1601, which stated that a part of the butts had been used as a bowling green 'since times immemorial'.

Here perhaps is the reason for the date of 1540 suddenly appearing after the First World War.

But can these musty records be found today? Despite extensive enquiries, sadly not.

Case study

Hereford Bowling Club

Our final case study from the Tudor and Stuart period takes us to Bewell Street, a narrow paved thoroughfare in the centre of Hereford, where stands, next to a Tesco superstore, the Tudoresque Bowling Green Inn (*below right*). The building's two gabled bays on its west side, belong to the pub. The single bay to the right – its half-timbered detailing subtly different – has its own door and a glazed ground floor frontage. This is the Grade II listed clubhouse of the Hereford Bowling Club, on which the plaque above appears. It dates the clubhouse to c.1768. And the bowling green? 'Probably the oldest in the UK'.

By now readers will be aware of how difficult it is to determine which bowling green is the oldest, and also how futile it might be to attempt a definitive judgement.

A case in point is Bewell Street, where Hereford Bowling Club celebrated the 500th anniversary of its green in 1984.

But on what grounds?

For example, when John Speed drew up a plan of Hereford in 1610, a year before his map showing the green in Southampton (*see page 71*), Bewell Street was clearly marked. A bowling green was not.

Not until Isaac Taylor's effort of 1757 (*see opposite*) does the present day green appear on a map.

That said, as research by David Whitehead has shown (*see Links*), bowling of some sort did take place in Hereford as early as 1533. In that year, various persons were presented to the courts 'pro custodiendo le boullynge'.

Then in 1557 a game of 'boules' was reported in the garden of a man called Gregory ap Rees Esq.

It is possible that Rees' garden lay at the back of Bewell Street. There were several long gardens belonging to houses in Widemarsh Street, off Bewell Street, plus, in the vicinity, some orchards (ideal cover for bowling alleys, as we saw at Southampton).

But as Whitehead found, several men called Rees lived in Hereford at the time. From *An Historical Account of the City* published in 1796, we also know that before the 1640s there was a bowling alley elsewhere in Hereford, on Castle Green, 'all which was ruined' during the Civil War.

So yet again we must wait until the 17th century for a confirmed reference to the green in question.

It comes in 1697, when properties in Widemarsh Street were sold to pay off the debts of Francis Griffith, a scrivener in London. Included within the sale was the 'Bolling Green... lying near All Saints Church' (on the south side of Bewell Street).

Among other documents relating to the sale was an earlier deed entitled 'Bowling Green', This indicated that Griffith had owned the green in 1684, when he had bought an adjoining garden.

The story next moves to the 1760s, when the then owner of the Widemarsh Street properties and bowling green bequeathed them to the Mayor, Aldermen and citizens of Hereford, in order to help fund the salary of a chaplain at the County Gaol.

The main house on Widemarsh Street became the Mansion House, for the use of the Mayor and circuit judges. Meanwhile, in 1768 the Corporation leased the bowling

green to an inn-keeper, Matthew Thomas, for £15 a year, with the proviso that he could not 'dig, plough or break up' its turf.

Thomas became the proprietor also of the building on Bewell Street that overlooked the green.

Described in 1768 as a 'Billiard Room', this is the present day clubhouse (complete with skittle alley on its upper floor).

Thomas was clearly a character, and a keen bowler, as we see from his poem in the *Hereford Journal* on May 5 1790, trumpeting the game's superiority to archery.

Three verses will suffice.

The Bowling-green, my fav'rite theme
Is pleasant, smooth, and even;
Great Jove himself began the game –
His Bowling-green in Heav'n...

Fair Atalanta too confest
The charms of nicely rolling,
And clasp'd her lover to her breast,
When he began his bowling...

Then boast no more of bow and dart,
Away with Quivers from us;
And all consult the Bowling art
On Green of MATTHEW THOMAS.

Thomas was the perfect host. Every year during Hereford Races he laid on a 'Publick Breakfast'.

In 1766 a Friendly Society formed at the Billiard Room, and it also staged regular meetings of Freemasons (who in England generally were often bowlers too).

In August 1784, a hot air balloon took off from the green.

As for bowling, a regular club

From Taylor's map of 1757 we see again how central bowling was in the life of an English community.

was also instigated, with Thomas advertising Monday dinners every fortnight 'when the favour of the Gentlemen's company is requested.' (This notice ran every April in the *Hereford Journal* for many years.) Another club met from 1783 onwards, at five o'clock on alternate summer Tuesdays, for 'Coffee, Tea, Cards, and Dancing'.

By the early 1790s the Mansion House, whose garden backed onto the green, had fallen into a state of disrepair. As a result, the Corporation put the property up for sale, intending to use the proceeds to meet the original charitable purpose of funding a chaplain.

The Mansion House formed one lot. Another, dated 1793, was for the 'Bowling Green Coffee House' with 'green, garden and appurtenances'. But there were no takers and they had to re-advertise in 1795.

Throughout this Matthew Thomas remained at the helm, until his death in 1796 at the age of 62. Such was his reputation that an obituary appeared in *The Gentlemen's Magazine*.

Thomas, it stated, 'was a man generally known and respected by all ranks. By early reading and a retentive memory he became the pleasant companion of his numerous friends.'

By 1817 regular bowls meetings had switched to Thursdays, to fit in with half-day closing. Venison was a favourite accompaniment.

In 1840, the business was offered for letting in the *Hereford Journal*. 'The Bowling Green is ornamented with well fitted-up Alcoves, and surrounded by a most productive Garden, walled in, and well planted with choice Fruit Trees in a full state of bearing.'

(The gardens to the rear, incidentally, were absorbed by the neighbouring Hereford Brewery, founded in 1834, on the site of which is now the Tesco car park.)

By now the clubhouse was known as Albert's Billiard Rooms, after Prince Albert. The green also had a skittle ground.

Next door, the Bowling Green Inn also dates from this period, even though it has never had any direct link to the green.

As of 2015 there were some 50 members of the Hereford club, who hope, having agreed to purchase the clubhouse from the brewers Whitbread, to be in sole ownership by 2018.

One question remains, however. Why choose the date 1984 to celebrate the 500th anniversary, when there is no record of the green being mentioned in 1484?

We can only conclude that someone, at some point, misread the date of that original deed. The one that was actually dated 1684.

To the east of the green was the Mansion House, fronting onto **Widemarsh Street**. Writing in the 1970s, David Whitehead noted that a blocked entrance and window in a wall, also on the east side of the green (since demolished) may have formed part of a summer house belonging to the Mansion House, offering access to the green. If so, it serves only to emphasise how important bowls was in municipal life, as we saw also at Chesterfield.

Overlooking the green in 2007 (*above left*), as in 1757, is the 14th century spire of **All Saints**.

Apparent also is that the green is now a flat green. Hereford adopted the rink game in the 1920s and played a leading role in forming the county association in 1928.

Since then much around the green has changed, not least the supermarket next door. But not the red brick clubhouse. For Hereford's green may or may not be the oldest, but its clubhouse, in use since at least 1768, is one of only four bowls related clubhouses extant from that period and still functioning (the others are at Bishop's Castle Ellesmere and Great Torrington).

How proud Matthew Thomas would be, looking down from his very own 'bowling green in heav'n'.

Chapter Six

England 1688–1830

Georgian gentlemen enjoy a game of bowls, as depicted on a copper panel created by FT Callcott for the Grade II* listed Black Lion on Kilburn High Road, London, at the time of the pub's reconstruction in 1898. That no records exist of there ever having been a bowling green at the pub matters little. Bowls was by then firmly part of an idealised view of English life, no less than cricket on the village green might be considered today.

By the late 17th century bowls had evolved into a game that would be quite recognisable to players of today; a game similar to modern crown green bowling, played on grass in summertime, without fear of censure from the courts and often with the blessing of local authorities.

Various banning orders from the days of Henry VIII may have remained on the statute books, but they ceased to carry any weight.

Nor, in an age of muskets and cannons, could bowls be blamed any more for distracting men from archery practice. Instead, archery was set to become popular as a sport, especially amongst the aristocracy, as was another sport newly emerging in Kent, Hampshire and the south, cricket.

In the previous chapter we showed how bowling greens had started to take root as hubs of community life. In this chapter we trace the beginnings of a recognisable club culture, remembering always the necessity to distinguish between the creation of a green and its later use by a club. Thus to recap, as

an example, while bowling on the green at Southampton was recorded in 1600, the club we know today did not form there until over a century later.

In fact the 18th century was to witness the birth of at least 24 clubs that are still in action today. These were not only in the locations featured in the previous chapter, such as Lewes, but in the likes of Croydon in Surrey, Blackburn in Lancashire, Bedale in North Yorkshire, Haddington in East Lothian and Kilmarnock in Ayrshire, each playing to their own, subtly different set of rules.

For sure this evolution was assisted by the emergence of newspapers, which so often carried notices advising readers that a club or society was about to be formed, or of matches and dinners taking place.

Yet despite this newfound respectability, in the eyes of some, bowls remained tainted by its association with gambling and drinking. It was for this reason that the famous itinerant cleric, the Rev George Whitefield, often preached from bowling greens.

In 1739, an estimated crowd of 7,000 heard him speak at the Hannam Mount green in Bristol.

Of his visit to Oxford in January 1739, he recorded in his journal:

'God put it into the Hearts of some Gentlemen to lend me a large Bowling-Green, where I preached to about five thousand People… Blessed be God, that the Bowling-Green is turned into a Preaching-place. This, I hope, is a Token that Assembly-rooms and Playhouses will soon be put to the same Use. O may the Word of God be mighty to the pulling down of these strong Holds of the Devil!'

It was no doubt the moralising of Whitefield and others that led to bowling being cited in anti-gaming legislation enacted between 1739-45. But even then we need to be cautious, for the term 'bowling' still also applied to games that we would consider as skittles. One version, popular at 18th century London inns and pleasure gardens, for example, involved bowling a ball along an angled plank of wood at a set of nine pins (as featured in *Played at the Pub, see Links*).

There can be no greater indication of how seriously 18th century aristocrats took bowls, or at least the socialising that accompanied it, than the sophistication of the pavilions built to service their greens. This is the Grade II* Bowling Green House at Wrest Park in Bedfordshire, designed by Batty Langley for Henry Grey, the 1st Duke of Kent, in c.1735.

Nor in a semantic sense should we forget that the reason the delivery of a ball in cricket is called 'bowling' is because until the 1760s cricket balls were indeed 'bowled' along the ground, underarm.

As will become apparent, the use of the term 'bowling alley' for outdoor greens also persisted into the 18th century. This was particularly so in the context of country house gardens.

For the aristocracy and social climbers of the Georgian period, having a bowling green was a sign of wealth and sophistication. So if a substantial house was put up for sale or to let, and it had a green, this would be listed prominently, often in capital letters.

In addition to their social status, greens also fitted perfectly into the symmetrical style of garden design in vogue from the 1630s until the mid 18th century.

Influenced by French gardens at Fontainebleau and elsewhere, this style rejoiced in compartmentalised parterres, clipped hedges, ornamental trees and water features. Stephen Switzer, in his *Ichnographica Rustica, or the nobleman, gentleman and gardener's recreation*, published in 1718, described the kind of parterre which the English had made their own, 'viz. Bowling-green or plain Parterres, the method of which they [the French] own to have received from England... the beautifullest with us... on account of the Goodness of our Turf, and that Decency and unaffected Simplicity which it affords to the eye of the Beholder.'

But fashions change, and by the late 18th century bowling greens fitted less well into the more natural landscapes propounded by Capability Brown.   »

▲ Painted in 1695 by the Flemish artist, **Jan Siberechts**, frequently described as the father of British landscape art, this panoramic view shows **Wollaton Hall** in **Nottingham** from the east. In the foreground, the D-shaped bowling green sits on a raised terrace with a banqueting house on its southern side.

Two figures in the centre of the green appear to be pointing out the lie of the land to the player nearest the house, who is about to bowl, while the pair nearer to us examine the position of the woods.

Siberechts was one of many artists to come to England from the Low Countries following the Glorious Revolution in 1688. His speciality was the 'country house portrait', showing off the wealth and taste of his noble clients, in this case Thomas Willoughby. The green and its formal surrounds had been laid at Willoughby's behest, while the house, by Robert Smythson, dates from the 1580s.

Wollaton Hall today is a museum. In the grounds, only a hint of where the green lay can be discerned amidst a clump of trees, bound by a path which follows the curve of the road in the foreground.

▲ From the collection of the British Museum, this engraving by James Tinney, dated c.1702, shows in the middle distance the bowling green at **Hampton Court** in **Surrey**, shortly after the completion of four corner pavilions, designed by William Talman under the direction of Sir Christopher Wren. The green itself had been commissioned by Charles II in 1670, the same year that his laws of the game were published.

Only one of the pavilion survives. Now listed Grade II* and much altered since to serve as a private residence, in 2012 it was put on sale for £10 million, making it undoubtedly the most valuable bowling pavilion ever recorded.

In contrast to the formal setting at Hampton Court, the scene at **Claremont** in **Esher**, also in **Surrey**, portrayed in 1738 by John Rocque (*below*), shows an early example of the more naturalistic English landscape style. Stephen Switzer is thought to have been involved, but the chief designers were Charles Bridgeman and John Vanbrugh.

Note how relaxed is the scene, with one man in the foreground about to bowl, whilst all around other men, women, children and dogs enjoy the green.

Although no longer used for bowls, this landscape largely survives, as does Vanbrugh's **Belvedere Tower** in the distance.

≫ For the wider populace, meanwhile, especially the burgeoning middle classes, bowling only grew in popularity. Increasingly greens were found in pleasure gardens and in spa towns such as Bath. At pubs and inns too.

Newspaper adverts for them were plentiful. Typical is an entry in the *Norfolk Chronicle* in December 1777 for the George Inn, East Dereham. This is described as 'a most delightful Bowling Green with Summer-house and Arbors, surrounded with Gardens and pleasant Shrubberies'.

It is from newspaper notices that we also learn much about the nature of early clubs and societies.

Many appear to have started as dining clubs, in which, as at Hadley Heath, subscribers combined to book a green at an inn for a specific time each week, after which a set meal, referred to as an 'ordinary', was enjoyed.

Another example was the Black Swan, Darlington, where according to the *Newcastle Courant* in January 1739, there was 'a Bowling-Green, where a Company of Gentlemen meet, and raises a Sum of Money by Subscription, there are two Drinking-rooms adjoining it, very commodious.'

Similarly in the *Norfolk Chronicle*, a notice to let the Black Lion at Walsingham in 1781 described it as 'well calculated for Road Business, and publick Amusements, viz large Assemblies in the Winter Season, and in Summer a commodious Bowling Green, to which there is about Fifty Subscribers, and a Billiard Table'.

As reported in the preceding case studies, bowling greens of this period were by no means sacrosanct, as they are today.

Rather, they hosted an array of colourful events.

A 'Match at Foot-ball, play'd by six young Women of a Side' was staged on a green at Bath in 1726, for the 'Divertion of our polite Gentry'. The green at Southwark in London hosted an annual fair and occasional boxing matches. At Scarborough in 1732 there was a foot race around the green.

Hot air balloon launches were also popular; in 1784 on the Forth Bowling Green in Newcastle and at Leominster, where live animals in a cage were sent skywards.

During the summer of 1742 the green at the Cold Bath in Leicester hosted illuminated concerts every Thursday evening, 'to the general satisfaction of the Gentlemen Subscribers'.

For women, such events were the only time they ventured onto most bowling greens, as guests, for it was not until the late Victorian era that we find them actually bowling in earnest.

As for Scotland, the birthplace of the rink game which would transform bowling south of the border in the late 19th and early 20th centuries, bowls clubs would develop along similar lines during the Georgian period.

Indeed it was in Scotland that we see the first glimpses of what may be described as a bowling industry, evidenced by a notice placed in the *Caledonian Mercury* in July 1720 by Gavin Godsman, an ivory and wood turner based in Edinburgh. Among the first items offered in a long list of products was biased bowls. It was also in Scotland, in the 1790s, that Thomas Taylor of Glasgow became the first business to specialise in bowls equipment.

In common with many of the clubs and greens that emerged in this period, Taylor remains happily in business to this day.

▶ Depicted here in 1712 by Dutch draughtsman Jan Kip, **Badminton House** in **Gloucestershire** is best known in sporting circles as the home, since 1682, of the Duke of Beaufort's Hunt, as the place where the game of shuttlecock gained its modern name in the 1860s, and more recently as the venue for the Badminton Horse Trials. But in the 18th century there was only one game to be had in the immediate environs of the house.

Seen in the centre foreground, the bowling green at Badminton was possibly as level as it was square. But as this was almost 200 years before the rink game arrived in Gloucestershire, the minute figures drawn on the green are playing at angles across it.

Kip's engraving is one of a series of similar works reproduced in Robert Atkyns' compilation, *The Ancient and Present State of Gloucestershire*. But Kip is equally known for his collaboration with fellow Dutch artist, Leonard Knyff. Together this pair produced another collection of drawings of country houses in 1707, entitled *Britannia Illustrata*. This included the engraving on the right, showing **Chatsworth House** in **Derbyshire**.

Laid out in the 1690s at the same time that the house and gardens were rebuilt in a daringly modern Baroque style, the bowling green can be seen on the left of the central garden axis. Note the square **Bowling Green House**, seen from the rear. When the grounds were restyled after 1755 by Capability Brown, this building was relocated and the green fell out of use.

Other great houses with greens drawn by Knyff and Kip included Haigh Hall at Wigan, Barrington in Gloucestershire, Bryanstone in Dorset and Hamstead Marshall in Berkshire.

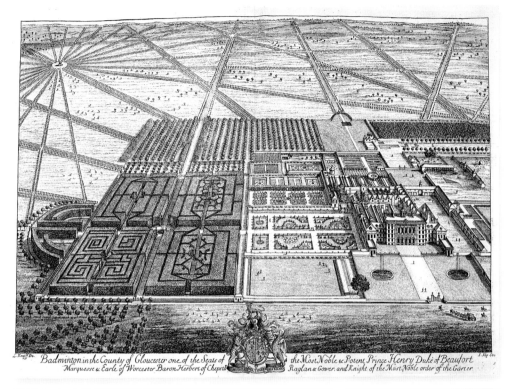

Badminton in the County of Gloucester one of the Seats of the Most Noble & Potent Prince Henry Duke of Beaufort Marquesse & Earle of Worcester Baron Herbert of Chepstow Raglan & Gower, and Knight of the Most Noble order of the Garter.

Nowadays the former bowling green at Chatsworth forms part of private gardens reserved for the resident Duke of Devonshire. But the Grade I listed former Bowling Green House (*above*) can be visited. Built in 1693-95, probably to the designs of William Talman, it was relocated in c.1750 to the immediate east of the house, and is now known as Flora's Temple.

▲ It is not only in the gardens of dukes that early bowls related buildings have survived.

Above, in the midst of rural **Cumbria**, is one of a matched pair of Grade II* listed corner pavilions, built c.1700 or possibly earlier, to serve a bowling green at **Maulds Meaburn Hall**, originally the seat of the Lowther family.

The family, whose most famous scion in sporting circles was Henry Cecil Lowther, the 5th Earl of Lonsdale (after whom Lonsdale belts and the modern sportswear range were named), moved from Maulds Meaburn in the 18th century to Lowther Hall (also drawn by Messrs Knyff and Kip).

Amazingly it is possible to trace the outline of the original green.

However the pavilions might easily be mistaken for outhouses. Indeed one was, at some stage, converted into a communal privy.

◄ Also in **Cumbria** is this Grade II listed garden house in the grounds of **Cockermouth Castle**.

Built in 1682-83 on a terrace overlooking the bowling green (now a lawn), it is, in common with several other surviving examples, octagonal in form. Steps lead up to the principal room, which served as a space for dining, drinking, card-playing and the like. Underneath was a food preparation and cellar area, reached by a back door on the lower level. Today the pavilion serves as the gardener's office, with a potting shed below.

Bowling fitted in perfectly with the romanticism of the times, offering an ideal expression of the picturesque. This is especially so at **Kymin Hill**, a mile east of **Monmouth** in **Wales**. There, a castellated tower known as the **Roundhouse** was built in 1794 (*below left*). Again its upper floor consisted of a dining room, with the kitchen below.

Listed Grade II* and owned by the National Trust, the Roundhouse was funded by subscribers, led by the Duke of Beaufort and eight MPs, to the Kymin Picnic Club. This met every Tuesday for 'dining together and spending the day in a social and friendly manner.'

Close by lay a bowling green, surrounded by a dry stone wall.

In 1784 the Rev John Wesley recorded in his journal, 'Tues.10. I took a walk to what is called the Bowling-green house [no doubt the predecessor to the Roundhouse]...

'I have hardly seen such a place before. A gravel walk leads through the most beautiful meadows, surrounded on all sides by fruitful hills, to a gently rising ground; on the top of which is a smooth green, on which the gentry of the town frequently spend the evening in dancing.'

▲ Between the 1770s and 2014 there was no sign of a bowling green at **Hanbury Hall**, near **Droitwich** in **Worcestershire**. Like so many greens at country houses of the period it was swept away when garden design switched from formalism to naturalism.

▲ Church, pub and bowling green – a wonderfully evocative image of Georgian England at peace with itself, captured in watercolour by **Michael Rooker**, some time in the period after 1788 when he began a series of annual autumn tours around the southern counties.

But although Rooker may have used a little artistic licence, this was no fantasy. For the church, pub and bowling green can all be visited today. The church is the Grade I listed **St Nicholas**, whose 17th century castellated tower has changed little (even if it stands further away than depicted).

The pub is the Grade II listed **Castle Inn**, which at the time Rooker visited was called the Bunch of Grapes. And the setting is a corner of the village of **Hurst** in **Berkshire**, just east of Reading.

As for the **Hurst Bowling Club**, whose badge features a bunch of grapes, they have long since converted the green to that of a standard flat 'Association' green, so that there are now neat ditches separating the green from the pub terrace. It appears also that either the pub has undergone major alterations or Rooker has transposed a more attractive gable end of the building that faces east, overlooking the pub garden, rather than portray the more prosaic gable end that we see today facing the green, to the south. Predictably the white timber staircase has been replaced by a steel fire escape.

But whether in the late 18th century or the early 21st century, it seems churlish to nitpick in the presence of such a harmonious rural village scene.

Legend has it that Charles I played here while on hunting trips in the Windsor Royal Forest. For its part Hurst BC dates its formation to 1747, based on the diary entry of a Mr Belchin, who visited the inn that year.

'This house is very pleasantly situated and has belonging to it a large and handsome bowling green for the diversion of those gentlemen who please to play.

'Being all assembled together we sat down and smoked our pipes and drank some wine in a very sociable manner.'

The original of this Rooker watercolour is now held in the Paul Mellon Collection in Washington DC. But a copy hangs in the club's modest 20th century pavilion, which stands almost exactly on the site of the tree seen on the right.

But recently the National Trust decided to reconstruct elements of the original parterres and walks, which had been designed, it is thought by George London, at the same time as Hanbury Hall itself was built, in around 1701.

Apart from recreating the green, two timber corner pavilions were constructed with tiled, square bell roofs, based upon designs drawn up by a Worcester surveyor, James Dougharty, in 1732.

Nor are these just for show. As in the 18th century, visitors are invited to play on the green, either bowls or croquet. Flat shoes only, naturally.

Drawn & Engraved by Rob.t Cruikshank.   *Published by Sherwood & C.º August 1. 1825.*

The Bowling Alley, Worcester, or Characters of the Hand and Glove Club.

▲ After the rural idyll of Hurst, **Robert Cruikshank** offers a rather different view of bowling in Georgian England, this from *The English Spy* published in 1825, a 'satirical and humorous' portrayal of social habits during the reign of George IV.

Writing under the pseudonym Bernard Blackmantle, the author, Charles Malloy Westmacott and Cruikshank (referred to as 'Transit') call in on members of the **Hand and Glove Club** in **Worcester**, at one of their summer evening meetings at a Subscription Bowling Alley (which, note, clearly is a green). The club, we learn, is composed of the town's 'most respectable' inhabitants.

Whilst sketching, Cruikshank chats 'with a sporting Reverend, whose taste for giblets had proved rather expensive; and who was most desirous of appearing in print: a favor merry Stephen Godson, the lawyer, requested might also be extended to him. "Ay," said John Portman, "and if you want a character for your foreground rich in colour, my phiz [face] is much at your service; and here's George Brookes, the radical, to form a good dark object in the distance."'

Other characters who presumably also appear above included Will Shunk, a supporter of the reformist politician Francis Burdett, Sam Swan, who sang 'a good chant', Joe Shelton, 'an artist in economy', Probert the frugal schoolmaster, Dr Davis, who regulated the town's clocks and played a double bass, and the pompous Captain Corls, fresh from his campaigns in India.

'In this way,' wrote Westmacott, 'the evening passed off very pleasantly.'

In the 1820s half of England's gloving industry was based in Worcester, hence the club's name.

But where was the alley?

One thought is that it was in the Sansome Fields pleasure gardens, a section of which re-opened as the Arboretum in 1859. It was there that the Arboretum Bowling Club, the forerunner of the present day Worcester Bowling Club, based on Wood Terrace, formed in 1867.

Also of interest in Cruikshank's drawing is the shelter on the right, similar in form to those still in use at Hadley Heath (*see page 65*), a few miles to the north of Worcester.

Indeed a copy of this lithograph hangs in the pub adjoining that green, the Bowling Green Inn, and it could be said that the Hadley Bowling Club, which meets there every Thursday, is one of the few private member clubs left in bowls that continues in the tradition of the Hand and Glove Club.

▶ 'A large smooth plain extends its verdant brow' after the scythesman has shaved its 'peeping flowers' and 'unripen'd crop', then tugged the heavy roller to press the turf 'and every rising prominence' subdue.

And so to play. The bowls lad takes a rest in front of the roller. The woods lie all around the jack. And the bowlers? They are in dispute, mostly with themselves.

Unlike the emerging game of cricket, other than occasional ironic allusions linking bias, life and the rub of the green – tropes that were well mined by Shakespeare – bowling has rarely been the focus of narrative prose. There are nevertheless themes that will be familiar to modern day players in **The Bowling Green**, a poem written in 1727 by **William Somervile**, for which this engraving, by John Thurston and Charlton Nesbit, served as a frontispiece when it was re-issued in 1813 (in a collection that included Somervile's better known work, *Hobbinol*).

The language is dense, the references obscure. But in essence this is the tale of a doubles match involving four characters, Bendo, Zadock, Griper and Nimrod (he of the 'sinewy limbs and solid brawn' on the right).

Although not depicted in the woodcut, Somervile describes 'the motley tribe' that attends from the sidelines, all betting on the outcome. 'Attornies spruce, in their plate-button'd frocks, And rosy parsons, fat and orthodox: Of every sect, whigs, papists, and highflyers, Cornuted [cuckolded] aldermen and hen-peck'd squires: Fox-hunters, quacks, scribblers in verse and prose, And half-pay captains, and half-witted beaus…'

From the commentary we learn that the jack is biased and that the 'large smooth plain' is anything

but. Thus after a decidely weak shot Bendo is heard to curse 'the mountains that obstruct his way', and so 'on the guiltless green the blame to lay'.

Zadock proves no happier, despite having found cheer in 'three black mugs'. With pain in his hams he bends to bowl, finds his wood blocked by Bendo's short bowls, and flies off in a rage to hide his head 'in thick mundungus clouds'.

It is left to Griper 'a veteran well skill'd' (perhaps the player pointing with his stick) to settle the game.

Fondly he kisses the winning wood to the loud applause 'of every betting friend'.

Somervile, a Warwickshire squire and hunting enthusiast who drank rather too much and died in 1742, clearly knew his bowls. But even more, he captured brilliantly the antics of the players as they pursued each wood across the green, hoping that their invocations and contortions might somehow steer them to the jack.

But if all this brings a wry smile to the reader, it should be added that by the time *The Bowling Green* was reissued in 1813, 86 years after its composition, it was already a period piece. In fact the general consensus amongst bowling historians of the 20th century

was that, by the dawn of the 19th century, bowls was dying out.

It had already fallen out of fashion amongst the aristocracy. In 1763 Benjamin Martin thought the greens at Epsom were less frequented than before by the gentry, while in 1801 Joseph Strutt, in *The Sports and Pastimes of the People of England*, wrote that although bowls had been 'a very popular amusement' in his youth, in London, at least, few greens remained and none 'were so generally frequented' as before.

Could this have been true? Was bowls already being regarded as a quaint leftover of bygone days?

◀ If the consensus was correct and bowling did go through a lean period during the late 18th century, then this observation must at least be counterbalanced by the number of clubs that did manage to endure.

As noted earlier, 24 current clubs may reasonably claim to have their roots in the 18th century.

As ever, we need to be cautious about dates. Three of the 24 clubs are in Scotland, one of which, Kilmarnock, dates its foundation as 1740. If this could be proven, Kilmarnock would be the oldest club in Britain.

In England, in Croydon, Surrey, as we learn from Valerie Nurcombe's excellent history (*see Links*), there was a green in the town as early as 1695, shown on a John Ward map as lying by the side of the Archbishop's Palace.

However, the **Croydon Bowling Club** (*top left*) takes its foundation date of 1749 from the year in which bowling was first recorded at the Three Tuns Inn on Surrey Street.

But there is no evidence of a club forming then, and not until 1857 are there any reports of matches.

Croydon's current green, incidentally, dates from 1922.

Similarly, **Helston Bowling Club** in **Cornwall** is based on a green laid on the site of Helston Castle (and which since 1834 has been overlooked by the Grylls Monument). As seen from its badge (*centre left*) the club considers itself to have formed in 1760. But it also fully acknowledges that the modern Helston club was actually re-formed in 1905, after years of its predecessor lying dormant.

At **Brampton Bowling Club** in **Cumbria** meanwhile (*above right*), all that can be ascertained of its early history is that its green belonged originally to a coaching inn, the Howard Arms, and that it

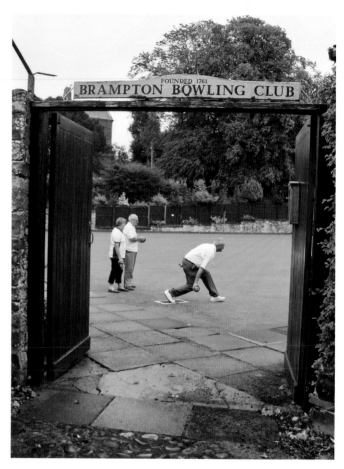

certainly existed in 1860 when the inn was advertised for sale.

But as to why the club claims to have been formed in 1761, no-one in living memory has been able to say, other than that the claim is of long standing and so must therefore have some substance.

As well it might. For there is plenty of evidence of other bowls clubs forming around that time.

One is **Blackburn Subscription Bowling Green Club** in **Lancashire**.

According to a shield in its possession (*lower left*), clearly some of its members believed at some point that its formation date was

1749. Other sources say 1734. But as we noted earlier, the actual date is 1753, and this makes the club, in common with Lewes, the oldest in Britain to have a fully documented formation date.

For this reason the full story follows in Chapter Eight.

Otherwise what emerges from these and other stories is that while a number of clubs have indeed manipulated historical evidence in order to gain more bearing, it is equally a sign that bowlers of every generation love to place themselves within an historical continuum... which of course they are.

▲ Tucked behind the **George Inn** in **Solihull**, **Warwickshire**, the bowling green dates from between 1693, when the inn bought the site, and 1783. We know the latter date because that year the green was reported as having been the scene of a public spat between Dr Parr, the Curate of Hatton, and the Rev Charles Curtis, Rector of St Martin's in the Bull Ring, Birmingham.

In 1790, as reported in the *Gentleman's Magazine*, mourners at the funeral of William James, an assistant at the green, played a match there, as he had requested, on their return from his burial.

Note the curved edge of the green, which indicates that it is a crown, rather than a flat green. This is to accommodate an old yew, which in the 19th century was trimmed by a topiarist into the shape of a giant peacock. Ever since, the **Solihull Bowling Club** has had a peacock as its symbol.

Close to Solihull is another club with its roots in the Georgian period, as its name suggests.

Ye Old Knowle Bowling Club (as it has been known since 1937) may now occupy a site laid out only in 1994, but it was formed by a group of local gentry at The Mermaid Inn,

now The Greswolde Hotel, in 1780. There is, furthermore, evidence that bowling took place on the village green at Knowle in c.1742.

Over in **Suffolk**, the old gates of the **Hadleigh Bowling Club** (*right*) stated its origins as 1754. This in truth is the earliest date known for the green, rather than the club, but it is genuine. The green was attached to the White Lion and was advertised as such in the *Ipswich Journal* of June 1 1754.

Both the gates and the green survived until 2010, when the site was sold for a care home. But thanks to the sale the club lives on at a new green on the outskirts of the town (*see page 210*).

The early years of the **Banbury Chestnuts Bowling Club** (*right*) are a little less clear, because the club's early records were lost in a fire in 1976. However it is known that there was a green in Banbury as early as the 16th century, near the Reindeer Inn, and that it was there, it is thought in 1780, that the present club formed.

It takes its name from the site where it has been based since 1893, a site distinguished by large horse chestnut trees.

Lastly, in **North Yorkshire** we find the **Bedale Bowling Green Society,** formed in 1792 and playing on the same green, at Wycar, since 1794.

As noted on page 40, its records remain wonderfully intact, including its early rules. Rule One states: 'The Game 3d each; for four players, 5 [points] is the Game, six Players 7'.

The members paid £5 12s for the club's first 'Bowling Green House', plus 2s 6d for a roller.

Today the Bedale green is distinctly level, having been converted as recently as 1990, while the current pavilion was built in 2000. Needless to add it cost rather more than £5 12s.

▲ 'Let no man be biassed' reads the inscription on the **Bowling Green House** at **Newark Town Bowling Club** in **Nottinghamshire**.

As recorded on its pediment – now sadly without its original finials – this splendid Grade II listed edifice was built in 1809, the year in which the club's 80 subscribers moved here from Newark Castle, where they had played since 1790.

Described in the *Nottingham Journal* as 'delightfully situate, with a fine salubrious air' the new green looked 'fair to cement that union amongst the inhabitants so universally conspicuous'.

Until 1958 the bowls house doubled as a residence for the greenkeeper. But since then, as its fabric deteriorated and the club increasingly found it unsuited to members' needs, a bungalow-style pavilion was built alongside. Then in 2006 – shortly before this photograph was taken – faced with a repair bill of £85,000, the club opted to sell it to a developer who, as part of the deal, financed new changing rooms and toilets in the adjoining pavilion.

At the time of writing the building is being converted into a private house, with its terrace separated from the green by railings. On which note the green itself is now a flat one, having been converted to rink play in the 1920s.

One of Newark's oldest rivals is Mansfield BC. Tracing its roots to 1700, Mansfield left its historic, town centre green and quirky 1914 clubhouse, by the Bowl in Hand, for a new green in 2009.

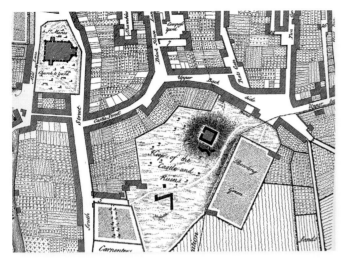

▲ Returning to castle greens, this town plan of **Guildford** in **Surrey** in **1739** shows a rectangular green to the east of the Norman keep.

Bowling in Guildford goes back further than this, for in a lease of 1612 there is mention of an acre of land lying in 'the great Close next the Bowling Alley.' Also, on the 1739 map (but not shown here), north of the castle, on what is today the corner of North Street and Leapale Road, is marked the 'Old Bowling Green' (perhaps the alley referred to in 1612).

Other references to bowling in Guildford appear in the journal of antiquarian William Bray. As a youth in the 1750s he bowled often, and on one occasion stayed on at the bowls house to play whist late into the night. (Bray's diaries are otherwise noted for including one of the earliest references to the game of 'base ball', in 1755.)

By 1885, when the Castle grounds were sold to Guildford Corporation, the bowling green was marked as tennis courts. However bowls returned in 1911 thanks to the formation of the **Castle Green Bowling Club**.

Today the Castle still dominates (*above right*). But note also that in order to conform to the rules for rink play, the green is now squared off, with a slight bank dividing the playing area from the rest of the still rectangular green.

Another club overlooked by a Norman keep, this one circular, is **Tamworth Castle Bowling Club** in **Staffordshire** (*below*).

Accessed via a discreet doorway on Ladybank, and occupying a terrace high above the wooded banks of the River Tame, the green

was certainly in use shortly in or around 1814, when the Castle, the adjoining Castle Inn and its gardens were sold by Lord George Townshend to John Robins.

However, as the inn was a busy coaching stop on the London to Chester road it is possible the green may have existed prior to this.

The club itself dates from at least 1845, when its earliest surviving records begin. A member at this time was the local MP and Prime Minister, Sir Robert Peel, while the club steward was Mr Hanson,

landlord of the Castle Inn. Amongst his expenses were £1 10s to pay a green boy and kit him out with boots, jacket and cap.

In the 1880s the club went into abeyance but was revived in 1893.

In 1905 it hosted an early crown green county match, Staffordshire v. Warwickshire. To mark the occasion, a five-pound cannon from the Crimean War was fired twice.

Another celebration took place in 1977 when the club raised £4,000 to buy the green's freehold.

Included within its boundaries are two unusual, early 20th century hexagonal brick shelters, and a Grade II listed single storey brick clubhouse (seen on the left of the bowlers). This has elements dating from the mid 19th century and stands immediately next to another, much larger, two storey Victorian building that used to belong to the town's brewery and is now an annexe of the Castle Hotel.

In fact if the door to the green in Ladybank is not open, then the only way to see this most private of greens is from the annexe, or, of course, from the battlements of Tamworth Castle.

Case study

Great Torrington Bowling Club

Another castle green, but this time a hexagonal pavilion, perched on a corner of the green at Great Torrington. Seen in 1862 (*above*), and in 2014 (*right*), and listed Grade II, it is thought this building is the one referred to in accounts of 1717, showing that Etheldred Davey, four times mayor of Torrington, was reimbursed £3 7s 4d for 'new building the summer-house in the Castle-green'.

When the City of Plymouth decided to celebrate the 300th anniversary of the Armada in 1888, they could find no local bowlers to re-enact Sir Francis Drake's fabled game on the Hoe. In fact they could find only one bowls club in the whole of Devon.

Forty miles north of Plymouth, the Great Torrington Bowling Club gives its date of formation as 1645.

This date derives from the fact that when one of the most decisive battles of the Civil War took place at Torrington in 1646, the Royalist forces under Ralph Hopton had been stationed on 'Castle Green'.

As we have already noted at Southampton, the use of the word 'green' is not, in itself, proof that bowling took place there. But there is possible evidence of bowling in the Torrington area around the time of the Civil War.

Firstly, a mile or so from the Castle Green is Torrington Common. Within this is an area long known as 'the old bowling green'. It is similar to the Hoe, being relatively isolated and so ideal for illicit games at a time when the game was prohibited.

Secondly, when one of Oliver Cromwell's favourite preachers, John Howe, gave a sermon in Torrington in 1654, he employed a bowls metaphor. He said, 'And as men (in that bodily exercise) when the bowl is out of their hands variously writhe and distort their bodies, as if they could govern its motion by those odd and ridiculous motions of theirs; so we are apt to distort our minds unto

uncouth shapes and postures, to as little purpose...'

Had Howe observed bowlers in the town? Or had he perhaps read John Earle's graphic description, published in 1628 (*see page 52*)?

Moving to the Castle Green – or Barley Grove as it was also known, 'barley' being a possible corruption of 'bailey' – we know that a summer house was built there in 1717 (*see left*). But was it the one we see today?

And was it built for bowling?

Quite possibly both, because in 1741, local accounts show that John Squire was paid 5s for laying turf on the 'bowling green'.

Similarly, in 1756 is this entry:

'Rec'd by subscriptions for repair the Bowling House... £1 0s 10d... George Towle for Repairing the Bowl House... £1 14s 10d.'

Not only does this confirm the

Castle Green's use for bowling, it also suggests a regular group of players paying a subscription.

Clearly not all visitors to the green behaved, because in his *Picturesque Sketches of Devon*, the itinerant Rev John Swete reported how in 1789 the 'pleasure house' had been put out of use by John Rolle, the Lord of the Manor, following unseemly behaviour.

However in 1837 Rolle granted the Council a 25 year lease at 2s 6d per quarter, 'specifically for the purpose of a bowling green'.

Because it was now in the public realm the bowlers did not enjoy exclusive rights. In 1838, for example, the green staged celebrations for Queen Victoria's coronation, including children's sports and dancing. Presumably this public use continued after the lease with the Rolle estate expired,

for, at some point between 1862 and 1883, ownership of the green was conveyed to the Council.

By this time the 'pleasure house' was at least a century old (or more if indeed it was built in 1717), and was in much need of repair.

Thankfully the bowlers recognised its worth. In 1887 (which is when the club's earliest records begin) they opened a subscription fund 'to make the bowl house look not only respectable, but something like an ornament to the green'. A few months later, heritage called again in the form of that invitation to play at Plymouth.

But if playing on the rough turf of the Hoe seemed familiar to Torrington players, visitors to the Castle Green were less impressed. No doubt inspired by the Armada celebrations, bowls clubs had formed in Bideford and Torquay in 1889. But when bowlers from Barnstaple visited Torrington in May 1890, according to a newspaper report penned by 'Cast Ball' they found 'the peculiar levels' of the green to be 'fair baffling'. There were also references in reports to the use of 'thumb' and 'finger' bias, terms standard in crown green bowling.

We can get an idea of conditions from a photograph taken from the Castle Mound in 1903, during a match v. Torquay (*above right*).

As is evident, the green follows an irregular shape with games taking place in all directions. In other words, typical of the pre-rink age, but one that in Devon, at least, was fast becoming anachronistic.

So in 1911 the club relaid the green to make it level, square, and edged by ditches.

Tellingly, within months of this task being completed, Great Torrington recorded its first ever loss on home turf.

▲ Seen in 2014 from the same vantage point, the transformation of the **Castle Green** is obvious. On the far side stands the club's current pavilion. Before it was built in 1988 excavations revealed evidence of a domestic building on the site and ramparts connected to the castle. This suggests that the green's boundary walls were built using masonry from the castle, perhaps when Torrington mayor John Yeo 'laid out and planted' the green in the early 1800s.

Least changed of all is the corner summer house, now in use for storage. That it may have been built as a vantage point, rather than specifically for bowls, is suggested by the fact that under the floor is a ten foot drop, and there is a blocked up basement window facing out over the river valley, 300 feet below. Certainly when it was listed Grade II in 1951 (along with the green's walls) it was described as a gazebo.

Whether it can be considered the oldest purpose-built bowls pavilion in Britain therefore remains open to challenge. But for sure it is one of the oldest structures in use at a bowling green and, no question, one of the most handsome.

Case study

Ellesmere Bowling Club

A striking feature at Ellesmere is that the bowling club owns not one, but two crown greens, both irregular in shape and at different levels. Above, viewed in 2012 from the lower green, is the rear of the pavilion serving the older, upper green. The white rendered section of the pavilion, to the left, is the original, dating from 1763. Below right, the OS map of 1901 shows the older green occupying the motte of Ellesmere Castle. The lower green, which straddles the wooded area and field to the north of the motte, was laid in 1989.

Half way between Shrewsbury and Chester, Ellesmere is one of three Shropshire towns featured in *Bowled Over* to possess a castle green, along with Clun and Bishop's Castle.

Ellesmere's green is also the oldest belonging to any club currently affiliated to the British Crown Green Bowling Association. Bowlers have been climbing the slopes of the castle mount since at least the 1760s (whereas, for example, Blackburn Subscription Club, of a similar vintage, no longer plays at its original green).

Now designated as a Scheduled Monument, the motte on which Ellesmere Castle was built in the 11th century was formed, unusually, by glacial moraine. That is, its heights were deposited by the same process that, at the end of the Ice Age, created the 'meres', or lakes, that are so much a feature of the surrounding area.

According to the antiquary John Leland, little of Ellesmere Castle remained when he visited in 1540.

But two centuries later, clearly the motte offered the perfect, picturesque spot for the town's bowlers, being relatively level, almost circular (at about 57 yards in diameter) and offering wonderful views.

The two earliest references to the green both date from 1763. At that time the castle grounds were owned by the Egerton family. In fact it was Francis Egerton, the 3rd Duke of Bridgewater, who planned to build a canal linking Ellesmere to the Cheshire coast (hence the town of Ellesmere Port).

The first reference comes in the accounts of the Bridgewater Estate and relates to the building of the square pavilion, still in use today (*see left and opposite*).

The second, from Benjamin Martin's *Natural History of England*, says of Ellesmere '... and what

is more remarkable, here is a windmill about the middle of the town; and near it, on the highest part of the rock, a very pleasant bowling-green'.

John Cary in his *New and Correct English Atlas* (1787), was especially impressed by the view from the green. It took in, he noted, one city, parts of seven counties, one large inhabited castle and the remainder of two, three market towns, 16 churches, four chapels, 30 gentlemen's seats, and 40 mountains and hills.

Given this natural advantage, as we have noted at other greens of the Georgian period, Ellesmere's could hardly remain the sole preserve of bowlers.

Just two examples. In 1810, to celebrate George III's Golden Jubilee, a huge bonfire was lit on the green. This cannot have pleased the bowlers. Nor a series of dances organised annually by a local women's club from 1811 onwards.

In the absence of club records from this period, the archives of the Bridgewater Estate have been useful in drawing up a picture of the green's early years.

We know that once elected to membership, subscribers paid one shilling to join. Also that bowls lads, or green attendants, wore the Egerton family livery, and that on important occasions, the Egerton colours were raised on the club's flagpole.

But in the present context, it is the surviving elements of the pavilion that are of chief interest.

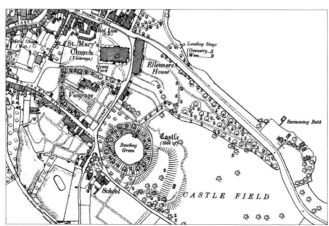

◀ Photographed in c.1890, with its flagpole alongside, the square pavilion at **Ellesmere Bowling Club** faces south over the almost circular green. In front stands, presumably, the greenkeeper with his waistcoat, watch-chain and straw hat.

Three other Victorian images of the pavilion have survived, each celebrating its picturesque qualities.

One, a print c.1880, shows only a modicum of ivy growing up the chimney on the left, and two finely dressed ladies promenading on the green. Another, dated c.1900, by which time ivy covers much of the building, shows the same greenkeeper joined by a gent in a smart suit, while two couples look down from the wrought iron balcony. A third, also possibly from the 1890s, shows two heavy rollers by the pavilion and a woman clearly trying to be out of the shot. Perhaps the greenkeeper's wife.

All suggest that here was a popular beauty spot, as at Great Torrington and Kymin Hill, and that as such the pavilion was designed to offer views from its balcony towards the Welsh hills to the west, and from its rear, as seen below, over the town and The Mere.

From the accounts of the Bridgewater Estate we learn that the pavilion was built in 1763.

Bricks from the Estate's own brickworks were used, together with 3,000 slates, the final cost amounting to £39 13s 6d. The roof was then re-slated in 1813 and a year later, 14s worth of hedging was planted, some of it still evident.

Today, as seen centre left in 2012, with junior members practising on the green, the core of the building survives, but with somewhat unsympathetic extensions on its flank. Note also that the flagpole, chimney and iron balcony have gone. (The loss of the latter, in the late 1960s, supposedly on safety grounds, is still mourned by some older members.)

Had it remained intact, no doubt the pavilion would have been a candidate for listing. Together with its counterparts at Bishop's Castle, Hereford and Great Torrington, it is one of the few genuinely 18th century structures still functioning at a modern club green.

But a modern bowling club has very different needs to its Georgian predecessors, and now that the club owns the site it has priorities that go beyond the purely picturesque.

Photographed from the rear of the pavilion extension, with the Mere in the distance, this view shows Ellesmere's lower green, laid in 1989. It was necessary because after years of playing only friendlies the club joined the Whitchurch, Oswestry and Wrexham Leagues, and so needed the extra green (even if site constraints meant that a square green was not possible).

Ironically the new green is more challenging than the old, having more undulations and steeper falls. Meanwhile a new weathervane adorns the roof of the old pavilion (*above*). It was donated in 2005 by Ron Roberts. Most clubs elect a President. At Ellesmere, however, Roberts was one in a long line of members to bear the alternative title of 'Mayor of the Green'.

Case study

Bishop's Castle Bowling Club

This is Minute Book III of the Bishop's Castle Bowling Society, covering the years 1872–1986. (It changed its name from Society to Club in 1918). But what of Books I and II? Alas the former, once held by a local solicitor and then returned to the Society, went missing in 1904, while the latter was last recorded around the same time in the hands of the proprietor of the Castle Hotel (who was also the Society's landlord). Were both destroyed, or, tantalisingly, do they survive somewhere, hidden away? As at Lewes, the loss of such early records at Bishop's Castle is a painful one, still felt keenly today.

Located less than two miles east of the Welsh border and four miles from Offa's Dyke, we need hardly be surprised that, as at Ellesmere, and as the name suggests, the bowling green at Bishop's Castle occupies the motte of a Norman fortification.

Or that a list of Bishop's Castle's opponents includes teams with names such as Battlefield, Castlefields, Ludlow Castle, Stokesay and Newcastle.

Where once the English fought the Welsh tooth and nail, today they play crown green bowls.

But there are other reasons to pick Bishop's Castle as a case study. Firstly, on the north side of the green stands another 18th century octagonal pavilion, one that is Grade II listed and rather wonderfully serves a green that is itself octagonal, as may just be made out in the aerial view below.

Secondly, at the same time as restoration work was carried out on this pavilion, in 2007-08 (thanks to a grant of £49,200 from the Heritage Lottery Fund), local historians were asked to research thoroughly the origins of the pavilion, the green and the club.

Their efforts, conducted under the auspices of the Bishop's Castle Heritage Resource Centre, may be read in a series of publications (see Links) that provide a record arguably more detailed than exists for any other 18th century green.

Two of the papers are available online via the website of the South West Shropshire Historical and Archaeological Society.

The story they tell, at least for readers of Bowled Over thus far, is a familiar one.

The castle in question, which served also as a palace for successive Bishops of Hereford, fell into ruins during the 17th century, its masonry plundered for buildings in the town below. One of them, it is thought, was the Castle Inn, opened in 1719.

Now called the Castle Hotel, this is the grey slated detached building in the centre left of the aerial view below, with extensive gardens at its rear. For most of its life the bowling green has formed part of the hotel's

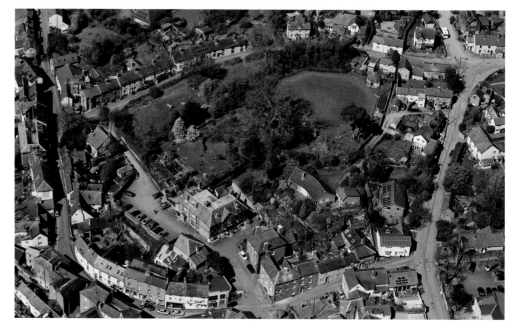

property, and indeed is still linked to it by a pathway winding through the hotel grounds.

As this was at a time when the aristocracy and emerging middle classes were starting to travel more widely within Britain, many of them inspired by a romantic, nostalgic passion for all things medieval, it was an obvious business move for the landlord of the new Castle Inn to prettify the motte in his backyard and build a summer house, where guests might take tea and enjoy the view. This could well have been the original purpose of the pavilion (as was also possibly the case at Ellesmere and Great Torrington).

Or the summerhouse and the bowling green may have been created in tandem, in 1719 or some time after. The Castle Inn was, after all, a busy coaching inn, and as we have ascertained, many of these laid on bowling greens for local tradesmen and passing travellers.

Unfortunately for historians, however, no advertisements or reports mentioning bowls at Bishop's Castle have been found in any newspapers of the period.

Instead, the earliest main source of reference is a visitors' book from the Castle Hotel starting in 1884, and that precious Minute Book III (*see opposite*), which starts in 1872.

From analysis of these minutes, supplemented by census returns and trade directories, it appears that the club could have formed in *c*.1800, or possibly as early as the 1770s. Certainly the bowling green was in place by 1809 when it appeared on a town plan.

Moreover, in a letter written in 1894 to the club's landlord, the 4th Earl of Powis (owner of the Castle Inn), the secretary wrote that the club had enjoyed 'the privilege of using the green for bowling for at least two hundred years'.

Even allowing for exaggeration on the secretary's part, this suggests a formation date nearer to 1719, and certainly before the 1770s. It also tallies with the formation of clubs such as Blackburn Subscription and Lewes (both 1753).

One reason for the secretary's letter, incidentally, was that the club's 'ancient rights and privileges' concerning its use of the green were being challenged, a challenge echoed in other locations during the 1890s, among them Southampton and Cannock.

A further concern was that repeated use of the green for dances and other communal events was affecting the quality of the turf, another familiar story.

Back in the 21st century, meanwhile, as restoration of the pavilion continued, analysis of its timbers, brickwork and roof led to the conclusion that like the bowling green, it could well date

from between 1719 and 1730, and certainly no later than *c*.1820. The king post in the roof timbers, it was also noted, was itself octagonal.

Concerning the membership, within the published research there is much of interest. Clearly many men were both active in the bowls club and in council affairs (a closeness mirrored at Chesterfield, to name but one location).

In 1872, a total of 21 members were listed. In 2015 there were 30.

Apart from restoring the pavilion, one of their most important recent achievements has been to purchase the freehold of the green from the Castle Hotel in the 1980s, for a relatively nominal sum.

Which means that, added to the fact that it sits within the boundaries of a Scheduled Ancient Monument, Britain's only octagonal green appears, like its listed pavilion, to be in thoroughly good shape.

▲ Seen on the day of its official re-opening in June 2008 – with members suitably attired in period costume – the Grade II listed pavilion at **Bishop's Castle** stands proud after its restoration.

It needed dampproofing, rewiring, re-rendering and, using sandstone tiles prepared by craftsmen trained at nearby Acton Scott, re-roofing.

A 20m stretch of the old castle battlements flanking the pavilion was also repaired.

Inside is a surprisingly capacious room with a cornice and fireplace.

During restoration much effort went into the two sash windows. From old photographs it appeared that at one point these had been replaced by an unmatched pair.

Now all is symmetrical, as the Georgians would have insisted.

To them it was but a simple summer house. But for bowlers of the 21st century, truly, it is an architectural treasure.

Case study

Barnes Bowling Club, the Sun Inn

The sign on the gate gives the formation date of Barnes Bowling Club as 1725. But either the evidence for this claim has been lost, or the signmaker misread the instructions. For it was actually nearer to 1775 that the Sun Inn opened, opposite the pond in the heart of this once rural Surrey village. Today, few of its clientele realise that at the back of this Grade II listed 18th century pub, in this now highly desirable suburb of south west London, lies a bowling green. Fewer still that this particular green is unique.

It is not only the green at the Sun Inn that is unique. Its resident club, the Barnes Bowling Club, is pretty unusual too. So combine the two and even if parts of the early history remain a little hazy, here in SW13 lies a repository of sporting heritage at its best, both tangible and intangible.

As explained on page 11, the green at the Sun Inn is neither crown green nor flat green but is rectangular, with its long edges sloping slightly down to form a relatively flattish basin, albeit with gentle undulations.

As at Lewes, everyone plays with lignum vitae woods. Also as at Lewes, the bias is much stronger than found in modern forms of bowling. A number 7 biased wood is the minimum, as stated in the club rules, but 12-13 is the norm.

The result is the curved trajectory illustrated on page 11.

As also seen on page 11, the jack in use at Barnes is, on the other hand, non-biased; a typical Victorian-style ceramic jack such as would commonly be used on flat greens (see page 12).

But there is more, because not only is the green at the Sun Inn the only surviving pub green in the whole of London, it is also the oldest green overall in the capital.

Plus, it is home to a club whose members do not, how should we put it, conform exactly to the ethos typical of flat green clubs elsewhere in the Home Counties.

In short, everything about the Barnes club seems to echo the old traditions of pub bowls – no dress code, no pomp, plenty of wine – whilst still managing to appear entirely on trend, if in a retro way.

Even within the club's constitution is the avowed aim 'to promote the historic game of 'Elizabethan Bowls'.

Given such a noble expression it seems churlish to point out that probably a closer approximation to Elizabethan bowls is the version played at Lewes. Or that the earliest reference to bowling in the Barnes area dates from 1693, 90 years after Elizabeth's death.

Listed in parish records that year is a 'cottage and land called the Bowling Green' on a site next to the Barnes village pond.

Although little more is known of bowling on that site, in the early 18th century there were regular press reports of bowling nearby, on Putney Common.

Of highwaymen too, preying on gentlemen returning home from a game of bowls, perhaps the worse for wear.

By 1775 the lease of the cottage by the Barnes pond had been conveyed to the parish by the local landowners, the Hoare family of Barn Elms, for use as a school. The bowling green became a garden and playground. Today this site is occupied by a day centre, with the adjacent pond still a focal point.

It was around 1775 that either the Sun Inn came into being, complete with a new green, or that the pub, already in existence, offered the now displaced bowlers a home in one of the gardens or orchards at its rear.

Whichever, it seems likely from archive maps that the green has never been large, and may possibly never have exceeded its current size of just 20 x 30 yards (a third of the area of a standard green).

If so, this would explain the distinctive form of 'corner to corner' bowls that survives at Barnes to this day. Not so much Elizabethan as simply tailored to local conditions.

Elsewhere, 'corner to corner' is a description sometimes used to describe the form of bowls that preceded rink bowls, that is, played corner to corner, but also in any direction. Yet the 'corner to corner' style played at Barnes does not fit that description. It really is played only 'corner to corner', and so may instead be the last vestige of a form of play that was local to London. (It is possible for example that 'corner to corner' was also the style in place at the Six Bells pub in Chelsea, see page 134.)

Returning to the Sun Inn, in the early 1800s the pub and green were bought by a local brewer, John Waring. This may explain why some accounts of the club's history put its formation date as 1805. Even so, no mention of the club can be found in any local newspapers of that period, while the club's earliest records date back only to the early 20th century.

These tell us that at that time it remained male only, with membership limited to 40. Most, according to one club history, were drawn from the professions or were managers in industry and commerce, thus reflecting a local demographic that had been transformed by the construction of Hammersmith Bridge in 1827, and by the opening of Barnes station in 1846, from that of a village into a London suburb. (Amongst its Victorian residents were leading figures in early football and rugby, and rowing, for Barnes lies close to several Thames boat clubs and the finishing line of the University Boat Race at Mortlake.)

Hardly surprisingly, given how many pub greens have been lost in London, life for the Barnes Bowling Club has not always been easy. After membership fell during World War One, in 1922 the landlady at the Sun Inn announced her intention to turn the green into a more profitable tennis court.

To which one local paper countered, 'It seems little short of sacrilege to abolish this historic green which cannot be replaced.'

Thankfully the club rallied, following a range of social events and friendlies against clubs from Ealing, East Sheen and the Tower of London.

More recently, the club has had to face a hike in its rent from £60 a year to £4,000.

Furthermore, although the pub is listed, the green is not. It does however fall within the Barnes Green Conservation Area and, in 2014, was designated an Asset of Community Value by Richmond Borough Council.

Hopefully this will be sufficient. For at a time when every square inch of the capital is being eyed up by developers, it represents a tempting morsel. Which leaves us only to repeat those words of 1922.

To lose this historic green would be 'little short of sacrilege' not only to Barnes, or to London, but to British sport as a whole.

◀ In the midst of a metropolis dominated by clubs playing in rinks and adhering to strict dress codes, **Barnes Bowling Club** stands out as a maverick, even Bohemian crew.

Surrounded by greenery and high walls, there is a simple, timber framed clubhouse at the pub end with basic facilities and storage for the club woods (some thought to be at least of Victorian vintage).

As explained, play takes place from corner to corner. In order to deliver a bowl, as seen centre left, players must stand with their front foot on a paving slab, off the green.

Each player has two woods (as in crown green bowls). The jack is deemed dead if it leaves the green and to count, woods must end up 'within the stick' (four feet from the jack). These and other rules (as listed on the club website) remain subtly different from the norm.

Hence the impression that they were tailored to a narrow green.

At the same time, this very narrowness is possibly the reason the club never adopted Association rules. To do so they would have needed a minimum of four rinks, impossible in the space provided.

Yet how fortunate. For it is surely the quirkiness of the Barnes game, and its setting, that has helped attract such a diverse membership. Currently limited to 80, it includes, or has included such figures as the poet Roger McGough, the musicians Alan Price and Roger Chapman, DJs Richard Skinner, Larry Page and Mike Reid, and a number of individuals from that other BBC.

Women are also much to the fore and there are even floodlights.

So progressive, yet traditional; not only in respect of the bowls played but in the informal ease that makes Barnes, surely, a genuine throwback to the spirit of the game as it was in the pre-Victorian era.

Chapter Seven

Scotland to 1892

Starting out as makers of violin cases in 1770, Thomas Taylor's company turned in 1796 to the production of bowls, billiard balls and artificial limbs. In 1871 it was Taylor's who developed a machine lathe and slate bed testing table that enabled identical sets of bowls to be produced with a reliable degree of bias, thereby ushering in a completely new era in the game. But this was only one of several advances to originate in Scotland.

Few major sports played in Britain today have not been enhanced in one way or another by the Scots, particularly during the 19th century; by their enthusiasm, by their penchant for rules and regulations, and by their talent for technological improvement.

This contribution was especially pronounced in golf – a Scottish game, after all – and in football.

But it applies equally to bowls, if not more so. For as noted in Chapter One, it is no exaggeration to state that the Scots more or less invented modern flat green bowls.

For years bowlers south of the border called this the 'Scotch game', before they learnt to call it the 'Association game' (after the Scottish rules were adopted by the newly formed English Bowling Association in 1903).

So how did the 'Scotch game' make such inroads when faced by centuries of tradition in England?

Firstly, as noted in Chapter Two, the Scots did so by perfecting the art of creating flat greens, thereby allowing clubs to play each other without the hosts having too much of a home advantage.

In other words, they literally created a level playing field.

Secondly, by standardising not only the greens but also the bowls and jacks – thanks to the advances made by Thomas Taylor's – they paved the way for bowling to become a national, and then international sport.

Thirdly, by dividing their level greens into rinks, with each team playing in fours, they were able to maximise the use of greens in the most efficient manner possible.

Now up to 48 bowlers could play on a green at any one time and not get in each other's way.

And where did they get this idea? From the Scottish game of curling, whose timeline – starting in 1511 near Stirling and in 1541 at Paisley Abbey – closely parallels that of bowls.

The word 'rink' (from an Old Scots word 'renk') denotes an area of combat. Curling in rinks, it was found, made better use of the ice, and was safer. Moreover, when the Grand Caledonian Curling Club formed in 1838 (becoming the Royal Caledonian Curling Club in 1842), its rules followed

the practice of clubs in Edinburgh and Kilmarnock by having teams of four curlers per rink, each playing with two stones, the same as would become the norm in the 'Scotch game' of bowls.

The games share several terms too; 'wick', 'guard', 'draw', 'drive' and 'tryg' or 'trig' (as used still at Hadley), denoting the place from which curlers and bowlers release their stones or bowls (shortened from 'tricker' or 'trigger').

Also worth noting is that Scottish bowlers (who included many curlers) first met to co-ordinate their activities in 1848. This was just a year after curling's first great North v. South match took place in 1847.

It was also at least 30 years in advance of their counterparts in England even organising regional matches, let alone sitting down to formulate any shared rules.

Of course other factors were involved in smoothing the way for this transformation, on both sides of the border. One was urbanisation, which broke down old traditions and thrust strangers together in new environments.

Castle greens were common in Scotland, examples being at Banff, Brechin, Cupar and Dirleton. This John Wood map of 1825 shows the castle green at Lanark, in use since at least 1750, originally as a public green, and as home to Lanark Thistle Bowling Club since 1918. It is the oldest green in Scotland to remain in use. Robert the Bruce held court in the castle in 1321.

Bowls, football, cricket, indeed any sport helped to forge new identities and build communities.

Road improvements, combined with the coming of the railways, gave ordinary people more of a chance to travel, to pick up new ideas; to play each other at sport.

Finally, it is feasible that bowls benefitted from the advent of longer, warmer summers from the 1830s onwards, caused by what climatologists now describe as the ending of the Little Ice Age.

But before all this, before the mid 19th century, bowls in Scotland looked pretty much like it did in England.

As in England, it had been fashionable amongst the nobility.

Robert Stewart laid a bowling green at Birsay Palace on the Isle of Orkney in the 1570s. Earl Patrick did the same at Glamis Castle in the 1680s. During the same decade greens are recorded at Holyrood Palace, at King's College, Aberdeen, and at St Andrews.

Just as in England there were expanses such as the links at Leith, Bruntsfield and Aberdeen, where, as well as golf and horse racing, less privileged bowlers could play.

But for all the similarities with England, there were differences.

The Scots, as will become apparent, were at the forefront of providing greens from the public purse or through charitable donations. In 1552 in Edinburgh a burgess wrote to the 'Provost, baillies, deacons and other honest men' urging them to grant land to the community for 'recreation in archery, shooting with culverins [hand guns] and bowling'.

From the council minutes of Haddington on August 18 1662 we read that 'efter much deliberation' it was ordained that William Allen, a merchant and former treasurer

of the Kirk Sessions, was to give Patrick Young 'a sum of Scottis money for building of ane house at and wall aboot and laying the ground of ane bowilling grein on the sandis of the said Burgh'.

As noted on the right, this particular green was not a success. But others would be, laid by councils and then let out to individuals to operate on a negotiated lease. By doing this councils retained control of green fees (ensuring they remained affordable), and also, crucially, were able to clamp down on gambling and drinking.

As a result, pub greens such as Cameron's Bowling Green Tavern in Glasgow and the Castlecarry Inn at Cumbernauld were, by the 1840s, rare. Even today only four operate in Scotland (see page 26).

Finally, we cannot forget that it was largely the Scots who, apart from influencing bowling practices south of the border, throughout the 19th century played a leading role in the export of bowls to the likes of Canada, Australia and New Zealand, thereby laying the foundation for the 'Scotch game' to become the 'world game' as we know it today.

Almost certainly the oldest green in Scotland, albeit no longer in use, is this one in **Stirling**, laid in 1713 under the auspices of an almshouse known as **Cowane's Hospital**.

Two clubs are known to have played on it. **Stirling BC**, formed in 1854, moved onto their own green soon after in 1858 (see page 31).

Meanwhile a second club, **Guildhall BC**, formed there in 1856 and played on well into the 20th century until, finally, restrictions on its width led to formal bowling coming to an end.

A similar story can be told at **Haddington** in **East Lothian** (left).

This, it should be noted, is not the green referred to in the council minutes of 1662. That green lay due west of Nungate Bridge roughly where now stands a listed dovecot, built in 1771 in what is called Lady Kitty's Garden.

This green lies about 50 yards away, just north of Nungate Bridge. It was first leased in 1749, and therefore might well be Scotland's second oldest green, or at least a contender for that claim along with the green at Lanark (see opposite).

As at Stirling, the green proved too small to cope with demand and so the town's current green, at Wemyss Place, was laid in 1890.

But the old green lives on, as the **Normandy Memorial Garden**.

As to the **Haddington Bowling Club**, it claims to have originated in 1709 and therefore to be the oldest club in Scotland. But alas (a now familiar story), no evidence can be found and so we must ask, was the date a misreading of 1749?

Or even an attempt to trump the claims of Kilmarnock, who claim a foundation date of 1740?

Either way, allied to the records from 1662, the former green is old enough for Haddington to merit a special place in bowling history.

▶ **Glasgow** today has a higher concentration of greens than any other city, a trend that started in the 18th century, as we can see from **John McArthur's map** of **1778**.

(1) South of **Gallowgate**, this green was, in 1750, run by John Orr of Barrowfield 'for the diversion of Gamesters' and had 'a Stately Pair of Butts' for archery. It was built over in c.1802 by Kent Street, now part of the famous Barras Market.

(2) Laid out in 1695 and known as **Mungo Cochrane's** (after its first proprietor), this green on **Candleriggs Street** was public, charging in 1804 'only a trifle'. A market place was built on the site in 1816, now the Merchant Square complex.

(3) Part of Glasgow University, **College Gardens** was depicted in 1762 by Robert Paul with three bowlers playing on its Middle Walk. This site is now High Street car park.

(4) Shown here as an orchard, by 1804 this site on **St Crispin's Place**, by a hospital and almshouse, was leased by Glasgow's earliest known club, the **Society of Bowlers**, whose members paid an annual subscription of 10s 6d (the same as charged by Glasgow Golf Club).By 1828 a gasworks occupied the site. Today it is halls of residence for the University of Strathclyde.

(5) It is thought the Society of Bowlers then moved to this site, south of **Drygate** – the last green in the town centre before the development of the West End – but that this was built over by the 1850s. The site is now occupied by flats overlooking Cathedral Square.

In **Edinburgh**, **William Edgar's map** of **1765** (*right*) shows the location of four greens in the city, of which three were next to hospitals.

(6) Accessed from **Candlemaker Row** this green was opened in 1691 by the Merchants Company,

which two years later bought ten pairs of bowls. At one point it was known as **Tamson's Green** (after its lessee, Mr Thompson), and was the base of Edinburgh's own **Society of Bowlers**, until its closure in 1766. A small car park occupies the site today, opposite Greyfriars Kirkyard.

(7) Nearby in **Argyle Square**, this green, recorded first in 1702, was attached to the **Trades Maiden Hospital** (which despite its name was a charitable school for girls).

In April 1732, the *Caledonian Mercury* described the green as charging 3d entry, whether bowling or not. The site is now covered by the Royal Museum of Scotland.

(8) This green lay between **George Heriot's Hospital**, a school for poor boys, and the Town Wall.

After leaving Candlemaker Row (6), in 1768 the Society of Bowlers petitioned the hospital governors to issue them with a 21 year lease for the plot, known as the 'wilderness'.

Among the regulars there was the **Waverley Club**. After the Town Wall was demolished in 1788, many of the bowlers moved to a new green laid behind the Royal Archers' Hall in 1791. (In 1848 they formed the Edinburgh Bowling Club and played on until controversially evicted by the Royal Archers in 2008). The Heriot's green, meanwhile, is now lawns flanking the school's main entrance on Lauriston Place.

(9) The green of the **Merchants Maiden Hospital** lay opposite the College but had been built over by 1784. On the site is now a listed church, occupied by the University, on South College Street.

Two other greens on Edgar's map, not shown, were at Holyrood (now lawns), and a tiny green west of Canongate Church, now a yard behind 181-183 Canongate.

Clearly, even in the 18th century, space was at a premium.

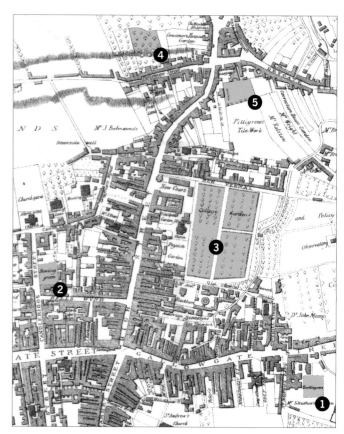

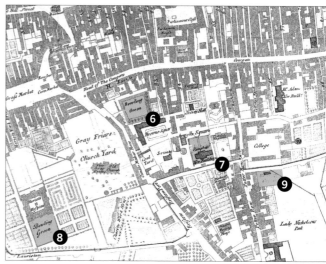

▲ From the **National Museums of Scotland**, this 10 inch tall collection of silver medals and a solid silver jack offers gilt-edged evidence that the **Society of Bowlers** in Edinburgh comprised men of means and influence. As noted opposite, the Society had laid a new green in the grounds of Heriot Hospital in 1768. Three years later one of their members, William Tod, a merchant, donated the silver jack as a trophy.

Such trophies were then much in vogue in Scottish golf (and of course silver medals were introduced at Southampton too, in 1776). The idea was that each year a winner's medal would be attached to the jack. In this collection there are twelve, dating from 1771-87, each bearing the winner's name and a Latin inscription.

Interestingly, the rules of the competition survive too. They reveal a game in which at least one element of what would eventually become the 'Scotch game' was already in place; namely that 'the bowl that carys the Block [jack] into the Bank is a counting bowl'.

However, two other rules stated, 'the Block is to lye wherever it's thrown' and the trig [the mat or marker] has to be laid 'within four feet of the place where the Block lay the last end'. These rules suggest that play was still all over the green rather than in rinks.

▶ If Haddington BC's claim to be the oldest bowling club in Scotland, with a formation date of 1709, is unfortunately not backed by evidence, what can be said of the claim of **Kilmarnock Bowling Club**, as seen on its gates, to have been instituted in 1740?

Remember that the earliest verifiable date for the formation of any club in England is 1753 for Lewes and Blackburn Subs. So what is the basis of Kilmarnock's claim?

It appears in an 1858 history of the town by Archibald McKay *(see Links)*. McKay quotes from a Council minute of March 5 1764, stating that in 'about the year 1740' a shooting prize of £5 had been placed in the hands of Mr Paterson (presumably Robert Paterson, the Town Clerk), and that this had been put 'towards erecting a bowling-green, and purchasing bowls, as being thought a more agreeable diversion than shooting'.

Once again we cannot assume that this was the birth of the club. But we can at least trace links between senior figures in Kilmarnock society and the bowls fraternity of that period.

The poet Robert Burns too.

That first green from c.1740 was laid at the foot of Back Street (now the bus station). Next to it was an inn known as Bowling Green House. Burns visited this inn on several occasions owing to his friendship with various locals, including Tam Samsom, whose son-in-law, Sandy Patrick, was the licensee.

In 1797 the Back Street green was advertised for sale in the *Caledonian Mercury* by its owner, Robert Paterson's son, William, a solicitor, who had succeeded his father as Town Clerk.

But Kilmarnock's bowlers did not have far to go, for a new green was laid almost across the road, on

a site that extended from Portland Street to Garden Street, as can be seen on a John Wood map of 1825.

Its proprietor was Thomas Bicket, who sold spirits on Fore Street. We know this because it was during his tenure that in 1814 the green was frequented by a young William Mitchell (of whom more later).

In 1827 there appears to have been a split, possibly caused by the construction next to the green of the George Hotel (which still stands).

One group of bowlers went off to lay a new green on part of a nursery that had belonged to Tam Samson, on the east bank of Kilmarnock Water, off London Road. The remaining bowlers then joined them in c.1843 when the railway sliced through the old green.

This third green is where the club has been happily based ever since.

Only in one sense was the move to prove unfortunate. In 1852 all the club records were destroyed, it is thought when the river flooded.

Hence, frustratingly, yet another important piece of bowling history must remain unresolved.

▲ From the collection of the **Scottish National Portrait Gallery**, this is the oldest known photograph in the world to depict the game of bowls, taken in c.**1845** by **John Muir Wood**, a music publisher and piano manufacturer in Glasgow.

Wood was clearly an early adopter, for the 'calotype' process he employed had been invented by Henry Fox Talbot only four years before. What we see is, of course, a studiously posed composition, as all photos would be until at least the 1870s. This was because early cameras required such long exposure times that each subject had to hold his or her position for several minutes. That some of them could not explains why faces are often blurred, as seen here.

Where the image was taken is not known. If not in Glasgow, the most likely location would be a private garden or pleasure ground in the west of Scotland, in Argyll, Arran, the Ayrshire coast or the Clyde valley, where Wood liked to travel. But wherever it is, the presence of that octagonal gazebo might yet offer a clue.

▲ Thought to date from **1862**, this photograph shows members of the **Hawick Bowling Club,** formed eight years earlier, at their green on **Bridge Street** (now the site of the Baptist Church). In a town whose wealth derived from knitwear and hosiery, the bowlers seen here include two drapers, two engineers and a framesmith, as well as a

cabinet maker. Second from the left stands the Provost, a skinner.

In 1870 the joining fee at Hawick was 20s, and the annual subscription 10s, both fairly typical for clubs at that time.

By contrast, **St Vincent Bowling Club** in **Glasgow**, photographed below in **1860**, a year after the club's formation, charged 42s

and 21s respectively. For as the backdrop makes clear – showing the sweep of St Vincent Crescent, itself only recently constructed – this was a club for the prosperous middle classes.

Even so, by 1864 the club had 140 members and was one of the largest in Scotland.

One attraction no doubt was that in addition to its clearly charming pavilion and large green, 47 x 47 yards square, it had a curling pond, thereby allowing members to play all year round.

On which note, although the photograph at St Vincent is clearly posed for effect, it contains a hint that a form of rink game was being played at the time. For whereas the white jack in John Muir Wood's photograph of c.1845 is relatively large, that seen at St Vincent is more akin to the small non-biased jacks that would become standard in rink bowling.

A small white jack also appears in the Hawick photo.

Hawick, incidentally, left the green shown opposite in the 1870s for the club's present home on Buccleuch Road, where their green lies next to that of Buccleuch BC.

For its part St Vincent now has two greens – the curling pond was decommissioned in 1878 – with a rather plainer pavilion, and has two other bowling clubs as neighbours.

The green of the University of Glasgow BC lies over the fence on the west side, and beyond this is based Corunna BC. Behind them, handsome as ever, stands St Vincent Crescent, now listed.

Yet across the road to the south looms the futuristic hulk of the Armadillo, or Clyde Auditorium.

In this context, how little bowls has changed, comparatively, since the 1860s, while the world around has moved on.

▶ For such a pivotal figure in bowling history, remarkably little was known of **William Wallace Mitchell** (1803-84), at least until recently. Not only were all his papers lost, but so too was a portrait of him. This sketch, from an 1893 book by Humphrey Dingley, *Touchers and Rubs*, is the only image that survives.

Most accounts of Scottish bowls describe Mitchell as a Glasgow solicitor. But as revealed by new research by Gerry McCready of the Portland BC, Kilmarnock, Mitchell followed a quite different path.

His earliest games of bowls took place when he was aged 11, on Tom Bicket's green on Back Street, Kilmarnock, close to where he grew up. Originally apprenticed to a tinsmith, after developing eye problems Mitchell went to work for a carpet weaving company owned by Thomas Morton. It was possibly in connection with this business that in c.1817 he moved to Paisley, the home town of his wife, Agnes.

From there Mitchell crossed the Atlantic to Connecticut, to set up a carpet factory in Thomsonville (now Newhaven), for the Kilmarnock firm of Gregory & Thompson. But although he took up American citizenship, after the death of his father, and of Agnes (in 1835) he returned home and in partnership with his brother George took over a firm of cotton bleachers and finishers in Glasgow.

Mitchell was aged 45 when he was one of some 200 bowlers to attend a dinner at Glasgow Town Hall in November 1848. According to the *Falkirk Herald*, this was 'for the purpose of forming a general brotherhood' and to find a common set of rules, something that Scottish curlers had arrived at following the formation of the Royal Caledonian Curling Club ten years earlier.

It was around this time that Mitchell reduced his business commitments, which meant that when a second gathering of bowlers took place in Glasgow in March 1849, to appoint a rules committee, he was well placed to take on the role of secretary.

Well suited too. Reports suggest that Mitchell was a real stickler for detail. Over the next few years bowling lore has him corresponding with various Scottish clubs, some who supported the move to uniformity, some who were reluctant to ditch their own rules (as happened in other sports too, such as football in the 1860s).

Records show that during this period Mitchell retained sporadic membership of two Glasgow clubs, Wellcroft and Willowbank, where his brother George was a regular.

But as McCready has found, this had nothing to do with Mitchell's commitment levels. It was because he continued to travel to America.

Perhaps because of this it was not until 1864 that Mitchell unveiled his first set of rules. These he published in his *Manual of Bowl Playing,* a booklet he financed himself at a cost of £5, and which included advice on how to construct a green. It was the first publication devoted solely to the sport.

Clearly Mitchell leaned heavily on rules that were already in place at Willowbank, as set down in their minutes of 1835. His Rule 15 echoed one taken from the Edinburgh Society of Bowlers, going back to 1771. This stated that bowls that touched the jack but then went into the ditch should 'count the same as any other bowl'.

(This was in contrast to the tradition in England that such bowls be deemed 'dead'.)

Because of this, even to this day Scottish bowlers can be heard

calling a bowl that has touched the jack before entering the ditch 'a Mitchell'.

Mitchell's rules were steadily adopted by clubs from 1864 onwards. He then updated his *Manual* in 1870, repeating in it a list of clubs from the first edition, to which we shall return later.

However it would not be until after his death in 1884 that moves to establish a national governing body finally reached fruition.

Formed in Glasgow in 1892, the Scottish Bowling Association would, like Mitchell's rules, have a transformative effect on the game of bowls, across Britain and the world.

But before coming to this, much else was going on in Victorian Scottish bowls besides.

◀ While three Scottish clubs, Haddington, Kilmarnock and Lanark Thistle may claim to have formed in the 18th century, at least 179 of Scotland's current clubs trace their origins to the period 1820-92. This, the first boom era of Scottish bowling, followed a period of social upheaval in the wake of the Highland Clearances and economic growth after the Napoleonic Wars; a period during which, despite steady emigration, Scotland's population doubled from two million in 1821 to just over four million by 1891.

Bowling clubs proliferated, and not only in the cities. Grangemouth BC, just outside Falkirk, formed in 1820, followed by Peebles (1829), Wigtown (1830), Newton Stewart (1831) and Dumbarton (1832).

Ayrshire, following in the wake of Kilmarnock's bowlers, became a particular stronghold.

Formed in 1834, **Ayr Bowling Club** (*top left*), is the oldest of nine clubs based in this seaside town (which is also home to Bowls Scotland), and the most central. Its green, on **Cassilis Street**, screened by stone walls and entered via a simple doorway bearing the date 1834, was originally the town's washing green (before the advent of the 'steamie'). Opposite one corner is Wellington Square, laid out in 1810-20 and lined by elegant Georgian terraces, whilst backing onto the clubhouse is the imposing Sheriff Court and South Ayrshire County Buildings, opened in 1822.

In other words, a green in the very epicentre of municipal life.

Eight miles north up the Ayrshire coast, the entrance to **Troon Bowling Club**, on **Dallas Road** (*left centre*) is marked by an ironwork sign bearing the date 1840. At that time the club was based on Shore Road. However in 1894 Troon's

committee began negotiations with the local landowner, the Duke of Portland, about moving to the much larger site at Dallas Road, intending to sell Shore Road.

It took three years before the move was settled, only for 41 club members to decide to stay put, under the new name of Troon Portland BC. (Note there is also a Portland BC in Kilmarnock.)

A further 25 miles up the coast, although the gate at **Largs Bowling Club** on **Douglas Street** (*lower left*) gives their formation date as 1860, the club actually formed four years earlier under the name Allan Park, based on a green where livestock grazed before going to slaughter. The club moved to the rather more salubrious Douglas Street in 1864.

Finally in East Ayrshire, ten miles south of Kilmarnock is **Mauchline Bowling Club**, on **Rankine Drive**, seen above during an **Eglinton Trophy** match in July 2012.

Formed in 1867, the club is one of several to have retained an old pavilion – in this instance dating from c.1890-1920, with a half-timbered gable typical of the period – while building itself a larger, if rather less attractive flat-roofed

clubhouse across the green, also typical of its period, the 1970s.

The Eglinton Trophy, first awarded in 1857, is the oldest bowling competition in the world.

The question is, was it played in rinks that year? Indeed it was.

Mitchell recorded how the Earl himself had played for Ayrshire at the Willowbank green in Glasgow, and had acted 'as a driver' (or 'skip') in the central rink on the green. But there are even earlier reports of rinks. From the *Glasgow Herald* in August 1846 we read that the annual match between Shotts and Hamilton was organised in rinks, as was a match between Wellcroft (Glasgow) and Priorscroft (Paisley) in August 1847.

As already noted, the concept of rink play came from Scottish curling, in which rings are marked in the centre of the rink as a target. Yet Mitchell's Law XII.5 on 'throwing the jack' stated, 'If it run too near the side of the space, it must be moved to a sufficient distance from it to allow both fore and back hand play.'

In other words, the jack was not yet centred within the rink, as it would become in later years.

Curling and bowling, especially
among the poorer classes of our
countrymen, will do more to promote
their comfort and welfare and tend
to their good conduct than all the
beer halls and Sunday-trading bills
the legislature has ever passed
Earl of Eglinton
1857

A blessing rest on Eglinton!
An' on his princely ha',
An' blessed be the memory
O' him that's noo awa'.
He greatly loved his fellow-men,
But saw a gap between,
An' closed it up, an' syne ilk class
Became ilk other's frien'
William Mitchell
1864

◄ A scion of one of Ayrshire's
leading landowning families, the
mutton-chopped **13th Earl of
Eglinton** drank and gambled with
the best of them in his youth. But
in his later years, at least until his
death in 1861 at the age of 49
(after a round of golf at St Andrews)
he devoted himself to sport.

He presented the first Eglinton
Trophy for curling in 1851. He
laid bowling greens in most of the
villages within the family estate.

And in 1857 he donated this,
the second **Eglinton Trophy**, or
'Jug', for bowls. This was as the
prize for a competition begun in
1855 by a Mr Mack of Ardrossan,
between bowlers in Ayrshire and
Glasgow. No mere bystander, as
noted opposite, the Earl played for
Ayrshire in 1857.

By 1905 over 3,000 bowlers
were taking part annually.

Still going strong today, each
July the two parties take turns to
act as hosts, with several clubs
staging games. In addition to an
overall winner, the name of the
club whose members clock up the
highest average of shots per rink is
engraved on the base.

The Earl said of bowls: 'Much as
I value the game for the pleasure
there is in playing it, I value it
still more for the way it brings
classes of the community
together, and promotes
good fellowship...'

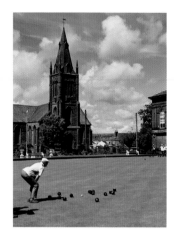

▲ In south west Scotland, on the Galloway coast, **Kirkcudbright Bowling Club** is to be found, as at Ayr, in the very heart of the town.

On one side stands the parish church, on the other the Town Hall.

Formed in 1855, Kirkcudbright was at the forefront of efforts by Scottish bowlers to organise competitions and generate public interest in the game. But whereas the Eglinton Trophy was limited to Ayrshire and Glasgow, the Kirkcudbright committee went further. As announced on a poster issued for its second tournament in 1864 (*right*) – the first was in 1861 – theirs was to be 'Open to Great Britain and Ireland'. Another poster stated '...such an opportunity of witnessing Britain's Greatest Bowlers has never occurred'.

Indeed it had not (other than perhaps in 1861). No earlier international events are known.

How many non-Scots there were amongst the 292 entrants is hard to say, but certainly some were from Ireland and England. Reporting on the event in his *Manual of Bowling*, published shortly afterwards, William Mitchell described hearing 'Cockney dialects', while a bowler named Woods is known to have travelled from Preston.

Clearly for the fishing port of Kirkcudbright, the tournament was an opportunity. A poster, now on display in the modern bowls club and aimed at visitors from Cumberland, advertised day trips on a paddle steamer, first from Maryport, then Whitehaven, both across the Solway Firth. Tickets cost 2s 6d but were free for bands of musicians not exceeding twelve in number. Such bands were offered free admission to the green.

Entry to the competition was also priced at 2s 6d.

Of particular interest are the competition 'bye-laws', showing as they do how the 'Scotch game' was already well defined. For example, each player was to use four biased bowls, 'the circumference of which shall not exceed 16¼ inches'.

Games were '21 up' with a minimum length for a mark of 20 yards. Also, five games were to be played at a time, suggesting that the green was divided into rinks.

Note that the prizes were not cash but objects of a specific value. Thus the winner, William Currie of Troon, took home 'a silver tea service of the value of £50'.

This form of award, common in Victorian sport, ensured that winners avoided the stain of being classed as a professional.

Speaking after the event, Provost Cavan called it 'the most brilliant

affair that has ever taken place in the history of bowling'.

Certainly it was a pioneering example of what was to become standard fare in the bowling world, combining match play with music, excursions and a holiday spirit.

But this was not the only form of competition. A few weeks later, in September 1864, another tournament took place on the Ribble-side green of Mr Poole in Preston, Lancashire. This, however, was a handicap match 'open to all England' but not beyond. (Amongst the entrants was J Woods, possibly the same Woods who competed at Kircudbright.) Another difference was that, as was commonplace in the north of England, the prizes were in cash. J Dewhurst, the winner, took home £8.

Another club in Galloway to have its green in a prominent location is **Garlieston**. Here, the village was laid out formally by the Earl of Galloway in the mid 18th century, but with no provision for a green. So when **Garlieston Bowling Club** formed in 1867, rather than go to the outskirts where a square green would have been possible, it settled on a narrow strip of turf on the waterfront, gifted by the Earl.

This means that, unusually, the Garlieston green is split into two halves, one of three rinks, the other of two. Unconventional for sure, but then look out over the bay and who would wish it otherwise?

Also prominently positioned is **Wigtown Bowling Club** (*left*) eight miles up the coast. Formed in 1830 and seen here in 2012, the green forms part of an elongated town square dominated at its east end by the County Buildings, a French Gothic edifice of the 1860s that originally housed the sheriff court, local library and assembly rooms. Nowadays Wigtown is best known for secondhand bookshops, several of which also face the square. Public gardens lie to the rear of the bowls clubhouse, capped at their west end by a market cross, erected in 1816.

To complete this perfect picture of Georgian town planning are ornate iron railings and lampholders on the north side of the green.

Alloa Bowling Club, the oldest of six clubs in this famous brewing town in Clackmannanshire – a town of fewer than 20,000 inhabitants – has been at its green on Coningsby Place since forming in 1845. Before then, an earlier green, created some time before 1811, lay in the town centre, behind the Tontine Hotel (now Ochil House) on Marshill.

In addition to its famous smokies Arbroath has four clubs. Arbroath Bowling Club is the oldest, with a pair of windswept greens looking out over the North Sea and the Bell Rock lighthouse, as depicted on the club's crest (*left*). Also depicted is Arbroath Abbey, the ruins of which overlook another pair of greens, belonging to Abbey BC, formed in 1878.

WE LYE;" be Careful

▲ When **William Mitchell** published his *Manual of Bowl Playing* in 1864 he included two drawings of hand signals. Used to denote which woods are counting at a particular stage of an end, both will be familiar to bowlers today.

But for historians, most valuable of all is Mitchell's fold out appendix, printed in both the 1864 and 1870 editions. Seen here almost in its entirety (missing out only the names of office holders in the right hand column), it lists 137 clubs, of which eight are in northern England. A further 12, he adds in a footnote, did not make returns. Although we have been able to trace a further 35 clubs that existed at this time, Mitchell's achievement in getting responses from as many as he did represents a worthy achievement.

Of the 129 Scottish clubs listed, 106 are still in action as of 2015.

NAME OF CLUB.	Year when Founded	WHERE SITUATED. Town or Parish.	County.	MEMBERS AND PLAYERS. Number of Members.	Match Players.	Entry Money.	Yearly Subscription.	THE GREEN. Size of, in yards. Length.	Width.	State or Order.	PRESIDENTS
Albany,	1833	Glasgow,	Lanark,	120	32	42/	25/	57	38	Excellent,	John Paris,
Allan Park,	1858	Largs,	Ayr,	30	12	...	7/6	42	34	Good,	George Main,
Alloa,		Alloa,	Clackmannan,								
Ardeer,	1857	Stevenston,	Ayr,	40	24	10/6 & 21/	3/	44	44	Good,	Neil Robson,
Ardgowan,	1841	Greenock,	Renfrew,	100	16	42/	10/6	48	48	Good,	Mat. Brown,
Ardrossan,	1842	Ardrossan,	Ayr,	40	12	15/	10/6	47	45	Good,	William M'Jannet,
Ayr,	1834	Ayr,	Ayr,	70	...	20/	21/	45	43	Excellent,	Captain Paton,
Ayr Citadel,	1858	Ayr,	Ayr,	65	32	20/	15/	50	37	Good,	P. B. Hill,
Annan,			Dumfries,								
Abercorn,	1860	Paisley,	Renfrew,	120	16	10/	10/	63	37	Good,	Andrew Faulds, Ju
Aberfeldy,	1862	Aberfeldy,	Perth,	27	20		5/	36	12	Good,	James F. Wyllie,
Airdrie,	1852	Airdrie,	Lanark,	65	40	15/	15/	42	42	Good,	Peter Marshall,
Argyll,	1860	Dunoon,	Argyll,	32	16	1/	10/6	40	30	Good,	David Dunn,
Bank End,	1852	Paisley,	Renfrew,	32	12	7/6	3/6	36	12	Fair,	Capt. William Carl
Bannockburn,	1859	Bannockburn,	Stirling,	36	20	20/	3/	36	27	Tolerable,	Alexander Wilson,
Barkip,	1863	Dalry Parish,	Ayr,	70	40	10/	2/6	42	37	Very Fair,	James Carrick,
Bellahouston,	1859	Glasgow,	Lanark,	140	20	21/	21/	73	40	Good,	James Wilson,
Belvedere,	1860	Glasgow,	Lanark,	46	12	Nil.	10/6	42	32	Good,	Jos. H. Wright,
Bladnoch,	1858	Wigton Parish,	Wigton,	18	16	20/	10/	48	26	Good,	Thomas M'Clelland
Bo'ness,	1864	Bo'ness,	Stirling,	52	30	...	...	43	32	Pretty Fair,	John Anderson,
Borestone,		Borestone,	Stirling,								
Bowling,		Bowling,	Dumbarton,								
Brampton,	1764	Brampton,	Cumberland,	51	15	Nil.	7/6	42	33	Very Good,	John Lee,
Bridgeton,	1851	Glasgow,	Lanark,	94	20	Nil.	21/	68	39	Good,	Alexander Murdoch
Bridge of Earn,	1859	Dumbarney Parish,	Perth,	20	12	...	...	Medium,	Medium,	Pretty Fair,	John Cowan,
Broughty-Ferry,		Broughty-Ferry,									
Bear's-Den,		New Kilpatrick,									
Calton,	1862	Glasgow,	Lanark,	45	16	21/	21/	40	30	Fair,	Robert Miller,
Carlisle,		Carlisle,									
Carron,		Carron,	Stirling,								
Castle-Douglas,	1860	Kelton Parish,	Kirkcudbright,	50	30	21/		43	37	Very Fair,	Provost Hewat,
Castle-Kennedy,	1857	Inch Parish,	Wigton,	33	24	...	2/6	50	30	Good,	Rt. Hon. Viscount Dalry
Claremont,	1840	Edinburgh,	Edinburgh,	39	20	21/	21/	46	25	Good,	David M'Brair,
Cockermouth,	1860	Cockermouth,	Cumberland,	70	30	Nil.	10/	46	34	Middling,	John Pearson,
Cumbernauld,		Cumbernauld,									
Cupar,	1853	Cupar,	Fife,	40	16		6/6	37	18	Good,	Andrew Russell,
Charleston,	1864	Paisley,	Renfrew,	90	24	10/	6/	60	38	Middling,	John Smith,
Dalbeattie,		Dalbeattie,	Kirkcudbright,								
Dalry,		Dalry,	Ayr,								
Denny,	1845	Denny,	Stirling,	47	24	7/6	7/6	42	32	Good,	Dr. Cuthill,
Dumbarton,	1838	Dumbarton,	Dumbarton,	32	12	21/	20/	40	40	Fair,	Allan M'Lean,
Dundee,		Dundee,									
Dundonald,	1854	Dundonald,	Ayr,	20	12	21/	5/	...	...	Good,	R. Gairdner, Sen.,
Dunoon,		Dunoon,	Argyll,								
Duntocher,	1853	Duntocher,	Dumbarton,	40	20		2/6	32	30	Middling,	John Walker,
Dreghorn,		Dreghorn,	Ayr,								
Dalkeith,	1857	Dalkeith,	Edinburgh,	54	36	30/	5/	45	40	Beautiful,	David Cleghorn,
Dunse,		Dunse,									
Dunfermline,	1852	Dunfermline,	Fife,	112	30	20/	10/	47	39	First-rate,	Wm. Brown,
Dumfries,		Dumfries,	Dumfries,								
East Linton,	1862	Prestonkirk Parish,	Haddington,	60	16	5/	3/	41	18	Fair,	Francis Storie,
Edinburgh, New,	1861	Edinburgh,		100	20	21/	15/	42	35	Very Good,	Thomas Paterson,
Eglinton,	1853	Eglinton,	Ayr,	30	18	...	...	76	41	Good,	Hugh Conn,
Falkirk,	1838	Falkirk,	Stirling,	65	24	2/6	12/6	42	40	Middling,	Henry Aitken,
Galashiels,	1859	Galashiels,	Selkirk,	52	30	21/	12/6	38	28	Do.	David Shiell,
Galston,	1850	Galston,	Ayr,	50	24	25/	7/6	45	45	Good,	John Hendrie,
Gatehouse,			Kirkcudbright,								
Girvan,	1841	Girvan,	Ayr,	50	32	5/	10/	41	27	First-rate,	John B. Ross,
Glengarnock,	1858	Kilbirnie,	Ayr,	59	28	...	2/6	44	33	Very Good,	John Cunningham
Govan,	1847	Glasgow,	Renfrew,	42	12	...	21/	40	38	Good,	George Wishart,
Grangemouth,		Grangemouth,									
Grosvenor,	1856	Greenock,	Renfrew,	128	24	25/	10/6	59	41	Good,	Robert Sellars,
Guildhall,	1856	Stirling,	Stirling,	60	40	2/6	1/	43	33	Good,	Archibald Walls,
Haddington,	1709	Haddington,	Haddington,	55	24	2/6	7/6	41	23	Do.	William Watson,
Hamilton,	1841	Hamilton,	Lanark,	100	32		10/6	50	40	Do.	John Meek,
Hawick,	1854	Hawick,	Roxburgh,	40	12	20/	10/	40	36	Fair,	John Laing,
Helensburgh,	1863	Helensburgh,	Dumbarton,	55	16	20/	15/	40	20	Tolerable,	Alex. Breingan, P
Hillhead,	1849	Glasgow,	Lanark,	140	40	21/	21/	42	42	First-class,	William Kirkwood

NAME OF CLUB	Year when Founded	Town or Parish	County	Number of Members	Match Players	Entry-Money	Yearly Subscription	Length	Width	State or Order	PRESIDENTS
Hillhead,	1849	Glasgow,	Lanark,	140	40	21/	21/	42	42	First-class,	William Kirkwood,
Hurlford,	1862	Hurlford,	Ayr,	24	12	10/6	5/	41	33	Very Fair,	J. H. Murray,
Hillton,	1849	Dundee,	Forfar,	30	28	20/	10/	41	11	Good,	Jno. Morrison,
Innellan,		Innellan,	Argyll,								
Irvine,	1849	Irvine,	Ayr,	60	24	43/	7/6	38	26	Good,	Robert Caldwell,
Jedburgh,	1859	Jedburgh,	Roxburgh,	44	25	20/	10/	40	26	Do.	William Veitch,
Kendal,	1826	Kendal,	Westmoreland,	30	24		10/	50	40	Do.	
Kerelaw,	1860	Stevenston,	Ayr,	36	16	21/	5/	46	25	Very Best,	William Lockhart,
Kilmarnock,	1740	Kilmarnock,	Ayr,	50	20	40/	15/	42	40	Good,	James Hannah,
Kilpatrick, Old,	1864	Kilpatrick,	Dumbarton,	26	16	Nil.	8/6	30	15	Middling,	H Carmichael,
Kilwinning,	1855	Kilwinning,	Ayr,	60	30	30/	7/6	40	40	Good,	John Carruthers,
Kingston,	1850	Glasgow,	Lanark,	114	56	15/	20/	51	40	Good,	William Tait,
Kirkaldy,	1858	Kirkaldy,	Fife,	63	16	60/	20/	50	40	Good,	Wm. Anderson, Jun.
Kirkintilloch,	1852	Kirkintilloch,	Dumbarton,	26	12	30/	15/	30	22	Very Good,	D. R. Stewart,
Kircudbright,	1856	Kirkcudbright,	Kircudbright,	45	30	21/	21/	50	33	Fair,	William Mure,
Kirkcowan,	1853	Kirkcowan,	Wigton,	18	16	12/6	4/	41	28	Very Good,	William M'Dowall,
Ladeside,	1860	Kilbirnie,	Ayr,	36	20	20/	6/	45	42	Middling,	William Knox,
Langholm, Working Mens',	1857	Langholm,	Dumfries,	60	36	3/	3/	69	35	Improving,	Adam Niven,
Lochmaben,		Lochmaben,	Dumfries,								
Leith,		Leith,	Edinburgh,								
Lanark, Waterloo Green,	1856	Lanark,	Lanark,	80	20	21/	6/6	36	35	Good,	William Irving,
Maybole,	1848	Maybole,	Ayr,	40	16	20/	12/6	37	36	Good,	Arthur Muir,
Maryhill,	1861	Maryhill,	Lanark,	70	20	21/	12/6	35	35	Good,	John Shaw,
Mildamhead,		Dumfries,	Dumfries,								
Moffat, Baths,	1827	Moffat,	Dumfries,					40	20	Good,	
Milngavie,		Milngavie,									
Newmilns,	1862	Newmilns,	Ayr,	40	20	20/	5/	40	40	Very Good,	F. F. Richmond,
Newton-Stewart,	1831	Newton-Stewart,	Wigton,	36	20	10/6	7/6	45	40	Capital,	Henry Stuart,
Partick,	1845	Partick,	Lanark,	107	20	21/	21/	49	40	First-class,	Andrew Dykes,
Peebles,	1829	Peebles,	Peebles,	50	12	5/	3/6	40	32	Good,	Archibald Donaldson
Peel Street,	1854	Partick,	Lanark,	60	16	2/6	7/6	40	40	Good,	John Anderson,
Penrith,	1729	Penrith,	Cumberland,	80	25	2/6	7/6	45	32	Very Good,	Joseph Hudson,
Perth,	1853	Perth,	Perth,	115	16	31/6	21/	50	40	Very Good,	S. R. Stewart,
Pollokshaws,	1854	Pollokshaws,	Renfrew,	43	16	10/6	10/	42	40	Good,	Thomas Watson,
Port-Glasgow,		Port-Glasgow,	Renfrew,								
Portland,	1860	Kilmarnock,	Ayr,	68	20	100/	12/6	55	43	Good,	John Horne,
Priorscroft,	1839	Paisley,	Renfrew,	100	32	25/	20/	45	38	First-rate,	William Craw,
Preston,		Preston,									
Rothesay,	1846	Rothesay,	Bute,	70	16		5/	41	35	Good,	John M'Ewan,
Rutherglen,	1862	Rutherglen,	Lanark,	52	32	21/	10/6	41	32	Do.	Bailie Murray,
Renfrew,	1851	Renfrew,	Renfrew,	40	12	20/	7/	40	28	Do.	Matthew White,
Saltcoats,	1861	Saltcoats,	Ayr,	57	20	21/	10/6	45	44	First-class,	William Brown, Jun
Shawlands,	1861	Eastwood Parish,	Renfrew,	64	31	10/	20/	38	30	Splendid,	Matthew Algie,
St. Mary's,	1859	Dumfries,	Dumfries,	56	20	21/	10/	43	35	First-class,	Lieut.-Gen. Johnsto
St. Rollox,	1857	Glasgow,	Lanark,	80	20	Nil.	25/	41	32	Good,	James Burns, Sen.,
St. Vincent,	1860	Glasgow,	Lanark,	140	50	42/	21/	47	47	Good,	F. A. Barrow,
Selkirk,	1856	Selkirk,	Selkirk,	29	20	20/	10/	40	18	Good,	Robert Paton,
Silloth,	1863	Silloth,	Cumberland,	120	24		3/	48	39	Good,	Major Jackson,
Stewarton,	1862	Stewarton,	Ayr,	31	12	21/	12/6	40	37	Very Good,	William Laughland,
Stirling,	1854	Stirling,	Stirling,	88	24	25/	10/	42	38	Capital,	Patrick G. Morrison,
Stranraer,	1859	Stranraer,	Wigton,	60	32	10/6	10/6	48	43	Capital,	Provost Guthrie,
Strathaven,	1862	Strathaven,	Lanark,	38	20	21/	9/	38	38	Good,	Thomas Tennent,
Thornhill,	1839	Thornhill,	Dumfries,	40	21		5/	60	29	Very Good,	David Crichton,
Troon,	1820	Troon,	Ayr,	40	16	20/	1d. p. day	40	40	Good,	A. B. Cowan,
Uddingston,	1864	Bothwell Parish,	Lanark,	70	30	Nil.	10/	40	30	Good,	James Barr,
Victoria,	1855	Girvan,	Ayr,	32	16	5/	10/	40	20	Do.	Robert Hannah,
Victoria,	1859	Paisley,	Renfrew,	94	36	10/	8/	48	30	First-rate,	William Cowden,
Warriston Park,	1852	Edinburgh,	Edinburgh,	32	24	10/6	21/	46	26	Pretty Fair,	James Nairne,
Waverley,	1856	Edinburgh,	Edinburgh,	19	12	2/6	11/	44	31		Mr. Contie,
Wellcroft,	1835	Glasgow,	Lanark,	120	48	21/	21/	53	41	Excellent,	James Pritchard,
Wellmeadow,	1849	Paisley,	Renfrew,	95	40	20/	14/	45	42	Excellent,	Robert Abercrombie,
Whitehaven,											
Whitevale,*	1837	Glasgow,	Lanark,	55	20	Nil.	21/	35	32	Middling,	John Brown,
Wigtown,	1830	Wigton,	Wigton,	30	24		10/	54	24	Good,	William Carson,
Wishaw,	1861	Wishaw,	Lanark,	80	32	20/	7/6	40	40	Do.	Henry Houldsworth,
Willowbank,	1808	Glasgow,	Lanark,	156	36	21/	25/	46	44½	Very Good,	W. W. Mitchell,
Workington,											
West-End,		Dundee,									
Wellington Park,	1853	Greenock,	Renfrew,	80	24	1/6	1/	2 Greens, 27×18		Very Good,	John M'Cowan,

"THEY LYE;" be Up

◀ Mitchell's survey shows just how greatly greens varied in size before standardisation. The smallest was Old Kilpatrick, just 30 x 15 yards. The largest was Bellahouston in Glasgow, which at 73 x 40 yards would eventually be split into two.

Clearly it was the clubs who described their own green's 'State or Order'. These range from 'capital' (Stirling) to merely 'middling' (Paisley), 'tolerable' (Bannockburn) and 'indifferent' (Cupar).

Fees and subscriptions provide a useful indicator of the relative social status of each club. Kilmarnock charged the most to join, at 100s, while the subscription at Glengarnock, a club associated with an ironworks, was just 2s 6d.

Note that Mitchell himself is named as President of Willowbank. On the full version of the appendix he is also listed as club champion in 1864. Truly, a real all rounder.

▲ Nestling on the banks of the North Esk River and with a thickly wooded ridge as its backdrop, this is **Dalkeith Bowling Club**, south of Edinburgh, formed in 1857 on land owned by the Duke of Buccleuch (who had had a circular bowling green of his own at nearby Dalkeith Palace, earlier in the 19th century).

As at Mauchline and several other Scottish clubs, Dalkeith has retained its original pavilion, whilst building a new one opposite. But at Dalkeith, unusually, both have merit. Seen above is the original, built soon after 1857 for £25 and thought to be the oldest building in use at a Scottish green. Now used for storage and as an extra dressing room, it appears basic, but has an immaculate wood panelled interior with an iron hand pump, used to draw water from the river.

It was from this pavilion in the 1870s that the greenkeeper was warned 'that if he or his wife were discovered selling drink on the green or in the house, dismissal would be instant.' Alcoholic drinks were finally allowed in 1896.

In 1920 the club purchased the site for £100. This allowed it to build a larger, but no less charming pavilion across the green in 1924.

▲ Bowls clubs are often hidden behind hedges or walls, but the only hint that **Hillside Bowling Club** in **Edinburgh** exists is a door tucked down a flight of steps beween the tenements on **Brunton Place**.

Formed in 1870 in Hillside Street, the club moved to this most private of enclaves, lying between Calton Hill and the Easter Road ground of Hibernian FC, in 1893.

When William Mitchell's *Manual* was published in 1864 there were seven clubs in Edinburgh and Leith (of which Leith BC and Lutton Place BC survive). Over the next 28 years, up to the formation of the Scottish Bowling Association in 1892, a further 20 or so more clubs formed (of which 15 survive, including Hillside, Edinburgh West End, formed in 1864, and Currie, Liberton and Northern, all formed in the 1870s). But as the *Edinburgh Bowling Annual* reported in 1903, the total then shot up again during the following decade at 'an alarming rate', to reach around 100 clubs.

Today only 50 are still going, and given that one of the latest casualties, Edinburgh BC, lost its green to development, Hillside might be glad to remain so out of sight.

Listed Category C, the pavilion at Galashiels BC in the Borders, formed in 1856, was opened in 1883 (*left*) and extended in 1930 to accommodate lady members. It is mirrored by that of Whitehouse & Grange BC in Edinburgh (*right*), where the club, formed in 1872, added the upper storey in 1912 to cater for the growing number of young players wanting to join.

main activities, both served by the pavilion seen here; an unspoilt Arts and Crafts delight, built in 1926 and distinguished by two hexagonal corner turrets.

Equally well preserved is its interior, with scrolled plasterwork in the main hall bearing the club's foundation date (*right*).

Listed Category C, the Ardgowan pavilion is one of 16 listed pavilions in Scotland still in use for bowls.

Paisley in Renfrewshire, once a great centre of weaving, has one of the highest concentrations of bowls clubs in Britain, 14 in total.

The oldest is Priorscroft, formed in 1839. But as this occupies a relatively new site, created in 1973, the Paisley club with the strongest heritage assets is **Abercorn Bowling Club**. Its red brick pavilion, which bears the club's formation date of 1860 (*left*), dates from 1898, when it moved to its current site on Garthland Lane.

On the north bank of the Clyde, **Yoker Bowling Club** (*right*) is based on Hawick Street, originally known as Harvey Street. This is because the Harvey family farmed in the area and, in the 18th century set up what would become one of the largest distilleries in Scotland.

In fact it was largely for workers in that distillery that William Harvey set up the bowls club, using a field next to his dairy (the site of which is now a business park), in 1850.

Lastly, to the immediate west of Glasgow, the **Partick Bowling Club** formed in 1844 and has been based on Fortrose Street (*above right*) since 1854, making this the oldest green in continuous use in the Glasgow area. Across the road lies the West of Scotland Cricket Ground on Hamilton Crescent where Scotland played England in the first ever football international in 1872.

▲ Another area of expansion in the bowling world lay to the west of Glasgow on both sides of the River Clyde. In **Greenock**, only a few hundred yards from the docks, yet in the midst of a solid, respectable residential district, **Ardgowan Bowling Club** (*top*) took its name from the square in which it made its home in 1841. In common with many other Scottish bowling clubs, Ardgowan was established as a multi-sports club, offering bowls, curling and quoits to its 132 original members, each paying an entry fee of two guineas plus a one guinea subscription.

Eventually the curling pond made way for a second green, while in 1875 tennis courts were laid on the east side of the square. Bowls and tennis remain the club's

◀ While cricket fans may be familiar with the three Ws of the West Indies team of the 1950s – Worrell, Weekes and Walcott – Scottish bowlers are more inclined to think of **Willowbank**, **Whitevale** and **Wellcroft**. All three clubs have been stalwarts of the Glasgow scene since the 1830s, and for almost as long have been debating which is the oldest.

Determining the age of Willowbank largely depends on how we define a club. As explained in the previous chapter, many bowlers in the 18th century met weekly at a specific green, drawn together as much by their love of drinking and good fellowship as by the game. Rarely did such groups own or even rent a green directly.

So it was that the story of **Willowbank** goes back to a green at the Sauchy Hall pleasure gardens, opened in 1816. When Sauchy Hall was earmarked for development, in 1833 some of the regular bowlers there clubbed together to build a new green on Elmbank Street. They called themselves the Willowbank Bowlers in memory of Sauchy Hall, 'saugh' being another word for willow. When this group then adopted a formal constitution, in 1835, the very first minute made clear 'That the club shall consist of the present subscribers to the Willowbank Bowling Green.'

Look closely at the pavilion at Wellcroft today (*right*) and its iron spandrels look familiar. They resemble both those on the pavilion at St Vincent (*page 108*), but more importantly, those on the pavilion Wellcroft built on Eglinton Street in 1851 (*page 17*). This pavilion, spandrels and all, is also depicted on 'the coffee pot', a Wellcroft trophy hallmarked in 1853.

In other words, they considered their formation to have been 1833.

That the minutes survive is a story in itself. After disappearing, they were bought from a 'Clydeside barrow' in 1913, by an eagle eyed member, AB McAuley.

Willowbank's members made their final move westwards to their current home on Downanside Road in 1896.

For its part, **Whitevale Bowling Club** started in the East End of Glasgow on a small green. The

club gives its foundation date as 1836, although there is a strong suggestion that it might have been 1835. Alas, no records have survived. What is for certain is that the club moved to its current green on Whitehill Street in Dennistoun in 1865.

Pictured above is the green of **Wellcroft Bowling Club**, with the tree-covered slopes of Queen's Park rising behind. A horse chestnut tree, trained to make a letter 'W', marks the entrance (*left*).

Wellcroft formed at the Wheatsheaf Inn on Clyde Terrace in January 1835, before inaugurating its green on Surrey Street, close to the Bowling Green Tavern, the following May. From there in 1851 the club moved to Eglinton Street, Govan, only for the site to be bought for railway use. Finally it settled in Queen's Park in 1876, where it may have been safe, but it was most certainly not alone.

▲ From the W-shaped tree outside Wellcroft, following around the bend of Queen's Drive to the gates of the **Queen's Park Bowling and Tennis Club**, is less than 600 yards.

But that is only for starters, because within a radius of only a mile and a quarter from the centre of Queen's Park, there are 25 bowling greens at 14 locations.

(This compares with 44 in 1929, at 21 locations.)

Nowhere else in the world has such a concentration of greens.

Queen's Park itself opened in 1862. But why was it such a magnet for bowlers? Primarily because as Glasgow expanded south of the Clyde in the mid 19th century, the Queen's Park area became one of the most popular new suburbs, with acres of space for sport and recreation.

The Queen's Park Bowling and Tennis club formed on the east side of the park in 1867 (nine years before Wellcroft arrived). Its plot was secured on a ten-year lease from the Corporation at £10 per annum. Spending over £1,200, the founders built an octagonal pavilion and had two greens laid under the direction of Duncan McLellan, the Superintendent of the Glasgow Parks Department. The turf came from Kilwinning in Ayrshire.

That same summer, just a few hundred yards away, the Queen's Park Football Club was also formed. And just as this club would become an important force in its sport, so too would the bowls club.

For the next two decades all the local clubs played each other on an ad hoc basis, until in 1888, the Glasgow Bowling Association was formed by 22 clubs. This was not Scotland's first regional association.

Others had been formed in the Borders (1872), Edinburgh and Leith (1878), Linlithgowshire (1882), East Lothian (1883) and Midlothian (1885).

But Glasgow, through its sheer weight of numbers, wealth and influence, became immediately dominant. Thus when the Scottish Bowling Association was finally formed in 1892 – 44 years after that initial meeting attended by William Mitchell – Queen's Park was the obvious choice for the inaugural national championships.

In fact it remained the venue for the next century or more, before the SBA finally switched the event, and its headquarters, to the Northfield Club in Ayr, in 1989.

There are three greens at Queen's Park. The original pair are the west, or 'wee green' and the east or 'big green', seen on the right (with the former Crosshill Queen's Park Church, built in 1872 and now flats, in the background). The third green to the south, the 'top green', was added in 1889, taking the place of three tennis courts.

But to return to the formation of the SBA in September 1892.

During the years 1820-92, as stated earlier, no fewer than 180 of the bowling clubs now playing in Scotland were formed.

Even so, it took repeated appeals in *The Scotsman* by James Brown of Sanquhar in Dumfriesshire

before 122 of them came together to form the SBA. Brown was elected Secretary/Treasurer and in the spirit of Mitchell published his own Manual. A year later the first national championships at Queen's Park saw Carluke reach the finals, where they lost, perhaps appropriately, to Kilwinning.

Readers interested in a more in-depth study of bowling in Glasgow should refer to *Played in Glasgow*, an earlier title in the Played in Britain series (*see Links*).

But we finish here by noting that when the SBA formed, it extended its offer of membership to clubs all over Britain. Not one outside Scotland actually joined. Or at least, not for a decade, as we will now go on to discover as we return south of the border.

Chapter Eight

England and Wales 1830–1914

While subscription clubs and societies were common in the 18th century, in the 19th century a new model emerged. The Gateshead Bowling Green Company was incorporated in 1865, initially with seven shareholders, each investing £190. This was enough to buy a town centre site and build on it a handsome pavilion, most of which remains in use. Gateshead is the oldest bowling club in the north east, an area that was quick to adopt the 'Scotch game'.

The reconfiguration of bowls in Scotland during the 19th century was to have a profound effect on bowling south of the border. But whereas in Scotland total uniformity had been achieved by 1892 – that is, the nation's bowlers had by then all switched to flat green bowls played in rinks – in England and Wales bowlers were to be irrevocably split.

As detailed in Chapter One, they divided into essentially four camps: those who adopted the 'Scotch game' in its entirety (and went on to join the English Bowling Association, formed in 1903); those who maintained traditional non-level greens and biased jacks (and came to call their game 'crown green' bowls); those who took elements of both codes (some of whom went on to form the English Bowling Federation in 1945), and those who ignored all these developments (such as in Lewes and Barnes) and carried on more or less as they were.

The differences that emerged during the Victorian and Edwardian eras were not confined to rules. They equally encompassed differing attitudes towards professionalism, to gambling and to the links between bowling and public houses. Indeed it was largely owing to these differences that the evolution of bowls in England and Wales was more fragmented, and therefore more gradual than in Scotland.

That said, the period witnessed a growth in bowls in every part of England and Wales that was no less comprehensive than in Scotland, or indeed in other major sports, such as football, cricket, rugby, tennis and golf.

Private bowls clubs, the natural successors to the subscription clubs and societies of the Georgian period, continued to grow in number from 1830, as did the number of pub greens.

At Gateshead (*see left*) and elsewhere, more bowlers chose share issues and incorporation as a means of securing their own greens. They were joined, moreover, by greens appearing not only in new areas, such as Devon, where as we noted earlier there was only one club in 1888, but also in new contexts.

These included greens in public parks (starting in Birmingham in 1859, as noted below), at seaside resorts, and attached to works or institutions, such as Conservative and Liberal Clubs. To give just one early example of this, in Worcester in 1857, a Working Men's Institute opened in Silver Street, with a bowling green, two skittle alleys and a quoits ground.

By the end of the century, sports and social clubs of this type would become almost as commonplace as pub greens.

The social and economic background to bowling's growth in England and Wales was exactly as outlined in the previous chapter on Scotland; that is, rampant urbanisation allied to improvements in transportation and communications.

As in Scotland these developments led to some clubs (albeit still a minority) seeking to play their neighbours on a home and away basis. For individuals, England's first open tournaments took place in the 1860s.

One of the drivers of these tournaments, it has to be said,

From a report on the creation of possibly the first bowling green in a public park in England, namely **Adderley Park** in **Saltley**, **Birmingham**

We were glad to see a plot of ground railed and laid out for a bowling green, and as it is in a forward state the lovers of that healthful, ancient and fascinating game may enjoy their bowls without having to go miles before meeting with a green deserving of the name, or at least open to the class it is intended to benefit.

Birmingham Journal 16 July 1859

was hard cash. Carrying on from the high stakes recorded during the Tudor and Stuart years, 19th century bowlers, in the north west of England especially, were well rewarded, even compared with other professional sports such as boxing and pedestrianism.

One early example: in July 1835, a match to '31 up' was staged in Chester between two locals and two players from Manchester. The visitors won 31-8 and took home £50. This was the equivalent of the annual wage of a labourer.

Seeing how popular such matches were, publicans with greens were more than happy to issue challenges via the local press. Or the players themselves did so, as reported in July 1849 in the *Nottinghamshire Guardian*:

'Three or six members of the Basford Bowling Club are open to play a similar number of any Green or Club in England, home and home game'.

Inevitably, as the stakes rose, but in amateur circles too, as more clubs started playing each other and becoming ever more competitive, the quality of greens came under increasing scrutiny.

As a result, bowlers grew much less willing to share their hallowed turf with non-bowlers, as had been the norm since the 16th century.

Thus in 1852, as noted earlier, bowlers in Lewes were minded to take over the lease of their green once and for all following the staging of a horticultural show.

Their actions were echoed in Winchester in 1867 when, after a fireworks display, some people about to dance on the green – 'the devotees of Terpsichore' as described in one local newspaper – were stopped abruptly by 'the lovers of bowls... seeing that the turf was likely to be damaged'.

The question of 'whose green is it anyway?' reached its head in Cannock in the 1880s, as a later case study will show. But aside from the legal aspects of the issue, it should be noted that by this time the quality of turf at many greens had improved immeasurably.

This, as noted in Chapter Two, was thanks to the availability of lawn mowers, introduced in the 1830s, followed in the 1890s by the arrival of petrol mowers, and to the use of sea-washed turf from Cumberland and Ayrshire, now able to be transported to all corners of the British Isles by the growing railway network. Not only for bowls but for golf, cricket, and from the 1870s onwards for tennis, football and rugby, the laying and maintenance of sports turf was now an industry in its own right.

So little wonder that by the late 19th century bowlers, and greenkeepers, would be far more protective than their forebears. No longer would they tolerate their bowling green doubling up as a village green.

This proprietorial tendency would even be manifested in public parks. Arising out of concerns for public health and welfare in Britain's increasingly industrialised, crowded and polluted towns and cities, public parks started to appear in the early years of Victoria's reign; for example in Preston and Birkenhead. Sports facilities were not originally on the agenda; parks were for perambulation, contemplation and for enjoying the horticultural and arboreal displays. But younger citizens made it instantly clear what they also craved by swamping these new open spaces with games of cricket, or by swimming in the newly created boating lakes. »

▲ As bowls increased in status during the 19th century, so too did the sophistication of clubhouses. Even so, the pavilion of **Old Trafford Bowling Club**, built on **Talbot Road, Manchester**, in 1877, and seen here in 2004, was and remains unusually substantial.

Located just east of Old Trafford cricket ground and within the former boundaries of the Trafford Park estate, the bowls club occupies a corner of what had been, from 1847-57, the ground of the Manchester Cricket Club (which became Lancashire County Cricket Club in 1864). In fact one of the bowls club's founders was described in the original minutes as the manager of the cricket club.

Given his involvement, and all the other activity in the area, it therefore seems likely that the pavilion was built with more than bowls in mind. To the north lay the Botanical Gardens. To the south, from 1881-1908, was the Northern Tennis Club, and to the west, where the cricket club were

based, stood pavilions built for the 1857 Treasures of Art exhibition. From 1887-91 this site was home to the Manchester Athletic Club.

The bowls club was thus in good company, in an area already filling with detached villas, built on either side of a new rail link to Altrincham.

Reflecting this, its founders were mainly businessmen; a tallow chandler, a jeweller, and merchants of cotton, timber and cigars.

Today the pavilion is surrounded by busy roads, offices and retail outlets. It needs a new roof, repairs to a collapsed sewer, and repainting. In 2003 alone the club had to find £14,000 for the green.

But on the positive side, being so close to both Lancashire CCC and Manchester United, the club profits handsomely from parking revenue and bar takings on big match days.

Plus they have a few big match days themselves amongst their 150 members, 20 of them juniors.

So plenty of challenges at Old Trafford, but plenty of spirit too, just like their sporting neighbours.

>> Probably the first local authorities to provide public greens in parks were Leith, outside Edinburgh, where two greens were laid on Leith Links in 1857, and Birmingham, as noted on the previous page, in 1859 (although strictly speaking Adderley Park was a philanthropic rather than a municipal initiative).

Crucially, however, at Leith, while one of the greens was reserved for members of the public wishing to 'pay and play' as and when, the other was allocated to a club. Fitz Park in Keswick had a similar dual set up (see page 129).

But even where only one park green was laid, clubs still formed, and in many cases their members became as proprietorial as any at private clubs, freezing out other casual bowlers in the process (an issue that persists to this day).

Other early parks greens were laid by Bolton Corporation, at the Heywood Recreation Ground in 1866, and by Manchester, at Philips Park in 1871. Thereafter park greens proliferated in areas where few private clubs existed, such as Leeds and Bradford, but were late to appear in cities which had long established clubs, for example London and Glasgow.

Concerning what form these park greens took, and what type of game was played on them, this varied according to the location.

As we saw in Chapter Five, the first known set of rules in England had appeared under Charles II's name in 1670. But as far as we know, these rules were not universally applied.

Meanwhile those sets of 18th century club rules that survive, for example from Rugeley and Bedale, each differ in a number of ways.

Yet another set appeared in the London sporting newspaper, *Bell's Life*, on June 15 1845.

These were the rules played at the Barrack Tavern, Sheffield.

They included the requirement for a minimum 'mark' of 25 yards, for the jack to be considered 'dead' if it entered the ditch, and that 'it is allowed to throw the jack to any part of the green, provided the centre is left unencumbered'.

This last rule, aimed at avoiding obstructions, survived in crown green until 1979 and was known as the 'button rule', because in order to enforce it a small disc was placed in the centre of each green.

The 1845 Sheffield rules show that whilst the Scots were preparing to meet in Glasgow in 1848 to discuss aligning their rules, in Yorkshire and other parts of the north and Midlands, a degree of common ground also existed, and that the essentials were not that different from the crown green code that would eventually emerge.

Considering that it was largely owing to WG Grace that flat green bowling became so ubiquitous in England, it is ironic that the only statue of him in a bowling context – completed by Rosemary Phipps in 1998 as part of a Millennium sculpture trail – is located in Victoria Park, Stafford, next to a crown green. There is of course also a statue of him at Lord's.

It is therefore no surprise to learn that bowlers in those crown green areas were also the first to organise on a formal basis.

In Scotland, it will be recalled, the earliest local associations had formed in the Borders in 1872 and in Edinburgh & Leith in 1878.

In England, Lancashire & Cheshire were the first to form a joint association in 1888. Yorkshire followed in 1892, as did the Isle of Man (with its headquarters at the Bowling Green Hotel in Douglas).

Also formed in 1892 (the year that the Scottish Bowling Association came into being), was the Northumberland & Durham Bowling Association.

Further south, both the Midland Counties Bowling Association and the London & Southern Counties Bowling Association were formed in 1895. At this point there was still no obvious movement towards the formation of a national body, as in Scotland. But this all changed in 1903 with the arrival of the cricketer WG Grace on the scene, an intervention that led to the formation of the English Bowling Association (EBA) and large swathes of England and

Wales adopting the Scottish rules (as discussed opposite).

Unlike the split in rugby that took place in 1895, as a result of which Union and League went their separate ways, it took years before the divide in bowls settled along the lines we know today.

In parts of Gloucestershire and Norfolk the decision to take one route or another, crown green or flat green, was often down to individuals. In Suffolk, when in 1910 a club formed at the Derby Road Hotel in Ipswich (later to become the Marlborough BC), it adopted flat green rules only because its landlord, Sam Dobbin, was Scottish. Prior to this, bowlers in Suffolk had mostly used strongly-biased Framlingham woods (see pages 10 and 79).

Meanwhile at St Albans Bowling Club, formed in Clarence Park in 1903 – the year of the EBA's formation – it was agreed to lay a crown green, apparently at the behest of a northern member.

But then another member said that he had heard talk of a new way of playing. So, a crown green was laid, but with flower pots arranged to mark out rinks. Only in 1921 was the green finally levelled and squared off, thereby bringing St Albans in line with other EBA clubs in Hertfordshire.

In Cornwall too, when Helston Bowling Club – first incarnated in 1760 – was revived in 1905, according to the *Cornishman* newspaper in 1908, both the 'Scottish' and 'English' versions of bowls were played.

Perhaps the oddest aspect of how the 'Scotch game' caught on south of the border is that its spread was partly precipitated by cricketers, and, even more oddly, by cricketers not from England but from Australia...

▶ Seen in action for England in 1907 at the **West End Bowling Club** in **Newcastle-upon-Tyne** is the unmistakable figure of **Dr William Gilbert Grace** (1848-1915).

Tall, portly and famously hirsute Grace towered over English bowls in a manner that no man had ever done before, with the possible exception only of Sir Francis Drake.

For modern readers it is hard to overstate Grace's impact on the bowling world. After a dazzling career as a cricketing all rounder, he played his final Test match for England in June 1899, at the age of 51. He was still at that stage a huge celebrity, if one tainted by incidents of gamesmanship and a sense of his own worth, especially at the box office. He also remained fiercely competitive.

And so when the management of the Crystal Palace Company offered him the chance to oversee the formation of the London County Cricket Club at their ground in Sydenham – a few hundred yards from the actual Palace, and next door to their new stadium, which had recently become the venue for FA Cup Finals – Grace grabbed the chance (and the lucrative salary).

Ultimately the cricket club was no great success. By then Surrey and Middlesex were too well set up for any new London-wide club to succeed. But in any case Grace had developed another passion.

Among the Australian party touring England in 1899 was Major BJ Wardill, the Liverpool-born secretary of the Melbourne Cricket Club, and also a member of the Melbourne Bowling Club. The latter, Australia's oldest bowling club, had been formed by a Scotsman John Campbell in 1864, and had always played to Mitchell's rules. (Thus Australia adopted the 'Scotch game' long before the English.)

It was Wardill who suggested to a senior English bowler, SE Yelland from Hove, that their two nations should play each other in bowls as well as in cricket.

This led to the formation of the Imperial Bowling Association (IBA); an organisation originally intended not for governance but simply to arrange international matches.

Grace, of course, turned out to be rather good at bowls (if not as good as he had been at cricket, not that anyone would have dared to suggest as much), and in 1901 persuaded the management at Crystal Palace to convert tennis courts by the cricket ground into a bowling green. There he set up the **London County Bowling Club**, and in 1901 welcomed the first touring party of Australian bowlers.

But there was a problem. The IBA wanted to adopt the rules of the Scottish Bowling Association. Yet instead of welcoming this the SBA refused, claiming that the rules were its copyright.

Grace sidestepped this obstacle by simply enrolling London County as members of the SBA.

But a greater problem was that in May 1903 Grace went over the heads of the IBA and other existing associations by writing to 600 clubs in all parts of the country inviting them to join a new body he and others intended to form, the English Bowling Association.

The EBA came into being at a meeting of eight men in the cricket pavilion at Crystal Palace on June 8 1903. The following month Grace then played in a series of England v. Scotland matches at Crystal Palace and South London BC.

At a meeting in London, the next month, involving the EBA, IBA, the London & Southern Counties Association and the Midland Counties, the actions of Grace and

the EBA were called into question, precipitating what the *Edinburgh Evening News* described, perhaps with a certain *schadenfreude,* as 'The English Bowling Crisis'.

But it was a temporary impasse. Faced with an invitation from the great man himself, 44 clubs joined the EBA in its first year, among them all members of the London & Southern Counties association, including Southampton and Reading (whose rules of 1899 show that they were already bowling in rinks). Six of the clubs were in Carlisle. Another was the West End BC in Newcastle. Both cities were of course close enough to Scotland to align themselves with the new order without hesitation.

Also joining up were clubs in Bristol, where Grace had started his cricketing career for Gloucestershire.

Finally the IBA capitulated too, in 1905. Grace had prevailed.

A number of artefacts from this period survive. The photograph

above is one of several of its ilk, each cherished by whichever club Grace happened to visit. Below is one of his woods, mounted and preserved at the headquarters of Bowls England in Leamington.

There, also, are the EBA's original minutes, each adorned by Grace's familiar signature. Thus as club after club joined the cause, and in turn levelled their greens, Grace's inveterate letter-writing may be said to have proved that his pen did indeed turn out to be mightier than the sward.

▶ On display in the clubhouse of the North London Bowling Club in Highgate, this photograph, taken at Crystal Palace in July 1903, shows the first official **England bowling team**, with **WG Grace**, centre stage as always.

Grace, of course, played as skip, a position he would occupy until finally bowing out of the international scene in 1908. But what is also noteworthy is that in the English team, and in both the Welsh and Irish teams which also competed at Crystal Palace, there were numerous Scots.

Now it is true that Scots were active at clubs all over Britain. But the fact that they turned out for the other home nations suggests that in those early years there was still a dearth of home-grown players with experience of the Scottish rules.

Grace's legacy is immense. But not at Crystal Palace. The London County BC fizzled out in 1914, and of the green no trace remains. Also, the pavilion in which the EBA first met was demolished in the 1950s, (although the cricket pitch is still an open space). But on nearby Anerley Road, the Crystal Palace Indoor Bowling Club plays on. Formed by Grace in 1905, inside one of the Palace galleries, it is the oldest indoor club in Britain. It was not the first however. The first was, almost inevitably, in Scotland, as we will discover in Chapter Ten.

ENGLISH TEAM.
Captain W. G. Grace

Grace's competitive streak was not always appreciated. At Victoria BC in Weston-super-Mare in 1903 his 'skittling' tactics were said to have caused much unease amongst his hosts. Formed in 1900, as stated on its pavilion (*right*) – itself built in 1913 – the Victoria club was a strong advocate of flat green rules, and since 1914 has been home to the Somerset Bowling Association.

◄ After the EBA, the Irish Bowling Association was next to form, in January 1904, followed in May by the **Welsh Bowling Association**, whose founding members included a club with a strong Scottish connection. This is the **Mackintosh Institute** in **Cardiff**. Its distinctive clubhouse, built between 1780 and the 1830s, was once known as Roath Castle and was home to the Richards family, one of whose number, Harriet, married Alfred Mackintosh in the 1870s.

His influence is evident in the surrounding streets, among them Angus Street and Inverness Place.

In 1891 Mackintosh gifted the house and grounds for the benefit of the local people, who decided to lay a green and tennis courts.

In 1986 the Estate trustees tried to sell the site but, after a spirited campaign, the membership combined to buy the freehold for £170,000. Since then the Institute has added a community centre and an indoor bowling rink.

Another county quick to embrace the Scottish game was Sussex.

In **Hastings**, members of the **Alexandra Park BC** first bowled on public lawns in the park in 1893, until the council laid the green seen here (*left*) in 1907. The pavilion is more recent, built in 1988 after an arson attack destroyed the original.

Also based on the green is **Clive Vale BC**, formed in 1900.

▶ Such was the spread of the 'Scotch game' in the early 20th century that the bowling green that we now believe to be one of the oldest in Britain, if not *the* oldest, became one of hundreds in England and Wales to be levelled, thereby ending centuries of tradition.

This, in 1908, is the **Falcon Bowling Club** in **Painswick**, **Gloucestershire**, a green that may date back to the 1550s (*see page 76*). As can be seen, a substantial amount of earth had to be dug in order to level and square off the green, although the club insisted on first cutting away the old turf so that it could be relaid afterwards.

Gloucestershire was a county that enjoyed some contacts with crown green bowlers in the north. Even as late as 1907, when the British Crown Green Bowling Association was formed, there was a suggestion that the county might compete in its Crosfield Cup.

They did not, no doubt owing to the influence that WG Grace exerted in Bristol and the south of the county. The city of Worcester was similarly borderline. In 1907 all its clubs had crown greens. By 1939 they had all been levelled.

Some clubs compromised. At Speenhamland in Newbury, where the green was levelled in 1910, it was agreed members could still play 'corner to corner' if they wished, 'in keeping with local tradition'.

For manufacturers of green keeping equipment the growth of bowls represented good business. Greenkeepers too were grateful for the increased sophistication of lawn mowers. Advertising in 1884 (*right*), the aptly named Green's of Leeds and Southwark were among the leading companies, along with Ransome's of Ipswich and Shanks of Arbroath.

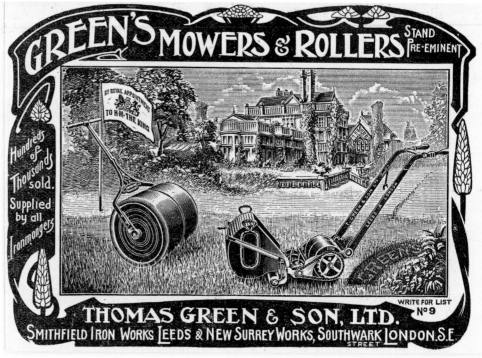

GREEN'S MOWERS & ROLLERS STAND PRE-EMINENT

Hundreds of Thousands sold. Supplied by all Ironmongers

BY ROYAL APPOINTMENT TO H.M. THE KING

WRITE FOR LIST No 9

THOMAS GREEN & SON, LTD.

SMITHFIELD IRON WORKS LEEDS & NEW SURREY WORKS, SOUTHWARK STREET LONDON.S.E.

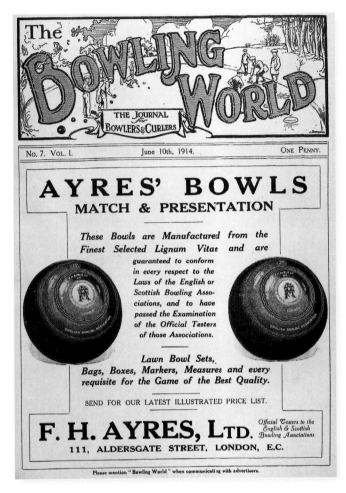

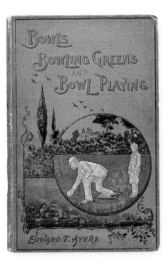

CT Car Works v Salford Municipal Guild, Balloon Co-op v Manchester Postal Clerks, and Leigh Railway v Warrington Cemetery. Other clubs represented the police, hospitals, breweries and newspapers. We also learn that Ladies' Days had become popular in Scotland. They afforded 'excellent opportunities for a mild flirtation in the mixed rinks'.

As can be seen from the cover, *The Bowling World* had set out to report on curling. But alas for WA Sims, the weekly managed only nine editions before it ceased publication, in June 1914, long before the curling season.

A few weeks later the Great War erupted, and not until 1933 would another bowls periodical appear.

bye-laws not from Scotland but from the crown green Lancashire & Cheshire Association. As was later the case in Gloucestershire (noted opposite), Norfolk & Suffolk even came close to playing inter-county matches in the north west.

Ayers describes a time when bowling in Norfolk was only slightly different from crown green. He refers to 'thumb' and 'finger' pegs and observed that 'some jacks are biased, but uselessly, I think'.

He did not think much of the 'Scotch game'. Level greens, he wrote, tended to 'sameness (not to say tameness) of play', and while playing 'all over the shop' rather than in rinks risked occasional collisions, this was more than compensated by the 'varieties of play' required when faced by 'perpetual changes of ground'.

After 1903 and the formation of the EBA a rush of books appeared.

Of these, *All About Bowls* by George Burrows (published 1915) is the best informed. This was because Burrows, originally based in the north west, had reported on many of the big money matches in the crown green world, but then saw the other side of the new order when he moved to London and became active in the administration of the English Bowling Association.

At least two of the investors behind *The Bowling World* had close links with the EBA. Its editor, WA Sims, was a former president, while the current president, John Gillespie, was one of the directors.

Despite this the journal did its best to cover crown green affairs as well as those of flat green.

There is much of interest to historians in *The Bowling World*.

The fixtures alone tell us just how many types of institutions and organisations had set up clubs.

Lancashire's fixtures included

▲ Launched in April 1914, *The Bowling World* was the sport's first dedicated periodical, but by no means the first publication devoted to the subject. In fact, following on from William Mitchell's *Manual* in 1864, some 20 books on bowls are known to have appeared before the First World War.

Most offered practical guidance. For example in 1868 *Routledge's Handbook of Quoits and Bowls* repeated Mitchell's rules and so helped sow the seeds for rink bowls in London and the south.

It was written by the MP and Old Harrovian, Douglas Straight, under the pen-name of Sydney Daryl.

More informative is *Bowls, Bowling Greens and Bowl Playing*, written by **Edward T Ayers**, and published in 1894 (*above right*).

Living in Yarmouth, Ayers viewed bowls from the perspective of East Anglia, a region then as now characterised by quirks such as the 'roving cot' (*see page 178*).

Also, Ayers had been a founder in 1894 of the Norfolk & Suffolk Bowling Association. This took its

Sunderland from Mowbray Park.

RELIABLE SERIES. K 1806

▲ Park greens form an important part of bowling's heritage. But they are also currently under the greatest threat, both from falling numbers of users and from swingeing cuts in local authority spending (the two often being closely related).

One of the largest concentrations of park greens in England is in the north east. As reported in *Played in Tyne and Wear* (*see Links*) of 112 greens in the area in 2010, all but ten were in parks. The oldest is at Brandling Park, Newcastle, laid in 1882. A year later followed the green above in **Mowbray Park, Sunderland** (which itself had been created in 1857). Seen beyond the pavilion, which is still extant, is the glass roof of the Winter Gardens, opened in 1879 and modelled on the Crystal Palace in London.

The importance of parks in the north east is highlighted by the fact that it was four park based clubs that set up the Northumberland & Durham Bowling Association in 1892. That same year in Glasgow, the Parks Superintendent Duncan McLellan was asked by the council to draw up a report on the usage of park greens in other cities. The council had considered park greens in 1869, only to dismiss the idea owing to the sheer number of private clubs already in operation.

McLellan visited 14 towns and cities across Scotland and the north of England, Newcastle included. In Edinburgh he found that the six park greens were used by 600-700 bowlers weekly, each yielding £50 per annum. He noted that whereas Salford charged 1d per hour per

Another example of string being used to mark out rinks is at Gladstone Park in Dollis Hill, London (*right*), where the park opened in 1901, followed by the green in 1908. It is sobering to note that although all three greens illustrated on this page remain, and at Swansea the pavilion was rebuilt on its centenary in 2007, at none is there still an active bowling club.

player, Manchester charged 2d. But overall, McLellan reported, park greens did cover their costs.

Even so it would be another decade before Glasgow laid its first greens, at Glasgow Green in 1903 and at Kelvingrove in 1905. By 1933 there would be 67 in the city, a total matched only by Manchester.

South Wales is another area with a tradition of park greens. The first was at Sophia Gardens, Cardiff, in 1878. But as Darryl Leeworthy has noted (*see Links*), this was in effect a private green reserved for Cardiff Bowling Club. Initially the Welsh Bowling Association would admit only private clubs. But in 1906

it relented, accepting park based clubs 'provided their greens were fit and proper'.

In **Swansea** the first park green to be laid was in **Brynmill Park**.

Now listed Grade II, the park had opened in 1878, with the green following in 1907. Two clubs were based there, Brynmill and St Gabriel's, and as seen above, strings were used to mark out rinks. This was at a time when in flat green bowls the jack could be sent anywhere within the rink, up to one yard from the edge.

In 1928 the EBA specified that jacks had to be centred in the rink, a rule that remains in force today.

Even amongst bowlers there is confusion as to which type of bowls dominates in which part of England.

This is one of two flat greens at **Fitz Park** in **Keswick**, **Cumbria**, a town that marks the unofficial boundary between flat green territory, to the north, and crown green territory, to the south (*as shown on the map on page 9*).

Both greens at Fitz Park were laid when the park opened in 1880, but unusually, they were located in different areas rather than side by side. This one, opposite Keswick Museum is reserved for **Keswick Bowling Club**, formed in 1882 and formerly called Fitz Park No 1 Club.

Parts of the pavilion are also thought to date back to 1882.

A hundred yards or so south across the park, on the banks of the River Greta, is the public green, known originally as the 'clog' or 'penny' green, for the use of those unable to afford annual subscriptions or who simply wished to 'pay and play'.

A club called Greta Side also played on this, before it merged with its neighbours in 1972. This has left the lower green for casual players and day trippers, who now pay £3.50 rather than a penny.

Sixty miles south in Lancashire, the **Fulwood Conservative Club** in **Preston**, (*left*) bears a distinctly Scottish baronial style, but is a bastion of crown green. Opened in 1899, it was designed by Myres, Yeevers & Myres, who also laid out the adjoining Freehold Park Estate.

Together with surviving elements of the nearby Fulwood Barracks and other Victorian buildings, the bowls club now falls within the Fulwood Conservation Area. Being a social as well as a bowls club helps too. Fulwood has 500 members and runs no fewer than 20 teams on its two adjoining crown greens.

▶ Bowling greens started to appear in pleasure gardens and spas in the late 17th century, and at **seaside resorts** in the 19th century. In Margate there was one laid at the Tivoli Gardens in c.1830. But it was in the early 20th century that the notion of public greens laid primarily for holidaymakers really took off, invariably on sites by, or overlooking, the seafront.

Seen here in 1913, this is **Clarence Gardens**, overlooking the **North Bay** at **Scarborough**, with the Clarence Hotel (now the Clifton), in the distance. Behind the rise to the left lies the splendid North Marine ground of Scarborough Cricket Club, opened in 1863 and home since 1876 of the famous annual cricket festival. During the Edwardian era the model of this festival was to be adopted in the world of bowls, with coastal resorts vying with each other to organise week long tournaments designed to attract bowlers on their annual holidays.

Bournemouth led the way in 1909, in Meyrick Park, followed in 1911 by Hastings, at the Queen's Road Cricket Ground (where a quoits competition was held too), and the Isle of Man, where the now famous crown green festival started as part of that year's Coronation and Jubilee Carnival in Douglas.

Clearly the scene here at Scarborough is rather more relaxed, with women joining men on the

green, apparently playing 'all over the shop' rather than in rinks.

Almost certainly this was a crown green. For, as can be seen on the map on page 9, the coastal towns of the North Riding, from Bridlington via Scarborough up to Whitby, stand out in an area otherwise dominated by flat green clubs. This, despite being more than 50 miles from the nearest crown green territory around Harrogate, is a result of the area's desire to attract crown green bowlers from all points west on holiday.

Today the green seen above is an area of lawns, while the focus of bowling in the resort now lies just beyond the Clifton Hotel, at the Scarborough Bowls Centre. Built in 1989 with both indoor and outdoor facilities, this is the venue for the Gambart Baines tournament, one of the oldest crown green open events, first held in 1919 following the gift of a magnificent silver trophy by the owner of the town's waxworks.

Bowling Ground & Pier Pavilion, Southport.

▲ **Southport** is among several west coast resorts favoured by crown green bowlers from Liverpool, Wigan and Preston. These greens were in **King's Gardens**, opened by George V in 1913 and running parallel with the town's celebrated Lord Street. In the background lies Southport Pier.

Today the greens are lawns and a play area, but at the other end of King's Gardens lie two more greens

which, since 1937, have been home to Southport BC, one of only five flat green clubs in Lancashire.

Then across the road, in Victoria Park, apart from the lawns of the Southport and Birkdale Croquet Club, are the three greens of Victoria Park BC (formed 1899).

Every August these host an open tournament staged in conjunction with the Southport Flower Show.

▲ While it is true that during the Edwardian era women made great strides in their efforts to participate more fully in sport – the 1908 Olympics marked a particular watershed – it is unlikely that the group posing here in c.1900-05 were members of a club. Especially since the green belonged to a pub, the **Royal Oak** in **Eccleshall, Staffordshire** (which survives, unlike the green, now a car park).

Instead, the occasion was almost certainly a Ladies Day, such as that held in 1908 at Southey in Wimbledon (a club formed in 1886 and still going today).

As described by George Burrows in *All About Bowls*, the 'prizes were costly and numerous, for local tradesmen as well as clubmen gave liberally'. Ladies Day was 'a red-letter day: an event for rolling out the red carpet, for hoisting gay flags and bunting and for the presence of a chorus of throaty tenors and lusty baritones who sang their bravest to the accompaniment of a little boy pianist.'

Not all women were content with such indulgences however.

At a time when the Suffragettes were starting to adopt militant tactics, which included attacking golf clubs, the numbers of women in archery, tennis, swimming, gymnastics and, ironically, golf, rose to new levels before 1914.

As for bowls, hardly a progressive sport, the prevailing male attitude was summed up by the Old Harrovian, Sidney Daryl, in his 1868 *Handbook of Quoits and Bowls*. The latter sport, he wrote, 'is a very nice game for ladies, and nothing can be more picturesque than to see the dear creatures – of course, in the most elegant and bewitching costumes – doing their best to cut Cousin Tom, Dick or Harry out of his advantageously near position to the jack! Such laughing and chaffing, such bright eyes and rosy cheeks, such panting and puffing when their turn is over!'

To such men, the idea of women playing bowls competitively was therefore quite shocking.

Among the first women to bowl in a regular set up were those in West Bridgford, Nottinghamshire (in 1904), Hook and Southborough, Surrey (in 1905), and in Oakham, Leicestershire, and Kingston-upon-Thames, Surrey (in 1910).

Women also started bowling at Birchfield Park, Birmingham, at Mandley Park, Salford, at Gorse Hill, Stretford, at Levenshulme, Manchester and in various parks in Sheffield. In 1906 the London County Council reserved one rink on each of its greens solely for women.

Make no mistake. Deep prejudice still ruled out women at most clubs.

But the advances of the 1900s were at least a start, or rather, a re-start. For before Victorian sensibilities kicked in, women were often recorded bowling. Mrs Pepys enjoyed bowls in the 17th century, while in May 1532 Anne Boleyn lost the considerable sum of £12 7s 6d after a bowls match against the Sergeant of the Cellar.

Mixed bowling? Even in 1914 that seemed like a step too far.

From the collection of Geoff Barnett, this card is one of a 1913 series on women in sport, issued in packs of Wills 'Scissors' cigarettes, a brand widely exported to British servicemen in India and the Far East. If meant to titillate it appears modest enough. Indeed the dress was actually quite progressive. For as George Burrows wrote in 1915, 'Elegant as were the flowing skirts and floral or feathered hats of the women who started the game in 1908, they were pre-eminently unsuitable for serious bowls, and the regulation costume has everything to recommend it.'

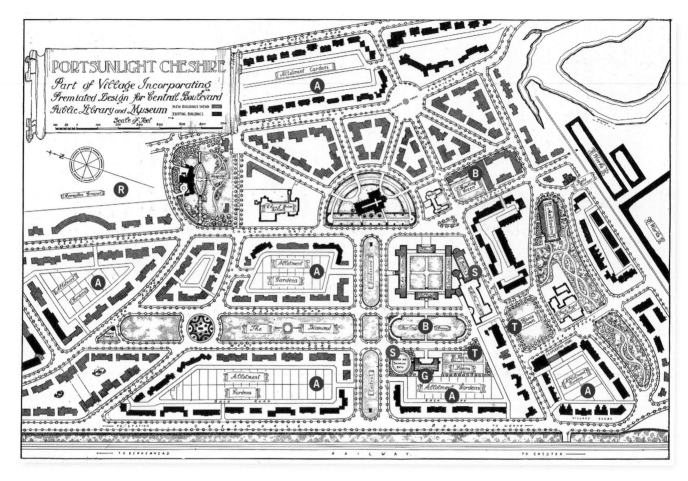

▲ As the 19th century drew to an end after decades of concentrated urbanisation and industrialisation, the Garden City movement emerged under the influence of Ebenezer Howard, with bold new ideas of how to plan communities around open spaces and sports facilities.

Although not directly part of that movement, landscape architect and town planner **Thomas Mawson** (1861-1933) embraced many of its ideas, as seen here in his plans drawn up in 1906 for William Lever, owner of the soap making works at **Port Sunlight** on the **Wirral**.

Born into a poor family in Scorton, Lancashire, Mawson enjoyed his most successful working relationships with other self made men like Lever, and well understood the importance of providing working people with good housing and plenty of access to fresh air.

Thus his plans for Port Sunlight comprised six sites for allotments (marked **A**), two for swimming, indoors and outdoors (**S**), two for tennis (**T**), a large recreation ground (**R**) and a gymnasium (**G**).

Mawson also provided for three bowling greens on two sites (**B**).

Mawson's trademark was the blending of two of the most dominant landscape design trends of the previous two hundred years, that is of formality and naturalism. Strongly influenced by the Arts and Crafts movement, he set out to balance beauty with utility.

It was a vision into which bowling greens fitted perfectly; an ancient game rooted in English culture and romance, yet in a progressive sense, suited to both genders and all ages. In addition, even when not in use, a green added a softnesss to its environs.

In this respect it is significant that his preferred description for the new field of town planning was 'Civic Art', the title he chose for his celebrated book on the subject.

All told Mawson was involved in the layout of over 20 parks, starting in the 1890s in the Potteries at Hanley and Burslem (both now listed Grade II*), where he made oval bowling greens the centrepiece of each plan. Later designs by his firm included Broomfield Park in Southgate, London (1902), Stanley Park, Blackpool (1922) and Central Park, Plymouth (1931).

▲ Before he took on commissions for public parks and town planning, **Thomas Mawson** established his reputation as a garden designer for wealthy private clients.

At a time when sport was once again considered fashionable in country house circles, croquet lawns and tennis courts became especially popular, often with a pavilion or teahouse alongside, just as in the days of William Talman, Stephen Switzer and Charles Bridgeman, two centuries earlier.

Seen above is the Grade II* listed pavilion designed as part of an overall scheme for a lawyer,

William Lethbridge, at **Wood House**, **South Tawton** in **Devon** between 1899 and 1905.

Working with Dan Gibson, who designed the Arts and Crafts house, Mawson located a croquet lawn to the immediate south of the house, with this loggia-style pavilion to the west, overlooking tennis courts and a bowling green edged by yew hedges. The pavilion is faced in granite sourced from nearby Dartmoor, and incorporates changing rooms on its ground floor, with a viewing terrace above accessed by steps leading up from the arched openings at each end.

The balustrade matches that of the house (which itself is listed Grade I, and in 2015 was being converted into a spa and medical centre).

At the same time Mawson worked on Wood House, he was commissioned to design gardens at **Foots Cray Place**, in **Sidcup**, **Kent** for Samuel Waring. Waring was a partner in Waring & Gillow, whose furniture factory was in Lancaster, where Mawson's office was based.

Extending to some 1,000 acres, the Foots Cray estate had already undergone two major redesigns. In 1754 it had been laid out in formal style around a Palladian villa. These gardens had then been cleared by 'Capability' Brown in 1781 in favour of a 'natural' landscape.

Mawson, again, opted for a mixture of the two approaches, formality near the house giving way to wildness on the perimeter.

At its core, on a rise, stood the imposing villa, with grand steps leading down to two terraced lawns, one for tennis, one for croquet. On Mawson's original plans drawn up in 1901 there was no bowling green, but by 1904 one existed; long, thin and lined by hedges, just like the alleys of the 17th century.

And at its southern end stood an enchanting pavilion (*above right*).

Listed Grade II, this was designed by Robert Atkinson (who later joined Mawson's firm), and completed c.1903.

A summer evening on the crown green at Port Sunlight, with the red brick and terracotta houses of Cross Street behind. On the original plans Mawson allocated this space for tennis (marked furthest on the right of the plan opposite). But although this and other elements were not implemented to the letter, the essential layout survives and remains a beacon of its time.

The upper octagonal storey is timber framed, clad with weatherboarding. Its domed roof is tiled and its windows, facing onto the green, are leaded. The upper room also retains much of its original timber panelling and plastered domed ceiling.

But alas this pavilion (now a private residence), the bowling green (now its back garden), some terracing, walls and elements of the stable block, are all that is left of Foots Cray. In 1949 the house burnt down and since then most of the landscaping has been lost or absorbed within the surrounding public park and open spaces.

A rare treasure then, and a reminder of how the monied classes once again, if only briefly, embraced bowls in the Edwardian period.

▶ Its clarity suggests that this is a photograph, but actually it is a watercolour and pencil drawing, signed by H & W Greaves, meaning the brothers **Henry** and **Walter Greaves**, and dated on the back August 9 1902, the day of Edward VII's coronation.

It depicts the rear of the **Six Bells** on **King's Road** in **Chelsea**, the last pub in central London to have a bowling green.

A narrow green it was too, which, taking into consideration the positions of the bowlers on each side of the picture, leads us to speculate that the bowls played there was 'corner to corner'.

That is, exactly as played today on the equally narrow green at the Sun Inn in Barnes, which is now the only pub green in the whole of Greater London (*see page 102*).

But whether this 'corner to corner' style was played only in two venues, or was a London phenomenon, or was found elsewhere remains unknown. As does the significance of the glass display case, possibly a fish tank, positioned on four table legs in the centre of the picture.

This being Chelsea, all manner of tales about the Six Bells abound; that bowls was played here in 1568, that Charles II was a regular, and that at one point the garden ran all the way down to the river.

None of them is at all likely.

Other, rather more reliable tales tell of the writers and artists who frequented the pub, such as Shelley, Carlyle, Turner, Augustus John and the American James Whistler, who taught Walter and Henry Greaves how to draw after renting boats from the Greaves' family boatyard on the Thames.

(The friendship did not end happily, and Walter died a pauper, but that is another story.)

As for the green, there was certainly a garden at the pub in the 18th century, known for its grape vines and hollow-stemmed mulberry tree. It is also recorded that a bowls club formed there in 1878, was revived in 1881, and that annual subscriptions were five shillings.

In June 1895, Philip Norman, one of the editors of the *Survey of London*, reported, 'Seeing a strip of grass which attracted my attention I entered and found a bowling green with arbours or little summer-houses, in the style of an old fashioned tea garden'.

Readers may wish to compare these arbours with those depicted at the Hand and Glove on page 90.

Norman continued, 'Here a bowling club was in full swing. It should number, according to the rules, 60 members, but this year there are 65. By the look of those who were playing they seem to be of the tradesman class, "fat and scant of breath". New churchwarden pipes are fashionable there.'

In 1900 the *Pall Mall Gazette* reported that the pub 'had known only two hosts in a hundred years'.

At the time that was written the whole front of the building was in the process of being rebuilt to designs by the pub architects GR Crickmay & Son.

Not that this is obvious from the Greaves' drawing. But the redesign is quite evident from the King's Road, and is the main reason the pub is listed Grade II. Bedecked in carved devils and black and white Tudoresque detailing, it was described in *Licensing World* in 1914 as a prototype of the newly fashionable 'Mock Antique Tavern'.

After the 1950s the pub went through a number of reinventions, as a jazz venue, an American restaurant, and most recently in 2015 as the Ivy Chelsea Garden Restaurant. Bowling was last recorded there in 1969, but if you eat there today you can still stand on this spot, and, amid all the tables, umbrellas and greenery, look back towards the building and get a real sense of what it must have been like, playing 'corner to corner' in this magical secret garden.

As noted at Hadley Heath, in 2015 there were 34 pubs bearing the name Bowling Green, of which only five still have greens. This is one of them, at Scotforth, on the A6 south of Lancaster. The green is small, rectangular and enclosed by a drystone wall, between a supermarket and a petrol station. The earliest reference to there being a green on the site is from the *Lancaster Gazette* of August 1 1807, when the sale of the Hazlerigg Estate was advertised to be at John Bagott's house, 'the sign of the Bowling Green'. On which note, eagle eyed readers studying the pub sign above might be wondering. Here, clearly is a flat green player, the large mat and white clothing being the obvious clues. Yet this is most definitely crown green territory.

▲ The arbours at **The Stile Inn** on **Harrow Road**, **Wolverhampton**, may be less ornate than those at the Six Bells, but the spirit of pub bowling lives on here, as it has since around 1890.

This is a crown green, but with a twist, for the green at The Stile is T-shaped (see page 23). Thus 'corner to corner' is fine, but not bowling 'around the corner' in such a way that an opponent cannot use opposite bias to reach the jack.

Note that the building seen here is an old stable, with the hay loft directly above the open door hatch. This dates from when the pub, which is locally listed, opened originally in 1860.

Running a pub green has never been easy. When the Bowling Green Hotel at Chapel Field in Norwich, was offered for let in 1848, a notice in the *Norfolk Chronicle* promised

that 'Subscriptions to the Bowling Green, &c., will pay the Rent and Taxes.' But that '&c' included regular events staged on the green, such as public sales.

By the end of the century such usage was taboo, which made the life of landlords even tougher, as ET Ayers noted in his book of 1894 (see *Links*). The proprietor of a green in Great Yarmouth, he wrote, found that the annual subscriptions paid by its 'many skilful players' had proved 'altogether inadequate to meet the heavy expense which keeping a green in order necessarily entails, unless the players spend unduly in "drinks", which is far from being the case... Under these circumstances it is not to be wondered at that the proprietor turned it to building purposes.'

At another pub with a green, reported Ayers, a sign had gone up

stating, 'Gentlemen are expected to spend sixpence each evening'.

Back at The Stile, such concerns can never be dismissed. And yet here is a classic local in a working class district where there are still enough pub greens in the area for there to be a South Staffordshire Licensed Victuallers' Bowling League... with two divisions.

All told The Stile puts up nine teams in seven different leagues.

Should you be in the vicinity, look out also for the pub greens at the Summerhouse and the Newhampton, but not at the Molineux Hotel, up the road, for reasons explained overleaf.

And if calling at The Stile, check out what greenkeeper Derek Cox is growing in beds around the green.

A bowler at the pub since 1955, his onions and green beans are apparently legendary.

▶ One business model of sport and recreational provision that did not endure beyond the Victorian era was the privately run pleasure ground.

Seen in 1920, up the road from The Stile Inn, these are the **Molineux Grounds**, **Wolverhampton**, viewed from the upper floor of the Molineux Hotel, originally a house dating from c.1720. In 1860 the house became a hotel and its grounds were opened to the paying public. In 1869 they hosted the South Staffordshire Industrial and Fine Arts Exhibition. But as happened at all Victorian pleasure grounds, the venture struggled and the proprietors increasingly turned to sport to bring in extra revenue. (It was the same at the Crystal Palace before it was transferred into public ownership in 1913.)

Where there had been terraced gardens at Molineux, a skating rink was created, later turned into the bowling green seen here. Where there had been an ornamental lake, tracks for cycling and athletics were laid. But these too were not enough, and in 1889 Wolverhampton Wanderers moved in, eventually building a bespoke football ground on the site from 1925 onwards.

The hotel and bowling green lived on as a separate entity. The green in particular became one of the leading venues in Staffordshire, with Jesse Gough its star player.

But in 1969 it was turned into a car park, and ten years later the hotel closed. Since listed Grade II*, it is now home to the city archives.

Similar tales emerge elsewhere.

In Birmingham, the Aston Lower Grounds, opened in 1865, comprised gardens, a menagerie, an aquarium, a concert hall and boating lake, plus facilities for cricket, athletics, skating and later cycling, before it went bankrupt and was taken over by Aston Villa

in 1897. Apart from a few Victorian buildings that survived into the 1970s, the only other survivors were two bowling greens.

One, behind the Holte Hotel (now owned by the football club), is a car park. The other, built over in 1966 but once popular with Villa players, is where there is a now a concourse featuring a statue of William McGregor, the Scottish founder of the Football League. (It is not known if he bowled, but he certainly enjoyed curling.)

On a smaller scale, the Grade II listed **Victoria Park Hotel** on **Victoria Road**, **Barrow in Furness**, built in 1900, offered tennis courts to the north, and a bowling green to the south, as seen on the right in the early 1930s. The courts have since been built over. The green, unsurprisingly, is now a car park.

Note how perfectly bowling greens and tennis courts slotted into the grid of Victorian and Edwardian town planning. Just the right size, and right on people's doorsteps.

▶ One key element of the *Played in Britain* series has been the study of 'sporting clusters', of which this one in **Southampton**, viewed in 1951, is a perfect example. Centred on **Northlands Road** (seen snaking south on the right), here is a cluster that, like so many, is grouped around a cricket ground.

To the left is **The Stadium** at **Banister Court**, opened in 1928 for those two great, but relatively transient crazes imported from the USA and Australia, greyhound and speedway racing. The stadium also staged stock car racing and boxing before it was redeveloped as housing in 1963. Charles Knott Gardens on the site is named after the stadium's original promoter.

Behind the stadium Knott's **ice rink** (in operation 1931-40 and 1952-88) and a later **bowling alley**, also made way for houses.

At the end of Northlands Road stands **The Dell**, from 1899-2001 the home of **Southampton FC**, now flats on Archers Road. Just visible at the far, Milton Road end of The Dell are its once famous 'Chocolate Boxes', three odd terraces on stilts.

However the main focus, in the foreground, is the ground of **Hampshire County Cricket Club**, in use from 1885-2000 (before the club moved to the Rose Bowl in Eastleigh). This much loved ground is now also housing.

Note two bowling greens on the right side of Northlands Road.

These belonged to **Banister Park BC**, formed in 1906, and hosted a Home International series in 1927. After the club relocated in 1989, also to Eastleigh, housing on Edwin Jones Close was built on the site.

So, five sporting venues, all built over by housing between 1963 and 2001, which leaves just two.

Both are on Northlands Road, abutting the top of the cricket

ground. On the left are the grass courts of **South Hants Tennis Club**, formed in 1878 and at Northlands Road since 1890, while next door is the **County Bowling Club**.

A founder member of both the London & Southern Counties Bowling Association and the EBA, its green opened in 1889 and was sometimes called the Upper Green, to distinguish it from the Old, or Lower Green, down by the docks (*see page 70*). One of its founders was the aforementioned Edwin Jones, a department store owner.

Victorian and Edwardian bowling greens were often next to cricket grounds; at Northampton County Cricket Ground, for example, where bowls, cricket and football all shared a site until the 1990s.

Now only a few remain, such as at Ashbrooke (Sunderland) and Aigburth (Liverpool).

One reason for the link is that, as WG Grace found, bowls is an ideal sport to take up in later life. Indeed a number of multi-sport clubs have been known to present a pair of woods to any cricketer whose knees have finally gone, if only to make extra sure that he remains a club member.

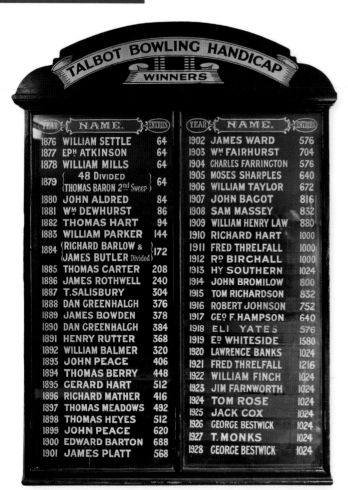

TALBOT BOWLING HANDICAP
WINNERS

YEAR	NAME.	ENTRIES
1876	WILLIAM SETTLE	64
1877	EPH ATKINSON	64
1878	WILLIAM MILLS	64
1879	48 DIVIDED (THOMAS BARON 2nd Sweep)	64
1880	JOHN ALDRED	84
1881	WM DEWHURST	86
1882	THOMAS HART	94
1883	WILLIAM PARKER	144
1884	RICHARD BARLOW & JAMES BUTLER Divided	172
1885	THOMAS CARTER	208
1886	JAMES ROTHWELL	240
1887	T.SALISBURY	304
1888	DAN GREENHALGH	376
1889	JAMES BOWDEN	378
1890	DAN GREENHALGH	384
1891	HENRY RUTTER	368
1892	WILLIAM BALMER	320
1893	JOHN PEACE	406
1894	THOMAS BERRY	448
1895	GERARD HART	512
1896	RICHARD MATHER	416
1897	THOMAS MEADOWS	492
1898	THOMAS HEYES	512
1899	JOHN PEACE	620
1900	EDWARD BARTON	688
1901	JAMES PLATT	568

YEAR	NAME.	ENTRIES
1902	JAMES WARD	576
1903	WM FAIRHURST	704
1904	CHARLES FARRINGTON	576
1905	MOSES SHARPLES	640
1906	WILLIAM TAYLOR	672
1907	JOHN BAGOT	816
1908	SAM MASSEY	832
1909	WILLIAM HENRY LAW	880
1910	RICHARD HART	1000
1911	FRED THRELFALL	1000
1912	RD BIRCHALL	1000
1913	HY SOUTHERN	1024
1914	JOHN BROMILOW	800
1915	TOM RICHARDSON	832
1916	ROBERT JOHNSON	752
1917	GEO F.HAMPSON	640
1918	ELI YATES	576
1919	ED WHITESIDE	1580
1920	LAWRENCE BANKS	1024
1921	FRED THRELFALL	1216
1922	WILLIAM FINCH	1024
1923	JIM FARNWORTH	1024
1924	TOM ROSE	1024
1925	JACK COX	1024
1926	GEORGE BESTWICK	1024
1927	T. MONKS	1024
1928	GEORGE BESTWICK	1024

Crowds of up to 2,000 could pack in to watch the Handicap at the Talbot Hotel, seen here in 1947.

◄ Although hundreds of crown green clubs have no links at all to pubs or breweries, there is no escaping the fact that the origins of the **British Crown Green Bowling Association** (BCGBA) and several of its foremost competitions are linked with licensed premises.

On display at the **Raikes Hall** pub on **Liverpool Road**, **Blackpool**, this is the honours board for the **Talbot Bowling Handicap**, the oldest 'open' tournament, not just in the crown green world but in the whole of British bowling.

It was initiated in 1873 by Robert Nickson, the landlord of the Talbot Hotel, also in Blackpool, where there had been a green since the pub opened in 1845. It could hardly have been better located. Across the road, opened in 1846, was Blackpool's first railway station (since rebuilt further up Talbot Road and renamed Blackpool North),

Joseph Fielding was the Talbot's first winner, taking home £5.

It must be emphasised again that at that time no-one used the term 'crown green'. As noted elsewhere, most bowling in Britain before the Scottish revolution was 'crown green', or at least not on level greens. As such it was only after the formation of the EBA in 1903

that those bowlers who did not sign up to the 'Scotch game' decided to organise themselves and adopt the name 'crown green'.

But it was about more than titles, biased jacks or types of green.

Where crown green bowlers differed from their counterparts elsewhere was that they attached no stigma to professionalism, to cash prizes, or to betting. The 'Blackpool Handicap', as the Talbot was originally known, was therefore only one of many such open tournaments whose roots went back deep into the 19th century.

Nevertheless, being in Blackpool, at a pub that was so easily reached, Nickson's tournament grew rapidly (even if, being held in late September it became known for being contested in gusty winds).

The honours board, which starts in the handicap's fourth year, shows how entry grew from 64 in 1876 to over a thousand after 1918. Young and old competed. Dan Greenhalgh, winner in 1888, was just 22.

As the numbers rose, so did the winnings. James Ward, an Oldham publican, won £50 in prize money in 1902, but was rumoured to have pocketed ten times that amount by backing himself to win.

In 1907 a rival handicap started up at the Waterloo, another Blackpool pub. That same year the BCGBA formed and set up its headquarters at the Gynn Hotel, near the North Shore Promenade.

In many ways Blackpool is still the spiritual home of crown green. But the Talbot, which stood on the corner of Topping Street, is no more. It was demolished in 1968 to be replaced by a multi-storey car park.

Hence the old honours board now resides at Raikes Hall, where the tournament has been held ever since. More on this and the Waterloo Handicap follows later.

Bowlers do seem to like the sea air. In flat green the earliest seaside tournaments were, as noted earlier, at Bournemouth in 1909 and Hastings in 1911.

In 1910 the BCGBA chose to stage its first **Merit Finals** in **Fleetwood**, six miles up the Fylde coast from Blackpool.

Seen here in July 2010 is the same event, staged at **Fleetwood Bowling Club** on the 100th anniversary. (Most know the tournament as the 'All England' – a title commonly used for competitions in the 19th century – despite the fact that some of the entrants are from North Wales.)

In 1910 the mostly northern spectators were said to have been shocked when the event was won by a 'southerner', 33 year old Enoch Peers, from Wednesfield in Staffordshire.

In 2010 the winner was Noel Burrows from Cheshire, a rare individual who has won honours in both crown green and flat green, and both outdoor and indoor.

Fleetwood and neighbouring Thornton Cleveleys is a real hot bed of bowling, with 19 clubs, one of which, the Strawberry Gardens Hotel BC, formed in 1848.

But they are not all pub based. Also in the area are clubs in various public parks, at a working men's institute, and attached to a cricket club.

Also attached to a cricket club – though the bowlers would say it is the other way round – is Spen Victoria in West Yorkshire. Formed at Cleckheaton Wesleyan Chapel in 1862, the cricket club set up the ground in 1865, adding the green (*left*) in 1894. Spen Victoria plays in the Mirfield League, probably the strongest in crown green, with 81 teams across eight divisions.

Case study

Blackburn Subscription Bowling Green Club

As its name suggests, the Blackburn Subscription Bowling Green Club has a venerable history. It is a history, moreover, that goes back to 1753. Why therefore does the club not feature in an earlier chapter? Firstly because the club's current home, its third, dates from 1869. Secondly, because it was in the Victorian period that the club's history became subject to close scrutiny by a local historian. This, it would appear, was the first time any historian had taken such a close interest in a bowling club. As such, his findings represent a watershed moment. However they also offer a valuable lesson to all historians, whatever their field.

On June 16 1888, Blackburn historian WA Abram began his usual slot in the *Blackburn Weekly Express* by stating, 'The Blackburn Subscription Bowling Green is, with the exceptions of the Parish Church and the Grammar School, the oldest foundation or institution still in existence in the town.'

'Its records, fortunately, have always been in the hands of faithful custodians, and have been carefully preserved.'

And so they remain, stored by Blackburn Library's Community History Department, having been handed over for safe keeping by a modern day local historian, and bowls club member, Ray Smith.

Note the date of Abram's article. This was just three weeks short of the 300th anniversary of the Spanish Armada. That is, 300 years after the period when bowling was starting to emerge as an integral part of British life.

In other words, the time was now ripe to consider the place of bowls in the nation's heritage.

Of course bowling clubs did not exist in Drake's era. They were a product of the 18th century. But as Abram wrote in 1888, even a club formed in the 18th century qualified as one of the three oldest institutions in a major town.

Earlier in *Bowled Over* we record the existence of a notice, dated May 4 1753, announcing the formation of the Lewes Castle Bowling Green Society (*see page* 60).

No other club's records predate this. But from the same records

that Abram cites in his article we are able to confirm that, by an extraordinary coincidence, the Blackburn Subscription Bowling Green Club also formed in 1753.

Kilmarnock claim to have formed earlier, in 1740, but as noted in the previous chapter, have no documentation to that effect.

Lewes and Blackburn Subs may therefore lay joint claim to being the oldest bowls clubs in Britain, and therefore the world, based on primary evidence.

On which note, as seen on page 92, Blackburn Subs own a shield on which its foundation date is given as 1749. Other sources have stated that the club was formed 'prior to 1749', while to muddy the waters further, Abram himself, in his exhaustive work, *A History of Blackburn*, published in 1877, stated that the club 'existed so long ago as 1734'. He adds, with authority, that 'the number of members in 1734 was 18'.

These contradictions offer a textbook lesson as to why historians insist that primary sources always take precedence over secondary sources.

Here is how the Blackburn tale appears to have unfolded.

Firstly, the club's first minutes make it absolutely clear that it was formed in 1753.

The first entry, seen opposite, states somewhat verbosely (as was the fashion for club secretaries): 'We whose names are hereunder written do hereby agree to all and every the within written Rules, and do hereby severally promise and

engage to stand to and perform the same, and do hereby also promise and agree that we will pay to John Sudell of Blackburn in the County of Lancaster Gentleman the Steward of the within mentioned Bowling Green, for the present year, the several sums of four Shillings, opposite our respective names, for the use of the said Green, being two Shillings each for the last year's Subscription, and two Shillings for the present year's Subscription, as witness our Hands this 17th day of May 1754.'

It then lists 19 subscribers who had paid up both for 1753 and 1754. (Abram may not have noticed a faded name at the foot of the page).

The club's green was, as Abram rightly stated, 'at the foot of the slope at Cicely Hole'. This was in fields near the town, roughly where the station is now, on land owned by John Feilden of Witton Hall. Feilden not only allowed the club to play there without charge, he even paid his subs.

The club president at the time of Abram's articles in 1888, Henry Backhouse, did surmise that this green might have been in use for a few years prior to 1753, but was in no doubt that the club itself was formed that year.

Why therefore did Abram write 1734 in his history of 1877?

Perhaps because he read the local newspapers, which also seemed confused about the club's origins. On May 19 1847, reporting on the club's relocation to a new green (after the railway swallowed up the original one), the *Blackburn Standard* described the club as having a list of subscribers dating from 1752.

This and other anomalies leads us to wonder if one or two pages might have been lost from the minute book when clearly it was rebound some time in the period between 1847 and 1888. For sure those early pages that do survive are delicate, with damaged edges and ink seeping through the paper (*as seen on the right*).

Then on March 11 1869 the *Blackburn Standard* reported on the club's next move, to its current green, this time stating that it had been formed in 1734.

This, note, was before Abram's opus was published in 1877 and may therefore have been the source of his error. Either that or when Abram was compiling the book he wrote 1734 by mistake, instead of 1754, or, just as likely his typesetters misread the date (a possible error encountered also at Barnes and Hereford). Certainly in all his later accounts Abram stuck to the formation date of 1753.

Finally a likely source for the claim 'Prior to 1749'.

This phrase also first appears in the *Blackburn Standard*, this time on December 18 1886. Reporting on a fund raising bazaar, the *Standard* reports speeches by local MP William Coddington (a subscriber to the club), and Henry Backhouse.

Presumably the expression 'prior to 1749' came from either man, or the reporter himself. That another date in the article is wrong (it cites 1746 instead of 1846) adds further to our suspicions.

All of which are finally settled by WA Abram in his aforementioned series of articles in 1888. 》

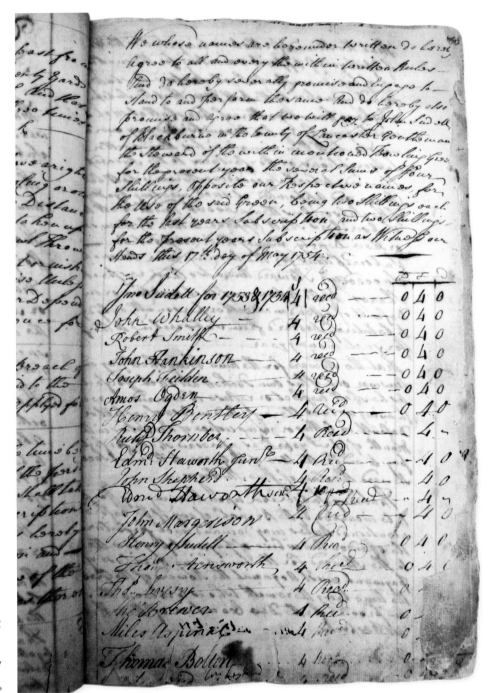

» What do we learn from this?

That, as emphasised before, secondary sources such as newspapers cannot always be relied upon (hardly a revelation), but nor can the utterings of club officials (especially as Henry Backhouse later went through the club records with Abram in 1888 who reported them faithfully).

But perhaps just as importantly we can sense in these various contradictory references to Blackburn Subs, all cited between 1847 and 1888, and in many others from the Victorian era relating to places such as Southampton, Chesterfield and Hereford, the very beginnings of a narrative, which however faulty, was to inform the history of bowling for the next century or more.

Their errors became our errors, just as our errors – for no-one is perfect – might themselves be passed onto future generations.

One final point. Club records apart, one reason why Abram, in his articles of 1888, was able to go into so much detail about the early subscribers to the Blackburn Subs was that almost to a man they were prominent in the town's affairs.

Thus could the story of the club be seen to mirror that of the town itself. Abram recognised this, and in so doing, opened a door for us all.

▲ Thought to date from 1899, this is one of several group photographs in the archives of the **Blackburn Subscription Bowling Green Club**, now held as part of the Cottontown collection at Blackburn Library.

In Chapters Five and Six it was apparent that bowling was a sport much enjoyed by members of the aristocracy, the merchant classes, the newly emerging industrial barons and generation after generation of municipal officials.

This fits exactly the profile of subscribers in Blackburn as listed in 1753-54 and researched by WA Abram in the 1870s and '80s.

They included John Sudell (gent), John Whalley (townsman), John Hankinson ('wealthy gent' and governor of the Grammar School), John Feilden (gent and landowner), Thomas Livesey (school governor and calico printer) and Edmund Haworth (textile merchant).

By 1899 more tradesmen were involved. According to the club archives members then included both local MPs (including WH Hornby, a distant relative of the author), a brewer, cotton merchant, jeweller, dry salter, school master, quarry master, bank manager, coal manager, druggist and several signed only as 'gentleman'.

What stands out are the names.

Not only are there several from the same families listed in the 1750s, but many of the surnames chime with individuals active in the early years of professional football in east Lancashire, surnames such as Sudell, Bentley, Haworth, Hindle and Charnley.

Attention must also be drawn to the pavilion. Built in 1869 after the club's second green was requisitioned for building work – it lay in the St Peter Street area – its architect is unknown. But it has often been likened to a railway station house.

Note the moulded keystone bearing the date 1869 above the central doorway. Shortly after this image was taken extensions were added at each end, so that the door was turned into the central window we see today. Apart from this and plainer bargeboarding, the building remains remarkably unspoilt.

BLACKBURN SUBSCRIPTION
ESTABLISHED PRIOR TO 1749
BOWLING GREEN CLUB.
PRESIDENTS
1881-93 H.BACKHOUSE 1930 R.EASTWOOD

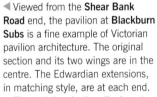

◀ The interior of the pavilion at **Blackburn Subs**, located on **Shear Bank Road**, on the edge of the town centre, consists of several, small interlinked rooms where members may read newspapers, play snooker or simply huddle around the fireplace on an autumn evening. In one corner, where members store their woods, there are four curling stones left over from when the Caledonian Curling Club used to meet at the green (until c.1965).

In the rules of 1754, members were ordered not to make bets of more than sixpence on club premises, to pay fines if caught swearing, and to play no more than three ends of '7 up' before allowing other members a chance to play.

Out on the green today, standard crown green rules apply, and since 1964 women have been admitted to membership.

◀ Viewed from the **Shear Bank Road** end, the pavilion at **Blackburn Subs** is a fine example of Victorian pavilion architecture. The original section and its two wings are in the centre. The Edwardian extensions, in matching style, are at each end.

The club has had to dig deep to keep the building in good order. In 1994 in particular it spent £6,600 on roof repairs, requiring the careful removal and refixing of each one of the original slates, some grey, some pink. Sections of the stone walls that enclose the green (which is cut into rising ground) have also had to be painstakingly rebuilt.

Otherwise the club's ethos has changed little since it was described, in 1852, as a place that offered 'a relaxation to those who are close to the business of the day, and whose body requires a change, as well as mind, from the toils of the shop and the counting house.'

Case study

Cannock Bowling Club

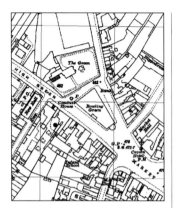

Town centre bowling greens, as found in Scotland in the likes of Kirkcudbright, Wigtown and Ayr, are rare in England, and mostly hidden away, as at Hereford. By comparison the crown green at Cannock, seen above on an OS map of 1918, could hardly be more central. Or more exposed. Slotted between the Market Place and a bandstand at one end, and an area called High Green at the other, the green dates back to at least 1753. It appears in this chapter however because in the late 19th century its very centrality thrust it into the midst of one almighty public row.

During the late 19th century one of the key issues facing bowling greens sited in the public realm (as opposed to in public parks) was the question summed up best as 'whose green was it anyway?' Was it the bowlers, who had been bowling on it for decades or even centuries? Or the public, who had a legal right of access?

This issue arose in several places, Southampton and Chesterfield included. But nowhere did it cause such a furore than in the Staffordshire town of Cannock.

In Stebbing Shaw's *History and Antiquities of Staffordshire* (published 1801) it was noted, 'In the middle of the town is a public bowling green, which in the year 1753 was encompassed with a handsome brick wall'.

One perhaps much like the wall seen in the photograph below.

Not seen in the photo is a stone, hexagonal Conduit Head, built in 1736. This provided water good enough for Cannock to become much visited as a spa, which in turn put the green centre stage.

From reports compiled by members of the modern day club,

led by Mike Hewitt, the green staged bare knuckle fights and pole vaulting competitions.

Following the formation of the Cannock Rifle Volunteers in 1861, its band played on the green each Wednesday evening for several summers. Tea parties and dances were staged by the Ladies Club.

And if ever the gates were locked, ladders were placed to allow people to climb in.

All seemed well, until, as happened elsewhere, changes in local government prompted council officials to review what sites they actually controlled. In Cannock that meant the newly appointed Local Board, which promptly called for a meeting of keyholders for the green. After the bowlers failed to respond, the Board had its views reported in the *Cannock Advertiser* on June 28 1878.

'It was felt by the Board that the ground was Parish property and should come under the Board's control.' Some members, it

added, objected to the fact that the Green was locked by the bowlers. They even suggested the locks be 'wrenched off' or part of the walls pulled down to allow public access. The green, it was said, could be turned into a flower garden, a veritable 'God's Acre'.

Eventually the bowls club secretary argued at a meeting that the green had been built by public subscription and that 'possession is nine tenths of the law'.

His members then put up notices warning that trespassers would be prosecuted.

For two years the dispute festered until the vicar of St Luke's unwittingly set it off again.

Every Saturday night he chose to stand inside the walls of the green and preach to the public gathered outside. But on one night in July 1881 he had been heckled so much by a drunk that he had given up.

Whilst reporting this, the *Advertiser*, in passing, praised the bowls club for at least allowing

This photograph of the bowling green in Cannock was taken from a Georgian villa on the High Green, known as the White House. The house, its gates (seen in the foreground) and the Conduit Head (out of view to the right) are today all listed, and with the green form the core of a Conservation Area. The image is dated 1896, a significant year, as will be revealed.

the vicar access. Whereupon a member wrote in angry response that no such credit was due. No-one at the club had ever been consulted on the matter, and many of them actively disapproved.

To which a Mr Frederick Cox responded that the club could not prove that it had any exclusive rights or authority over the site.

On August 11 1881, reported the *Advertiser*, despite constables guarding the gate, a Mr Moore led an invasion of the green, throwing his hat into the air and shouting 'Hurrah!' A club member tried to push him off but was repulsed by the crowd. Frederick Cox then stepped in. Trespass notices were torn down. The turf was damaged.

Only when two respected residents intervened was order restored and, finally, a resolution agreed demanding that the Board investigate the issue of ownership.

Cox meanwhile sought to reassure *Advertiser* readers that he wished not for any charges of assault to be made but for 'fair arguments', free of 'ill feeling or physical contention'.

Eventually the Board resolved to take possession of the green in November 1881. But the date passed with no action.

So the debate continued on the pages of the *Advertiser*.

One correspondent wrote that certain elderly gentlemen who had been around in 1810 recalled that at that time the walls around the green had been 'much broken down'. Nor had there been any turf, so heavily was it used as a playground and for other purposes.

In April 1883 Frederick Cox again urged the public to action.

'Go on [the green] fearlessly if you desire, nobody dare summonse you. The bowlers threatened your humble servant

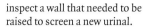

with proceedings but they know a trick or two of that.'

Another letter argued that if everyone went on the green it would become unplayable, and surely 'the general feeling of the town is in favour of bowlers having the green', even if that did not mean they should have the power to control it.

In July 1883 tempers frayed again when a bowler tried to stop a regular Wednesday night brass band recital taking place. The following week large numbers turned up to ensure that it would.

But presumably no bowler dared stop a Tradesman's Dinner taking place on the green in honour of Victoria's Golden Jubilee in 1887.

Eighty people dined, reported the *Advertiser*. 'Garlands of flowers and paper chains were stretched across The Green, from which were suspended Chinese and Japanese lanterns, making a beautiful show...' After the tables were cleared 'over one thousand persons, of all classes, were inside the boundary walls. The band then played for dancing, which was kept up until half past ten when the playing of the National Anthem brought to a close one of the most memorable events Cannock has ever witnessed.'

Five more years passed until an incident once again reignited the row. The Board's surveyor broke the lock on the gate in order to

inspect a wall that needed to be raised to screen a new urinal.

The bowlers went to court.

But when the case was finally heard at Walsall on July 19 1893 Judge Griffiths found against the club. So they appealed.

And in an indirect fashion, this time they won. At a Divisional Court on January 23 1894 the club argued that it had existed for over a century and had in that time built a pavilion, enclosed the green and maintained it.

Unable to agree a verdict, the jury was eventually discharged. But not before the foreman told the court that eleven of the twelve did not consider the green to be public. Although this had no legal effect, the bowlers at least felt vindicated.

Finally, in 1895, a solution was proposed. Just as the Conduit Head and its waters were looked after by a trust, so too would be the green. On October 23 1896, four members of the bowls club and four councillors were elected as trustees, their aim being 'to preserve the ground for ever as and for the purpose of a Bowling Green.'

In return, the club would be charged a peppercorn rent, as long as it could show that it had at least twelve members'.

As of 2015 it had 75 members, and all was well.

The same view in 2012, facing the bandstand end, where the green tapers to just ten yards in width, and above, the top end and the Conduit Head. Like Chesterfield, Lewes and Hadley, Cannock BC is male only and does not play in any league. Nor does it suffer much damage, thanks to having so many CCTV cameras around and a taxi rank at the High Green end.

Case study

Carlisle Subscription Bowling Club

This is 'Chalker', mascot of the Carlisle Subscription club. A 'chalker' is a bowl that touches the jack, meaning that, under flat green rules, it may still count if it ends up in the ditch. In times past players carried sticks of chalk to mark such woods. However William Mitchell, in his 1864 *Manual*, noted another method, that of spitting on the wood (which thus became a 'spittler').

The city of Carlisle may not be widely known for its sporting achievements, but in the world of flat green bowls it has been a genuine powerhouse.

In addition to Carlisle Subs and various other private clubs, there have been clubs for police and firemen, for ex-servicemen, for workers at British Rail, the Co-op, Electricity Board and County Council. There have been clubs at the Edenside ground of Carlisle Cricket Club, representing at least five local companies.

These were Cowans Sheldon (cranemakers), Stead McAlpin (fabric printers), Carr's (of water biscuit fame), Hudson Scotts (makers of metal boxes, including for Carr's), and Ferguson's, the textile manufacturers who at Holme Head in 1881 became one of the first British companies to lay a green for its workers.

In 1958, Godfrey Bolsover (*see Links*) listed 24 EBA clubs in Carlisle, and that did not include members of a 'Wet League', based at pubs built as part of Carlisle's pioneering State Management Scheme (*see pages 174-75*).

Carlisle Subs' bower (a word used across Cumbria for cottages and pavilions) was built in 1897 and is a smaller version of the pavilion at Edenside Cricket Ground. The central extension, clearly, is more recent. In 2014 the club received £50,000 from Sport England's Inspired Facilities fund to improve the toilets and changing rooms, and provide disabled access.

All this in a city of 75,000, with now just nine surviving clubs, of which Carlisle Subs is the oldest.

But not the first.

There had been a bowling green since at least 1746 at Spring Gardens, close to a racecourse on The Swifts. (Carlisle's current racecourse opened in 1904). Next to this was a pub known by 1837 as the Bowling Green Inn.

Reports of regular cash sweepstakes taking place on this green reveal a high proportion of entrants were tradesmen and skilled craftsmen, such as butchers, confectioners and joiners. It also seems likely there was a club there, as in 1851 bowlers from Penrith paid a visit.

But perhaps the green was not exclusive enough for some, for as reported in the *Carlisle Journal* in 1865, 'a party of gentlemen' was seeking subscribers to fund 'a private green'.

So was born Carlisle Subs, on a site rented from Lord Lonsdale behind Spencer Street, close to the city centre. With permission from the local council, turf for the green was cut from Stoney Holme, an area bordering the River Petteril and in later years occupied by a golf course, rugby ground and Brunton Park, home of Carlise United FC.

In April 1866 the club advertised for 'a steady and respectable man, who is competent to take charge of and keep in order the new bowling green during the ensuing summer.'

A year later, in July, the first visitors were Penrith, for six games of pairs played to '21 up'.

In 1879, the lease at Spencer Street was taken over by a coach-builder, forcing the club to move a few hundred yards east to its current home on Myddleton Street.

It is easily missed. Accessed down a cobbled alley, it is hidden by brick walls and hemmed in on three sides by terraced houses.

Amazingly, only a few streets away the green of Courtfield BC is in an almost identical setting.

◀ This is the **Carlisle Bowlers Shield**, presented by pharmacist CM Dalziel in 1903.

Initially the shield was awarded to the winner of a competition amongst the city's six clubs.

Apart from **Carlisle Subs** (in whose pavilion the shield is displayed) these were Courtfield, Holme Head, Stanwix and the West End Subscription Club, each of whom is still in existence, plus Edenside (based at the cricket ground but disbanded in 2010 after being twice hit by floods).

These six Carlisle clubs were amongst the earliest in England to adopt the Scottish rink game, and amongst the northernmost to join the English Bowling Association, soon after it formed in 1903.

An impressive impact they made too. Carlisle Subs won the first National Rinks Championships in 1905, to be followed by West End in 1907 and Edenside a year later.

Carlisle players also won two EBA singles titles, while one Subs member, William Johnson, bowled for England from 1904-11 and was EBA President in 1908.

After the First World War the scope of the Dalziel Shield, as it became known, was broadened into a new Border City Bowling Tournament. This became one of the most prestigious flat green tournaments in the north, and was won by the likes of Hexham, Dumfries and Annan, before the shield was retired in the 1960s.

Note incidentally that the bowler depicted on the copper shield appears to have been based on the character known as **'Toucher'**, who appeared on promotional material issued by the Glasgow company, Thomas Taylor (*see page 104*).

'Toucher' is also, of course, like 'chalker,' a term for a wood that touches the jack.

Case study

North London Bowling Club

Hampstead Heath is one of the great open spaces of London, with acres of meadows, woods and winding paths, a lido, running track, 29 ponds (three for swimming) and a public bowling green, home to Parliament Hill Fields BC. But hidden away on the Heath's Highgate borders is one of London's oldest bowls clubs. Set up on farmland in 1891, North London BC's first pavilion was a cowshed and its first tea lady the farmer's wife. Now its neighbours are multi-millionaire businessmen.

Considering how many bowling greens there were in London before the 19th century, it is telling how few remain in the capital that predate 1900.

The reason is simple. As London expanded throughout the Victorian period, old greens were swallowed up, one by one, forcing bowlers (and cricketers) into the suburbs to seek pastures new.

This was how the North London Bowling Club came into being. As told in the club's early history, compiled by WA Walton, North London's founders were members of a club in inner city Camden, whose green lay 'not far' from the statue of Richard Cobden. (Its location has never been identified but readers may know the area better as Mornington Crescent.)

Impelled to move in 1891, one faction of Camden bowlers found a site on Croftdown Road, near Parliament Hill Fields, and set up Mansfield BC (named after their landlord, the Earl of Mansfield).

The other headed further north towards the Earl's residence at Kenwood House, to Fitzroy Farm.

Even today the site seems isolated, albeit with houses and cottages nearby on unpaved roads and narrow lanes. But in 1891 it was positively rural, on the outer edge of Highgate Village and with but a few lodges and mansions, Kenwood House included, in the vicinity. The club's boundary with Hampstead Heath was formed by Ken Brook, which fed an adjoining pond (one that in 1926 was designated as the Ladies' Bathing Pond).

When North London became a founder member of the London & Southern Counties Bowling Association in 1895 its green had no ditches or banks. Its cowshed-cum-pavilion had a partition down the centre so that the committee could meet in private, and the farmer, Tom Ward, would turn up to play, often in carpet slippers, after a day's haymaking.

In 1905 the club set about converting the green to EBA standards, with a small 'nursery rink' alongside. This however was removed in 1910 when, having agreed a new lease of £50 a year with the Earl of Mansfield, a new pavilion was built (*see opposite*) and the green squared off and relaid.

How this relaying proceeded tells us much about club life at that time. As told by Walton, when the issue of new turf came up, the members were split. Some wished to send the greenkeeper,

Henderson (we are never told his first name), to the north, 'on a mission of search and enquiry'.

Others, like club secretary Carter, a man 'of autocratic bearing', refused, considering it 'infra-dig' to invest such authority in a mere greenkeeper.

Carter won the day, and turf samples were duly sent for and examined by the members of a sub-committee who, writes Walton, adopted an 'air of knowledge and wide experience'.

Their choice made, they then deigned to call in Henderson.

Henderson was not impressed. None of the samples was much good, he reckoned, but he supposed that one could at least be considered 'the least poor'.

This one, the committee was embarrassed to note, had been the sample they had thought the worst. So of course they ignored their greenkeeper and, of course,

the end result was found wanting, as may just be discerned from the photograph taken in 1912 of the London & Southern Counties Challenge Shield Final (*opposite*).

Walton concludes the episode by noting, 'It is to the credit of Henderson that he afterwards tended it as well as he did'.

More so, as we learn later, because at that stage he was still cutting the grass with a scythe and a hand mower. And even when his successor requested a petrol mower in 1956 he was turned down. Fortunately a group of members took pity and bought him one two years later.

Thus, one step at a time the club adapted to the modern era.

During the Second World War a gas-lit cabinet used to store the members' Havana cigars was removed. In 1966, 31 years after the matter had first been raised, women were admitted as full members, albeit on a three year trial period.

Walton tells another tale which has a bearing on the club's situation today.

In 1924 the club reformed itself as a limited company and secured the freehold of the green and Fitzroy Farm. It then sold the farm but placed a restrictive covenant on the site so that any plans for a building put up on it would have to meet the club's approval, and could not overlook the green.

The present dwelling, built in 2011-13 by a wealthy hotelier, is a contemporary 'grand design', but still, barely visible from the green.

Its scale confirms, nevertheless, just how valuable is the land on which the green lies, and how reassuring therefore that North London's share structure makes it difficult for members to collude and put it up for sale.

As happened in a roundabout way at Mansfield BC. Their site, where a large indoor bowls centre was built in 1971, and where the outdoor green was closed in 2011, is, as of 2015, the subject of a bitter planning battle between developers and former members who want to build on the site, and the local community, which wants to retain it as an open space.

In the 1950s, there were 240 clubs in Middlesex. Since then, along with Mansfield some 145 have fallen by the wayside. Hence North London finds itself the second oldest club in the capital, north of the river (after Bounds Green, formed 1887). But its green is the oldest. Not old by national standards perhaps, but in London terms a real, and spirited survivor.

 Built in 1910, the pavilion at **North London BC** is typical of early 20th century clubhouse design in that it is ranged around a large central hall, perfect for gatherings. Indeed the club has always prided itself on putting on a good show as well as a good spread, helped by the availability in this part of London of so many entertainers.

On the walls, it will be noted, are photos of every club president, plus those of other noted members, such as former Arsenal footballer Leslie Compton, who bowled here despite having an artificial leg in later life, and whose antics are fondly recalled in the club's annals.

The pavilion exterior (*left*) is also typical of the Edwardian period.

Before trees and lush vegetation hid it from the outside world, the green offered a clear view across to Hampstead Heath, whereas today most Heath walkers come across it only by accident. Those who do are invariably captivated. Some have even become members. As has the hotelier next door.

Case study

The Waterloo, Blackpool

Built for the Bolton-based brewers Magee Marshall in 1901, the Waterloo Hotel lies midway between Blackpool FC's Bloomfield Road stadium and the Pleasure Beach (both opened in the late 1890s). From Waterloo Road, as seen above, it looks much like any red brick, Tudorbethan public house of the period. But walk around the back and there stands the most substantial bowls arena in Britain, home of the famous Waterloo Handicap since 1907. Its first winner was James Rothwell from West Leigh (*right*). In 1886 Rothwell had won Blackpool's original handicap at the Talbot, a mile and a half to the north. But although both tournaments are still contested, it is 'The Waterloo' that has come to dominate.

Anyone with an interest in British sport knows of Wembley, of Wimbledon, of 'The Open' in golf and 'The National' in horse racing. Yet how many have on their bucket list 'The Waterloo' in Blackpool?

Not many, for sure, and yet they should. Without doubt the prime competition in the world of crown green bowls, 'The Waterloo' – named after the pub where it has been staged since its inception in 1907 – is by any standards an exceptional sporting and cultural phenomenon. It attracts the best crown green players, tests them on a tantalisingly challenging green, and is held in a compact mini-stadium, known almost inevitably as 'the Wembley of Bowls', in front of passionate, knowledgeable crowds, often topping the 2,000 mark. Accompanied by a heady mix of betting, booze and barracking, The Waterloo is the ultimate in pub bowling.

It is, furthermore, whisper it across the Pennines, another reason why Blackpool is regarded by many as the spiritual home of crown green bowls.

Certainly there had been two greens in the town as early as 1786, albeit both described as 'diminutive', when the population totalled less than 500 and visitors were just starting to arrive by stagecoach to sample the sea air.

But the real boom followed the arrival of the railway in the 1840s. Gradually, mill and factory owners across Lancashire and Yorkshire arrived at a schedule whereby

entire towns would effectively close down, one by one, so that their workers could head off *en masse* to the seaside for their 'Wakes Week' annual holidays.

Robert Nickson at the Talbot was, as noted earlier (*see page 138*), the first Blackpool landlord to recognise that many visitors not only enjoyed playing bowls but would also pay to watch top players in action. Starting in 1873 with 50 entries, the Talbot Handicap grew to 1,024 by 1913.

One factor in its rise was convenience. The Talbot and its green were literally across the road from Blackpool's main railway station. However as the resort expanded inland and south along the coast, rival pub greens emerged, such as the Belle Vue on Whitegate Drive (whose green is now a car park) and Raikes Hall (now host of 'The Talbot').

Built in an area known as South Shore, the Waterloo Hotel was itself handily placed for the opening, in 1903, of a new station, known as Waterloo Road (since renamed Blackpool South).

As for 'The Waterloo' handicap, this was the brainchild of the Waterloo's landlord Robert Selkirk, who was himself a keen player. When it commenced on May 3 1907 there were 320 entries.

Part of its appeal was that Selkirk's rules required only 17 points to win (later reduced to 16). This resulted in shorter matches and therefore appealed to a wide range of bowlers of all standards.

Most entrants started with four points in every round. Twenty nine were handicapped. Three 'back-markers' played off scratch, these being the cream of the money-match men; George Beatty from Burnley, Gerard Hart from Blackrod and James Rothwell of West Leigh (*left*), whose victory on the final day in October 1907 was reportedly witnessed by as many as 3,000 spectators.

Rothwell took home £50, a considerable sum, and as with James Ward at The Talbot in 1902 (and indeed most winners in such crown green competitions), earned much more from various side bets.

Not only did crown green bowls offer higher rewards than most other professional sports of the Edwardian period, it also offered individuals the longest potential career at the top, matched only by billiards.

Twenty one years separated Rothwell's victory at The Talbot in 1886 and his eventual triumph at The Waterloo in 1907. Yet amazingly, twice as many years would pass between Rothwell's son Jack winning his first Waterloo Handicap in 1914, when he was 23, and his follow up victory in The Talbot, in 1956.

Crown green bowls also gave professionals from other sports a chance to play on beyond their initial retirement. This was particularly true for footballers.

Of these the most stellar example was Jack Cox. Born in Liverpool in 1877, Cox played on the wing during two spells for Blackpool FC, with eleven years in between at Liverpool, where he played over 300 games, won two League championship medals and was capped by England on three occasions. Then in 1925 at the age of 49, fourteen years after hanging up his boots, Cox became the first and only individual to win both the Waterloo and the Talbot in the same year, a feat known as the 'Blackpool Double'.

Between them, the Talbot and Waterloo Handicaps were extremely good for Blackpool.

They put the Fylde Coast firmly on the bowls map during the Edwardian period and no doubt played a part in the decision of the British Crown Green Bowling Association to establish its first headquarters in Blackpool, at the Gynn Hotel, in 1908.

Indeed so important did bowls become to Blackpool's fortunes that the Council set up a dedicated sub-committee to oversee both the major handicaps.

Inevitably most of what is celebrated about the Waterloo as a venue concerns 'The Waterloo' as an annual tournament. »

▶ Despite the importance of the **Waterloo Hotel**, few images survive from its early decades. This faded clipping, reproduced in Alan Ward's history of the competition (see *Links*), is thought to date from c.1902, shortly after the green opened. Only a few benches are provided for spectators and just one building appears beyond the walls (although the area would soon sprout housing following the expansion of the Pleasure Beach amusement park nearby in 1903).

But if photographs are few and far between, fortunately the Waterloo's competition ledgers have been preserved by successive proprietors and bowls managers.

Below is an example, detailing the closing rounds in 1913. This was the only time a final has been contested by brothers. **Gerard Hart** from Blackrod, a real hotbed of Lancashire bowling, beat **Richard Hart**, by 21-19.

One quirk of The Waterloo was that rather than evening up numbers in the early rounds, as is usual in knock-out tournaments, byes continued to be granted in later rounds. Thus as we see in 1913 Gerard Hart and John Howarth, also of Blackrod, received byes as late as the seventh round.

Other contestants are listed from Blackburn, Barrow, Leigh, Newton-le-Willows and Chorley, while the South Shore favourite was Tom Richardson, runner up in 1907.

Also well known was the 33 year old former Manchester City, Fulham and Leicester Fosse winger, **Fred Threlfall**, whose victory in the Talbot two years earlier had earned him £468 plus bets. At a time when the maximum wage in football was £5 a week, small wonder that crown green professionals so loved the Blackpool air.

>> However it should not be forgotten that the green is in regular use throughout the season by the Waterloo's resident club, and remains popular with visitors, keen to experience the hallowed green for themselves.

In addition, as the financial burden of running such a large establishment throughout the year grew ever more onerous, especially once the pub ceased to run as a hotel, successive bowls managers have had to introduce extra tournaments to keep the tills ringing. Three competitions alone were launched in 1977; the Spring Waterloo, the Junior Waterloo, and, to the mild displeasure of some diehards, a Ladies Waterloo, which gained 256 entries in its first year and drew a crowd of 500 to its inaugural final.

Also established is a Champion of Champions event. Staged since 1974, this involves 32 players who have won their county's individual merit competition or one of the selected open tournaments, The Waterloo included.

Perhaps the most propitious event was a televised competition, inaugurated in 1968. This ran on the BBC in various guises (singles and pairs) until 1986. The BBC also covered the Waterloo Handicap throughout the 1970s and '80s, a period during which the entries rose to an all time peak of 2,048.

But alas this level of interest could not be maintained. In the late 1980s the BBC dropped crown green from its schedules, a crushing blow both to the game and the Waterloo. And although cameras did return briefly in the 2000s, courtesy of Sky Sports, this was only after the BCGBA offered to cover Sky's production costs.

Since then live coverage has been via the internet.

Meanwhile, entry to The Waterloo has ebbed sharply, falling to 512 since 2008.

Higher entry fees (introduced by an increasingly anxious management) and rising travel costs have been largely to blame, deterring those club bowlers who in former years used to bulk out the field, literally by the coachload.

Attendances have also declined.

Of equal concern, the Waterloo itself has come under threat. In fact in 2006 it seemed as if the end was in sight, when in common with many British pubs ownership of the Waterloo passed from the brewers (in this case Greenall

Whitley, its owners since 1974) to a property company. Faced with mounting losses, this company submitted plans to redevelop the pub as flats and build a nursing home on the green. A further setback came when an application to have the pub listed was turned down by English Heritage in 2012.

In the end, the plan for flats failed when the property company went into liquidation. The plans for a nursing home, meanwhile, were stymied by a covenant which protects the green and its surrounds, including the car park, from development.

Throughout this period the pub went through a series of crises, most recently re-emerging in early 2015 under the supervision of bowls manager Mark Audin. But there are no guarantees and at the time of going to press no-one can be sure of how long the Waterloo, and therefore 'The Waterloo' can survive in the current climate.

Queuing on finals day in 2014 (*right*). Until around 1990, a ticket for the finals of 'The Waterloo' was as coveted as that of an FA Cup Final. Today entry can be had on the day. Above, those gathered in the Waterloo's main bar gain a view of the action from a bay window overlooking the rear of the south terrace.

As is the case at so many of Britain's historic sporting venues, it does not require great architecture to engender great atmosphere.

Having made do with temporary stands in its early years, **The Waterloo** started to take on its current, stadium-like appearance in 1961, with the construction of the **North Stand**, seen here in 2008. This raised the green's capacity to just over 4,000. Two further stands were built in 1983, after Greenall Whitley took over the Waterloo.

Originally seating 1,040, the cantilevered, **West Stand**, which cost £150,000, can be seen in the lower photograph, on the far right. Safety measures have since reduced its capacity to just 256. The more basic **East Stand** (from which the photo was taken, also in 2008) seats 128 (reduced from 677). This replaced an iron and glass cover damaged by gales in 1983.

As can be seen, the fourth, south side of the green features a terrace for standing spectators, also built in 1983, backing onto the pub.

With such tightly knit enclosures, there is an intensity at the Waterloo – part football ground, part Centre Court – that still takes first-time visitors by surprise, and requires an especially cool head from players.

Plus there is the green itself.

Although fairly flat by crown code standards, it rises up towards the terrace and pub corner, and is one of the largest on the circuit, able to stage up to six games at any one time on its 43.6 yards (39.6m) by 44.4 yards (40.4m) expanse.

This means that to succeed, players must be able to play 60 yard long marks from corner to corner, a skill admirably displayed by **Simon Coupe** from Walton-le-Dale, seen in the yellow shirt, and destined to be a Waterloo winner in both 2010 and 2011.

▲ It is not only the stands that are tightly knit at the **Waterloo**. So too is the crown green community, for whom big match days are like the gathering of a tribe. Most of the referees, such as Larry Whiteley (*above*) are local, and are also club players. As are most of the spectators, many of whom stay in Blackpool for a week, starting on

the Saturday in September when The Waterloo is whittled down to the last 32. This total is then reduced to 16 on the Monday, then 8 on the Tuesday, before the finals take place on the following day.

Meanwhile a number of other competitions are held in the area during the same period, including The Talbot, whose final, at Raikes Hall, often takes place the day after The Waterloo, thereby giving the crowds the benefit of an action packed week in the resort.

Two of the best known regulars at The Waterloo finals are **Rita and George Booth** from Blackpool, seen here in 2008 (*below left*), sitting behind the scoreboard in the West Stand. It is their custom to mark cards day in, day out, throughout the tournament, and the custom of the winning player to reward them and other volunteers with tips.

Most of the players are familiar faces too. Seen here on course to win his first Waterloo title in 2008, **Gary Ellis** of Whitefield (*above right*) went on in 2014 to become only the second man to win five Waterloo titles overall (following on from Brian Duncan, who set the benchmark between 1979 and 1992). Still only in his 40s, one of Ellis's greatest assets is to have mastered all the marks that the Waterloo green has to offer, not only corner to corner but down the edges too.

Unique in bowls, the South Terrace at the Waterloo (*right*) is built along the same lines as a football terrace, crush barriers and all, and as such has seen its capacity halved from 800 to 400 by more stringent safety regulations. This is where much of the atmosphere at tournaments is generated, and where those other great Waterloo regulars gather – the bookies.

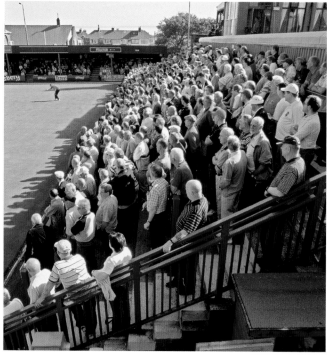

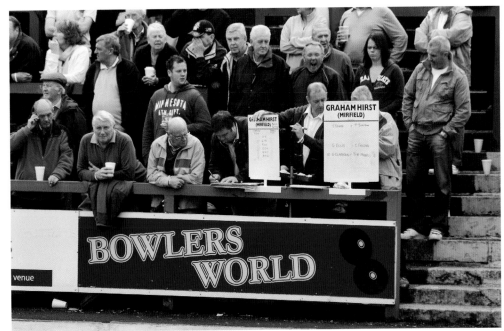

▲ In crown green bowls as in horse racing and greyhound racing, wherever there is action there are bookmakers. Pictured here on the **South Terrace** at **The Waterloo** are three of the five licensed firms whose presence has long been part of the scene on finals day.

Bill Forber from St Helens comes from a famous bowling family and also travels to every Isle of Man festival. **Graham Hirst** operates out of Mirfield, West Yorkshire. Seen on the right, on duty at the 2008 finals to the left of the JP Doyle sign, is **'Charlie' Tattersall**.

Known to all in crown green circles as 'Tat', he was a respected player, then bookmaker for many years before his death in 2013.

'Tat' and his colleagues have witnessed a host of changes in the last few decades.

Punters in the crowd still 'shout for their money'. Players still need a thick skin at times to withstand the barracking. But The Waterloo is no longer a handicap in the true sense.

Originally, as we saw in 1907, top players played to scratch and lesser players were given points in each round. Then after 1945, previous winners and runners-up were handicapped too. This however changed during the reign of bowls manager Jim Parker, who ran the Waterloo from 2001-13.

In 2003 Parker made all players equal and dropped the shorter game format in favour of a full '21 up'. This had the effect of reducing the chances of an ordinary club bowler advancing in the tournament.

Since then the shorter format of '16 up' has returned, and off the green there have been other positive changes. In the stands, for example, white plastic seats have been brought in from Old Trafford cricket ground, extra safety concerns have been met and the pub itself has received a long overdue makeover.

Even so, there exists a general consensus that the atmosphere is not as lively as it was. Readers may judge for themselves by viewing clips of past matches on the internet. The 1980 final between Vernon Lee of Blackpool and Glyn Vernon of Winsford is particularly recommended, showing Lee

dancing around the bowls as the crowd roars.

That passion, that intensity may have dissipated. But under the Waterloo's new management there remains plenty to play for.

And for any reader who has yet to experience it, there is no better way to judge than by attending The Waterloo in person. Odds on it will prove an eye-opener.

Case study

The Panel

Another Blackrod man to make his name in crown green bowling was Jimmy Cunliffe (1912-86). In common with Fred Threlfall and Jack Cox this was Cunliffe's second sporting career. In the 1930s he played mostly at inside right for Everton, winning a Championship medal in 1939 and one England cap. Then, after losing much of his footballing career to the war, he took up bowling, joined 'the Panel' in 1958 at the age of 45 and proved to be one of its leading players throughout the 1960s.

After 'The Talbot' and 'The Waterloo' we turn next to a rather different form of crown green competition, also originating in the Edwardian era.

Launched in 1908, the Lancashire Professional Bowling Association (LPBA), more widely known as 'the Panel', was and nominally remains a group of professional bowlers who play each other not in a single competition but in an ongoing series of matches.

At the Panel's peak these matches could draw crowds of 2-3,000 in locations spread across the region mapped below, but centred on the triangle between Chorley, Wigan and Bolton.

Yet today the Panel takes place at just one green, on Wigan Road, Westhoughton, and is rarely watched by more than a handful of spectators. Plus, across the road from the green, the pub with which the Panel has been most closely associated in recent years, the Red Lion, was, after years of neglect, demolished in 2015 to make way for a care home. (This was despite the pub having elements dating back to the 17th century and lying within a Conservation Area.)

The Westhoughton green, at least, is safe for the time being, as will become apparent. But the Panel itself, a throwback to an era when high-stakes professional bowling was a real phenomenon in Lancashire, hangs on by a thread.

Primarily the LPBA was formed to meet the demand for gambling.

And because for gamblers it is vital to have faith in the quality and integrity of the contestants, the LPBA had a committee to vet bowlers wishing to join its roster.

Or 'Panel', as it was dubbed.

The LPBA did not spring out of nowhere. As we have noted, betting has played an integral part in bowling since the 16th century. It is mentioned in the rules drawn up in 1670 (*page 53*), and grew more popular still in the 19th century, particularly in the coal mining and mill towns of Lancashire. Towns exactly like Westhoughton.

Most of the venues were pubs and social clubs. Most Panel bowlers were local, for as the *British Bowls Annual* commented in 1923, 'The Lancashire man turns to bowls as ducks go to the water'.

On average there were and still are about a dozen bowlers on the Panel at any one time.

At the same time, the public could join the LPBA as members, in order to get reduced admission and other benefits.

Being on the Panel was no sinecure. Matches were, and still

are played from Monday to Friday, all year round, apart from Good Fridays and Christmas Days. Also as we shall see, the show must go on, whatever the weather.

On the other hand, until recently, the rewards could be considerable. Before the Panel, in the late 19th century players such as Gerard Hart of Blackrod and Thomas Taylor of Bolton (known as 'Owd Toss') were amongst the highest paid sportsmen in Britain.

Prize money of £50 was not uncommon, and as noted earlier, this could be topped up by side bets and by a share of the gate receipts.

In 1900, James Rothwell played George Beatty at the Bamfurlong Hotel in Wigan for £340. This was roughly three times the average annual wage of a labourer.

For ex-professional footballers and cricketers entering the circuit, these were rich pickings, and, moreover, they were free from the stigma and prohibitions that the governing bodies of football and cricket attached, at least outwardly, to players who were caught betting on their own sport.

Matches were long, even to 'IOI up', as this allowed for plenty of ebb and flow in the betting markets. Thus it was common for big money matches to take place over two days, sometimes even split between two venues.

In the middle of this stood the pub landlords. They often acted both as promoters and stakeholders for the players and their backers, and as bookmakers.

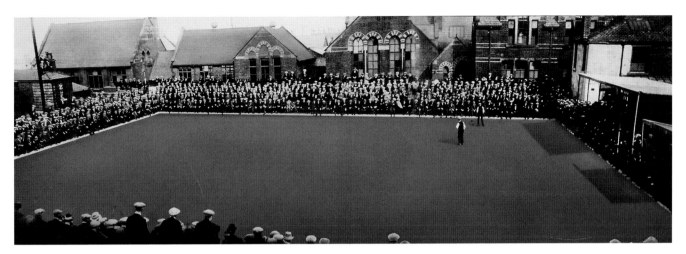

In fact the forerunner of the Panel was an organisation known as the Lancashire Licensed Victuallers Bowling Green and Players' Protection Society. Its job was to regulate matches and ensure that fixtures did not clash.

Meanwhile the bowlers formed their own group, the Professional Bowlers' Association, aimed at weeding out players who were prone to throwing matches in return for backhanders.

Eventually in October 1908, representatives of the two bodies met in Manchester to agree to merge under the new name of the LPBA. Its aim, reported the *Sporting Chronicle* was to 'leave no stone unturned to purge the game from those undesirable elements which have crept into it.'

So began the Panel, with great success over the coming decades.

But with this success, not surprisingly there came an uneasy relationship with amateurs in the crown green game. (There were never any professionals in the flat green code.) For example in 1921 professional bowlers were told not to enter the Talbot or Waterloo. In the 1950s they were limited to

entering no more than five open tournaments a year and barred from playing for their counties.

Even so, compared with other sports, the lines between professionals and amateurs were not so strictly drawn up, and even 'amateurs' were free to enter competitions for which the prizes were cash (such as the Waterloo).

By comparison, in sports such as rowing or athletics, anyone even taking part in a competition for which cash prizes were on offer, whether they won or not, would be deemed a professional.

(The EBA was similarly strict. In 1933 a member of one club was banned from competing in a competition because, as a full-time greenkeeper for the Corporation, he was deemed to be a 'professional'.)

Like the modern day tennis, golf and darts pros, the Panel bowlers worked their way around a circuit.

Before the Second World War this included the Yarrow Bridge and Robin Hood at Chorley, the Springfield Hotel at Wigan (next to the football ground), the Hulton Arms at Four Lane Ends and the Seven Stars at Standish. The

summer season even saw the Panel take up a residency in Blackpool.

But after the Second World War this all changed. Before the war, bowling had been considered as lying outside the remit of the 1934 Betting and Lotteries Act; firstly because it was classified as 'a game', and secondly because all bets placed at Panel matches had been based on credit (whereas in horse and greyhound racing bets have to paid for up front).

Faced with an investigation in 1947, the LPBA was told that if it did not want the Panel to fall under the jurisdiction of the 1934 Act, which it did not, it would have to agree to certain restrictions.

Firstly, no green could stage more than eight days of play per year. Secondly, the LPBA secretary had to write to the police in each town at least seven days in advance of every booking.

The 1950s were thus tough years for the players, with reduced crowds and less money coming in. On the other hand, the restrictions on greens meant that the Panel was forced to spread to other areas, such as Southport, Nelson, Hyde and Irlam.   »

▲ Four miles from Westhoughton, the **Gibraltar Rock Hotel** on **Deane Road**, **Bolton** – shown here in 1926 during a Charity Handicap match in aid of Bolton Infirmary – was one of several Panel venues in the immediate area.

Clearly the photograph, now displayed on the walls of the Railway Club in Bolton, has been doctored by whichever publication reproduced it (the identity of which remains unknown). Nevertheless it illustrates the level of public interest in professional crown green bowls in the early part of the 20th century, and is a reminder that from its early years, charitable fundraising formed an important part of the game's ethos.

The green at the Gibraltar Rock would later feature in a series of photographs taken by Humphrey Spender in 1937 as part of the Mass Observation study known as 'Worktown' (available to view online). As Spender's images show, the Rock was akin to a small scale football ground, with terracing and shelters on all four sides of the turf.

Today the green is covered by a car park, while the pub survives as a Spar convenience store.

≫ Finally in 1957 the landlord of the Robin Hood at Chorley decided, with the approval of the LPBA, that he would apply for a licence under the terms of the 1934 Act. If it did help his trade, it was not for long.

Four years later his pub closed. But then four other pubs also applied for licences, and these now became the main venues; the aforementioned Hulton Arms and the Springfield Hotel, plus the George and Dragon at Whelley and the Red Lion at Westhoughton.

Albeit on a smaller scale, the Panel now entered a new golden age, with bowlers such as Ingham Gregory from Burnley, Glen Howarth from Haslingden and the diminutive 'dancing man', Vernon Lee from Chadderton.

Since the 1980s however, the Panel has again diminished, so much so that today, as noted earlier it can be found only in one place, Westhoughton.

The recent loss of the Red Lion has dealt a further blow, meaning that punters can no longer sup on a pint as they follow the action.

But the green at least is secure. In 2005 the LPBA bought the freehold for £12,000. Not bad value for a green which is in use 52 weeks of the year, which appears in fine fettle, and which acts as a channel for more than a century of bowling history.

▲ August 2008 and **Chris Morrison** and **Paul Dudley**, two of the Panel's leading players, play on the green at **Westhoughton**, with the tower of St Bartholomew's marking the centre of the town nearby. When this photo was taken the Red Lion still stood behind the houses, on the other side of Wigan Road. Now the green exists as a separate entity.

None of the players on the Panel today are true professionals. Bets apart, the maximum each can win in a game is £30, and just to play costs £10 per player. So, they tend to be on shift work, or are either unemployed or retired.

As a result there is no longer any divide between the LPBA and the BCGBA. Panel players are free to play in county matches, open competitions or local leagues.

Each weekday sees two matches on the green, the first starting at 1.00pm. Players are handicapped according to ability and form, with the weaker man receiving a number of points start and always sending the jack at the first end.

Some concessions have been made to modernity. A standard jack is now used, whereas once players had their own selection, each with a bias to match their woods.

When the Panel utilised multiple venues, each man had his own favourites. But at least Westhoughton offers challenges of its own, with a significant climb towards the covered side and a steep fall on the scoreboard edge.

There remain a number of differences between Panel rules and those of the BCGBA. Matches start from the centre. Players get a second throw of the jack if they

send it off the green or fail to set the minimum length of 19 metres. Also, the circular mats in use are smaller and are left behind by the last player to bowl at each end.

In addition, games are played to '41 up', compared with '21 up' in a regular crown match.

However the most unusual aspect of the Panel is that when two bowls cannot be separated using conventional measures, a '**standard**' is used. That is, a straw is cut precisely to length.

Seen here in the 1960s (*left*), Ron Kellett has just cut a straw and balanced it between his bowl and the jack. His opponent must then place this same length of straw between his wood and the jack.

If he can make it 'stand' he wins the end. If it falls, Kellett does.

This method, precise and time consuming, was once common. One of the earliest references to it appears in John Earle's *Microcosmographie*, published in 1628.

Now only at the Panel can this age old drama still be witnessed.

▲ Perhaps it is the cussed spirit of all involved. Maybe it is that other sports events, especially horse races, will have been postponed. Or is it simply the novelty of seeing a referee search for the jack in a thick fog or snowstorm, using a lantern or torch? Or watching bowls turn into snowballs as they skid along the surface? Over the years, Panel players have tried various methods to deal with the cold and maintain some grip on their bowls; buckets of hot water placed around the green, foil-wrapped jacket potatoes kept in pockets, and even coconut oil rubbed onto the woods to stop them picking up snow.

Seen here in January 2013, volunteers clear the snow so that **Mark Foster** and **Mike Geraghty** can get on. Below, the game is poised at 33-31 as most spectators huddle in the shelters, bemoaning the local authority for closing down the green's refreshment room on health and safety grounds.

No need for any risk assessments for the bowlers however. **The Panel** must play on.

▲ On a brighter day in August 2008, two **Panel** institutions study their liabilities, **Jackie Edwards** on the left, **Brian Duncan** on the right.

Edwards is a stalwart of the betting fraternity. A former Rugby League player for Warrington, his son Shaun followed in his foosteps and played for Wigan and Great Britain before becoming a coach to the Welsh Rugby Union team.

Duncan meanwhile has crossed the rail from being a Panel player himself between 1969-76, one of the greatest. As noted earlier he won the Waterloo five times and countless other major competitions.

For 'bettors' (as they were referred to in the 1670 rules), the attraction of the Panel has always been that as well as 'backing' a bet, bets can also be 'laid' (as is now also possible via various internet betting exchanges).

In other words, an individual may offer odds and take someone else's bet (on credit). Then, a minute later, he can take the odds offered by someone else.

Thus notebooks get steadily filled with numbers and jottings, with money changing hands only once the result is known. Most regulars, it has to be said, end up more or less even, but it is possible to lose heavily from a series of wrong calls.

For the first time visitor none of this will make much sense. But no doubt someone will explain. And then regale you with tales of legendary players, epic matches, infamous betting scams and even police raids of old.

Friday is the most popular day at Westhoughton. Come rain or shine. Or snow...

Case study

Old English Bowls

Our next case study concerns not one bowling club but six, clustered on the south coast around the city of Portsmouth. Pinpointed on the map above, five of the clubs are in Hampshire. They are Titchfield, BC near Fareham (1), Alverstoke BC in Gosport (2), Bellair BC in Havant (3), Emsworth BC (4), and Hayling Island RBL BC (5). Across the border, just inside West Sussex lies Bosham BC (6). Together these clubs form the Old English Bowling Association, an organisation founded in 1924, but with its roots in earlier times. The question is, how much earlier?

Speaking at the annual dinner of the Old English Bowling Association in 1937, the chairman of Bellair Bowling Club, Eden Smith, said, 'I don't want to disparage the EBA game, because any game that can command such a multitude of supporters... must have a kick in it somewhere.'

However, he assured his audience that the form of bowls that they were playing was indeed the game that Francis Drake had played in 1588.

Smith concluded with a toast to the OEBA: 'May its motto still remain: Biased woods for unbiased players'.

So, what do we have here?

A genuine throwback to the Tudor or Stuart era, as at Lewes?

Or is 'Old English Bowls', like the so-called 'Elizabethan' bowls at Barnes (see page 102), merely a name given to a southern English variation that, because it does not conform to flat green rules, and because crown green bowls does not exist locally, is automatically assumed to be of great vintage?

In one sense Old English Bowls does share a characteristic with bowls from Drake's era, in that it uses strongly biased bowls.

But as we have noted, such bowls are also in use exclusively at Barnes and Lewes, and by some players at Chesterfield, Hadley Heath and Framlingham, where the games are quite different.

And, unlike at these greens, the Old English bowlers of the south coast play in rinks, which almost certainly did not exist in 1588.

Another quirk of the OEBA is that its rinks are marked with white lines, in a unique fashion, as seen opposite.

But if not 'old', or even 'olde', when was this curious hybrid form of bowls first played?

The answer appears to be that it evolved between the 1870s and around 1910. In 1882 Bosham BC held a dinner attended by representatives from Southsea, Crystal Palace (a pub in Fratton) and Kingston Cross, while the earliest reference to a tournament come in 1889. This involved eight clubs in the Portsmouth & District area, including three from the Isle of Wight; Newport, Ventnor and Carisbrooke. Games were played in triples, rather than in fours, as would become the norm under EBA rules.

However, at this stage the term 'Old English Bowls' was not used, and nor was it in 1903 when eight clubs formed the Hampshire Bowling Association (HBA).

Interestingly, they were joined by Southampton Old Bowling Green Club, who played in the HBA's first Challenge Shield.

This competition, we learn from a retrospective article in the *Portsmouth Evening News* (on August 11 1926), had been 'open to clubs playing the wide bias wood game.'

The fact that the HBA disbanded after only one year suggests that while some of the nine clubs were leaning towards the Scottish way, as was Southampton (*page 73*), others demurred. This is confirmed in the *Portsmouth Evening News* article. JH Slater, a leading member of one of the HBA clubs, Saxe-Weimar BC (later renamed Southsea Waverley) is remembered as a great early supporter of the EBA games, despite in 1903 being 'forced by circumstances to play with wide bias woods'.

In the end it had to wait until 1920 for a new Hampshire County Association to form, this time firmly aligned to the EBA.

So it was that a dozen clubs still loyal to the 'wide bias wood game' struck out on their own by forming the OEBA four years later, in 1924.

This was cut to eight in 1935 when Havant Park, Hayling, Southbourne (Bournemouth) and Priory Park (Chichester) switched to the EBA . The loss of Priory Park, the oldest of the members, having formed in 1839, was a particular blow.

Since then the total has been reduced to six. Yet far from regretting that they did not fall in with the majority, the attitude of Old English bowlers today is exactly that of Eden Smith. Determined as ever that 'biased woods' still be used by 'unbiased players'.

▶ How does Old English Bowls differ from other bowling codes?

As seen here at **Alverstoke**, players step *on* to a mark to bowl, rather than stepping off it, as in crown and flat green bowls. Indeed outside the OEBA only at Barnes is this the practice.

Note also the existence of a baseline, behind which the bowl has to be delivered. When the HBA issued its rules in 1904, it stated that the jack must be sent a minimum of 75 feet. Hence, presumably, the need for a baseline (as can be seen on photographs taken in Portsmouth in the 1900s).

Alverstoke today is, incidentally, the spiritual home of Old English Bowls. Often referred to as 'the old ABCs', in the late 19th century the club was formed at the White Hart Hotel, before moving in the early 20th century to its current home in **Gosport Park**. Like all clubs in the OEBA, its green undulates gently rather than being crowned, or flat.

The second view of OEBA green markings (*right centre*) is from **Titchfield**, whose green was opened in 1923 and boasts a smart new pavilion built in 2014.

One condition of the club's tenure is that no play ever takes place on a Sunday.

As can be seen, at both ends of the rink, four yards from the baseline, is a box four yards square. Either side of this are lines to mark the extent of each rink. When these lines were introduced is not known.

Note also the absence of ditches or banks.

Under OEBA rules the jack must come to a halt inside the box, but does not need then to be centred (as in flat green bowls). In this respect Old English Bowls is akin to the 'roving cot' game as played at Cambridge, featured in the next chapter.

Bowls, however, may finish outside the box and still count, as long as they are within four feet of the jack. (For this reason four foot wooden rules, some in one piece, some hinged, are placed around the green for measuring.)

The rules also allow for the jack to leave the box, if knocked by a bowl, provided it remains within the base and sidelines.

But if none of these rules can be traced back definitively to before the late 19th century, the use of 'wide bias' woods does at least link the game with the distant past.

The usual measure of bias for woods associated with the OEBA is that set by John Jaques of London – a games manufacturer first established in 1795 and now based in Kent – that fulfilled a role similar to that of Thomas Taylor in Scotland. The standard Jaques bias for woods in the Old English game is often stated as 6-8 (compared with 12-13 at Barnes). However, in the records of Priory Park, Chichester, members of the OEBA until 1935, are cited woods with a bias ranging from 6-20, with one set at least reaching a bias of 25.

In recent years, Titchfield has managed to source reconditioned sets of sufficiently biased lignum vitae woods from Pershore Bowls in Worcestershire. However at Alverstoke, Jock 'the bowls doctor' obtains the required bias using another method; that is, he drills out the mount of an existing wood, adds lead, and then replaces the mount with a coin; for example a 1947 halfpenny (*right*).

Before machine lathes came into use in the 1870s, this method was common around the bowls world.

Thus the OEBA can be said to be keeping alive at least one tradition that most certainly was common in the lifetime of Francis Drake.

Chapter Nine

Britain 1918–1939

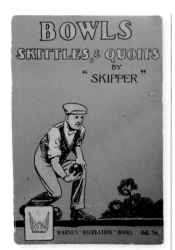

'Rest assured that bowls can and does call for a high degree of skill,' wrote 'Skipper' in this 1928 guide, adding that the game 'is by no means as slow as it appears', and provides exercise that 'although of the mild kind, goes a long way towards the maintenance of physical and mental fitness.' As for skittles, once a national game, it remains popular in the south west and East Midlands, but quoits survives only in a few locations. So perhaps in the end, mild is better.

During the First World War, like most sports, bowls carried on but at a much reduced level. Many a club turned its attention to fund raising for the war effort, or in some cases to opening up its facilities to the troops or to the war wounded. The EBA suspended its championships between 1915-18.

But almost immediately after hostilities ended, the country that David Lloyd George promised would be 'fit for heroes' took to its sports fields with renewed vigour.

As had been only too shockingly revealed by the poor physical state of many of those who enlisted during the war, Britain needed sport for more than just its morale. And although not necessarily a young man's game, bowls benefitted from this increased commitment to recreation at both a local and national level.

Surrey County Bowling Association, for example, the largest county in the EBA, expanded from 29 clubs in 1911 to 89 by 1923, and 174 by 1933.

One of the hundreds of new clubs that formed in the 1920s was directly connected to the war effort. This was in the Westfield Memorial Village, Lancaster. Built for soldiers of the King's Own Royal Regiment, the village was designed by Thomas Mawson, with, as was his common practice (*see page 132*), a bowling green and tennis courts in the centre. The green can still be seen today.

Municipal greens were created in ever greater numbers too, as part of a nationwide surge in park provision. Glasgow increased its number of park greens from 30 in 1914 to 67 by 1933.

A similar boom took place in company sports, with thousands of workers given access to subsidised sports facilities.

In London, the Business House Bowling League consisted of teams from virtually every bank, insurance company and government department, some of whose greens, including those of the Bank of England and the Civil Service, were lavishly maintained.

Bowls also weathered the Depression well. Even those who could not afford tennis gear or golf clubs could hire woods from a park keeper's hut and play for only a few pence. For the better off members of private clubs, wider ownership of motor cars made it easier for teams and individuals to enter competitions further afield.

In 1933 the newly launched weekly, *Bowling World*, estimated that 3,000 people were joining flat green clubs every season. 'No game, bar golf, is attracting more young men than bowls.'

A further characteristic of this period was that in most parts of England and Wales those clubs still wavering as to which type of bowls to play, crown or flat green, made their choice, thereby establishing the bowls map we know today. (Scotland had of course gone through this process before 1900).

The exception was the east of England, extending from

BOWLING MATCH NORFOLK v NOTTS HARLESTON MAGPIE JUNE 28/29.

Northumberland to Lincolnshire, the East Midlands and East Anglia.

In 1927 Norfolk, Lincolnshire and Nottinghamshire combined to form the Midlands & East Anglian Bowling Federation.

Derbyshire, Northamptonshire and Suffolk joined two years later, and eventually this grouping would lead to the English Bowling Federation forming in 1945 – the third and last major strand of English bowls to organise.

We will return to Federation bowls on later pages, but for now take note of the photograph opposite. This was a Norfolk v. Nottinghamshire county match played in 1929 at the Harleston Magpie pub. Pub greens were still numerous in Norfolk at this time, but although the Grade II listed pub survives (renamed the JD Young Hotel), the green is one of many to have disappeared.

Note that the players were still bowling in 'civvies' rather than in regulation dress.

Another group of bowlers to organise between the wars was women, at least in flat green circles. As noted in the previous chapter, the first ladies clubs or ladies sections of clubs had formed in the 1900s. By 1928 there were sufficient numbers to form a county association in Somerset, followed by Leicestershire in 1930.

Then in September 1931 Clara Johns of Sussex organised the first open tournament for ladies, at Eastbourne. A total of 240 entered.

Encouraged by this, at a meeting of 200 clubs in London a few weeks later the English Women's Bowling Association was formed. Its counterparts in Wales and Scotland followed in 1932 and 1936 respectively. (An association for ladies in crown green bowls had to wait until 1969.)

By 1939, 11,500 women were registered with the EBA's roster of 1,800 clubs. This was few compared with the 191,800 men, but there was plenty of optimism for the future. And as George Burrows of the EBA was to write before the 1939 season, one of the most encouraging aspects of the game at that time was how many young men were now to the fore.

However 15 months later most young men had other things on their minds, as, in the midst of the Battle of Britain, Winston Churchill told the nation, 'We must regard the next week or so as a very important period in our history.

'It ranks with the days when the Spanish Armada was approaching the Channel, and Drake was finishing his game of bowls...

Thirteen counties sent players to the fourth annual championships of the **English Women's Bowling Association** at **Wimbledon Park**, London in August 1935.

Note the strict adherence to whites – a policy that the EWBA adopted before the men – and that every bowler wears a hat. The only colours permitted were those of the players' counties on their hatbands, with the proviso that hatband bows had to be worn on the left side.

Predictably not all male bowlers welcomed women's involvement.

In 1929 members of the Pymmes Park BC in north London wrote to Edmonton Council to say that if women were chosen to play in a forthcoming match against the Council they would not take part.

In response, Mrs LR Ithell, one of the recently elected female councillors told the press, 'I once applied for membership of the Park Club on behalf of a few other women bowlers, but in reply I received a copy of the club rules, and was politely referred to the rule, "ladies not admitted". But the greens are public property, and women will go on playing there...'

This, she added, was despite criticism even by other women.

'A woman who saw me playing with other women said one day, "Just look at those women playing bowls. I shan't let my husband go there again".'

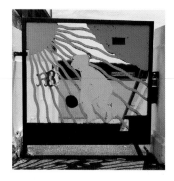

▲ A sunny welcome for visitors to the **Ramsgate Bowling Club** in **Kent**, formed in 1929 and with a dashing Art Deco gate to match.

As a small plaque on the gate informs passersby, the club's two greens were actually laid in 1924.

This was as part of a scheme by Ramsgate Corporation to boost the town's appeal by building a new road linking up the old town to the, as yet undeveloped, chalky cliffs to the west.

Overseen by the architects John Burnet and Partners, this new Royal Esplanade can be seen in the postcard from the mid 1920s (*top right*). Part-financed by the government, it opened in 1923.

As was the pattern established at other resorts (*see page 130*) the coastal side of the Esplanade was divided into sections; for public lawns, for croquet and for bowling.

This work, which required a considerable amount of engineering and landscaping, was completed in 1924 at a staggering cost of £160,000. However the plan was to recoup this by a development on the inland side of the Esplanade (that is on the right of the postcard).

To kick start this, the Corporation spent another £63,000 acquiring 76 acres of the Westcliff House estate and various adjoining plots, before commissioning architects Franklin & Deacon to design an estate on what was billed as 'the most perfect building site on the south coast'.

At the same time, two structures by Basil Deacon bookended the lawns and greens; at the west end, the Westcliff Lift, at the east end an Italian Renaissance bandstand and tea pavilion (now a bathing pool). Thus intending buyers into the estate could see that the amenities were already in place when the first houses were completed in 1929.

Today this grand vision is still very much in evidence.

Least altered is the pavilion of **Ramsgate Croquet Club** (*centre right*). Like Mawson's pavilion at South Tawton it has a viewing area on the roof, accessible from and at the same level as the Esplanade.

Its identical twin is the bowls pavilion. As can be seen (*below right*) an extension now obscures the frontage. However as it does not compromise the core structure, this has not prevented the building being listed Grade II, as is its croquet counterpart.

Together with the Westcliff Lift and tea pavilion, the croquet and bowls pavilions form part of the Royal Esplanade Conservation Area, a perfectly balanced example of 1920s planning, enticing to holidaymakers, yet equally desirable as a place in which to live.

Best time to visit? The club hosts a two-week open tournament in late July and early August (partly why that extension is so necessary).

However not all in Ramsgate is sunny. Cutbacks have meant that the bowls club might find itself liable for repairs, a prospect increasingly faced by clubs on public greens.

Exposed to the sea air, in a listed building, in a Conservation Area – that represents quite a challenge when all you really want is to play bowls and watch the ships sail by.

LAWNS & BOWLING GREEN, WEST CLIFF, RAMSGATE.   LP 251.

226 BOWLING GREENS, GREAT YARMOUTH

RHYL - WEST PROMENADE, SHOWING TENNIS COURTS AND BOWLING GREEN.

▲ Three inter war postcards illustrate how town planners in other resorts placed bowling greens in as central a location as possible; indicative of the game's status in early 20th century popular culture, and also of how greens brought life and colour to the townscape.

Seen above is one of two greens laid in the 1920s on **Marine Parade** in **Great Yarmouth**.

Before these, Great Yarmouth's principal green for visitors had been in the privately run Vauxhall Gardens, created a century earlier.

The prominent building seen in the postcard is the **Royal Aquarium**.

Built in 1876 opposite the entrance to the Britannia Pier, it failed as an attraction and in 1883 was converted into a theatre, and then a cinema, which it remains.

Bowling meanwhile has not only stayed in fashion but become an integral part of the local economy.

The two greens above have been joined by three more, forming a line on North Drive. Together these host Great Yarmouth's annual **Festival of Bowls**, which since 1945 has taken place over four weeks in September and currently attracts over 1,800 entrants, making it the largest bowls event in Britain.

(On the inland side of North Drive, incidentally, is the Wellesley Recreation Ground, home to one of the oldest grandstands in Britain, built in 1890-91, a tennis pavilion and ticket booth, all listed and all designed by Yarmouth's Borough Engineer from 1882-1922, JW Cockrill, who almost certainly oversaw the layout of the Marine Parade bowling greens too.)

At Great Yarmouth and at resorts across Britain, a significant impetus for holding summer bowls tournaments was the 1938 Holidays with Pay Act. This guaranteed all workers one week of paid leave between May and October.

The success of such tournaments also helps explain why bowling greens in certain resorts have outlived most other attractions.

A case in point is **Rhyl** in **Wales** (*above*). Seen here in the 1920s, next to red shale tennis courts, are two greens (one only just visible) on the East Parade (not the West, as stated on the postcard), with **Rhyl Pavilion** in the distance. The pavilion was replaced in 1991 but the greens live on. Indeed there are now three; one home to the **East Parade BC**, two for public use. One of the greens has a bank of seats, a leftover from when the East Parade served briefly as the **Welsh National Crown Green Bowling Centre**.

Inevitably one of the issues now facing greens such as in Great Yarmouth and Rhyl is that whereas once they were continually monitored by attendants, today they are more vulnerable to vandalism and to casual mis-use.

PROMENADE, BOWLING AND PUTTING GREENS, ILFRACOMBE   A 623

Even at seaside towns where level ground is at a premium, as at Ilfracombe, north Devon (*left*), a bowling green was still considered an essential. This was for holidaymakers. Locals had their own club inland, formed in 1893. The greens seen here still exist as public gardens, but since the buildings on the right have been cleared the setting is quite altered.

▲ By the inter war period many a bowls club formed prior to 1914 had grown so large – in some cases by starting up ladies sections – that its original pavilion was no longer big enough. One such was **Dover Bowling Club**.

Bowling is first recorded on Dover's foreshore in 1605, but the port's four surviving clubs today all date from the 20th century.

Dover BC began life in 1907 as the Dover Institute BC, moving to its current council-owned green in 1911. Watched over by the battlements of Dover Castle, it lies in **Maison Dieu Gardens**, named after a monastic 'House of God' that stood nearby as an overnight halt for medieval pilgrims going to Canterbury (as did God's House Hospital in Southampton).

The pavilion seen here was built by the council in 1935, the year the club adopted its present name.

Since then the only major change has been that its verandah has been enclosed. The building also experienced a near miss when a shell destroyed the green in 1944.

Patently its style harks back to Arts and Crafts influences, being timber framed, weatherboarded and

with Kentish clay roof tiles. But if it appears to be yet another example of how bowlers in the 1930s steadfastly refused to countenance modernism, in Dover they have good reason to be wary.

For what cannot be seen from this angle is that the opposite side of the green lies in almost permanent shadow courtesy of an ugly 1960s office block.

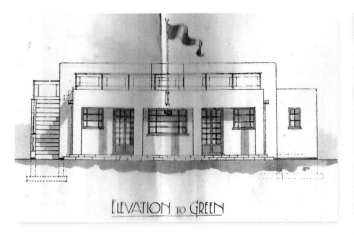

ELEVATION TO GREEN

The Avenue Bowls Club, Newmarket.

A view of the green and club house.   Photo : Frank Briggs, Newmarket.

▲ While most bowls pavilions built between the wars echoed the architectural styles of the pre-1914 era, there were a few exceptions.

One is the Modernist pavilion of **Newmarket Avenue Bowling Club** in **Newmarket, Suffolk**, a town known most of all for horse racing, since at least 1622. Although local inns may well have offered bowling to racegoers in the years since, the earliest club was formed at the Memorial Gardens in 1921. Then, keen to find a better, and more private green, in 1935 a group of members formed a limited company and purchased land on **The Avenue** (hence the club's name).

The club commissioned the long established firm, J & D Provan from Glasgow, to lay its green with Cumberland turf.

But instead of going for a traditional pavilion it approved what to other clubs must have seemed a daringly modern design, by local architect Cecil Rayner. Faced in white concrete render it featured Crittall windows and a flat roof which doubled, as at Ramsgate, as a viewing terrace, accessed from steps at the side.

Seen on this page are extracts from Rayner's plans, and above right, a local newspaper cutting from June 1936, reporting on the official opening, by the racehorse breeder and owner, Walter Raphael.

For all its modernity the pavilion (and green) cost a very reasonable £2,000, and occupied a prime site, close to the station and next door to the town's huge bloodstock auction mart (to which Tattersalls relocated

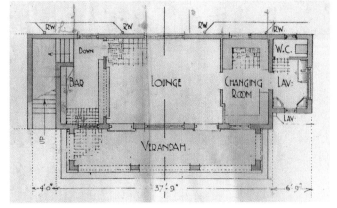

its entire operation in 1939, so that today its two main entrances flank the bowling green).

Since then, the Avenue club has opened its door to ladies, in 1957 (they played formerly at the Jockey

Club), and extended the pavilion on both sides, as seen in 2006 (*below left*). This has been at the cost of the rooftop viewing gallery, but not, fortunately, of the building's clean lines and 1930s ambience.

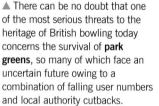 There can be no doubt that one of the most serious threats to the heritage of British bowling today concerns the survival of **park greens**, so many of which face an uncertain future owing to a combination of falling user numbers and local authority cutbacks.

And of course attached to most park greens stands a pavilion.

Above is an especially fine example at **Spencer Park** in **Earlsdon, Coventry**. Built in 1915 and designed by the Borough Engineer – to serve two bowling greens and ten tennis courts laid a few years earlier – the pavilion was closed in June 2015 after Coventry City Council sought to reduce the £30,000 annual costs of running the building and its associated facilities. A petition organised by the Friends of Spencer Park and signed by 3,000 local residents just weeks before the pavilion's centenary was due to be celebrated failed to reverse its closure.

But at least one of the two bowling greens was saved for the time being.

The question is, which one?

Unusually, Spencer Park has both a crown green and a flat green alongside each other (as had also been the case at the nearby War Memorial Park, at least until the crown green was converted into a putting green in 2010).

This juxtaposition, also once seen at two Birmingham venues, is indicative of Coventry's location on the border between the two codes.

At Spencer Park it was the crown green that gained a reprieve.

Even then it was saved not for public use – since the pavilion is now out of bounds – but for the sole use of the **Albany Bowling Club**, who pay an annual subscription to the Council.

In west London, the pavilion at **Acton Park** (*top*) was built in 1936 when the park's original green, laid in 1911, was relaid with a second green alongside. More recently that second green was turned into a flower garden, while the other has just gone into limbo after **Acton Park BC** folded in January 2015.

Before that, the club occupied the main core of the pavilion, with the end section serving as a café to the public. At **Cambridge Square Gardens** in **Southend** (*above*) it is now the other way round.

When built in 1925 the pavilion was for bowlers only. But since membership has declined – it stood at only 27 in 2014 – the club has been shunted into a room at the near end and the main section converted into a restaurant.

Langdale Bowling Club in the village of **Elterwater** is the most northerly crown green club on the west side of England.

This is a legacy of the fact that before boundary changes in 1974 created the new county of Cumbria, this part of the Lake District lay in Westmorland, a county which leaned more towards Lancashire, in the south, whereas to the north lay Cumberland, where flat green dominates. It is a legacy that requires the 20 or so Langdale members to travel many miles south on rural lanes in order to fulfil their fixtures in the Rothay, Kendal and South Westmorland districts.

But there is another reason to pick out Langdale. As noted earlier, after the First World War had exposed how unfit so many British men were when they enlisted, a number of charitable bodies started to campaign for the provision of more playing fields and recreation grounds, especially in cities.

Of these, the most effective was the **National Playing Fields Association**, set up in 1925 by Brigadier General Reginald Kentish.

Some 1,000 fields were laid out by the NPFA between the wars.

It was the NPFA, moreover, that in 1934 set a minimum recommended level of provision for local authorities. This was that at least six acres per 1,000 residents should be provided for 'outdoor recreational activity', of which four acres should be set aside for 'team games, tennis, bowls' and the rest for children's playgrounds.

Such was the importance attached to this mission that when King George V died in 1936 it was decided that instead of erecting statues in his memory, funds would be raised to either create or to enhance existing playing fields.

Shortly after this the Physical Training and Recreation Act of 1937 sought to address the same need; that of encouraging Britons to be active at a time when Germany was once again flexing its muscles.

By the time the fund was wound up in 1965 and its responsibilities handed over to the NPFA, a total of 471 **King George's Fields** had been endowed. At barely a third of an acre Elterwater's field was one of the smallest – the largest was 128 acres in Cardiff – and also possibly the only one to feature a bowling green and nothing else.

Indeed in an area currently with only a minority of permanent residents, Langdale BC is the only sports club representing the village. As such it is grateful for any green fees paid by holidaymakers (who can get the key to the green from the Britannia Inn opposite).

Yet another measure of how bowls, perhaps more than any other sport, is ideally suited to even the smallest of rural communities.

In most cases it is easy to identify a King George's Field, for as at Langdale (*left*), two Portland stone panels usually adorn the main gateway, one of which bears the inscription 'George V – AD 1910-1936'. The panels were designed by George Kruger Gray, known also for designing much of the coinage circulated within Britain and the Commonwealth between the wars.

▲ Looming in the distance, the unmistakable hulk of the 74,500 capacity **Millennium Stadium** in **Cardiff**, opened in its present form in 1999 and home of the Welsh Rugby Union, international football, rock concerts, speedway and much else besides under its sliding roof.

In the middle distance, the somewhat lower concrete and steel ribs of **Cardiff Arms Park**, the 12,500 capacity ground of **Cardiff Rugby Club**, formed in 1876.

And in the foreground, least obtrusively of all, the single green of **Cardiff Athletic Bowling Club**.

South Wales witnessed a surge in flat green bowls clubs between the wars, following the formation of county associations in mid Wales, Glamorgan and Monmouthshire in the period 1922-24.

Formed in 1923, Cardiff Athletic was, and remains a branch of the **Cardiff Athletic Club**, a body established the previous year by the merger of two much older amateur clubs based on the Arms Park site; **Cardiff Cricket Club**, formed in 1845, and **Cardiff Football Club** (that is the rugby club), formed in 1876. They had merged in order to form a company to buy the Arms

Park site from the Marquess of Bute for £30,000. In addition to cricket, rugby and bowls, further sections were formed between the wars for tennis, hockey, golf and even, briefly, baseball.

In 1914 there were just 20 clubs in the Welsh Bowling Association.

By 1939 there were over 170, including 38 in the Cardiff and East Glamorgan district alone.

▶ Outside **Wrexham** in North Wales, the **Llay Institute** is one of the largest and most lavish examples of a type of combined social, educational and sports centre that was to emerge in Britain's coal mining communities between the wars, courtesy of the **Miners' Welfare Fund**.

The fund, set up as a result of the Mining Industries Act of 1920, was an initiative whereby mine owners contributed a levy of 1d per ton of coal produced, going up to 2d in 1926, but then falling to a halfpenny per ton in the 1930s in the wake of the Depression.

Initially the fund focused on the provision of basic necessities such as pithead baths, canteens and changing rooms. But as the 1920s wore on it was extended to help fund a wider range of social and sporting facilities, including libraries, swimming pools and sports grounds.

In some locations the Miners' Welfare Fund developed facilities from scratch. In others it helped build on foundations that had already been laid, as happened at Llay. There, the Main Colliery had only just gone into full production in 1923 when its proprietors laid on leisure facilities for its workers at Llay Place Hall.

Its bowling green was opened on June 8 1923 with a doubles match between four pillars of the village; WL Halpin, managing director of the Colliery, partnered by Dr Morris Jones, against the Rev J Lewis Evans and Edward Stuart Clark, whose family owned the Hall.

Over the next few years so rapidly did the colliery expand – by 1929 it was the largest in North Wales, producing more than 1m tonnes of coal a year and employing 3,000 workers – that its sports and social clubs needed more space.

So it was that with a £20,000

grant from the Miners' Welfare Fund more land was bought from the Llay Hall Estate, and a Mold architect, F Roberts, commissioned to design a new clubhouse and institute.

Seen above after its renovation in 2005, this was opened on June 20 1931, and offered extensive halls and rooms for dances, meetings, classes and, at the rear, two crown greens. Despite the addition of an unsympathetic extension facing the two greens (*below left*), the Institute and a detached pavilion in a similar Italian Baroque style, serving the Institute's cricket and football grounds, are now listed Grade II.

Both are still well used too, despite the closure of the colliery in 1966, as is the case at most former miners' welfare clubs around Britain, most of them now run by trusts or local authorities.

Other miners' welfare clubs of note in a bowling context include the listed clubhouse at Denbeath in Fife, Scotland, built in 1924, and Backworth Hall on North Tyneside, a Grade II listed 18th century house that was bought by the Miners' Welfare Fund in 1934 and, like Llay, offers facilities for bowls and cricket, as well as golf and archery.

▶ 'Forty years ago,' reported *The Bowling World* in May 1933, 'it would have been regarded as folly for a business house to cater for the healthy enjoyment of its employees by providing a fully equipped sports ground.' Yet by the 1930s, it was able to report, 'what a change has come over the directorate of the large firms!'

By then, most British cities were dotted with company grounds, many including bowling greens.

On this page are two from the Scottish town of **Alloa**, both of which are listed and remain in use.

On the right is the **Co-operative Bowling Club** on **Sunnyside Road**.

With contrasting white rendered walls and red clay roof tiles, it was designed by George Alexander Kerr and opened in May 1925.

Below is the pavilion of the **Patons & Baldwin Bowling Club** on **Tullibody Road**. Designed by William Kerr of John Melvin & Son, this was built in 1926 for workers at Patons & Baldwin, the largest wool spinning company in Britain.

In its heyday the ground hosted football, tennis, hockey and bowls. However since the closure of the mill in 1999 and the sale of much of the sportsground for housing, only the bowling green survives.

Other prominent companies with greens still in use include Cadbury's (Birmingham), Rolls Royce (Derby), and Tata Steel (Port Talbot).

CO-OPERATIVE SPORTS GROUNDS, ALLOA

PATONS SPORTS PAVILION AND PLEASURE GROUNDS, ALLOA.

▲ In the Victorian and Edwardian periods bowling greens at pubs, especially in urban areas, and even more so in Scotland, were often denigrated for encouraging betting and excess. But come the 1920s, a time when breweries were looking at ways of making pubs more attractive to women and families, and car owners, bowling greens came back into fashion.

One of the best places to see the results of this trend is **Birmingham**, where as part of the **Reformed Pubs movement** a number of substantial, eclectically designed pubs were built on main arteries and on major roundabouts in a number of new suburbs, often resembling grand country houses of the Elizabethan or Stuart periods (hence the term 'Brewers' Tudor').

The **Black Horse** pub on **Bristol Road**, **Northfield** (*above*) is a prime example. Designed for Davenports Brewery by Francis Goldsborough in 1929 and now listed Grade II, it features several spacious rooms served from a central bar, with a baronial function room upstairs. But if the attention to detail in the interior is impressive, so too is that applied to the structures serving the crown green at the rear. These are a small pavilion with wooden roof tiles and with its own cellar, and a decorative colonnade built from Cotswold stone (just visible above).

Over on **Shirley Road** in **Hall Green**, meanwhile, the brewers Mitchells & Butler opted for a more Moderne style at the **Three Magpies**. Designed by Wood, Kendrick & Reynolds and opened in 1935, the pub's bowling pavilion (*above right*) matches the pub itself in its use of brown brickwork, metal windows, terrazzo flooring, wide timber eaves and a flat roof.

Despite both the pub and pavilion being listed Grade II in 1997, the closure first of the pub, in 1998, followed two years later by the bowls club, appeared to signal the end. But then in 2001 Greene King bought and refurbished the 'Maggies'. Even better, in 2006 members of the Greet Inn BC, who had lost their own pub green, took over and spent over £4,000 restoring the green and clubhouse.

However this was an exception. As of 2015, 23 pubs built in the Birmingham area between 1919-51 still have functioning greens, but a further 53 have been lost.

Built for the Cobbold Brewery in 1936 and named after a local heroine, the Grade II* Margaret Catchpole pub on Cliff Lane, Ipswich (*above*), designed by Harold Ridley Cooper, is exceptionally well-preserved, with its wood panelling and other interior details largely intact. Unusually, its bowling green was a later addition, in 1948.

Case study

Carlisle State Management Scheme

Seemingly ready for business, this is the bowls storage cupboard at the Redfern pub in Carlisle, the fourteenth and last pub built under the Carlisle State Management Scheme. Another pub in the scheme was the Horse and Farrier on Wigton Road, built in 1929 and closed in 2010. Four years later its bowling green was still gathering weeds as the future of the site remained in limbo (*right*).

In terms of design and strategy, there was much in common between Birmingham's Reformed Pub movement and the Carlisle State Management Scheme.

Not least, both resulted in a flurry of pub greens being laid between the wars, in defiance of those who continued to argue that, if offered the likes of bowls, skittles, quoits, darts or billiards, people were likely to drink more.

In fact, as the Mass Observation investigation into public habits conducted in Bolton from 1937 onwards observed, it was usually the opposite. Pub goers who engaged in games actually drank less, and more slowly.

But the Carlisle scheme had its roots in a rather different problem.

During the First World War, in 1915 the otherwise rural area to the north of Carlisle, around Gretna Green, became home to a vast workforce of some 25,000 munitions workers, brought in mainly from Ireland and Glasgow.

It was dangerous work and led hordes of men to congregate in Carlisle on a nightly basis.

After a year or so of escalating absenteeism and 953 convictions for fighting and vandalism, the Government decided to nationalise the entire Carlisle brewing industry at a stroke, pubs included, and put it all into the hands of a Central Control Board.

Similar schemes were set up in other areas where sensitive war work was in hand; for example in the Cromarty Firth in Scotland and Enfield, north London.

In all parts of Britain in 1915 pub opening hours were cut to aid munitions production, a cut not fully reversed until 2003.

But in Carlisle the restrictions went further. These included the provision of weaker beer, the payment of landlords with a fixed wage (rather than one based on sales) and the introduction of a 'no treating' rule, meaning that no-one could buy rounds of drinks.

At the same time over a third of all Carlisle's licensed premises were simply shut down.

In 1918, instead of reverting to pre-war market forces, supervision of the city's pubs was devolved to the Carlisle and District State Management Scheme, or SMS.

It was this scheme that then went ahead with an ambitious programme of pub construction along lines similar to those in Birmingham; that is, each in a distinct, light and airy architectural style, designed to be more welcoming to women and families, to serve snacks and food, with smoke extractors as standard, and equipped with a range of pub games.

Architect Harry Redfern (1861-1950) was put in charge of the programme. Based in London, Redfern seemed an unlikely choice, having done his most extensive work before then in various Oxbridge colleges.

But working with assistant Joseph Seddon, Redfern's 'Model Inns' were just that. Starting in 1927, 14 were completed in Carlisle, four with bowling greens.

The greens were no mere add ons. Redfern insisted on clinker beds under the turf – Cumberland turf, naturally – to ensure good drainage. At the Horse and Farrier the building was designed in an L-shape, on a north west to south east axis, so that the green received maximum sunlight.

Clearly the SMS greens were popular, for in 1938, E Mitchell, president of the SMS Bowls League, called for more to be made available as those in the scheme were having to host 480 matches in fourteen weeks.

Indeed the SMS was a great success with the public overall, and its pubs remained profitable until in 1971 the government decided to auction off the scheme's assets. Greenall Whitley bought some of the pubs and took on sponsorship of the league but, with dwindling numbers of bowlers (caused partly by the steadily deteriorating quality of the greens), fixtures came to an end in 1993.

As of 2015, seven of the SMS pubs in Carlisle remain in use as pubs. As for the bowling greens...

◀ Last but not least – opened in 1940, **The Redfern** on **Kingmoor Road** in **Etterby**, **Carlisle** ranks as one of the most sumptuous of the fourteen SMS pubs built between 1927-40, and is accordingly listed Grade II. Its architect was Joseph Seddon, but it was named after Harry Redfern as a tribute to all the work he had done in making the SMS such a success.

Note how the end bays were canted, with a verandah and first floor balcony offering prime views over the bowling green – a green which, sadly, by the time the author tried it out, as seen here in August 2012, was barely playable.

It is a familiar dilemma for a pub that no longer has a resident club. A well maintained green can bring in business, but an average or poor quality green has no appeal at all, even to casual bowlers.

Over at **The Magpie Inn** on **Victoria Road**, **Botcherby** the scene, also in 2012, appears more promising. Opened in 1933, this Redfern designed pub, also listed Grade II, demonstrates again his attention to detail. Every angle, every finish, was carefully considered. Redfern even specified the varieties of shrubs and flowers to be planted on the terrace.

And when in 1949 Seddon proposed glazing in the verandah to create a darts area, he made sure to get Redfern's approval first.

In 2010 the Magpie was restored to its sparkling best and the green made playable for casual games amongst the regulars.

But in 2013 the shutters went down, as they did too at the Redfern in January 2015.

Since then, Samuel Smiths Brewery has rescued the Magpie and the green. At the time of going to press, however, the Redfern remained boarded up.

Case study

Paddington Sports Club

Proving that bowls can be a young man's game, 21 year old David Bryant (on the left) and Reg Harris, both representing Somerset, pose before entering the EBA Pairs Championships at Paddington in 1953. This would be the first of many Paddington appearances for Bryant, who went on to become the most successful flat green bowler of all time, winning numerous national titles, three World titles and four Commonwealth Games golds, in between his career as a schoolmaster.

Compared with the governing bodies of other sports, those in the world of bowls have shown much less propensity either to build or to occupy signature headquarters, let alone to establish self-supporting national centres, such as Lord's, Wimbledon, Twickenham or Wembley.

Rather, they have preferred to live modestly by renting offices and staging their major tournaments at existing greens.

From 1928-56, the preferred venue for EBA championships was the Paddington Sports Club in west London. No doubt this had something to do with the fact that throughout those years the roles of both Secretary and Treasurer to the EBA were dominated by men from Middlesex and Surrey, and of course the Association had been born in London, in 1903.

But there were other well appointed greens elsewhere in the capital, and certainly ones with better parking and more space for spectators. So what was it that made Paddington become, as described by Godfrey Bolsover (see Links) and other commentators of the mid 20th century, the 'Mecca' of bowls (as opposed to the 'Wembley' of bowls, a tag later ascribed to the Waterloo)?

Firstly Paddington was handy for London's main rail terminals, compared with most of London's suburban clubs. Secondly, it had two greens, which in London between the wars was not common, other than in parks.

But thirdly, there was something atmospheric about Paddington's enclosed, urban environment that set it apart from other venues, in EBA circles at least (whereas in Glasgow several venues were equally boxed in).

The Paddington Bowling Club itself had come into being in modest circumstances in 1905, renting a two rink green at the nearby Paddington Recreation Ground (which had opened in 1888), occupying some stables as its first pavilion. However the club soon started winning honours, and gaining friends in high places; so much so that it was once said that 'the training ground for the Paddington Mayor's parlour was the Paddington Bowling Club'.

Two MPs were also amongst the membership.

In the mid 1920s the committee began looking for a more spacious long term home and identified only a few hundred yards away what was described as a 'waste ground' in the midst of mansion flats on Castellain and Delaware Roads (possibly used to dump spoil excavated from digging Underground tunnels). At one stage part of the site had also been used as a tennis club.

The hundred or so members formed themselves into a limited company, secured the

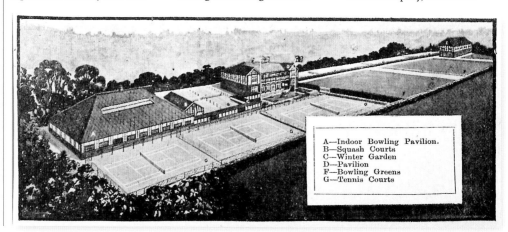

A—Indoor Bowling Pavilion.
B—Squash Courts
C—Winter Garden
D—Pavilion
F—Bowling Greens
G—Tennis Courts

necessary funding and after the groundworks had been completed, a grand ceremonial opening was held on July 21 1928.

As seen from the club's 1947 brochure (*opposite*), the narrow grounds housed a central two storey clubhouse, in the usual Tudorbethan style, together with nine tennis courts laid by the Leicestershire company, En-Tout-Cas. Tennis was to prove an important bedfellow for the bowlers, bringing in a steady, daily income and attracting members from the surrounding flats.

On the opening day lawn tennis's glamour couple of the day, Wimbledon champion Kitty Godfree and her husband Leslie, played an exhibition match. Also on the site was a putting green, two practice bowling rinks and two greens, laid with Cumberland turf by J & D Provan of Glasgow.

Before long Middlesex County matches were being staged on the two greens, followed in 1930 by the first international, against Australia. In 1931 the EBA switched its national championships to the club also, and in 1934 it hosted the bowls tournament of the Empire Games.

The following year an indoor bowling green was added too (as featured in the next chapter).

For the next two decades Paddington was the centre of the EBA universe. But in the end the Association moved its affairs to the Watney's Sports Ground at Mortlake, in south west London, where there were three greens, and crucially, better parking facilities.

Since then Paddington has gone through ups and downs but is currently on a definite up. It now offers two squash courts and a gym, and while there is only one outdoor bowling green, there are

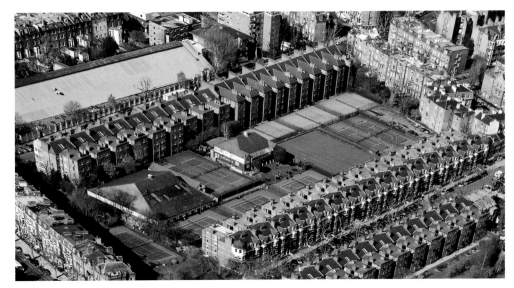

now ten tennis courts. Inevitably some tennis members would prefer the indoor bowling centre to make way for more courts, and with over 500 of them compared with only 40 or so bowlers, that is a battle that looks unlikely to go away. But for now bowling carries on determinedly, played by the few, watched over by the many (in the flats at least).

▲ Other than the immediate neighbours, most residents in Paddington have no idea that the **Paddington Sports Club** exists. Even the entrance on **Castellain Road**, in the foreground, on the right hand edge of this aerial view, is easily missed. Note to the left of the clubhouse (*seen also below left*) is the **indoor bowling centre,** built in 1935. Its interior can be seen on page 187. Note also the grey roof on the far side of **Delaware Road**. Built in 1910, this originally housed the largest indoor roller skating rink in Britain. Since 1935, however, it has been better known as the Maida Vale Studios of the BBC.

Case study

'Roving cot'

A jack and a mat, the starting point for any game of bowls, it might be supposed. But look closer, for what we have here, at the Dog at Dunley in Worcestershire, is an unbiased jack – that is a type usually associated with flat green bowls – and a small, circular mat, more commonly used in crown green. Plus, the green at the Dog at Dunley is undulating. Thus we come to a unique, hybrid version of bowls played in and around the Kidderminster and Stourport areas. Here, some greens are flat, some rise and fall. Bowlers set marks in any direction, and yet the jacks are those designed for rink play. How did this come about?

Following on from the examples of Lewes and Barnes, and of Old English Bowls on the south coast, further evidence that not all British bowlers in the early 20th century were prepared to slot neatly into either the crown green or flat green codes comes in two distinct pockets of England, in Worcestershire and in Norfolk (as marked on the map below).

Norfolk is arguably the most complicated county in England in terms of bowling heritage.

Firstly its clubs are split between some 65 currently affiliated to Bowls England (the former EBA and EWBA), and 87 affiliated to the English Bowling Federation.

However, 30 of those clubs are affiliated both to Bowls England and the EBF, indicating that their greens are flat but that the members play both codes.

The issue is complicated further by the fact that some EBF clubs in west Norfolk actually affiliate to North Cambridgeshire.

In addition, there are a further 90-100 Norfolk clubs not affiliated to either organisation, the majority of which are thought to play to Federation rules.

Secondly, Norfolk is the only county outside crown green territory to have had a significant number of pub greens.

It is calculated that 81 pubs in Norfolk had greens attached at one point during the 20th century.

Inevitably this number has dropped, so that as of 2015, only twelve pub greens survived in Norfolk, all but one with clubs

affiliated to the EBF. Some of these greens, it should be added, are now operated independently of the pub. At others, the pub is no longer a pub (see opposite).

But in the present context, of greater importance is that many Norfolk clubs play a form of bowls known as 'roving cot'.

In local dialect 'cot', meaning something small, is used to refer to the 'jack'.

But the term 'roving' requires a more detailed explanation.

Before the rink game took hold in England, as we saw at places such as Lewes and Framlingham all jacks were allowed to 'rove', in the sense that they could be delivered anywhere on the green.

Hence clearly a game in which the 'cot' is allowed to 'rove' has much in common with older forms of bowls. As to when 'roving cot' became distinguishable from crown or flat green bowls, there is a popular story in Norfolk that the term actually derives from the Second World War, when at the conclusion of matches an extra end with a roving jack was played for pennies, which were then

donated towards the purchase of children's cots at the Norfolk and Norwich Hospital.

But 'roving cots' were around long before this. ET Ayers, who was based in Yarmouth, used the word 'cot' in his 1894 book, Bowls, Bowling Greens and Bowl Playing.

He also made it clear that the game in Norfolk at that time was in a definite state of transition.

'On some greens old-fashioned brown jacks of wood are still used, but usually, nowadays, jacks of wood or earthenware, white or so painted, are used, and are much to be preferred as showing up clearly on the turf. Some jacks are biased, but uselessly, I think.'

Despite this greater visibility, by opting to use unbiased jacks on non-level greens the 'roving cot' bowlers of Norfolk were choosing the most difficult way of playing possible. This is because on non-level greens a biased jack acts as a pathfinder for the woods (see page 13), whereas an unbiased one can act only as a partial guide.

For this reason, in 'roving cot' matches all home teams have a distinct advantage.

There is evidence that rules incorporating 'roving cots' were in place in 1901 when the Norwich Bowling Association was formed, and in 1928, when a Business House League and a City Bowls League were formed in the city.

But what seems extraordinary is that in 1933 another league was formed, also based on roving cots. This one, however, was 150 miles to the west, in Kidderminster.

◀ Two bowling greens in Norfolk where 'roving cot' is the preferred game are at **The Bush** in the village of **Costessey** (*left*), where the pub is still very much in business, and **The Mitre** in **Norwich** (*below*), where the pub is now a Chinese restaurant and the green is run by the **Mitre Bowling Club** as a separate entity.

Note that at The Bush, as seen here in 2013, the jack is a standard unbiased jack, and that in this instance the end is taking place from 'corner to corner'. Many home players choose to do this because the 35 yard square green slopes appreciably down from the pub to the River Wensum, and therefore going 'corner to corner' maximises the challenge for their opponents.

Five miles away on **Earlham Road** in **Norwich**, the green of the **Mitre BC** (itself formed in 1900) started out as a standard square but had a corner cut out, as seen on the left, when the pub – a classic Tudorbethan design of the inter war period, now locally listed – was rebuilt in 1927.

Seen here, also in 2013, Mitre is in action in its annual friendly match against Felixstowe.

The club does also play in leagues, but only since 1986. It also now admits ladies, since 1997.

However one rule that has not changed is that in order to get from mat to jack, rather than cross the line of other matches taking place, players must walk around the outside of the green.

Incidentally, between these two greens there is another traditional pub green where 'roving cot' is played. This is the Crown Inn in New Costessey, a Reform pub built in 1931. Its licence was granted only on condition that another pub in the village close down. That was the Red Lion, built in 1756 and also with a bowling green.

Bowled Over **179**

▲ Back at the **Dog at Dunley** near **Stourport-on-Severn** another 'corner to corner' end is being played with an unbiased jack.

That the form of bowls found in this part of Worcestershire – centred upon **Kidderminster** – is, as in Norfolk, another hybrid, is quite understandable.

Crown green dominates the bowls scene in Birmingham, to the north east, as it does in Shropshire, to the immediate west. Yet in the rest of Worcestershire, to the south, it is the rink game that holds sway.

So what should we call this hybrid version? The locals appear to be undecided. Some call it 'open green bowls', yet some use the term 'federation bowls', even though there is no link, geographically or by affiliation, to the English Bowling Federation, played on the east coast. However the Kidderminster hybrid could equally be described as 'roving cot'.

How two such distinct areas of England, one in Norfolk, one in Worcestershire, ended up adopting such a similar form of bowls is,

alas, not known. But we do know when it first presented itself in the Kidderminster area in a formalised fashion. This occurred shortly before the First World War with the inauguration of the Eric A Knight Cup, a competition in which singles was played to '15 up'.

Among the early entrants were bowlers from the Kidderminster Town Bowling Club, based at the Cricketers' Arms (where the green is still in use), from the Franche Village Club, and from the parishes of St Ambrose and St John's.

In 1933 these clubs formed a **Midweek League** on Wednesday evenings, along with clubs from two local carpet manufacturers, Brinton's and Tompkinson's, plus another from the town's sugar beet works, and one in Wolverley. (Of these, Franche, St Ambrose, St John's and Wolverley survive.)

A total of 40 teams played in five divisions, with a Thursday afternoon league added in 1998.

No members of these midweek leagues were or are permitted to play their matches on a pub green.

For pubs, separate competitions were organised on Saturdays and Sundays known as the **Kidderminster Weekend Leagues**.

As seen at **The Dog at Dunley**, the ambience is notably relaxed, with more of a 'wear what you like, say what you like and drink what you like' attitude prevailing.

A further characteristic of Kidderminster's pubs is that they include some of the smallest greens in Britain, able to accommodate only two matches at a time. The green at the Dog, for example, measures just 18 yards down one edge and 21 down another.

Below, the green at the **Weary Traveller** in **Kidderminster** is 24 yards along its shortest edge.

In both the Midweek and Weekend Leagues a number of distinct rules apply.

For example the minimum length for a 'mark' (the distance the jack must travel before play commences) is 20 yards. The maximum is 40 yards.

Also, two throws of the jack are allowed. That is, a player may have two attempts to set a legal mark. This rule, once widespread in English bowls, also still applies in the Panel (*see page 156*).

Other Kidderminster rules are that an end is dead if the jack is knocked off the green (as in crown green), and that at the conclusion of an end, the mat may be moved back by any number of yards so long as it remains on the line of the previous end.

It is fair to say that along with the 'roving cot' game of Norfolk, the Kidderminster variant is the most difficult way to play bowls.

But it is not the only form played in the area. At least two local clubs play in rinks as well.

One is the Stourport Bowling Green Club, formed as a quoits club in 1853 and affiliated to Bowls England.

Another is Bewdley. Formed in 1902 this club plays both 'roving cot' in the Midweek League and in competitions that are rink based, even though its green is far from flat, with an 18 inch drop from the top edge (known by members as 'the cabbage patch') down towards the River Severn.

One more example of how in Worcestershire, as in Norfolk, and indeed as was almost certainly the case in all of England before 1900 or so, not all bowls clubs fit neatly into one category or another.

◀ Another version of 'roving cot' to have become formalised in the early 20th century is that which is played in **Cambridge**. This version differs from Norfolk and Kidderminster in being closer to flat green rules than to crown green rules.

Seen here and below in 2014 at the **Cambridge and County Bowling Club** – a flat green club formed in 1928, based on **Brooklands Avenue** on the edge of the Botanic Gardens – the first thing to notice is that the game, taking place in the **Cambridge & District Bowls League**, is being played in rinks that are marked out with strings (as was once common practice).

As the competition's website proudly declares, this is a league with 'extra challenges'. By this it means that unlike in standard flat green rules, neither the mat nor the jack have to be centred within the rink (a rule that the EBA formalised in 1928).

Instead, the mat may be placed anywhere as long as it is at least one yard from the ditch and from the strings along the rink edges.

Played in triples, the lead player may have two attempts to set a legal mark (as at Kidderminster), and may send the jack anywhere within the rink as long as it stops a yard or more from the rink edge.

Bowls must be within one yard of the jack to count and are dead if they touch the string.

Unlike in normal flat green rules, 'touchers' that end up in the ditch do not count, and if the jack leaves the rink, the end is deemed 'dead'.

Skips may also juggle the order of the players during the game.

Arguably this is a game with more variation, if one that tends to favour the home team (who even on a flat green are inevitably more familiar with the surface). But it is clearly popular, for the League has more than 50 teams playing in five divisions.

Other survivals of this form of the game can be found in the North Yorkshire and South Durham Works' League, centred on Middlesbrough, and in parts of Cumbria, where it is known as 'swing jack'.

Cambridge & County BC has not one but two inter-war pavilions; the first, designed by JW Pate, opened in 1930 (*left*) and above, a T-shaped pavilion housing indoor rinks, opened 1933 (*see page 187*). The grounds used to belong to Brooklands House, across the road, which had its own bowling green and is now, coincidentally, the regional office of Historic England.

Case study

Norfolk Bowling Club, Norwich

A. J. KIRCHEN

Amongst the portraits of past presidents framed under the thatched eaves of Norfolk Bowling Club's charming pavilion, that of Alf Kirchen (1919–99) will be familiar to fans of Norwich City Football Club and of Arsenal, for whom he starred in the 1930s. Capped for England both in football and clay pigeon shooting, Kirchen became a farmer in his later life, and a keen bowler. He served as club captain in 1974 and club president in 1980.

For our final case study of the inter war period we stay in Norfolk, at a club whose story takes us up to the point where the expansion of the 'Scotch game' – a process that commenced south of the border in 1903 – reached its furthest extent yet, in the 1930s.

As noted in the previous case study, bowling in the Norwich area can be a confusing matter. But, as would be expected of a city that until the Industrial Revolution was the second largest in England, it does have a long history.

One of Norwich's earliest bowling greens, in the 1770s, was known after the proprietor of the adjoining pub, as Back's Bowling Green. This lay immediately west of the Theatre Royal. Later, Back's widow took it over, and after her death the pub became known as the Bowling Green Inn.

Virtually all Norwich's early greens were attached to pubs, and as recorded by the Gospel Temperance Union in 1892, there were plenty of them – 631 licensed premises in total. (In fact as late as the 1960s there were still some 20 pub greens in the city.)

Also on display in the clubhouse is this hand-tinted view of Norfolk BC's annual friendly v. the EBA, in 1936. This was shortly before the thatched pavilion was expanded to its current size, and a second green laid on what had been allotments. Another thatched structure at a Norwich bowling club is that of the Victoria BC on Trafford Road, built in 1925 (see page 219).

For those gentlemen who wished to bowl in more salubrious quarters, the Victoria Club formed on Trafford Road in 1870. There, as at Cannock and Chesterfield, no matches were played against other clubs. Instead the emphasis was on social interaction (as it remains to this day at the Victoria).

But still this was not enough for some bowlers, and so in 1920 three of them, WC Webster, Arthur Rudd and James Batterbee, decided that the city needed a club that could offer more competitive play, but not in a pub environment.

Initially their issue of 2,005 shares of £1 each was sold amongst prospective members, some of whom were already playing at the Gladstone Bowling Club on St Giles Street. But then a wealthy shoe manufacturer, Sir Henry Holmes, bought up the remaining stock, thus enabling the company to purchase a site amidst the highly respectable detached villas on Unthank Road, and build a thatched pavilion that perfectly befitted its surroundings.

In a city where, as noted earlier, other clubs were still playing a

hybrid sort of game more akin to crown green bowls, Webster was keen to promote the rink game, and thus arranged for the EBA to send a team for the green's formal opening, in June 1922.

At this stage, there were few flat green clubs in either Norfolk or Suffolk, so Webster affiliated his new club to the Essex Bowling Association.

Hence the club was named the Norfolk County Bowling Club, as it did, in effect, represent the county. Or at least did so in EBA circles, for there was already a Norfolk & Norwich Bowls Union, which represented the many clubs playing the old way, often on smaller pub greens.

Despite being so outnumbered, the Norfolk BC did manage to persuade the EBA that one East Anglian bowls tradition was worth embracing. That was the playing of triples matches, a form of competition unknown in the EBA at that time.

The club's efforts also paid off in terms of encouraging other East Anglian clubs to adopt EBA rules. This led in 1934 to a Suffolk

& Norfolk County Association forming with six clubs between them (the minimum required by the EBA), before finally in 1936, Norfolk BC, with WC Webster again to the fore, managed to get seven other clubs to agree to go it alone and form the Norfolk County (EBA) Association.

(Note that it was named as such to distinguish it from its counterpart which represented Norfolk's non EBA clubs and which confusingly became known later as the Norfolk County Bowls Association, a branch of the English Bowling Federation.)

Among the other founding members were Gladstone (the only other EBA club in Norwich), Great Yarmouth and Harleston Magpie.

Suffolk meanwhile formed its own association, also in 1936.

And so, county by county, the EBA extended its reach. After Norfolk and Suffolk, all that was left was for the EBA to establish a foothold in the otherwise Federation or crown green areas of Nottinghamshire (where the EBA's county association was formed in 1938), followed by Lincolnshire (1949), Lancashire (1950) and Derbyshire (1951).

Soon after 1936, Norfolk County BC dropped the 'County' from its own title, extended its pavilion, laid a second green, and saw membership rise steadily to some 250. In 1968, as seen on the right, it built a superb indoor facility, whose popularity would so outstrip the outdoor greens that the second green, seen in the distance on the right, is now maintained for occasional use only.

In the 1920s, Norfolk County blazed a trail for the EBA.

It would appear to be doing exactly the same for the indoor game today.

▲ Playing in front of the thatched pavilion at **Norfolk BC** – a revelation as one approaches the green down a narrow, anonymous drive off **Unthank Road** – is club member **Rebecca Field**, shortly after she became World Indoor Champion at the age of 23 in 2013.

Norfolk may appear to be conservative. But it would certainly never countenance any 'roving cot'.

Its pavilion, built in 1922 and extended in the late 1930s, is a classic, timber-framed clubhouse, festooned with honours boards and pennants (*left*), in many ways a time capsule of bowls culture from between the wars and beyond.

But what makes the club stand out further is that across the two greens, as seen on the left, is an indoor facility that when built in 1968 was absolutely cutting edge.

Extended since to seven rinks, its surface is now state of the art. And of some 570 members in 2015, over 400 play indoors. Not that this is anything new, however, as we shall now discover...

Chapter Ten

Indoor bowling

Britain today has some 330 indoor bowling clubs, the oldest of which is Crystal Palace IBC, set up originally in one of the Palace galleries by WG Grace, who realised that coconut matting – a material used for cricketers' winter net practice – offered a suitable surface for bowlers too. Thirty years later Crystal Palace was among a number of clubs to erect its own, purpose-built indoor facilities. Because few of these have architectural merit, indoor bowls tends to get overlooked in heritage terms. But the game has a long history, starting not in the 1930s, nor even 1905, but in the 19th century, where else but in Scotland.

On November 28 1849, around the time that Joseph Paxton was showing Prince Albert his designs for a giant iron and glass hall to house the proposed Great Exhibition in Hyde Park, the *Aberdeen Journal* carried a story headlined 'Novel Bowling Green'.

Several gentlemen in Glasgow, it reported, had taken over the Old Sugar House on High John Street, in order to practice bowls during the winter months.

'The floor is laid with a green carpet of about half an inch in thickness, and a barrier is erected around, stuffed with hair for the purpose of resisting the balls.'

Thus began the long search for materials that would, as closely as possible, replicate the texture and resistance of high quality turf, thereby allowing those bowlers who were not keen on curling to play bowls all year round.

Bowling under cover was itself hardly new. Half-bowl was played indoors on stone or wooden floors, and many a Tudor skittle alley was under cover too. But as is so often the case in sporting history, it was the Victorians, and more especially the Scots, whose experimentation would pave the way, as it were, for the modern indoor game to emerge.

In 1888, for example, William Macrae of the Drumdryan Bowling Club, Edinburgh, experimented with sawdust spread over the cement floor of a drill hall. He also placed rubber bands in the grooves of his woods to slow them down.

It was also in Edinburgh that Britain's first proper indoor club was formed. Known as the Edinburgh Winter Bowling Association, most accounts give its date of formation as 1905 (perhaps confusing it with Crystal Palace).

In fact the Edinburgh club formed earlier, in December 1899, playing in the gas-lit cellars of the Synod Hall on Castle Terrace, a former theatre which also hosted Hislop's Cycling Academy.

The rinks were short, just 27 yards in length, with 18 inch sticks placed across the centre of each rink to prevent driving shots.

The *Edinburgh Evening News* described the flooring as 'being of slightly roughened cement covered with cocoa-nut matting, the friction of which, it is claimed, is about equal to that on an ordinary good green.'

The Edinburgh club enjoyed a long life. James Pretsell, President of the Scottish Bowling Association in 1898, was a leading member, and it remained active until finally forced to disband in 1965, when the Synod Hall was closed by Edinburgh Corporation. (The site is now occupied by an office block called Saltire Court.)

Meanwhile, as noted earlier, coconut matting was also used at the Crystal Palace in 1905, until once again the Scots came up with an alternative, woven jute carpet.

This was the surface laid at the Glasgow Indoor Greens, opened in 1913 inside the magnificent Industrial Hall, a legacy of the 1901 International Exhibition in Kelvingrove Park.

Unlike the Synod Hall and Crystal Palace, this new Glasgow venue was a commercial venture, with sizeable cash prizes on offer. For example the winners of its 1914 pairs' tournament shared £25.

Sadly the hall, a somewhat fantastical design by architect James Miller, burnt down in 1925, to be replaced by the much plainer Kelvin Hall. By then there were several indoor rinks around the country, all in existing buildings; at Alexandra Palace (London), the Kursaal (Southend), King's Hall (Wimbledon), and, as noted on the right, at the public baths in Kingston-upon-Thames.

Further indoor greens had been laid by local authorities in Bexhill, Bognor and Hastings, while the first Welsh indoor club to form was Sully Athletic, in 1922.

Experiments with flooring continued. One of the more intriguing took place in Yorkshire County Cricket Club's 'practice shed' in Leeds, in 1911, where members of the local Headingley crown green bowling club created a rink measuring 32 x 7 yards, covered with felt and with canvas protecting the heads of the rink.

Regular crown woods were used, but with an unbiased jack.

However it was in the 1930s that the first purpose-built indoor facilities were built. As will be seen, most were utilitarian shed-like structures. But their flooring was rather more sophisticated.

One option was Basa-Weave, as advertised in the 1938 EBA Handbook (opposite). This was a form of jute matting. Another was Rolphelt, marketed by the bowls manufacturers Taylor-Rolph and fitted at the new indoor rinks in Cambridge and Ayr. This was wool-based and resembled the green baize of a billiard table.

▲ While most indoor facilities of the 1930s were built as stand-alone entities, or by outdoor clubs, the **Alexandra Bowling Centre** in **Sunderland**, opened in 1937, was designed by W & TR Milburn as an extension to the **Alexandra Hotel**, a pub in the Grangetown area.

Note the steel framed, clear span roof with glazed rooflights, the viewing area to the right, backing

onto a bar, and the sign requesting bowlers, 'Please do not smoke on the green. This means you!'

Such signs were common, given the susceptibility of the flooring to scorch burns and the likely replacement costs.

After the Second World War the indoor green was turned into a dance floor. Today it forms part of a dining area in the pub.

In the public sector, meanwhile, during the winter months at least, bowls was often laid on in swimming baths where one of the pools was boarded over in order to save on heating costs.

The earliest known example of this was the public baths in **Kingston-upon-Thames**, shortly before the First World War, but seen here (left) during a ladies match in January 1934. The green was of course flat, although in 1955 the firm of Thomas Royle Ltd installed a trial crown green on wooden boards inside Bradford Baths in east Manchester at a cost of £1,000. A second was installed at the celebrated Victoria Baths in Manchester in 1957, followed by Joseph Street Baths in Leeds.

But whereas a flat green was essentially a roll of carpet laid on existing boards, a crown green required a bespoke wooden structure, and the idea did not spread.

▶ Inspired by the Crystal Palace IBC and its counterpart at Alexandra Palace (f.1908), eight outdoor clubs in London opted to build indoor facilities during the 1930s. The oldest surviving of these facilities (and the oldest in Britain) is that of **Temple Bowling Club** on **Sunset Road, Herne Hill**. Formed in 1881 and named after William Temple, licensee of the Golden Lion pub in Denmark Hill, the club moved to its present site in 1931 and hired architects Leslie H Kemp & Tasker to design a two storey clubhouse.

Measuring 140 feet in length, its ground floor was set out to service two outdoor greens, as seen here in 2011, while the upper floor housed three indoor rinks, galleries for spectators and a small bar.

Reporting on its opening day on May 6 1933, *The Bowling World* explained that a key decision had been to install a reinforced concrete and hollow block floor for the indoor rinks that was lightweight, dead level and strong enough to 'obviate deflection and deviation'.

Since then the original jute surface has been upgraded on several occasions and in 1996 the building's roof was reclad.

A set of murals on the end wall has, sadly, been painted over.

Otherwise, the clubhouse has been well preserved and, compared with most indoor bowling facilities, looks rather handsome too.

◀ Built in 1931 for **Crouch Hill Bowling Club** on **Hillrise Road** in **north London**, this extraordinarily large, L-shaped clubhouse was the first in Britain to incorporate a purpose-built indoor facility, with three, felt covered rinks on its upper floor (at the far end of the clubhouse as seen here, and below).

In 1933 Crouch Hill joined eleven other clubs, Crystal Palace and Temple included, to form an Indoor Section of the EBA. By 1939 there were 50 clubs, a third from London, a third from seaside resorts, such as Bournemouth, Margate and Southend, and several based in public baths.

Ultimately the scale of Crouch Hill's building worked against it and the club folded in the 1960s.

Thereafter it became a recreation centre before, in 2011, Ashmount Primary School was built on the site, along with a children's nursery, appropriately called 'Bowlers'.

◀ Opened in October 1933, the indoor hall at **Cambridge and County BC** on **Brooklands Avenue** (*see also page 181*) was built with the permission of the club's landlord and benefactor, Percy Cunliffe Foster of Brooklands House, on condition that it included a room large enough for two billiard tables.

Its two rinks were originally felt, laid on timber flooring. Today they are described by the suppliers, Greengauge, as pure semi-worsted polypropylene yarn. But however resilient – and it needs to be as the club's 140 or so indoor members use it almost on a daily basis – the old rules (*above*) still apply.

On the left is the six-rink indoor hall at **Paddington Sports Club**, **Castellain Road**. When opened in 1935, the steel framed building was said to have been the largest of its kind. Today two of the rinks are used for mini-tennis and golf, and as noted on page 177 (where there is an aerial view of the facility), there is an outdoor green on site, surrounded by tennis courts.

Because indoor facilities can appear rather stark, Paddington's has been jollied up with a mural. Depicting a castle in a rural setting, this was the work of **Edward W Holland** in 1948. Whether he was also the creator of the murals at Temple BC, now lost, is unknown.

CRYSTAL PALACE INDOOR BOWLING GREEN
(picture by courtesy of Bowls News)

▲ When the new home of **Crystal Palace Indoor Bowling Club** (CPIBC) was opened on **Anerley Road** in October 1937, as the club history records, it 'spoke volumes for the British workman'. For although in essence a utilitarian structure, as seen here, with six rinks (three on either side of its central columns), it had taken just ten weeks to complete.

But if the building, with respect, is unremarkable (albeit thoroughly modernised), Britain's oldest indoor club is anything but.

As noted earlier, it formed in 1905 when WG Grace and 35 others started bowling on coconut mats in one of the main galleries of the Crystal Palace. Intriguingly the club's first president was listed as RP Grace. Yet to date no-one has ever been able to trace any RP in the Grace family tree.

On which note, among the club's archives are two cheques signed by WG, presented as prizes for a tournament held on the outdoor greens at Crystal Palace in June 1904; one of five guineas, one of two guineas. Clearly, however vehemently amateur was the EBA,

which he had helped to found the year before, Grace himself, as he had shown throughout his cricketing career, had no moral objections to the award of prize money.

In 1909 the CPIBC transferred to one of the basements at the Palace. But after the site was taken over by the Royal Navy in 1914, the club went into abeyance.

Its next home, in 1924, with four rinks of 37 yards long, was the Australia Pavilion, a leftover from the 1911 Festival of Empire Exhibition (located behind the main stand of the ground where FA Cup Finals were staged). It was in this pavilion that in 1935 the CPIBC defeated Cambridge & County to become the first winners of the Denny Cup, the EIBA's most prestigious trophy.

The club won it again in 1936, when it beat Crouch Hill.

By this time the club knew it had to find another home, as plans were afoot to revamp the Palace grounds.

But this need became suddenly more acute after the massive fire on the night of November 30 1936 that laid waste to the Palace.

Earlier that afternoon the club had hosted a match against the

White Rock IBC from Hastings, and although its players had departed before the fire, six CPIBC members found themselves trapped in the Australia Pavilion as the flames took hold, up the hill. Fortunately all escaped, fleeing through the grounds as the pavilion roof caved in under a shower of debris.

Also fortunately a wealthy club member, businessman Fred Goodliffe, owned some land on Anerley Road, and while that site was prepared, the club won its third Denny Cup in succession, beating Paddington at the Cyphers IBC (itself newly opened a few miles away in Beckenham).

Matching the efficiency with which the CPIBC's new premises were completed was the speed with which the costs were paid off by the 100 or so members. Amounting to some £3,000, this included central heating, a kitchen, a card room and a billiard room (including a table bought secondhand for £15).

Yet once again, no sooner had the club settled down than war intervened. The building was requisitioned for storing the effects of bombed out families, the roof

was peppered with shrapnel and the club secretary was killed by a V2 rocket. Not until 1951 was the club able to resume playing.

(Cyphers IBC had to wait even longer. Their new building was all but destroyed by a bomb and could not be rebuilt until 1956.)

Since those eventful years the CIPBC has made a number of improvements. After buying the freehold for just £500, in 1952 a ladies section was finally created, its members gaining full equality in 1974. This required the billiard room to be converted into their changing rooms. But it was worth it as membership reached 800.

Then in 1982 £163,000 was spent on a new, column-free roof and the addition of a seventh rink.

More recently, a further refit took place during the years 2000-02, this time costing £120,000.

This included the electrification of the **Fred Goodliffe Memorial Scoreboard**, seen above.

Today membership is around 275. Yet the club does lack one thing. Since moving to Anerley Road the CPIBC has failed to win the Denny Cup again.

◀ Despite being in the vanguard of indoor bowling, only in 1951 was a Scottish Indoor Bowling Association formed by five clubs. Of those, only the **Ayr Indoor Bowling Club** on **Lothian Road** survives, and does so moreover at its original home.

As at Crystal Palace, the building in question – its Art Deco signage apart – is perhaps of less interest than the story of the club itself.

It was the brainchild of Edouard Ecrepont, a Belgian who came to Britain initially to recover from injuries sustained in the First World War, but soon married and set up a business importing Belgian roof tiles. He and his wife then moved to Ayr, where he started building houses. Quite when or where Ecrepont caught the bowling bug is not clear, but as his business grew more prosperous he decided that he would build the town's first indoor bowling centre.

It is possible that he got the idea from *boulodromes* in his home country. Like indoor bowling rinks, these were set up in various parts of France and Belgium to provide year round facilities for pétanque.

Using his own workers and materials, Ecrepont built the Ayr centre on land at the back of his builders' yard (now West FM Radio). Initially it had three rinks, covered in the same felt used for billiard tables, and a tea room on a balcony overlooking the rinks.

Back in London, this is Croydon BC, where the outdoor greens, laid in 1922, were joined by six indoor rinks in 1937. Heated, welcoming, with a bar and café, the popularity of centres such as this has led to concerns that the outdoor game will one day die out. By offering both, historic clubs like Croydon, Norfolk and Cambridge & County may thus represent the future too.

A photograph on display in the centre today shows Edouard and his wife Lilly posing proudly on the opening day.

Ecrepont had more than a business interest in the game however. He was a fine bowler, representing Scotland in its first indoor international matches played in 1936, and remaining a member of the team until 1957. He also took a regular summer holiday to play in seaside tournaments, both to Weston-super-Mare and Torquay.

During World War Two, as at Crystal Palace, the Ayr centre was requisitioned, in this instance as a store for grain and sugar.

As at Crystal Palace it was also later extended, in 1965, to five rinks, and with a suspended ceiling added in order to reduce the heating bills. (The indoor season runs from September to April.)

After Ecrepont's retirement, his grandson, Edward, took over the centre, but he sold it in 2001 to Gordon Neil, coincidentally also an international bowler, both indoors and out, and the owner of a local building firm. Hence, as seen on the left, the centre has enjoyed a makeover, with new lighting and the latest Greengauge surface.

Membership today stands at around 500, making Ayr one of the leading indoor clubs in Scotland, of which there are now 58, all based in premises built since the 1960s.

Chapter Eleven

Britain 1945–1990

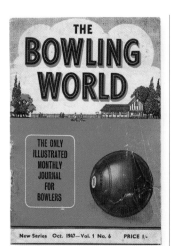

A sure sign that bowling was back in business after World War Two was the re-emergence of *Bowling World* in 1947. Edited by Herbert Collings, the journal estimated in 1949 that the number of clubs in Britain had risen since 1939 from 1,500 to over 2,000, and that the EBA National Championships for men had attracted a record entry of 43,000. Few of them appeared to be buying the journal, however, and later that same year *Bowling World* ceased publication.

Even though the bowls scene in Britain had been completely transformed during the fifty or so years prior to the Second World War, it had been, in essence, a quiet revolution.

For most onlookers in post war Britain, bowls, still, was a game shrouded in conservatism and played mostly by old people.

So in a world of shifting social trends and technological innovation, memorably celebrated at the 1951 Festival of Britain, could 'old men's marbles' possibly compete? Unquestionably it could.

Far from being cast aside by a generation that, as Prime Minister Harold Macmillan put it in 1957, had 'never had it so good', bowls in Britain reached a new peak during the post war period.

Throughout the 1960s and '70s, moreover, it proved able to attract widespread televised coverage, and therefore also commercial sponsorship.

We can take with a large pinch of salt an estimate in a bowls handbook dated 1957 that there were then four million bowlers in Britain, two thirds of them playing crown green bowls. Even half that number would have been extraordinary. But even if there were only (only!) one million – twice as many as today – certainly this was a golden era.

The steady rise in EBA club numbers reported in *Bowling World* in 1949 (*see left*) continued, so that by 1956 the total had risen to 2,375. This meant that for the first time since the formation of the EBA in 1903 it was possible to imagine flat green bowls one day outgrowing crown green.

This was a scenario EA Lundy aluded to in an article of 1961.

EBA clubs, he warned his crown green readers, were forming in greater numbers. EBA club members paid on average higher annual subscriptions (as remains the case today). And crucially, while the flat green game was continuing to spread around the globe, crown green players and officials remained resolutely, if contentedly, inward looking.

One factor in flat green's post war spread was that every four years it gained a publicity boost thanks to its status as a core sport within the Empire Games, renamed the Commonwealth Games in 1954.

This was especially so when British cities acted as hosts, as in 1958, in Cardiff, when the bowling tournament centred on Sophia Gardens, followed in both 1970 and 1986 by Edinburgh, where Balgreen formed the focus.

Only in one staging of the Commonwealth Games did bowls not appear on the schedule, in 1966, when the host city Kingston, in Jamaica, was unable to provide greens. That year instead a new event, the World Championships, was held in Sydney, Australia, with entries from sixteen nations.

It was held again in 1972, this time in Worthing, which became the new *de facto* centre for EBA tournaments. Worthing hosted it a second time in 1992, with Aberdeen staging it once in between, in 1984. Since then it has also been held in Ayr, in 2004, by which time the number of countries involved reached 24.

But for all flat green's growing international stature, crown green still had little cause for concern

Popular on the London bowls circuit in the 1950s were two itinerant showbiz clubs. The Concert Artistes BC, whose badge this is, included amongst its members actors Rob Wilton and Hattie Jacques, while the Stage Eccentric Bowling Society featured actor Jack Hawkins, boxer Freddie Mills, several magicians and BBC TV announcer Sylvia Peters.

during these years, given how popular the game remained with its core working class audience.

Just as in football, cricket and rugby the post war decades were marked by a surge in attendances and participation levels – albeit tailing off gradually during the 1950s – crown green events at the likes of the Talbot and Waterloo, consistently drew packed houses.

In 1969 crown green even caught up with its counterparts when women in three counties, Shropshire, Staffordshire and Warwickshire, combined to form the first ladies association.

As more counties joined, the association was renamed the British Crown Green Ladies Bowling Association in 1979.

By 1989 there were 21 affiliated counties and areas, including the Isle of Man, before in 1994 Wales joined, to complete the roster.

It was also during these years that gender barriers started falling within clubs. A typical tale comes from Cambridge and County BC, as chronicled by Stephen Harper-Scott (*see* Links). At the club's AGM in 1956 one former president had announced that if women were allowed to join the club he would never set foot in it again. But he could not prevent one concession being granted; that ladies be allowed to play on the outdoor greens on two afternoons a week.

This led in 1958 to a Ladies section being formed. But they were still not allowed to use the club's indoor rinks. Only in 1964 was that 'privilege' extended.

Similar accounts abound in the bowling world during this period.

Meanwhile, as more women took up bowls, its traditional target age group also grew. In the early 1930s life expectancy for the average British male stood at around 60. By 1971 this had risen to 68 for men and 72 for women.

Thus the 1950s saw a rise in the number of midweek, afternoon leagues aimed at pensioners.

In fact the number of leagues rose overall, and of competitions at seaside resorts, thanks to shorter working hours, longer holidays and greater mobility, car ownership included. Some leagues formed purely thanks to floodlighting. Possibly the first public greens to have been floodlit were in Fleetwood in 1938, while after the war, two clubs known to have experimented in this fashion, both in 1956, were Barnes BC in London, and Ayr BC in Scotland, where eight Altrilux lamps on 22 foot poles went up.

In crown green areas, where bad weather is seen merely as a minor inconvenience, floodlights also allowed the season to start earlier, in March, and extend right up to the end of October.

Inevitably not all was rosy in the glow of post war Britain.

Even at the height of the game's popularity, magazines and newspapers published warnings that could easily have been written today. The *Manchester Guardian*, for example, noted in May 1961 that four parks greens had been converted to putting greens. Why? Because 'there was not sufficient support from the bowlers to justify the cost of maintaining them.'

In particular, 'young middle-aged' men were not taking up the sport as before; some, perhaps lured away by the new fangled ten-pin bowling alleys that had arrived that year from the USA.

In his seminal book of 1969, *Corner to Corner and Over the Crown*, John Vose saw the signs.

'If the game is to spread then it must be advertised...'

▲ Flat green meets crown green in a *News of the World* **Challenge** at **Paddington** on September 20 1947. Spotting who is who is easy.

The home team wear their usual white flannels and dark blazers.

Three months earlier *Bowling World* had shown its own colours by commenting, 'It will be many moons before the crown green player becomes so well organised and disciplined as his flat-green colleague. The thought of donning special dress – flannel bags, blazer and Panama hat – for an important game of bowls would never occur...'

'But it must not be assumed that crown green players are a slovenly lot,' insisted the journal. 'Far from it. They come from all walks of life and many are really well dressed'.

How such condescension was met by the crown green contingent can be imagined. One of them, **James Heyes** (fourth from the right on the front row) was a 62 year old labourer from Aspull who had been playing for 47 years. But apart from two practice sessions before the Paddington encounter he had never played on a flat green.

Unsurprisingly, the home team won, 44-32, while in the return, held at the Railway Hotel, Lostock Hall, near Preston in May 1948, as expected, the crown green team gained revenge, winning 156-128.

Heyes was one of the great crown green players of his time.

Pictured again (*below left*) at the **Empire Services Club** in **Preston** – with **J Cottom** from **Pemberton** (wearing a muffler) – he won the Talbot in Blackpool in 1932 and the *News of the World* Lancashire tournament in Preston twice, in 1947, and in 1956.

The year before, when he was 69, Heyes completed a hat-trick of crown green triumphs by winning the Waterloo in heavy rain and wind. Not that he was so old. In 1957 the Waterloo was won by Bill Lacy, aged 76.

▲ In an era when Guinness was proud to tell the world 'Guinness is Good For You...' – and print score cards for bowls clubs which added '... every man jack of you!' – the relationship between beer and bowling became closer than ever.

Most brewers even had their own clubs. Above is the badge of the **Guinness BC**, formed in 1940 at the company's well appointed sportsground by its headquarters in Park Royal, west London.

How close was this relationship is encapsulated by an oil painting by the artist **Bernard Venables** (*right*), better known as the creator of 'Mr Crabtree', a cartoon strip about fishing in the *Daily Mirror*.

Commissioned for a celebratory book *Inns of Sport*, produced by the Whitbread Brewery in 1949, Venables' subject is the bowling green at the **Cherry Tree** in **Welwyn Garden City**, **Hertfordshire**.

The original Cherry Tree had been a timber cabin-style restaurant built by the Welwyn Garden City Company next to the new town's railway halt, with a bowling green added in 1925. Spotting its potential, Whitbread bought the site (but not the bowling green) in 1932, and in 1935 built the much larger Cherry Tree pub and restaurant in its place; a modern pub in every sense, car-friendly,

family friendly, in a growing town brimming with optimism.

In 1942 **Welwyn Garden City Bowling Club** formed on the green, and by the late 1940s – by which time Welwyn had been officially designated as a 'New Town' – the Welwyn Garden City Company had invested over £3,000 in relaying the green with Cumberland turf and landscaping its surrounds. The

company also paid for the green's upkeep and charged the club a reasonable rent of £200 a year.

For its part, the club became one of the most prestigious in the county. That much at least can be construed from the blazers and flannels in Venables' painting.

Yet fast forward to 1986, and the Cherry Tree, now best known as a music venue – Led Zeppelin played

there in April 1969 – was sold and in 1990 reopened as a Waitrose, with a car park in place of the bowling green. Welwyn Garden City BC, at least, managed to survive, and is now based at the Digswell Park cricket ground. But not so Guinness BC, or its green, now a block of flats on Lakeside Drive.

All this, come and gone, in barely half a century...

▶ July 1948 was a significant month in Britain. As well as seeing the foundation of the National Health Service and the staging of the Olympic Games in London, there took place an archery match that was to signal the birth of what we now call the Paralympics.

The venue was **Stoke Mandeville Hospital** in **Buckinghamshire**.

As told by Martin Polley in his account of the British Olympics and the early paralympic movement (*see Links*), the match was the brainchild of **Ludwig Guttmann**, a neurosurgeon who had fled Nazi Germany in 1938. During the war, Guttmann helped to revolutionise the treatment of patients suffering from spinal injuries by encouraging them to participate in sport.

Initially those attempted – the likes of archery, basketball, table tennis and fencing – depended on the range of wheelchairs available. But as wheelchair design evolved, using lightweight materials and differing wheel configurations, more sports became possible.

Seen here is one of the early wheelchair bowlers on the green at Stoke Mandeville in 1964.

This was four years before bowls first featured at the International Stoke Mandeville Games (the precursor of today's Paralympics), followed by its appearance at the 1970 Commonwealth Paraplegic Games, held in Edinburgh.

Another watershed was the opening of the **Lady Guttmann Indoor Bowls Centre** at **Stoke Mandeville** in 1974 (*above right*). In 1982 this became the base of the newly formed **British Wheelchair Bowls Association**.

When British bowlers then won three golds at the 1988 Paralympics in Seoul, followed by six more at Atlanta in 1996, it seemed that bowls had at last

Godfrey Bolsover (*below*) was a Nottinghamshire bowler and solicitor who in 1958 despatched an estimated 15,000 letters to every flat green county and national association in the world. Amazingly, most of them replied, the result being the *Who's Who and Encyclopedia of Bowls*, published in 1959. Extending to 1,300 packed pages, there are pen pictures of nearly 1,500 bowlers (from Britain, Canada and the USA), articles on a wide range of topics, on Cumberland sea-washed turf, on the duties of a marker, and of course on the origins of bowls and the Francis Drake story. Though not itself an historical work, and lacking any reference to crown green bowls, it is a truly monumental work of reference, and of huge value to historians.

established itself on the Paralympic scene. Yet it has not appeared since 1996, and in 2013 the Stoke Mandeville Centre was closed.

Bowls has nevertheless continued to evolve as a multi-disability sport. It featured again on the programme of the Commonwealth Games at Glasgow in 2014, and while there are now some 21 clubs affiliated to the BWBA, this represents only a fraction of the clubs where bowlers who use wheelchairs now play alongside able bodied players on a routine basis.

Added to which, continuing in the pioneering spirit of Guttmann and the Stoke Mandeville bowlers, the wheelchair of choice today is the ingenious Bradshaw Bowls Buggy, designed and manufactured in Bristol.

▶ Two miles south of where Billy Butlin established his first holiday camp at Ingoldmells, on the east coast of Lincolnshire, in 1936, the three greens of **Skegness Foreshore Bowling Club** play host to one of the largest seaside bowls festivals in Britain, first contested in 1957.

Itself formed in 1937, Skegness Foreshore BC is one of a number of flat green clubs on the east coast that affiliates both to Bowls England (the former EBA), and to the English Bowling Federation, which, as noted earlier, formed in 1945. But the Skegness festival is very much a gathering of Federation players and officials, with banners, badges and even chains of office very much in evidence.

Located next to the Pleasure Beach, with a tenpin bowling centre and putting green alongside, the foreshore greens offer an ideal setting. On the beach side is a raised viewing terrace (*above*) while on the North Parade side is the **Sun Castle Entertainment Centre** (*above right*), with bars and a terrace of its own. When opened in 1932, behind the neo-Gothic building's crenellations was a flat roof made of Vitaglass. This, a manifestation of how sun worship became fashionable between the wars, transmitted health-giving ultraviolet light to those gathered below, creating a giant solarium. A veritable 'sun castle' in fact.

Not that bowlers need much persuading of the benefits of sunlight or sea air. Anyone entering the qualifiers for Skegness has to commit him or herself to be available for the week long tournament in August, which sees 800 bowlers contest singles, pairs and triples. This last category is the traditional favourite in the Federation game. Under its rules, a 'rink' consists not of four but of three players. In addition, instead of each player always playing with two bowls, in one Federation triples event, each has three.

Seeing 18 woods all jostling for position around the jack – compared with 16 under Bowls England rules – is quite something.

And given the setting at Skegness, there is no better place to watch it unfold.

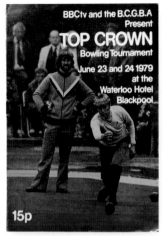

▲ While Federation bowlers flock to Skegness, the holiday destination of choice for many crown green bowlers – Blackpool notwithstanding – is **Douglas** on the **Isle of Man**, where an annual tournament has taken place since the 1920s.

Seen above is the winner of the 1960 Men's Singles tournament, **Bob Sephton**, a player from the Green Dragon pub in Whiston, Prescot, on Merseyside.

Despite the tournament's popularity over the years, precious little archive material has survived, so this and the adjoining image, thought to be from the 1960s, both from the collection of Don Lyons, provide a rare glimpse of its peak years. Its main venue then was the **Villa Marina**, near the centre of Douglas, where a green had been laid by a hotel of that name in the late 19th century.

In July 1913 the hotel and green were acquired by the Douglas Corporation and re-opened as an entertainment complex.

When the first open bowls tournament took place there in June 1922, there were 165 entrants, the winner being W Baker from Wolverhampton.

A ladies tournament was added in 1947 – Don Lyons' wife Maureen ended up running it – until so large did the event become that in 1969 a second week long tournament was added to run each September.

Entry levels reached a peak in June 1976, with 1,127 men and 392 women playing, and with greens all over the island being used for the early rounds. (Currently there are twelve crown green clubs on the island.)

Today both the Isle of Man week-long bowls festivals are centred on the three greens at **Nobles Park**, as seen below in 2012. Close by is an Edwardian bandstand relocated from the Villa Marina, and on the park's north side, the main grandstands for the TT Races.

Another fixture at Nobles Park is bookmaker Bill Forber from St Helens. His father, also Bill, won the Men's Singles in 1959, when he beat Bob Sephton.

Bowls festivals are like that. A place to renew old acquaintances, to play a bit, have a flutter and, above all, to enjoy a week's holiday.

▲ Crown green bowls reached a new peak in the 1960s when the BBC started televising some of its leading tournaments, such as this two day event at the **Waterloo** in 1979, in which two legends, Brian Duncan and Noel Burrows, met in the final. This exposure, combined with sponsorship, mainly from alcohol and tobacco companies, saw prize money in the game reach unprecedented levels.

Known initially as the Crown Green Masters, the Top Crown tournament was televised first in 1968, and enjoyed annual coverage until 1986. But then, almost imperceptibly, the tide turned and bowls dropped off the schedules.

It was a blow from which, many agree, the game has yet to recover.

Thanks to increased media coverage of bowls during the 1970s and '80s, David Bryant, a member of Clevedon BC in Somerset, became arguably the first bowler in Britain to achieve national renown (WG Grace aside), and certainly the first to have a beer named after him (brewed by Mauldon's of Sudbury in Suffolk). This beer mat is part of Bryant's collection of artefacts on display in Clevedon's clubhouse (*see page 38*), which was opened in 1973 at the height of his fame. Bryant, as noted on page 176, first came to wider attention at Paddington in 1953, started playing for England in 1958 and continued winning national and international honours into the 1990s. In 1980 he was awarded a CBE.

▲ David Bryant and his England team mates line up with their counterparts from Ireland, Scotland and Wales at the opening of the **1969 Home International series** at the **Watney's Sports Club** in **Mortlake**, south west London.

As recorded by Murray Hedgcock (*see Links*), Watney's had laid out the seven acre sportsground next to their Stag Brewery in 1919.

Located on the Surrey bank of the Thames, the brewery forms a backdrop to the closing stages of the University Boat Race.

In common with many large companies in the 20th century, Watney's lavished considerable

For bowlers visiting Mortlake these gates offered a familiar welcome. Dating from the mid 17th century, they originally stood in front of Cromwell House, whose grounds Watney's took over in 1929. The house was then demolished in 1947 but the gates survived, and now stand, restored, in front of houses built on the former bowling greens, on Williams Lane.

investment in its sports facilities. Six full time groundsmen were employed, while the Watney's Sports Club had over 2,300 members, each paying 3d a week.

Apart from providing for football, cricket, hockey and tennis, there were two bowling greens, one laid in 1929, another added in 1946.

As a report to the Welsh Bowling Association by Wyndham Jones in 1957 concluded, 'There is no doubt that for the future, new greens will be laid only by the big industrial firms and the public authorities'.

Indeed the costs of maintaining greens had been one reason why the EBA had left Paddington.

In 1954 one bowls reporter, 'Skip' of the *Western Morning News*, complained that the greens there 'have become so out of true level, and so full of tricks, that not even the finest bowler in the world can play a shot on either of them with the slightest confidence.'

To help rectify these faults the EBA gave Paddington a loan in January 1955, but the grumbles continued and so in 1958 its championships were relocated to Watney's, five miles to the south.

As can be seen, temporary stands were erected on two sides, while tents on the sportsground provided extra hospitality.

After the EBA switched again in 1974 (*see opposite*) the Mortlake greens stayed in use until finally the Watney's Sports Club closed in 2000. Today the much reduced brewery is owned by Anheuser-Busch, and the cricket and football pitches on Williams Lane are used by local schools. But flats and houses on Wadham Mews now cover the greens, with the flats seen above as their neighbours.

▲ Also on display at **Clevedon** is this pennant, won by **David Bryant** in the EBA singles championships at Mortlake, his second of six titles (added to which were nine others in the pairs, triples and fours).

Playing for Somerset, Bryant was also a four times winner of the Middleton Cup. In the 1950s this prestigious inter-county competition had been dominated by Surrey, which by 1959 was the largest county in the EBA, with 319 clubs (Watney's included). Yet since then a noticeably high number of players and teams from a range of counties, in all parts of England, has shared the honours.

Small wonder then that the game's centre would shift away from London, though perhaps surprising that in 1974 the EBA relocated its championships to **Beach House Park** in **Worthing**, down on the south coast of Sussex.

By doing so the EBA confirmed at least one part of Wyndham Jones' prediction. For whilst Jones was wrong to suggest that new greens would continue to be laid by companies, the post war years did see local authorities in resort towns continue to invest in greens as a way of boosting visitor numbers.

The council at Worthing had laid two greens at Beach House Park in 1924, added a third in 1929, a fourth in 1934, and a fifth in 1967.

For the EBA, apart from the obvious attraction of the seaside setting, the clincher was the quality of the Worthing greens, all tended under the supervision of the Scot, Jock Munro, himself a regular club and county champion.

Seen here at the **2005 EBA Championships**, Beach House Park offered plenty of room for temporary stands, for circulation and parking.

Added to this was a large park pavilion, built in 1925 (seen above in the distance), and a modern clubhouse built by Worthing Council in a corner of the complex for the 1972 World Bowls Championships (the first time this event had come to England). This clubhouse became the home of Worthing BC, and was joined in 1987 by the construction of new head offices for the EBA itself. This was the first time a governing body in British bowls had built premises (rather then rent an existing building).

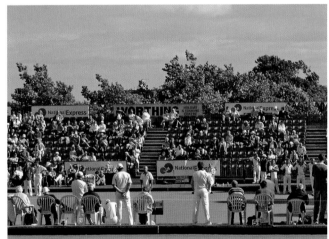

For the local council, Beach House Park proved a triumph. The World Championships made a small profit, and returned in 1992. In the interim, the Women's World Championships were staged in 1977. A year later Kodak sponsored a new Masters' Tournament, which was televised by the BBC.

During this time David Bryant carried on winning, becoming the only man to win honours at Paddington, Mortlake and Worthing.

He also won six indoors world titles, paired with Tony Allcock from Leicestershire, one of the few flat green bowlers to come close to matching Bryant's achievements, and who was destined, as its chief executive, to lead the EBA into the modern era and, eventually, away from Worthing.

▶ Photographed in 1949, a bowls maker at an unidentified company turns a **lignum vitae** 'wood', in what appears to be a basic workshop.

But even if the same process were to have been photographed at a large bowls manufacturer, the equipment would not have been that much more sophisticated.

Nor is it today, with one important difference. The handful of companies that nowadays turn lignum vitae bowls for their specialist customers do not do so from raw supplies of the wood, as this bowlsmaker is doing. Rather they recondition old woods.

The beginning of the end for lignum vitae bowls making came in 1931, when, after years of diminishing supplies, and of unsatisfactory experiments with vulcanised rubber bowls, an Australian, William Hensell, came up with a 'composite' alternative, made from phenolformaldehyde.

Within a few years British firms were in on the 'Henselite' formula, among them **Taylor-Rolph**, whose **Fitzgerald Works** in **East Sheen**, a mile or so from the Watney's SC in Mortlake, had a test bed, seen on the right in 1936, similar to the one pioneered in the 1870s by Thomas Taylor's in Glasgow.

Taylor-Rolph's early composites were marketed as 'Rolphite' and, as can be seen, could be supplied with a wood-like grain.

The Fitzgerald Works were flattened by a bomb in 1944, a huge blow not only to Taylor-Rolph but also to John Wisden & Co., whose cricketing equipment was manufactured there too.

Up to 1939 there had been around a dozen companies in Britain making bowls. In addition to Thomas Taylor and Taylor-Rolph, in London there was John Jaques, FH Ayres, TH Prosser and George Bussey (whose own composites, made in Peckham, were sold under the brand name 'Rolloids').

George Royle, meanwhile, was long established in Manchester, and in Edinburgh there was RG Lawrie, established in 1882.

Then after the war – a period in which even more supplies of lignum vitae had been used up in supplying parts to ships and even Mosquito aircraft – bowls makers fell by the wayside.

For lignum vitae, the 'wood of life', the final death knell was sounded in 1968, when Thomas Taylor gave up production in order to concentrate on plastics.

In a nod to history, however, one of their lines is still called 'lignoid'.

It was a similar tale at EA Clare Ltd in Liverpool, where their new plastic bowls were, and still are sold under the name Drakes Pride.

In 1982 Drakes Pride became the first bowls makers to use computerised lathes.

These two British companies, plus Henselite in Melbourne, and a relatively new Australian company based in Sydney, called Aero Bowls, are now the only four companies worldwide that make bowls approved by World Bowls, the international governing body for the flat green game.

That does not mean, however, that no lathes survive, or that lignum vitae has disappeared…

old woods. Ideally these are woods designed for flat green bowls. Being larger, they can then be cut down in size and reshaped for use in crown green, in which smaller bowls are the norm (*see page 11*). Some of the equipment used by Crawshaw in this process came from the former workshops of George Royle, in Sackville Street, Manchester.

Who buys these woods?

For a small number of bowlers, there is still no substitute for lignum vitae, rather as in the world of music there are those wedded to vinyl. As noted in previous chapters, lignum vitae is still used exclusively at Lewes and Barnes, and by some members at Chesterfield, Hadley Heath and at clubs playing Old English Bowls.

However in crown green bowls there are many more players – estimates vary between 10-15 per cent of the total – who have either never given up their lignum vitae woods or maintain one set for special circumstances, for example in cold temperatures (when plastic bowls can feel like ice) and in the early or late season, when greens can be wetter and heavier.

Plus, there are customers who simply want reconditioned woods to have on display, to touch and appreciate them as any antiques lover might.

Two things are for sure.

Firstly, lignum vitae woods will never be produced again. The wood is now on the endangered list.

Secondly, however, until the demand and desire for them ceases, there should still be enough lignum vitae woods around to satisfy demand.

After all, some of the woods still in use are a century or more older, some say even 200 years old.

Most, say the experts, will outlive us all.

▲ Photographed in 2015, **Ronnie Scott** is the last man in Scotland to turn his hand to the business of lignum vitae woods.

Based on **Blackfriars** in the centre of **Edinburgh**, his company still bears the name of **George Mackay**, its founder in 1805.

Scott does not manufacture plastic bowls, but is licensed to test them. On one long day and night during the Commonwealth Games in Edinburgh, in 1986, Ronnie and his brother Dennis had to test and stamp 140 bowls while a Games official stood watch.

But what Scott can do that no-one else in Scotland can – since Thomas Taylor's placed its last remaining lathe on display in its museum – is to restore old woods.

South of the border, that same service is offered by Pershore Bowls, in Worcestershire, and by **Premier Bowls** in **Stockport**.

Run by **Robert Crawshaw**, as seen on the left in 2004, what Crawshaw and his counterparts in Pershore do is source supplies of

▲ While it is true that since the 1930s bowlers have embraced modernity by taking up plastic bowls, they have proved less keen when it comes to pavilion design.

In this respect, with only a few exceptions – such as Newmarket Avenue (see page 167) – British bowls clubs remained steadfastly conservative; so much so that most clubhouses built between the wars might easily have been designed at any time between 1870 and 1914.

Only gradually, in the 1950s and '60s, was a break made with the past, as seen from these examples.

At **Wythenshawe Park** in **Manchester** (top left), the pavilion was designed by City of Manchester Architect Leonard Hewitt and opened in 1960.

T-shaped in plan, it has an upper floor supported on a single column, housing dressing rooms and a club room overlooking two crown greens to the north, and a set of tennis courts to the south.

Old Shrewsbury Bowling Club (top right) on **Victoria Avenue**, Shrewsbury, built its current pavilion in 1964; not, admittedly, out of a desire to modernise but

because its original pavilion, built in 1908, had been destroyed by fire.

In Devon, the pavilion of **Tiverton Bowling Club**, **Devon** (above left) was opened in 1977, while perhaps most unusual of all is the clubhouse of **Lutton Place Bowling Club** in **Edinburgh** (above right). Formed in 1860 and a founder member of the Scottish Bowling Association – WG Grace played on its green in 1901 – the club could hardly be more hemmed in. Accessed down a narrow path, on two sides are tenements. On the third the buttresses of St Peter's

Church, built also in 1860, come within inches of the green, and on the fourth side is the church hall.

So when the club decided to admit ladies in 1967 the members rolled up their sleeves and built themselves this new pavilion, with a timber-clad upper floor projecting over the green to create a few vital extra square feet of floor space.

Barely 40 people can squeeze in for tea (and that must include the visitors). But for a self-built effort, it is nevertheless impressive, and still looks the part as it approaches its half century.

▼ On the 400th anniversary of the **Spanish Armada** in July 1988, bowlers celebrated much as they had done in July 1888, by dressing up as Elizabethans and playing a game on Plymouth Hoe.

But whereas in 1888, as noted earlier, there were no bowls clubs to be found in Plymouth, and therefore a team from Great Torrington had to be drafted in, by 1988 there were over 20.

In fact 30 years earlier Bolsover listed 25 clubs in the city, including the Sir Walter Raleigh BC, on Victoria Road in St Budeaux (now defunct), the Sir Francis Drake BC on Whiteford Road, and two clubs, the City of Plymouth BC and Plymouth Hoe BC, who shared a public green on... the Hoe itself.

The green, actually tucked back slightly inland from the seaboard side of the Hoe, on **Lockyear Street**, had been laid in 1907 in response to a comment by 'Erasmus' in the *Western Daily Mercury* in January of that year.

'The town of all England, indeed all Britain, which should possess a bowling green, has none. That is Plymouth.'

Thus the Hoe and Recreation Grounds Committee of Plymouth Corporation was approached and at a modest cost of £65 the green was laid, and named, inevitably, the Sir Francis Drake Bowling Green. Also that year 130 men joined the newly formed Plymouth (Sir Francis Drake) Bowling Club, each being required to wear galoshes for the first season in order to protect the new surface.

In 1922 the club moved inland to Whiteford Road, where it remains to this day. But other clubs have since made use of the Hoe green, three of which are now in occupation; the **City of Plymouth BC**, the **Plymouth Hoe Ladies BC** and the **Visually-Impaired BC**.

Below left, seen in 2014 with the City of Plymouth bowlers in action, is the pavilion at the green.

Built in 1968 to replace one that had been destroyed in the Second World War, it was designed by the City Architect, HJW Stirling, who masterminded much of Plymouth's post war reconstruction.

It was on this green that the 400th anniversary match was held.

For old time's sake bowlers from Great Torrington were invited to form the 'home' side, while, as in 1888, the opposition came from Headingley (from the Original Oak BC). Some of the players ventured out onto the Hoe for a re-enactment of the original Armada encounter, mainly as a photo opportunity.

There they were urged on by a Francis Drake lookalike, Brian Whipp, who in his day job was a financial consultant with Manulife, the event's sponsor.

Then it was back to the green, where the Devonians exacted revenge for their defeat in 1888 by beating the visitors 99-63.

In 1888 it had been agreed that the Leeds bowlers would keep the original Plymouth Cup in perpetuity. Thus in 1988 a new cup was awarded, plus medals for all the players. These were presented at a civic tea held in the Council House.

The event marks an appropriate moment to bring to a close our account of bowling history.

From one Elizabethan age to another, from woods to plastics, from undulating grasslands to flat greens, from Tudorbethan pavilions to flat roofed modern clubhouses, bowls had undergone a complete transformation. And yet here we were again, commemorating an event that may or may not have taken place, involving a national hero who may or may not have played the game.

With provenance like this, there must surely be every chance of a rematch in 2088.

Chapter Twelve

Bowls today

Chloe Wordingham of Higham Ferrers BC in Northamptonshire is one of hundreds of young bowlers competing at national level. In 2014, aged 17, she won the inaugural Sutton Winson trophy for Under 18s at Leamington. Indoors, playing at Wellingborough Town, she often plays alongside Jamie Walker, Young Bowler of the Year in 2014. Bowls England reports that entries to youth tournaments often exceed the entry limit. So is the future of bowls bright, even as the woods themselves may be orange?

Announcing the launch of the Coalition Government's new Localism Act in August 2011, Eric Pickles, the Communities Secretary, told the press, 'Bowling is one of the nation's most popular pastimes and the bowling green has long been part of the fabric of our towns and villages. The new powers we are proposing can help to preserve this part of England's sporting and cultural heritage for years to come.'

Under these new powers, members of the public were invited to bid for bowling greens – or any other potentially vulnerable community asset, such as a pub, swimming pool, or open space – to be registered with their local planning authority as an Asset of Community Value (ACV).

Since 2011 it is understood that around a dozen bowling greens have been registered (although this may be an understatement because, appropriately for a measure promoting localism, no central records are being kept).

Among them are the greens at West London BC, the Marlpit pub in Norwich, and the Summit in Heywood, Rochdale. Gaining ACV status offers no guarantee of halting development. Rather it gives local groups a six month window to formulate a bid to take control of the asset.

Furthermore, not all greens designated as ACVs have survived, while critics of the measure point out that while it is all very empowering for, say, a bowls club to take over a council-owned park green, the raising of the £7-10,000 a year needed for maintenance is, for many, too much to take on.

As one club secretary thrust into this position told *Played in Britain*, 'I am 77, and this has become practically a full time unpaid job.'

On the opposing benches of the House of Commons from Eric Pickles, another ally of bowling has been the Labour MP for Barrow & Furness, John Woodcock.

A crown green player in his youth, in April 2011 Woodcock introduced a Private Member's Bill seeking greater protection of bowling greens.

To publicise the campaign he organised a bowls match at Westminster, on College Green (*see below*). Forty six MPs offered their support. But it was not enough.

He raised the subject again in April 2014 by launching, with Hove & Portslade MP Peter Kyle, a Labour Bowlers' Charter.

Among its proposals were that bowlers be enabled to buy their green at the going market rate as a green, rather than as a potential development site, and get support in the same way that, in football, the Supporters Direct organisation assists fans seeking to save their clubs from rapacious owners.

No doubt these campaigns and others have helped to raise the issue of green losses. But in the meantime, those losses have continued at a depressing rate.

In the south of England, between 1959 and 2015 the number of clubs in Middlesex fell from 242 to 94, and in Surrey from 311 to 137. Some of these losses, it is true, can be attributed to the merger of men's and ladies' clubs, a process that mirrored the merger of the EBA and EWBA in 2008 (to form Bowls England). But the downward trend overall is undeniable.

Labour MP John Woodcock (*left*) plus three members of the King Alfred Bowling Club from his Barrow and Furness constituency take the message to Westminster in July 2011. In the 1990s alone, seven greens had been lost in Barrow, although at the time of writing the latest news is that the one at the King Alfred appears to have been saved.

The situation is no different in crown green bowls. In 1991, for example, the Preston & District League consisted of 142 teams and 14 divisions. By 2015 only 68 teams remained in seven divisions. In the area covered by the league, over 30 greens have been lost since 1970.

On page 213 we show the findings of our own *Played in Britain* research into club numbers and club membership in 2014-15.

One sobering conclusion is that if the losses continue at the present rate, bowls in Britain will disappear by 2050.

It is not usually the business of *Played in Britain* to comment on the current state of any sport, unless and if only this impacts upon the specific heritage of that sport.

But as this book has sought to show, and as Eric Pickles and John Woodcock agreed, so ingrained is bowls in the fabric of everyday British life – in all manner of contexts, sporting, social and cultural – that the loss of clubs and greens, whether of historical interest or not, must be considered as harmful to the character of Britain as most of us have known it in our lifetimes.

That said, we must not assume that all is doom and gloom.

In Scotland, the total number of clubs affiliating to the SBA (now Bowls Scotland) has actually risen, from 762 in 1959 (as recorded by Bolsover) to 857 in 2012.

In the flat green, southern half of Wales during the same period, the numbers have also risen, from 249 clubs to 286.

Meanwhile in England, equally heartening stories have also emerged. In Oxfordshire the loss of clubs has been only slight, from 41 in 1959 to 37 in 2015, while in Cornwall, the number has actually risen, from 40 in 1959 to 47 in

THE MITRE MIXED B.C. 2000 A.D.

WHY NOT MIX IT – WITH FLOODLIGHTS

'The Happy Days Ahead'

2015. (It is of course possible that some of these clubs already existed but chose to affiliate only later.)

In terms of competitive play, there has also been a marked increase in the number of teams participating in afternoon leagues, and especially in leagues where mixed teams are the norm.

In addition, new clubs are being formed all the time.

To mention but two: Ashbourne BC in Derbyshire formed in 1998, its pavilion and two greens funded by £100,000 from Sport England; and Wanborough BC in Wiltshire was established in 1999.

Since then Sport England has continued to offer support to bowls, but with a condition.

Throughout the 20th century, one of the game's weakest points had been that, in England at least, the various governing bodies never shared information or resources, and therefore never had the same bargaining powers as other, more unified sporting codes. Hence in order to meet Sport England's conditions for grant aid, in 2004

six English governing bodies came together to form the Bowls Development Alliance (BDA).

These were the representatives of flat green bowls – the EBA, EIBA and EBF – plus their counterparts from crown green, short mat and carpet bowling.

Such unity, however, was shortlived, as political infighting led to four of the organisations dropping out, leaving the BDA in 2015 with just two members, Bowls England and the English Indoor Bowling Association.

And yet the BDA has achieved some success. In the period 2009-13 it secured almost £1 million from Sport England, followed by a further £2million for the following four year cycle up to 2017.

In this second cycle, the BDA has set itself two targets.

Firstly, to recruit 10,810 new bowlers aged 55 or over (thereby achieving a percentage gain on existing numbers), and secondly, to recruit an extra 2,800 bowlers who have a disability and are over the age of 16. »

From the Mitre Bowling Club, Norwich, in the 1950s, a cartoonist predicts the future as it might appear in the year 2000, should clubs open their doors to women. Inevitably the men will find themselves badgered by their wives and children, or distracted by girls in short skirts. Couples will canoodle on the sidelines. In fact, integration was well in train by the 1980s, and was finally cemented in the flat green game by the merger of the EBA and EWBA in 2008. Indeed most clubs now actively seek to recruit women and children. Floodlights, on the other hand, are still relatively rare.

▶ Three different London parks, three different scenarios.

Battersea Park (*top*) was the first London park to offer bowls to the public, in 1891. But according to James Manson, writing in 1912 (*see Links*), all was not well.

In the Midlands, the north of England and Scotland, he reported, public greens were enjoyed by artisans 'in great numbers', whereas in London, but in other towns and cities too, 'poorer persons, eager to play' were being 'crowded out by their brethren of more fortunate purse... men well able to afford the subscription of a private club'.

Still worse, he went on, many of 'these "use and wont" players have gone even further, and formed themselves into clubs... thus monopolising on occasion three or four rinks of a municipal green for perhaps three hours at a stretch'.

Manson called this 'a manifest abuse of public greens'.

A century on and membership of **Battersea Park Bowls Club**, formed in 1891, had dropped to just ten members. Moreover, the local authority, Wandsworth Borough Council, could not tell exactly how many casual bowlers were using the green, because in the absence of a parks attendant there to take bookings it was left to members of the club to let the public onto the green and take in the fees, if they happened to be there.

But even if they were, the club rather treated the place as its own private domain.

Of all the sports it caters for, says Wandsworth, bowls is the most expensive per head. A parks green (any green indeed) can cost between £7-10,000 a year to maintain. In these times of public sector cuts, something has to give.

In 2014 it did. Battersea Park BC folded, leaving the Council with a green to maintain for occasional corporate hirings.

One solution where clubs do still exist is for the members to take on the responsibility for greenkeeping, by offering voluntary labour and by sharing the cost of materials such as fertiliser and top dressing.

Another is to raise the green fees.

Either way, the result is that to belong to a parks club in 2015 is now in many instances more expensive than to belong to a private club. In parts of the north it is even twice as expensive, typically £70 a year against £35 a year.

This, it would seem, is a manifest reversal of what was intended.

The situation is further compounded when councils cut down on greenkeeping, or employ contractors more used to cutting football pitches on large mowers than tending to the more precise needs of a bowling green. As the greens inevitably deteriorate, so more bowlers go elsewhere, or just give up. In Middlesex, north of the river Thames, five or six parks clubs disband every year.

In Edinburgh, usage of the park greens fell by 70 per cent in the period 2007-2012.

At **King Edward Memorial Park** in **Shadwell**, east London (*centre right*) the drop off was even steeper.

The park's tennis courts are well used. The five-a-side pitches too. But these days few local residents come from cultures in which bowls is a recognised sport. And because no-one plays on the green, there is no-one to show them. So the green has been mothballed.

A third way, back in south west London, is at **Wandsworth Park** (*right*). Bowling greens are ready made play pens. Bowling green pavilions are ready made nurseries.

Add a café and soon there is new life.

>> Both targets reflect the BDA's aim to 'help people live longer, healthier and more fulfilling lives'.

Like motherhood and apple pie, it is hard to fault this ideal, even if many argue that as much effort should be concentrated on attracting young players.

But how to meet these targets?

One route chosen by the BDA has been to support a number of 'Play Bowls' road shows. These are in effect open days at selected clubs in which members of the public are encouraged to attend and be taught the basics.

Crucially however the emphasis is not on competition but on the social benefits of joining a club.

This, after all, is still the prime motive for most people in the game, as it was in past decades when hundreds of clubs appended to their handbook entries the words 'friendly games only'.

Only in 2017 can we assess how successful these recruitment drives have been. But the emphasis on over 55s is worth noting.

As reported in the previous chapter, by 1971 life expectancy for the average man and woman in the UK stood at 68 and 72 respectively.

In 2014 the Office for National Statistics reported a significant rise on these expectations, up to 78 for men and 82 for women.

On the same note, on page 213 we report that Sport England's data for 2014 shows bowls to be the 12th most popular participation sport for individuals over 16.

However, by analysing the statistics for specific age bands we see that amongst the over 65s, bowls leaps up to become the fourth most popular sporting activity, behind swimming, golf and attending a gym.

So the emphasis on recruiting older players is understandable >>

▲ When park greens are lost, they at least tend to remain as green spaces. Pub greens, on the other hand, tend to be built upon or turned into car parks. This was what happened, ironically, at the **Bowling Green Hotel** on the **Isle of Man**.

Built in 1873 and, in its early years, offering bowls, croquet, a game known as grass billiards and, in winter, a skating rink, the pub became the home of Douglas Bowling Club, and the unofficial headquarters of bowling on the island as a whole. But in 1983 the green became a car park, and Douglas BC moved down the road to the green at Villa Marina.

Thirty four pubs still stand in England bearing the words 'bowling green' in their name. Of these, only five still have functioning greens.

Since the 1930s, at least 39 other 'Bowling Green' inns or hotels are known to have been demolished or converted into other uses.

Many would argue that the least worst scenario for a pub green is for it to be converted into a children's play area or a beer garden.

The latter was not the original intention of the brewers Matthew Brown, owners in 1984 of the **Withy Trees** pub in **Preston**.

Their intention was to cover the green in tarmac.

Members of the crown green club based there launched a last ditch appeal, and although unable to stop the bowling green being closed, the judge and the local council were sufficiently persuaded that the turf should not be sullied.

And so, as seen below during the summer of 2012, a rather pleasant and spacious family-friendly beer garden is the result.

But do not expect any crown green bowlers to celebrate. All they see here are the original banks, a familiar bump here or rise there, and an expanse of turf that with only a few passes of a mower with its blade set low might easily be made playable in a matter of weeks.

Where there is grass, there is hope.

▲ It is not only parks and pub greens that have been lost. Many a private bowls club has closed also, often because the land on which it sits has become too valuable for its owner to resist development.

Or sometimes because the community around which it was based has contracted.

This was the green in the village of **Deanston** near **Stirling,** a village laid out between 1791-99 for workers at the Adelphi cotton mill.

In a street named 'First Division', stood a line of terraced houses reserved for managers at the mill.

These are the houses seen on the left. (Lower grade workers, as if they needed reminding, lived on streets named 'Second Division', 'Third Division', 'Fourth' and 'Fifth'.)

Being in a such a small, tight knit community dependent on one local employer, the **Deanston Bowling Club**, formed in c.1880, struggled after the Depression, and folded in around 1933.

In 1965 the mill was then converted into a whisky distillery.

Look closer and you will see that the bowls clubhouse was converted too, into a garden shed.

» and, arguably, of wider social benefit. Added to which, as often stated in this book, so much emphasis is placed by other sports on recruiting youngsters, why not be proud of bowls' popularity amongst the older generation?

But this, in itself, creates problems of its own.

Put bluntly, without an influx of younger members bowls clubs run the inevitable risk of atrophying.

To attract new members today requires a range of skills, be it in website design, social media or public relations. And, as many readers will be all too aware – and as this writer can attest from his own experience as a club secretary – the level of bureaucracy required to administer even the smallest of clubs is now much greater than even a decade ago.

These issues are compounded further by the fact that as Britain's pensioners become more active, and in some cases affluent, they have more distractions and opportunities to travel.

Not least, many bowls clubs report that nowadays their members have to undertake more grandparenting duties than was ever the case in the past.

To these ongoing social pressures must also be added the pressure on bowls clubs occupying sites coveted by developers.

In fact this is hardly a new issue. Throughout history bowling greens, so often found in prime town centre locations, have been under threat, as exemplified by this auction listing for the Bell Inn at Tewkesbury: 'Lot 3 – All that very desirable and celebrated bowling green, adjoining to Lot 2 [the inn], with a Summer House, Arched Cellar, and other conveniences, forming a most desirable situation for building upon.'

The date? July 1825.

Since then, for sure, the statutory protection of open spaces has been beefed up by a raft of planning legislation. For example many an historic bowls club now finds itself located within a Conservation Area. A few have even had their pavilions listed.

But still until recently there remained a quirk of the planning system that allowed councils to draw up local development plans in which, although larger open spaces were offered a measure of protection, bowling greens, being small and often located in built up areas, were considered as ideal infill sites for development.

In 2012 the National Planning Policy Framework set out to address this and other gaps in the protection of sports facilities.

The crucial paragraph 74 states that: 'Existing open space, sports and recreational buildings and land, including playing fields, should not be built on unless:

• an assessment has been undertaken which has clearly shown the open space, buildings or land to be surplus to requirements; or

• the loss resulting from the proposed development would be replaced by equivalent or better provision in terms of quantity and quality in a suitable location; or

• the development is for alternative sports and recreational provision, the needs for which clearly outweigh the loss.'

But in practice, as a number of bowls clubs have found, private landlords can often easily circumvent these conditions by making life difficult for the clubs, thereby running them down.

Or, the simple failure of a pub or social club where a green is sited can see the bowlers locked out, in many instances with very little advance warning.

Moreover, once a club's membership has fallen to a certain level, arguing the case for retaining a green becomes that much harder.

Yet nor can it be denied that at certain clubs a rump of members has set out deliberately to run the club down so that they can then sell the site on to a developer and share out the profits amongst themselves.

This has happened recently at two clubs in London, where land values are at their most tempting, but in theory it can happen anywhere unless members take precautionary measures, as did those at North London BC (*see page 149*), and at Summerhill BC in Newcastle-upon-Tyne (*see right*).

Nor can it be denied that there exists within bowling an underlying culture of complaint and resistance to new ideas.

The game has a poor record in recruiting members from ethnic minorities. As noted elsewhere, in a number of public parks, club members resist sharing their facilities with the public.

Even in the now increasingly precarious pub sector there is often a reluctance to admit that the bowlers could do a good deal more to support their beleaguered landlords.

In most cases shortcomings such as these can be eased by the injection of new members with fresh ideas and energy.

For make no mistake, bowls is still a game that attracts dynamic individuals, and passionate ones too. But in order for these individuals to have an effect, they must still have access to a green.

Lose the greens and, whoever wants to play, the game is up.

▲ Summertime frolics at the **Summerhill Bowling Club** in **Newcastle-upon-Tyne** in June 2015, upon the very green that WG once graced, in a match against Scotland, 108 years earlier.

In those days it was called West End Bowling Club. Mostly its members came from the surrounding Georgian and Victorian squares and terraces. But although a peaceful haven, the city centre was barely a few hundred yards away, making it an attractive proposition for a much wider pool of respectable gentlemen.

Also nearby stood St James' Park, home of Newcastle United (whose forerunners had also been called West End).

During the First World War the bowls club's finances took a dip and in 1916 it went into liquidation. But the gap was soon filled, for in its place was formed Summerhill BC, named after the area as a whole.

Summerhill became a fine EBA club, the sort of club where at

9 o'clock in the evening it was customary for the club president to pass around a silver snuff box.

Many of its members played at county level. Several achieved national honours and high office.

During Newcastle's Race Week, the club's annual bowls tournament was a highlight of the sporting year. That was when local celebrities, the likes of footballers Jackie Milburn and Len Shackleton, would gather in the splendid pavilion, built in 1937.

By 2010, when Summerhill featured in *Played in Tyne and Wear*, its declining membership was struggling. Finally, painfully, in March 2011 the club folded.

Now in the normal course of events, a well positioned open space in a desirable area would be an obvious target for developers.

Instead of which, as in 1916, a new group stepped into the breach. Only this time it was not a bowling club but a charitable trust formed by local residents, calling itself the Friends of Summerhill.

The Friends were able to take over the club because, fortunately, a few years earlier Summerhill had been registered as a Community Amateur Sports Club, thereby ensuring its site could be used ony for charitable or sporting purposes (*as explained on page 220*).

A board of management was elected, members recruited, and bit by bit the bowls club and its pavilion came alive again.

The greens are still there, if not quite up to county standard. But the place is buzzing, with events, classes, tree planting schemes, allotments, and a palpable sense of community. And parties.

Dancing on the green at Dirleton Castle, brass bands at Cannock, fireworks at Milton Regis... bowling greens, as we have noted, have been used for all manner of gatherings over the centuries.

Summerhill continues that tradition. It is proof that the closure of a club need not automatically be followed by the loss of its green.

▼ As if maintaining park greens were not challenging enough in the current economic climate, recent years have shown an unfortunate rise in incidences of vandalism, of casual (and often wilful) intrusion by dog walkers and of youths seeking out a patch of turf for a game of football, frisbee or the like.

The result in many parks and exposed urban environments, as seen at **Boggart Hole Clough** in **Blackley**, **Manchester** (*below*), is the erection of security fencing, with W-shaped spikes to deter intruders.

No question such fences are effective, if unattractive. But remembering the words of James Manson in 1912 (*see page 204*), they separate even further the greens from the general public, making those bowlers inside feel understandably more proprietorial, and those outside feel less likely to want to play.

▲ To most bowlers they are anathema. To others they are the future, an inevitability.

Here in **Gloucester,** an artificial green lies between two turf greens occupied respectively by **Gloucester City BC** and **Gloucester Spa BC**.

In the background members of the former play a match. In the foreground, members of the public play on the artificial green.

The quest to create all-year-round, low maintenance bowling greens goes back to at least 1914, when in Scotland, Beith Council laid an experimental 'green' using tarmac mixed with sawdust. But the real breakthrough was the invention of Astroturf in Houston, Texas, in the 1960s. This and later variants found favour in bowls clubs all over the world, especially in hot countries such as Australia.

In British bowls, as in the football world, these early surfaces were considered too hard and too fast. Nevertheless one of the first flat green clubs to try an outdoor artificial green was Penryn BC in Cornwall, in 1980. There, the mild climate allows members to bowl outdoors for much longer than is possible elsewhere in Britain.

Since then artificial crown greens have also appeared. North Wales has several, two of which (at Betws yn Rhos and Bradley in Wrexham), have even hosted county matches.

Despite many players expressing unease at this, the advantages are clear. At £35-50,000 to install, depending on the groundworks necessary, the price is not cheap.

But artificial greens require no irrigation (saving on water bills) and virtually no maintenance. They also last on average for ten years.

So are they the future? In public parks, perhaps, as in Gloucester. But in private clubs?

Penryn (and Falmouth, also in Cornwall) have certainly kept theirs. And some say that as more bowlers become accustomed to the precision of indoor carpets, more outdoor installations are inevitable.

In addition, the new generation of needle-punch and woven fabric surfaces, especially if laid on a shockpad, offer a much closer simulation of natural turf than was possible back in the 1980s.

It might be thought that those bowlers tasked with greenkeeping duties would welcome maintenance-free greens. Yet as this writer can attest, there is a satisfaction to be had from a stripe well mown, from the smell of cut grass...

And as so many foreign visitors have pointed out, going back to the early 18th century (*see page 16*), greenkeeping is a skill of which the British can be proud. Neatly cut turf, surely, is part of our heritage.

▲ Nowadays the **Bowling Green Hotel** in **Brook Street**, **Chester** – the back of which can be seen above on the left – is better known as the **St Werburgh's Centre**, after the Roman Catholic Church that took it over for use as a social centre in 1975.

But what of the flats overlooking the green? These, it could be said, offer another glimpse of the future.

Concerning the green, its roots are very much in the past. When John Anderson, the Mayor of Chester in 1680-81, wanted to build a new house and garden he levelled two fortifications just to the north of the city walls. Both were named after sports, Jousting Croft Mount and Cockpit Hill Mount.

Anderson's nephew Robert then laid a bowling green in the garden in 1687. Maps from the 18th century reveal this green to have been around 50 by 40 yards and trapezoid in shape.

For almost a century the green was frequented by the leading lights of Chester society, until in 1778 the house was converted into the Bowling Green Inn and the green opened up to the public.

A hundred years on from this and the green found itself in the midst of mills and foundries, chemical and engineering works.

The Bowling Green Hotel we see today was rebuilt in 1914, and is now Grade II listed. But by the early 1970s, like the industries all around, it was struggling.

Meanwhile, Chester's housing market was on the up, and so in 1999 St Werburgh's decided to capitalise on what was now a prized asset and sold the land at the rear of the centre to developers.

The result, despite fierce opposition from the bowlers, and two failed planning applications, was what we see today; a green

more than halved in area, to just 30 x 30 yards, overlooked by two sides of a four storey sheltered housing scheme, like a square version of an Elizabethan theatre.

Initially, the turf was maintained only as a lawn, for the use of residents. But then the developers went into liquidation, and after a lengthy legal wrangle, a group of volunteers set about restoring the surface for bowling.

Today the green is shared between the 30-40 members of the club, and a number of the residents in the sheltered flats, which themselves have now been renamed **Bowling Green Court**.

As the benefits of remaining active in later life are more fully appreciated, and as developers sense the value of offering a bowling green as an added amenity, the likelihood is that schemes such as this will become more common.

Already similar juxtapositions can be found at the Prince of Wales Court Bowls Club in Porthcawl, Wales (next to a care home built in 1973), at Graythwaite Court in Grange over Sands, Cumbria (a housing estate built 2004-05), and at four developments built by the Richmond Retirement Village Company in Cheshire, Oxfordshire and Warwickshire.

In Sheffield, after consultation with residents, the developers Urban Splash are also planning to make a bowling green an integral part of their overall regeneration of the famous Parkhill Flats.

Thomas Mawson would surely approve, as would John Anderson.

Here is a green that has been part of Chester's history for over 300 years, and which now, in its own small way, has carried on making history by showing a path to the future.

▲ Viewing the scene at the **Royal Leamington Spa Bowling Club** in **Victoria Park**, as the ladies of Kent, Cumbria, Huntingdonshire and Dorset line up for the Walker Cup semi-finals in August 2012 (*top*), readers can be forgiven for thinking that the pavilions date back to the club's foundation in 1909.

In fact, they were built in 1995, as part of a £420,000 redevelopment funded by the club's landlords, Warwick District Council, prior to Leamington staging the 1996 Ladies World Championships and becoming the national centre for the EWBA. The plan worked so well that the men moved here too, as did Bowls England, in 2013.

Leamington is hardly alone in its retro-style architecture. The timber pavilion at the **Boxford & District Bowling Club** in **Suffolk** (*above left*), located behind The Fleece pub – whose landlord formed the club in 1920 – was constructed in 1999 with the help of a £50,866 grant from Sport England.

Also in Suffolk, when **Hadleigh Bowling Club**, dating back to 1754, sold its green for redevelopment as a care home, the developers moved the club a mile north, where they laid an eight rink green and this single storey pavilion (*above*), completed in 2010.

Needless to add, none of the parties above were remotely interested in following a modernist approach. No flat roofs, no steel or concrete for them. Here there is nostalgia, but also an understated pride in every roof tile, timber slat, gable and verandah.

▲ It is ironic that of all the pavilions so far featured in *Bowled Over*, the most modern is in **Heaton Park, Manchester**, a Grade II listed park whose 600 acres house nine listed buildings, including **Heaton Hall**, a James Wyatt design of the 1770s.

The **Heaton Hall Bowling Club** is of a later vintage, having been set up in the park in 1926. It was the first EBA club to form in Lancashire, and therefore offered the ideal venue for the bowls tournament of the **2002 Commonwealth Games**.

Of course the £1 million bill for its construction, the work of DS One Architects, and its four new flat greens, was met by Manchester City Council and other public agencies.

It would therefore be unfair to compare its excellence with other new pavilions elsewhere.

Nevertheless, it is a handsome, angular confection of surfaces, voids and tones, with a light, curving club room looking out over the greens (one now used for croquet).

The 2002 Games are so often remembered for the stadium, pool, velodrome and arena. But here is a legacy that merits equal attention; an exemplar too of why bowlers need have no fear of modernism.

▶ More evidence of a step change in attitudes is provided by these three pavilions, the most striking of which is that of **Balornock Bowling Club** on **Wallacewell Road** in **Springburn, Glasgow** (*top*).

The club itself is young, having been formed in 1987 by residents frustrated by the lack of communal facilities in their post war estate.

In the early years a Portakabin served as a pavilion, until after a series of lively meetings the vote was to build not just a clubhouse, but a bold, modern one.

Loans were secured. Sponsors and members contributed. Studio KAP Architects were commissioned and in 2005 the £250,000 building was unveiled.

A decade on and opinions remain divided. Obviously shocking to traditionalists are the rouge coloured facings, although these are tempered by white walls and timber cladding at the Wallacewell Road entrance. Almost as radical is the flat roof, designed to prevent shadows on the green.

But overall most bowlers seem to approve and in 2006 the building won a coveted Civic Trust award.

Adopting a similarly low slung approach is the new pavilion at **Hillsborough Park** (*centre right*).

Designed for **Sheffield City Council** by Prue Chiles Architects, the pavilion opened in 2007 at a cost of £890,000.

Of this £660,000 was funded by the National Lottery, topped up by £19,000 raised by club members.

However the costs also included provision for a classroom, offices and other park improvements.

For the bowls element the need was to serve two crown greens on a split level site. On the Middlewood Road side, as seen here, a timber framed loggia looks out over the 'top green'. Behind this is a large, well lit clubroom, able to accommodate indoor bowling sessions and offering views over the park and the 'tournament green', located on a lower level at the rear.

While the exterior is restrained, clad in birch, the interior is full of colour; ideal, it would be thought, to attract younger users.

For Balornock the bigger issue is how to extend their building without compromising its architectural integrity. As noted often in this book, an unextended pavilion of any ilk is a relative rarity.

At Hillsborough Park, the issue is that since the building opened, local authority cuts have started to bite and the club is now being asked to contribute to running repairs to its fabric, and to the maintenance of both greens.

Membership, meanwhile has fallen from 140 to nearer 60. Nowt to do with the architecture. Just the way things are for park-based clubs in the midst of a recession.

Built at a cost of £146,000 in 2013 – to replace a 1920s 'bower' destroyed in an arson attack – the new timber frame bowls pavilion at Penrith Castle Park (*right*) was designed, by Eden District Council architect Paul Brunsdon, to enhance views of the castle ruins and to complement its stonework by the use of coloured laminate exterior panels.

Table 1: Bowling club numbers 2014–15

	England	Scotland	Wales	Totals
Flat green	2,081	864	402	3,347
Federation	905	n/a	n/a	905
Crown green	2,488[1]	n/a	107	2,595
Unaffiliated[2]	290	25	15	330
Indoor only[3]	207[4]	58	25	290
Totals	**5,971**	**947**	**549**	**7,467**

These figures are based on returns from the various governing bodies relating either to 2014 or 2015. Note that the number of clubs does not mirror the number of greens, some clubs having two or more greens. (n/a = not applicable)

1. includes 12 crown green clubs on Isle of Man
2. estimated figure, includes clubs playing Old English Bowls, Roving Cot, plus clubs such as Barnes, Chesterfield, Hadley Heath, Lewes and Cannock, and certain park-based clubs, and excludes organisations for which bowls is not the primary activity, such as Masonic Lodges and Townswomen's Guilds
3. excludes 'indoor carpet' and 'short mat' bowling clubs
4. excludes 93 clubs known to have both outdoor and indoor facilities (eg. Croydon BC), all of which are counted under previous heading

Table 2: Bowling club playing members 2014-15

	England	Scotland	Wales	Totals
Flat green	111,415	63,000	10,791	185,206
Federation	16,696	n/a	n/a	16,696
Crown green[1]	124,400	n/a	5,350	129,750
unaffiliated[2]	8,700	750	450	9,900
Totals[3]	**261,211**	**63,750**	**16,591**	**341,552**

These figures are based on returns from the various governing bodies applying either to 2014 or 2015.

1. estimates based on average of 50 playing members per club (following analysis of sample of 218 crown green clubs)
2. estimates based on average of 30 playing members per club
3. these totals exclude numbers for indoor clubs as the majority of their members are also members of outdoor clubs. One estimate is that there may be an extra 10-15,000 bowlers overall who play solely indoor bowls, taking the national total to approximately 350-355,000

For all the reasons outlined earlier in this chapter, interpreting statistics in the world of bowls is not easy.

Nevertheless, these statistics, compiled by the *Played in Britain* team, do at least present a guide to the current situation.

What they cannot do is tell us how many bowling greens there are.

Some clubs, as we know, have two greens. Leamington and Ayr Northfield have five each. But some greens, especially in parks, are shared by two or more clubs.

So we can only guess that if there are some 7,200 outdoor clubs, as shown in Table 1, there might be in the region of 8-9,000 greens.

In terms of club numbers and club membership, statistics from the past have always been patchy, mostly good in the EBA and SBA, less consistent in crown green, and non-existent in other areas.

As might be expected in the computer age, record keeping has improved. But even so, because statistics were sparse in the past, any modern data is of little use when trying to make historical comparisons that may be of value.

This difficulty is compounded by the fact that, arising from the mergers of the governing bodies for men's and women's flat green bowls in England and Scotland, in 2008 and 2010 respectively, hundreds of men's and women's clubs have themselves merged, muddying the statistics even further.

As for the numbers of bowlers, in 1957 the EBA counted 122,000 male bowlers. By 2001 this had fallen to 115,000, a drop of six per cent in 44 years. But by 2015 the figure had dropped to 75,000, a fall of 34 per cent in 14 years.

From 2001-15 the total for ladies fell also, by 29 per cent, although now the proportion of women in flat green bowls is marginally higher; 32 per cent, compared with 30 per cent in 2001.

One other source for comparison is Sport England's Active People Survey, which in April 2014 found that 312,000 over 16s in England played bowls at least once a week.

This compares with our total of over 341,000 in Britain as a whole.

To put this into context, other figures from the Active People Survey show bowls to be England's 12th most popular sport, more popular than basketball, boxing and rowing, and not much less popular than cricket or squash.

Of course everyone in the bowls world expects the overall figures to drop further. Bowls in this respect is no different from practically every other established sport in Britain.

But as our history has made clear, the game has dropped out of fashion before during the last 500 years, only then to bounce back.

And at least from these statistics we can see that bowls remains a sport of some importance, with a still substantial body of enthusiasts who believe in it, and in its core role in British life.

Moreover, who knows how the game might yet evolve? Could a shift in the culture of the game actually help to revive it?

Can bowls learn lessons from its own history?

This is the theme that we shall now explore.

▲ After decades, if not centuries, of out and out sexism – an issue prevalent in virtually every major sport in Britain – the full integration of women that has taken place in bowls in recent years has had an enormously positive impact.

The successful staging of the Women's World Championships at Leamington in 1996 was a particular watershed, for the EWBA and for Leamington's status as a bowling centre (so much so that the men followed in 2013).

At club level women have proved transformative too (as they have in many other sports, particularly athletics and rowing).

Women have also helped to change the way that bowlers present themselves. This process actually started in the 1920s.

At that time all bowlers dressed in their normal street clothes. But then in the flat green game the women started wearing regulation white uniforms (see page 163) and the idea soon spread to the men (whereas in crown green dress codes remained much less strict).

Then in the 1990s it was agreed that in order for more women to be attracted to flat green bowls, dress codes needed to be relaxed to include more colour. Trousers too were allowed instead of skirts, as seen at the **Royal Leamington Spa Bowling Club** (left), in 2012.

And once again, these ideas spread to the men's game, so that, bit by bit, the colour returned to flat green bowls.

As of 2015, girls and women constitute about a third of all bowlers in membership of Bowls England clubs, and a similar proportion in crown green bowls.

Most would agree that this is not enough and that more effort needs to be made to achieve parity.

Meanwhile there continues the BDA drive to attract more players with disabilities. Again, however, their presence on the green goes back a long way. At Stockport in 1851, one-armed James Tomlinson of Heaton Norris beat Edgeley 'crack' William Coppock in a money match, while in 1918 the runner up at the Waterloo, J Pimblett from Pemberton was also one-armed.

Currently fifty clubs belong to Visually Impaired Bowls England, an organisation founded in 1975, among them the Bridgwater VIBC in Somerset (right), itself formed in 1995. Each bowler is assisted by a sighted helper, and guided by a white string marking the centre of each rink (just visible here) running under the mat and from ditch to ditch.

Meanwhile in 1897 a one-legged bowler competed at the Talbot tournament in Blackpool, and according to the *Liverpool Mercury* was 'repeatedly applauded' (or was this because he had the nerve to be a crown green bowler based in the flat green stronghold of Keswick?).

After the First World War more disabled bowlers were in evidence. In Scotland greens were even set aside for blind ex-servicemen. On page 193 we also touched briefly on the pioneering role played by Stoke Mandeville Hospital in

advancing the cause of bowlers using wheelchairs.

No-one pretends that more could not be done. But it is probably fair to describe flat green bowls as one of the most integrated multi-ability sports currently played in Britain. At Heaton Park in the 2002 Commonwealth Games the matches for disabled bowlers were held in tandem with those for able bodied bowles, the first time this had occurred at international level. Both sets of bowlers were also treated as one within the Team England set-up.

It was the same at the **2014 Commonwealth Games** staged at **Kelvingrove** in **Glasgow**.

Seen in action above at those Games is bronze medallist **Paul Brown**. An auditor by profession, Brown not only plays for England but holds senior positions within the British Wheelchair Bowls Association, the Cerebral Palsy World Bowls Team and the umbrella organisation, Disability Bowls England.

Yet like numerous bowlers with disabilities Brown also plays regularly with able bodied players at his home club, Ross-on-Wye BC in Herefordshire.

▲ They may still be wearing shoes, or perhaps just socks, but for those young hipsters attending summer evening sessions run by the **Barefoot Bowls** events company in London, bowling is a rather different proposition from that seen at most other flat greens in Britain.

Born in Australia and exported to London in the last decade, 'barefoot bowling' is, as it sounds, a more relaxed way of playing.

Seen above in May 2015 it can often be found on the public bowling green at **Finsbury Square** in **Islington**. Laid on the top of an underground car park in 1962, the green has long been a favourite with office workers in the City of London, no doubt persuaded a little by the presence of a popular wine bar overlooking the green.

But it may equally be seen at park greens all over the capital, another favourite being the one at **Hyde Park**, opposite the **Albert Memorial** (*right*).

Most of London's barefoot bowlers tend to be from Australia, New Zealand or South Africa.

But casual though they may appear, most have grown up with the game and know exactly what they are doing.

And their influence is spreading. In south east London, for example, the Friends of Brockwell Park called upon casual bowlers to organise sessions at the green after the resident club disbanded. One of those who answered the call was a Siberian. Since then the Barefoot Bowls company has also staged events there, and on the greens at Clapham Common and Wandsworth Common.

Accompanied by DJs, with street food steaming on the sidelines, and craft ales and chilled wines being served at the bar, a Barefoot Bowls event appears to break every convention possible. To which the organisers would say that they have qualified coaches on hand to teach newcomers the basics.

And to which historians might add, surely this ethos echoes the game as it was played by 17th century aristocrats, with their banqueting houses and party spirit.

So could barefoot bowls be the future for urban bowling greens? For if it was good enough for lords and ladies three centuries ago, why not for the youth of today, barefoot or otherwise?

▲ He may not be barefoot, but the antics of young bowlers such as **Ben Harris** – seen here in 2014 playing for Warwick & Worcester in a county match v. Yorkshire at **Rastrick** – are still a far cry from the sedate game that most people think of when they think of bowls.

But that would only be people who are not familiar with the crown green code, where exuberance on the green has been part and parcel of the game for years, going back to the high stakes matches of the Victorian era.

And those who have not seen the 2003 film *Blackball*, based on the maverick flat green bowler Griff Sanders from Torquay.

It was Sanders who in 1998 was famously banned from flat green bowls for ten years after swearing at an official who dropped him from the county team for infractions that included eating chips and drinking

beer on the green, and even worse, wearing non-regulation socks.

Bowls, most bowlers would agree, finds itself at a crossroads in the early 21st century. Everyone is asking how might the game appeal to a new and younger audience?

Could flat green learn a lesson from its crown green counterparts, who at places like **Fleetwood**, seen above in 2010, revel in a football-like atmosphere, pint glass in one hand, betting slip in the other?

Is the answer more colour and pizzazz? Is it significant, for example, that when faced with a selection of modern plastic bowls – as displayed at **Raikes Hall** in

Blackpool (*below left*) – children attending introductory coaching courses choose any colour but black or brown?

Or that at the 'Crucible' of indoor bowls, **Potters Holiday Resort** in **Norfolk** (*below*), the green is actually blue, because that is what the broadcasters prefer?

▲ There is only one colour that counts in this climactic moment, captured on the greens at **Kelvingrove Park**, **Glasgow**, during the **Commonwealth Games** in July 2014. And that colour is gold.

Celebrating their victory in the final of the men's fours, against the 'Auld Enemy' England are Scotland's David Peacock, Paul Foster and Neil Speirs. Alex Marshall, having delivered the decisive bowl, celebrates out of shot at the other end.

It is no doubt wholly appropriate to conclude our account of British bowls by returning to Glasgow; the city where William Mitchell set out his rules in 1848, where Thomas Taylor perfected the art of creating matched sets of woods with a

prescribed bias in the 1870s, where the first national bowling association was formed in 1892, and where there is still the highest concentration of bowling greens and clubs in the country.

In total around 35,000 spectators turned up at Kelvingrove to watch the action unfold over the nine days of the Games in 2014. The Scots saw their men capture three golds overall. The South Africans were more delighted still to take home five golds. England managed one too, in the Ladies triples, plus three silvers to boot.

Other medals were shared amongst the bowlers, able bodied and disabled, from Wales, Northern Ireland, New Zealand, Australia, Canada and Malaysia.

And after the Games? With the Art Gallery and Museum a graceful presence in the background, the six greens at Kelvingrove constitute the single largest concentration of public bowling greens in Britain.

Since 2014 they have also been available to the public for no charge at all, seven days a week.

Being so close to the University of Glasgow, this is of course a great incentive to get students involved.

Sunday afternoons are reserved for Family Bowls and Barbecues.

On Monday afternoons the staff there run a two hour slot called 'Bowls and a Blether'(with a free cuppa thrown in for good measure).

This is followed on Wednesdays with a similar session called 'Blokes Who Bowl'.

The staff have also recently instigated a series of 'barefoot bowls' sessions.

No doubt the likes of William Mitchell, Thomas Taylor and WG Grace would be rendered speechless by much of what goes on at Kelvingrove today.

Men in shorts? Players celebrating with abandon? Women, for heaven's sake, playing the game, on the same greens and at the same time? And yet if the old game they loved so dearly is to flourish once more, surely anything and everything is worth a try.

In this respect what we learn most from history is that there is no one part of the heritage of bowls that is worth preserving that is more important than the game itself.

Chapter Thirteen

Conclusions

Tony Allcock amassed 15 world titles between 1986–2002, both indoor and outdoor, then did what few top bowlers have ever done. He retired, at the age of 47. In between breeding pedigree dogs and winning medals at Crufts, Allcock has since become the chief executive at Bowls England. This bronze statue of him, by Martin Williams, is at the Thurmaston Shopping Centre in Leicester, near to where Allcock grew up.

Given the enormity of the challenges facing the sport of bowls over the coming decades – the drive to recruit new players, the battle for media attention, the struggle to keep clubs alive, the search for more resources – any concerns over the heritage of bowls might seem marginal by comparison.

But as this book has sought to demonstrate, the unrivalled heritage of bowls should act as an inspiration, and as a foundation stone for all those efforts.

Increasingly we hear the word 'heritage' being appended to products; heritage tours, heritage fabrics, heritage windows, even heritage carrots and apples.

So what better or more deserved tag to append to bowls than that of a 'heritage sport'?

A sport that is played on some of the oldest sporting venues in the world.

A sport with rules that go back to before those of any other modern sport, to at least 1670.

A sport that numbers amongst its clubs two that were formed in 1753 (Lewes and Blackburn Subs),

older than the MCC, older than the All England Club at Wimbledon, older by a century or more than any club in football or rugby.

Because the story is trotted out so often, the game's association with Francis Drake has inevitably become something of a cliché.

Drake's form still crops up all over; on pub signs, on a stained glass window in a Glasgow clubhouse, in clubs bearing his name in Plymouth, Tavistock and Brockley, London (below), in the brand of bowls known as Drakes Pride, and in seemingly every article ever written on bowls for a lay audience.

But behind the legend, if a legend it be, lies the indisputable truth that in Drake's lifetime, and when Shakespeare was in his prime, bowls was the most popular sport in England. Horse racing and hunting apart, no other sport has such provenance.

So what now can the sport of bowls do to celebrate this extraordinary story, to strengthen its heritage, and in turn to use it as a platform for facing the future with greater resolve?

In this final, brief section, as in all *Played in Britain* titles, we lay out some ideas and suggestions based on our research and travels.

Recording history
It is time for bowls to take its own history more seriously.

This means an end to unsupportable claims of 'the oldest club in the world' or 'the oldest green in the world', and the adoption in its place of a narrative based on solid academic research.

Clearly, bowlers love their sport, and as such they deserve to know more of its fascinating history. Trotting out old tales and repeating mistakes from the past does no-one any credit.

Indeed, as we have found, the real stories are often far more revealing than the confection of myths and misunderstandings that the game appears to have inherited from self-serving narratives concocted by the Victorians and Edwardians.

Bowls has a brilliant story to tell. It has nothing to fear, and much to gain, from telling it properly.

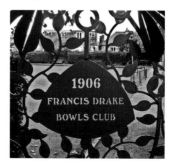

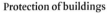

Protection of buildings

The bowling greens of Britain, as this book has set out to show, are served by an array of delightful and often quirky clubhouses and pavilions. But should more be done to protect them?

In England, as of 2015, there are 27 listed buildings that once served bowling greens, such as the pavilions at Swarkestone and South Tawton. This total includes pubs and even walls formerly attached to, or enclosing, greens.

In Scotland in the same category there are six such listed structures, for example the former pavilion of Melville BC in Montrose (above).

Concerning buildings still in active use, in England eleven buildings are listed that were purpose-built for bowls (such as the pavilions at Bishop's Castle and Newark), plus two more in use as pavilions after being converted (at Lewes, the former auricula theatre, and at Greenhill BC in Burnley, a former house).

This total excludes listed pubs adjoining greens, such as the Bowling Green Inn, Hadley Heath.

In Scotland there are 16 listed

purpose-built pavilions and clubhouses, including those at Alloa Co-op and Burntisland.

Only one bowls-related building in Wales is listed, the Llay Miners' Welfare Institute.

After visiting nearly 1,000 bowls clubs around Britain, the *Played in Britain* team considers the following pavilions to be worthy of consideration for listing (either on the national list or on local lists):

Blackburn Subscription BC (1869), Fulwood Conservative Club (1899), Sunderland BC (1906) and Victoria BC, Norwich (*above right*).

The two shelters at Hadley Heath are also considered to be rare examples of a once common feature at bowling greens.

Played in Britain would be interested to hear from readers if there are any other pavilions not featured in *Bowled Over* that should also be considered for listing.

Protection of greens

As noted in the previous chapter there exists a number of mechanisms for the protection of bowling greens. Some of the more historic greens, »

▲ Built in 1925, the timber framed **John Young Shelter** at the **Victoria Bowling Club** on **Trafford Road** in **Norwich**, forms a well proportioned and nicely detailed partner to the club's larger and also once thatched main pavilion, opened in the following year.

Both were designed by architect Albert Havers and built by John Young & Sons. That the former happened to be the club secretary, while John Young was club president, forms the nub of one of many engaging tales told by Norman Wordsworth in his history of Victoria, published in 1996 (see *Links*). It is an excellent book that every intending bowls club historian should read and learn from.

It is called, moreover, *Many Pleasant Hours*, that being the inscription written in Latin – *horae serenae* – above the clock on the front of the John Young Shelter.

Under this is written 'A welcome bower, 'neath sun or shower'.

In common with Chesterfield, Cannock and others featured in *Bowled Over*, Victoria is a club that, formed in 1870, remains unaffiliated and content to play games just amongst its members.

But does this shelter, however charming, merit protection? Or is it just one of many to be found at sports clubs and in parks all over Britain? It is, admittedly, easy to be seduced by such buildings. But this one, surely, stands out.

Formed in south west London in 1893, Balham Bowls Club (*left*) is indeed a great place, tastefully adorned with artefacts from the club's past. All it lacks is a bowling green. Instead, there is a block of flats at the rear. Meanwhile in Montrose (*top left*), after Melville BC were unable to pay a higher rent to the council in 2014, its pavilion was converted into a café.

▲ Not many bowls clubs have oil paintings hanging on their walls. But then not many clubs share the pedigree of the **Southampton (Old) Bowling Green Club**.

Seen here during its restoration in 2013, the portrait, dated 1857, depicts not a club president, as might be imagined, but 'faithful servitor' and greenkeeper **John Dymott**, whom we encountered on page 72. On his left arm is strapped a disc, perhaps lignum vitae, possibly a device for recording scores. Alas, unlike the 'clock scorer' at Lewes (see page 40), it appears not to have survived.

But the silver medal around Dymott's neck has. Awarded by the club in 1850, in grateful thanks for his years of service, it is one of a collection of medals which the club

had mounted in a display case in 1930, illustrated on page 75.

Thankfully both the case and the portrait survived the partial destruction of the pavilion during the Second World War.

As noted in the case study on Southampton, there are, it must be said, one or two disputed areas in the club's received history. But what the club cannot be faulted for is the range of its historic artefacts, going back to its earliest medal, dated 1784. Or the efforts to which a succession of Southampton members – **John Sanders** being the latest – have gone in order to keep the club's collection safe, in good order and, just as importantly, up to date (for how easy it is to imagine that the ephemera of today is of no value, when of course for historians of the future it will be priceless).

Every club, historic or otherwise, should have one person whose task it is to mind the archives.

At **Milton Regis**, that person is **Peter Luckhurst**. He has not only created a small exhibition area in a corner of the clubhouse (*above*), but has also, as is imperative, scanned every single item so that the originals can be kept safe, and only copies put on display (where

inevitably over time they will fade in the sunlight).

Throughout this book there are painful examples of where records have been lost, or left to moulder in a cupboard, or destroyed in a fire.

It was after their most recent fire that the members of the **Banbury Chestnuts BC** placed their records in a metal, fireproof trunk (*below*).

But the best strategy of all for any historic material is to do what the likes of Bishop's Castle and Bedale have done, and that is to hand it all over for safe keeping to the nearest local studies library, heritage centre or record office.

To any member of a bowls club reading this, the message is clear.

Look after your records and archives, and if the club cannot, hand the task to a professional.

such as at Lewes, Barnes and Southampton, lie within Conservation Areas, and therefore enjoy a measure of protection.

But what of the rest?

At the very least all clubs should consider registering as a Community Amateur Sports Club. This requires a club to have in its constitution a dissolution clause, specifying that in the event of the club folding, its assets must be redistributed within the sport or to a charitable organisation, thereby removing any financial incentive members might have to sell the site to a developer.

In addition, clubs with vulnerable greens should register them as an Asset of Community Value, under the Localism Act.

Bowling's governing bodies do provide advice and limited legal assistance to clubs under threat. In this respect, a useful checklist appears in the BCGBA handbook under the heading 'Guidelines for clubs whose greens face closure'.

But ultimately, for a green to be saved there has to be a strong will amongst bowlers and their local community to keep going and fight the good fight.

As for historic greens, it appears that they are unlikely to be deemed eligible for inclusion on Historic England's Register of Historic Parks and Gardens, under the criteria currently applied, although *Played in Britain* will continue to argue otherwise.

The Scottish Game

A definitive book on the Scottish contribution to the development of flat green bowls, and on Scotland's large concentration of historic private clubs, is long overdue.

On which note, Francis Drake, WG Grace and Tony Allcock; all are commemorated in one way or another. It is therefore time to give William Mitchell the recognition he most surely deserves.

Further research

The *Played in Britain* team has identified a number of gaps in bowls history that merit more detailed research. It would, for example, be helpful to find a source for that tantalising reference to the green at Painswick in 1554 (alluded to on page 76).

We should find out more about which other stately homes and great houses had bowling greens, and whether they have any plans or paintings as yet unidentified that reference bowling greens or pavilions. Based on what we have already discovered, such material must surely exist.

More research needs to be undertaken on pub greens, both past and present. As has been noted, only one pub green survives in London, one in Cornwall and one in the whole of Wales.

Ideally a national inventory would enable us to take stock and to identify pub greens whose protection should be prioritised. At the very least, East Anglia, once well blessed with pub greens, should be targeted for a pilot study.

Also of value would be professional analysis of the many vintage woods and jacks scattered around various clubs and museums. These sundry items need to be measured, weighed and compared and, if possible, subject to testing, dendrochronological or otherwise.

Some of these items, in one part of the country, appear to match those in another. Some are possibly not designed for bowls but for skittles or other games.

But until they are all properly assessed, we are none the wiser.

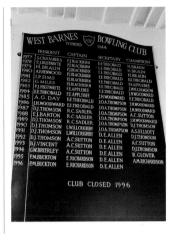

▲ Finally, on a sombre but practical note, what happens to the historic assets of a bowling club when it closes down?

All too often items are thrown onto bonfires or skips, snapped up by collectors, or stored away in former members' homes, to gather dust and be forgotten.

In the case of **West Barnes BC** in **New Malden**, **London**, formed in 1944, both the pavilion (now a children's nursery) and the green (a play area) survive, at the Sir Joseph Hood Memorial Playing Field. But of the club all that remains is this honours board, showing the club to have closed in 1996, before the identity of its last champion could be recorded.

Equally poignant is the story of **Christchurch BC** in **Dorset**. Formed in 1925, the club was based within the town's beautiful castle grounds on the banks of the River Avon.

The first blow came when the club lost most of its parking spaces to a housing development. That led to 40 members leaving. The remaining members were then asked by the council to contribute towards the costs of greenkeeping.

But as the standard of the green steadily deteriorated, so more bowlers left for other clubs, making the task of finding the required £9,000 a year even harder, until finally in 2013 the last 32 members called it quits.

Today, the club's classic colonial-style timber pavilion (*below*), extensively renovated as recently as 1988, lives on as a function suite for the neighbouring King's Arms hotel, with the bowling green forming a lawn in front. But the members are now all dispersed.

Such closures are desperately sad for all involved. They are even more regrettable when, as so often occurs, club records and artefacts are lost, destroyed or sold off in the process.

As noted opposite, they should always, as a matter of course, be handed over to libraries or county record offices, so that they can take their rightful place in the archives of their once host community.

But there is another reason for preserving materials. As the residents of Summerhill in Newcastle have shown, bowls clubs can rise again, particularly when, as at both West Barnes and Christchurch, the pavilions and greens remain.

The threads of history need not be lost. Should not be lost.

And just once in a while they are recovered. As happened in 2006 when an 84 year old member of the County Ground Bowling Club in Worcester was handed a black plastic bag by an anonymous donor.

In the sack were all the club records, going back to 1910.

In the *Worcester News* the 84 year old was described as being 'surprised and overjoyed'.

We prefer to say that he was 'bowled over'.

Links

Where no publisher listed assume self-published by club, organisation or author

Where no publication date listed assume published on final date within title, ie. 1860-1960 means published 1960

nd: no date

Websites – bowls

www.booksonbowls.co.uk
www.bowls.org (BCGBA)
www.bowlsclub.info
www.bowlsengland.com
www.bowlsscotland.com
www.disabilitybowlsengland.org.uk
www.eiba.co.uk
www.esmba.co.uk
www.fedbowls.co.uk
www.lscbowlers.co.uk
www.nationwidebowler.co.uk
www.pitchcare.com/magazine
www.scottish-bowling.co.uk
www.scottishbowls.co.uk
www.scotlawnbowls.com
www.talkingbowls.com
www.thesportofbowls.co.uk
www.vibowlsengland.org.uk
www.bwba.org.uk
www.welshbowlingassociation.co.uk
http://bowlsclub.org

General

Ayers ET *Bowls, Bowling Greens and Bowl Playing* Jarrold (1894)

Beauchampé S & Inglis S *Played in Birmingham* English Heritage (2006)

Bolsover G *Who's Who and Encyclopaedia of Bowls* Rowland (1959)

British Crown Green Bowling Association 1907-2007 BCGBA

Burrows G *All About Bowls* Hutchinson's Library of Sports and Pastimes (1915)

Collins T & Vamplew W *Mud, Sweat and Beers: A Cultural History of Sport and Alcohol* Berg (2002)

Cox R *Index to Sporting Manuscripts in the UK* British Society of Sports History (1995)

Daryl S *Routledge's Handbook of Quoits and Bowls* Routledge (1868)

Dickens C *Dictionary of London 1879* Howard Baker (1972)

Fisher J *World Bowls* The Normal Press (1956)

Hawkes K & Lindley G *Encyclopaedia of Bowls* Robert Hale (1974)

Haynes A *The Story of Bowls* Sporting Handbooks (1972)

Inglis S *Played in London* English Heritage (2014)

Inglis S *Played in Manchester* English Heritage (2004)

Linney E *A History of the Game of Bowls* TW Laurie (1933)

Manson J *The Complete Bowler* A&C Black (1912)

Mitchell W *Manual of Bowl Playing* Thomas Taylor (1864)

Physick R *Played in Liverpool* English Heritage (2007)

Pilley P (ed) *The Story of Bowls* Stanley Paul (1987)

Steadman C (ed) *Bowls Club Directory* PW Publishing (2001)

Strutt J *The Sports and Pastimes of the People of England* Methuen (1801)

Taylor A *Played at the Pub* English Heritage (2009)

Chapter 1. Bowls in Britain

Holme R *The Academy of Armory* (1683)

Recorde R *The Castle of Knowledge* (1556)

Chapter 2. Bowling greens

Evans RDC *Bowling Greens; their history, construction and maintenance* Sports Turf Research Institute (1992)

One Hundred Years: The Island Bohemian Bowling Club 1909-2009

Perris J (ed) *All About Bowls* Sports Turf Research Institute (2008)

Sorbiere S *A Voyage to England* Woodward (1709)

Museum in the Park, Stroud museuminthepark.org.uk

Chapter 3. Bowling clubs

Richardson BW *The Commonhealth: A Series of Essays on Health and Felicity, for Every-Day Readers* Longmans (1887)

'Stonehenge' *Manual of British Rural Sports* Routledge (1861)

Sudell R & Tennyson Waters D *Sports Buildings and Playing Fields* Batsford (1957)

Chapter 4. Medieval bowls, romance and bias

Inglis S *A Load of Old Balls* English Heritage (2005)

Mead WE (ed) *The Squire of Low Degree: A Middle English Metrical Romance* facsimile reprint Kessinger (2010)

Chapter 5. Tudors and Stuarts 1485–1688

Baddeley W St Claire *A Cotteswold Manor: Being a History of Painswick* Bellows/Kegan Paul (1907)

Baskerville T *Notes on Journeys in England* (c1680s)

Berkeley M *Old Worcestershire Inns* Worcestershire Archaeological Society Transactions (1924-5)

Brent C *Pre-Georgian Lewes c890-1714 – the emergence of a county town* Colin Brent Books (2004)

Breton N *The Court and Country* (1618)

Clancy J *The Story of Sittingbourne and Milton Regis* History Press (2003)

Cotton C *The Compleat Gamester* (1683)

Crowley R *Select Works 1559-1657*

Davies Rev JS *A History of Southampton* Gilbert & Co (1883)

Earle J *Microcosmographie* (1628)

Farrant JH *A Garden in a desert place and a palace among the ruins – Lewes Castle transformed 1600-1850* Sussex Archaeological Collections 134 (1996)

Gosson S *The School of Abuse* (1579)

Green R *The History, Topography and Antiquities of Framlingham and Saxted* Whittaker, Treacher & Co (1833)

Griffin R & Stephenson M *A Set of Elizabethan Heraldic Roundels in the British Museum* Archaeologia Vol 70 (1920)

Hall Rev G *History of Chesterfield* Whittaker & Co (1839)

Hawes R & Loder R *A History of Framlingham* (1798)

Head F & Holmes C (eds) *The Gentry in England and Wales 1500-1700* Sixteenth Century Journal Publishers (1996)

Hereford Bowling Club 1484-1984 HBC (1984)

Hyett FA *Glimpses of the History of Painswick*
British Publishing (1928)
Kent D *A History of Milton Regis Bowling Club 1540-1990*
Lee G *History of Ye Old Chesterfield Bowling Green*
Broad Oaks Press (1913)
Markham G *The English Huswife* (1615)
Newbury Bowling Club 1598-1998
Pepys S *Diaries 1660-1669*
Platt C *Medieval Southampton* Routledge Kegan Paul (1973)
Price J *An Historical Account of the City of Hereford* (1796)
Quarle F *Emblems, Divine and Moral* (1635)
Riden P (ed) *George Sitwell's letterbook 1662-66*
Derbyshire Record Society, No 10 (1985)
Shakespeare W *Complete Works 1589-1613*
The First 700 Years Southampton OBGC (1999)
The Game of Bowls at the Tilting Ground, Lewes LBGS (1986)
Vale M *The Gentleman's Recreations: Accomplishments
and Pastimes of the English Gentleman 1580-1630*
Rowman & Littlefield (1977)
Ward E *A Step to the Bath with a Character of the Place*
(1689)
Whitehead D *Hereford Bowling Green* Transactions of the
Woolhope Society Naturalists Field Club, Vol 41 (1973-75)
Williams G *A Dictionary of Sexual Language and Imagery in
Shakespearean and Stuart Literature* Athlone Press (1994)

Chapter 6. England 1688–1830
Abram WA *History of Blackburn* JG & J Toulmin (1877)
Addison J *Sphaeristerium, Poetical Works* (1698)
*A Guide to the History of the Ancient Tamworth Castle
Bowling Green and Club* (nd)
Atkyns R *The Ancient and Present State of Gloucestershire*
Bowyer (1712)
Bedale Bowling Green Society 1792-1992
Blackmantle B *The English Spy* Sherwood, Jones & Co (1825)
Brent C *Georgian Lewes* Colin Brent Books (1993)
Britannia Illustrata D Mortier (1707)
Cary J *New and Correct English Atlas* (1787)
Clark P *British Clubs and Societies 1580-1800* Oxford
Studies in Local History (2000)
Dezallier d'Argenville A, trans. James J *Theory and Practice of
Gardening* (1712)
Egan P, Stenson M & Theobald P *Part 1: The Bishop's Castle
Bowling Society* SW Shropshire Historical & Archaeological
Society, No 20 (2009); *Part 2: The Bishop's Castle Bowling
Society* No 21 (2010)
Fairfax T *The Complete Sportsman* J Cooke (1760)
Highways and Byways of Barnes Barnes & Mortlake Historical
Society (1992)
McKay J *A Journey through England* John Hooke &
T Caldecott (1714)

Martin B *Natural History of England* Owen (1759)
*Moll's A Compleat System of Geography, Ancient and
Modern (1711-1717)*
Nurcombe VJ *Croydon Bowling Club 1749-1999*
Schattner A *For the Recreation of Gentlemen and other Fit
Persons of the Better Sort, Tennis Courts and Bowling
Greens as Early Leisure Venues in 16th to 18th Century
London and Bath* Sport in History, Routledge (2014)
Somervile W *Hobbinol, Field Sports and the Bowling Green*
Ackermann (1813)
Swete J *Picturesque Sketches of Devon* (1792-1801)
Switzer S *Ichnographica Rustica* D Browne (1718)

Chapter 7. Scotland to 1892
Abercorn Bowling Club 1860-2010
Burnett J *Riot, Revelry and Rout: Sport in Lowland Scotland
before 1860* Tuckwell Press (2000)
Dalkeith Bowling Club 1857-2007
Dingley HJ *Touchers and Rubs* Thomas Taylor (1893)
Haynes N *Scotland's Sporting Buildings* Historic Scotland
(2014)
Houston DM *A Short History of Ardrossan Bowling Club
1842-1992*
McKay A *The History of Kilmarnock* (1858)
McLellan D *Glasgow Public Parks* John Smith & Sons (1894)
O'Brien G *Played in Glasgow* Malavan Media (2010)
Pococke R *Tours in Scotland, 1747, 1750, 1760*
Edinburgh University Press (1887)
Pretsell J *The Game of Bowls* Oliver & Boyd (1908)
Williamson E, Riches A & Higgs M *The Buildings of Scotland:
Glasgow* Penguin (1990)

Chapter 8. England and Wales 1830–1914
Anderson A *Bowls in Sunderland* Black Cat (2003)
Childs J *A Short History of the Mackintosh Estate, Roath*
Jeff Childs (2005)
Cooper C, Hewitt M & Horden W *A History of Cannock
Bowling Green* (2003)
Eeles F *Bowling Down the Years: History of the Portsmouth &
District Bowling Association* Woodfield (2000)
Howes D *The Presidents of Chesterfield Bowling Club
1852-1952* (2008)
Keswick Fitz Park Bowling Club 1882-2007
Leeworthy D *Fields of Play – the Sporting Heritage of Wales*
Royal Commission on the Ancient and Historical
Monuments of Wales (2012)
Mawson T *Civic Art: Studies in Town Planning, Parks,
Boulevards and Open Spaces* Batsford (1911)
Mawson T *The Art and Craft of Garden Making* Batsford (1912)
Pearson L *Played in Tyne and Wear* English Heritage (2010)
Platt J *Fifty Odd Years on the Bowling Green*

Websites – heritage
www.british-history.ac.uk
www.c20society.org.uk
www.cadw.wales.gov.uk
www.english-heritage.org.uk
www.historicengland.org.uk
www.historic-scotland.gov.uk
www.playedinbritain.co.uk
www.rcahms.gov.uk
www.savebritainsheritage.org
www.victorian-society.org.uk
http://canmore.org.uk
http://list.historicengland.org.uk

Websites – general
www.activeplaces.com
www.architecture.com
www.britishnewspaperarchive.co.uk
www.johnspeedmaps.co.uk
www.nls.uk/maps
www.old-maps.co.uk
www.oxforddnb.com
www.parksandgardens.org
www.publicpleasuregarden.blogspot.com
www.riba.org
www.scottisharchitects.org.uk
www.sportengland.org
www.sportinhistory.org (BSSH)
www.sports-council-wales.org.uk
www.sportscotland.org.uk
www.wellcomecollection.org
www.wikipedia.org
http://pubshistory.com
https://earth.google.co.uk

Gazette and Herald, Blackpool (1937)

Shaw S *History & Antiquities of Staffordshire* (1801)

Swain P *Bolton Against All England for a Cool Hundred: Crown Green Bowls in South Lancashire, 1787-1914* Sport in History, vol 33, no 2 (June 2013)

Walton WA et al *North London Bowling Club One Hundred Years 1891-1991*

Ward A *Bowling Legends* Alan Ward (2012)

Waymark J *Thomas Mawson: Life, Gardens and Landscapes* Frances Lincoln (2009)

Chapter 9. Britain 1918–1939

Busson C *Book of Ramsgate* Barracuda Books (1985)

Hunt J *A City Under the Influence – The Story of Half a Century of State Pubs* Lakescene (1971)

Macfarlane D *Crown Green Bowling on the Island from 1892 to 2000* Isle of Man CGBA (2001)

Seabury O *The Carlisle State Management Scheme: its Ethos and Architecture* Bookcase (2007)

Chapter 10. Indoor bowling

90 Years of Indoor Bowling at Crystal Palace IBC (1995)

Crystal Palace Indoor Bowling Club 1905-2005

Harper-Scott S *Cambridge & County – the end to the Cunliffe Foster Era* (2003)

Harper-Scott S *Cambridge & County – the early years* (2004)

Hotchkiss F *The Art of Bowls* Heinemann (1937)

Rigby T *The Paddington Sports Club Centenary* (2005)

Todd T *Carpet Bowling* (1950)

Chapter 11. Britain 1945–1990

Allan G *Tournament Summer – Seaside Bowls and Bowlers* The Alpha Press (2001)

Clevedon Bowling Club One Hundred Years of Bowls 1910-2010

Hedgcock M (ed) *Hand in Hand: Watney's Mortlake World* Barnes & Mortlake History Society (2007)

Hornby H *Bowling for a Living: A Century on the Panel* Sport in Manchester, Manchester Region History Review, vol 20 (2009)

Howarth G, Lyons D (ed) *Memoirs* unpublished (2003)

Polley M *The British Olympics* English Heritage (2011)

Vose J *Corner to Corner and Over the Crown* Strule Press (1969)

Wentworth Day, J *Inns of Sport* Whitbread Brewery/Naldrett Press (1949)

Chapter 12. Bowls today

Bowling along for 100 years: the story of Royal Leamington Spa Bowling Club 1909-2009

Bowls England Yearbook Bowls England (2014)

Callister S *The Old Bowling Green, Brook Street, Chester – a Case for Conservation* unpublished notes (c.1999)

National Planning Policy Framework Department for Communities and Local Government (2012)

Our Sporting Life exhibition, Tyne & Wear Museums (2011)

http://locality.org.uk

www.glasgow2014.com

www.glasgowlife.org.uk

Chapter 13. Conclusions

Hewitt I & Lloyd S *Immortals of British Sport - a celebration of Britain's sporting history through sculpture* (2013)

Wordsworth N *Many Pleasant Hours - A History of the Victoria Bowling Club 1865-1996*

www.cascinfo.co.uk

Reports

Active People surveys, Sport England (2015 and previous)

McLellan D *Report by Superintendent of Parks as to the Provision made for bowling greens in Parks in Towns in England and Scotland* Glasgow Council (1892)

Pettigrew W *Municipal Parks: Layout, Management and Administration* Journal of Park Administration (1937)

Provision for Sport The Sports Council (1971)

Review of Parks Outdoor Bowling Provision in Leeds Leeds City Council (2013)

Newspapers, magazines and journals

Aberdeen Journal; Ayr Advertiser; Banbury Guardian; Bell's Life; Birmingham Gazette; Birmingham Journal; Blackburn Standard; Bowlers World; Bowling World; Bowls International; Caledonian Mercury; Cannock Advertiser; Carlisle Journal; Chester Courant; Chesterfield Gazette; Cornishman; Country Life; Cumberland News; Daily Record; Derby Mercury; Derbyshire Times & Chesterfield Herald; Darlington & Stockton Times; Dundee Courier; East Kent Gazette; Edinburgh Evening News; Falkirk Herald; The Field; Framlingham Weekly News; The Gentlemen's Magazine; Glasgow Herald; The Guardian; Hampshire Chronicle; Hampshire Courier; Hastings & St Leonards Observer; Hereford Journal; Ipswich Journal; Kentish Gazette; Lancashire Evening Post; Lancaster Gazette; Licensing World; Liverpool Mercury; Morning Advertiser; Newcastle Courant; Norfolk Chronicle; Nottingham Journal; Nottinghamshire Guardian; Pall Mall Gazette; Portsmouth Evening News; Reading Mercury; Richmond & Twickenham Times; Southampton Daily Echo; Southampton & Hampshire Observer; Sporting Chronicle; Sports Argus; Stamford Mercury; Sunderland Daily Echo & Shipping Gazette; Sussex Agricultural Express; Taunton Courier; The Scotsman; The Times (and Times digital archive); Western Daily Mercury; Western Morning News; Worcester Herald; Worcester News; World Bowls

The series
Played in Britain 2004–15

Played in Manchester
Simon Inglis (2004)

Played in Birmingham
Steve Beauchampé and
Simon Inglis (2006)

Played in Liverpool
Ray Physick (2007)

Played in Tyne and Wear
Lynn Pearson (2010)

Played in London
Simon Inglis (2014)

Played in Glasgow
Ged O'Brien (2010)

Engineering Archie
Simon Inglis (2005)

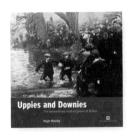

Uppies and Downies
Hugh Hornby (2008)

Played at the Pub
Arthur Taylor (2009)

A Load of Old Balls
Simon Inglis (2005)

Liquid Assets
Janet Smith (2005)

Great Lengths
Dr Ian Gordon and
Simon Inglis (2009)

The British Olympics
Martin Polley (2011)

Bowled Over
Hugh Hornby (2015)

www.playedinbritain.co.uk

Credits

Photographs and images

Please note that where more than one photograph appears on a page, each photograph is identified by a letter, starting with 'a' in the top left hand corner of the page, or at the top, and continuing thereafter in a *clockwise* direction

All Historic England photographs listed are either © Historic England or © Crown Copyright, Historic England. Application for the reproduction of these images should be made to the Historic England Archive, The Engine House, Fire Fly Avenue, Swindon SH2 2EH

Ordnance Survey data: contemporary maps © Crown Copyright and database right (2015); archive maps © and database right Crown Copyright and Landmark Information Group Ltd (All rights reserved 2015)

All the badges featured on the inside jacket, front and back, are from the Eric Cook Collection and reproduced courtesy of Clevedon Bowling Club

Historic England Archive

Aerofilms Collection: 137; Alan Bull: 1, 33ab; Steve Cole: 34a, 59, 62ac, 63; Nigel Corrie: 74abc, 75d, 84a, 148a, 149a, 177bc, 187c; James O Davies: 93a; Damian Grady: 22d, 55a, 79a, 177a; Derek Kendall: 11a, 103ac; Patricia Payne: 84b; Bob Skingle: 199b, 209

Photographers

Simon Gill: 11c, 14b, 20b, 21b, 24c, 27a, 32eg, 34c, 35a, 37, 38ce, 41a, 42a, 64a, 65ab, 76ab, 77bc, 81abcd, 92ad, 93c, 96b, 97b, 123b, 124b, 125a, 166, 170, 181ab, 187ab, 208a, 214c, 220bc
Peter Holme: 2, 7, 13b, 15abc, 18ab, 23b, 25b, 26a, 30c, 32a, 47a, 64b, 88ab, 92bc, 98a, 99bcd, 129ab, 135ab, 138a, 139ab, 140, 142b, 143abc, 145ab, 146b, 147, 150a, 152a, 153ab, 154abd, 155abc, 158a, 159abcd, 169ab, 174a, 175a, 178, 179ab, 180ab, 183abc, 200a, 205b, 206, 212c, 216abd
Hugh Hornby: 10, 11b, 13ac, 21c, 27cd, 28a, 30b, 50b, 78ab, 79b, 93d, 110acd, 113c, 133a, 152b, 160b, 161abc, 171a, 175b, 194abc, 195d, 205a, 210bc, 211, 219a, 221b
Simon Inglis: back cover abcd, front flap, 16, 19a, 25a, 27b, 28b, 29, 30ad, 32bcdfhi, 35c, 36abc, 38bfg, 40b, 41cd, 42bcd, 48, 60a, 62b, 63b, 66a, 68abc, 69ab, 70a, 73ab, 74d, 83a, 93b, 94, 102, 103b, 105b, 113d, 116ac, 117de, 118e, 119a, 121, 125b, 133b, 146a, 149b, 154c, 164acd, 168abc, 171b, 173ac, 174b, 188b, 189c, 196c, 197bc, 200bc, 204abc, 208a, 215b, 218b, 219c, 221a, 232
Iona Shepherd: 26b, 31a, 34b, 41b, 105a, 107b, 110b, 112a, 113ab, 117ab, 189ab, 212a
Stuart Wallace: 12bc, 14a, 19b, 22a, 35b, 36d, 38ad, 39a, 111, 118abd, 119b

Steve Beauchampé: 95c, 173b, 214a; Garfield Bennett: 200d; Sally Chapple: 10; John Church: 202a; Steven Cole: 51; rosemarycripps.co.uk: 122; Colin Everett: 31c; Tony Hammond: 57a; Brian Hanchett: 219b; ©tonyhowell.co.uk: 88c; Jo Kibble: 202b; Sampson Lloyd: 218a; Malcolm MacCallum: 199a; Roger Matile: 14c; Eddie Melluish: 201ab; Ged O'Brien: 118c; Lynn Pearson: 120a; Richard Perry: 31b; Martin Polley: 24a, 47b; John Sanders: 70b, 75a, 220a; Bob Saunders: 210a; Patricia Theobald: 100a; Neil Tough: 116d; Jay Watson: 82ab; Reed Ingram Weir: 207; David Whyte: 186a; Jonty Wilde: 212b; Arnie Withers: 193d; Jason Wood: 167d

Geoff Barnett archive

12a, 20a, 52, 72b, 104a, 109, 114ab, 115ab, 126a, 127b, 130b, 131b, 138b, 164b, 165abc, 186bc, 188a, 190a

Archives, agencies, collections and clubs

©Christopher Barnes/Alamy: 95b; ©Andrew Fox/Alamy: 24c; ©David Lyons/Alamy: 133c; TR Annan & Sons: 17b; Bob Croxford/Atmosphere Picture Agency: 49b; Bath in Time: 54; Berkeley Castle Charitable Trust: 56a; Blackburn Central Library/cottontown.org: 141, 142a; The Bodleian Libraries, University of Oxford (MS BODL, 264, folio 63): 45; Bowls England archive: 184b; Brent Archives: 128c; Bridgeman Images: 86b, 87c; Yale Center for British Art, Paul Mellon Collection, USA/Bridgeman Images: 89a; Private Collection/The Stapleton Collection/Bridgeman Images: 90; ©British Library Board: 91(J/11631.h.17), 127a; ©Trustees of the British Museum: 86a; Buckinghamshire County Museum Collections: 6; Cambridge University Library: 71; ©Devonshire Collection, Chatsworth, by permission of Chatsworth Settlement Trustees: 87b; Chesterfield BC: 67; Clackmannanshire Council/Alloa Library Archives: 172ab; Clevedon BC/David Bryant Collection: 192a, 196a, 197a; Colorsport: 136a; ©Country Life: 55b, 56c; Crystal Palace IBC: 184a; Daily Herald Archive/National Media Museum/Science & Society Picture Library: 198b; Ray Farlow: 99a; ©Andy Gammon: 58a; Getty Images: front cover, 130a; Great Torrington BC: 43, 96a, 97a, 201c; Steve Grudgings: 136b; Hawick BC: 108b; Murray Hedgcock: 196b; Hereford Local Studies Library: 83b; Michael Hewitt & Gerry Hindley: 144b; Hugh Hornby: 162ab, 191ab; Hull & East Riding Museum, Hull Museums: 46a; Simon Inglis: 190b; Kirkcudbright BC: 112b; Landmark Information Group Ltd: 98b, 144a; The Landmark Trust: 57b; Look and Learn: 56b; Don Lyons: 195ab; Mary Evans Picture Library: 126b, 163; Mary Evans Picture Library/Douglas McCarthy: 50a; Milton Regis BC: 80ab; Mirrorpix: 185b; The Mitchell Library: 108c; Mitre BC: 203; ©Museum of London: 134; ©National Library of Scotland: 104b, 106b; ©National Museums Scotland: 107a; ©National Trust Images/David Hunter: 89b; Newbury BC: 39b; Newmarket Avenue BC: 167abc; Norfolk BC: 182ab; North London BC: 124a, 148b; North Yorkshire County Record Office (ZTG 7/1): 40a; Paddington SC: 176b; Painswick Falcon BC: 77a; Lynn Pearson: 128a; Plymouth City Council, Library Services: 49a; Robert Pool: 117c; Potters Resort: 216c; Press Association Images: 4, 176a, 214b, 217; Raccoon

Galleries: 215a; Railway Club, Bolton: 157; © RCAHMS (Aerial Photography Collection). Licensor www.rcahms.gov.uk: 116b; Rex Features: 198a; RIBA Library Books & Periodicals Collection: 87a, 132; Southampton Old BGC: 44a, 72a, 75bc; Staffordshire Museum Service: 131a; John Muir Wood, A Game of Bowls/Scottish National Portrait Gallery: 108a; University of Strathclyde. Licensor www.scran.ac.uk: 106a; Summerhill BC: 123a; by permission of Surrey History Centre: 95a; Sussex Past: 58b; Waterloo Hotel Archive: 8, 151b, 195c; ©webbaviation.co.uk: 61, 100b; Wellcome Library, London: 193ac; West Glamorgan Archive Service: 128b; Yale Center for British Art, Paul Mellon Collection: 85

Printed sources

Anderson A *Bowls in Sunderland* Black Cat (2003): 185a; Bolsover GR *Who's Who & Encyclopedia of Bowls* Rowland (1959): 193b; Hall Rev G *The History of Chesterfield* Whittaker & Co (1839): 66b; Perris J (ed) *All About Bowls* Sports Turf Research Institute (2008): 17a; Strutt J *The Sports and Pastimes of the People of England* Methuen (1801): 44b; Sudell R & Tennyson Waters D *Sports Buildings and Playing Fields* Batsford (1957): 21a; Ward A *Bowling Legends* (2012): 150b, 151a, 156a, 158b; Wentworth Day J *Inns of Sport* Whitbread & Co (1949) image ©Bernard Venables: 192b (with permission of Eileen Venables)

Acknowledgements

In common with all the books in the Played in Britain series, *Bowled Over* owes much to the efforts and dedication of Simon Inglis and Jackie Spreckley.

Played in Britain is grateful for the support received from English Heritage (now Historic England), especially John Hudson, Clare Blick, Barney Sloane, Tim Cromack and Allan Brodie, and for the generous sponsorship received from NFU Mutual, with thanks to Susan Barley in particular.

The author wishes also to thank all the Played in Britain team, notably Steve Beauchampé, Ged O'Brien, Doug Cheeseman, Peter Holme, Lynn Pearson and Martin Polley.

Bowled Over has proved to be a mammoth undertaking and the author wishes to thank the many hundreds of bowlers and bowls officials who, over the past decade, have proved every bit as friendly and helpful as one would expect from this most civilised of games.

Of particular value have been the knowledge and support of Geoff Barnett, David Brailsford, Roger 'Sam' Bunton (Norfolk), John Chaplin (Lewes), Don Lyons (Isle of Man and Panel), Stuart Marshall, Phil Martin, Gerry McCready (William Mitchell and Kilmarnock), Gerald Merry (Chester), Graeme Moir and Peter Swain.

Others who have helped in various ways include Gordon Anderson (Mitchell Library), Mark Bath (Wainwrights of Southampton), Phil Brown, Peter Chalk, Peter Clare (EA Clare Ltd), Dave Clarkson, Albert Clayton, Barry Cotterell, Robert Crawshaw (Premier Bowls), John Crowther (BCGBA), Steve Davies, Mel Evans, Alan Fidler, Adrian Garside, John Ingleby, Malcolm MacCallum, Neil McDade (Thomas Taylor), Chris Metcalfe, Grant Sandilands, 'Charlie' Tattersall, Len Williamson, Matt Wordingham (Bowls England) and Tracy Wraight.

Thanks also go to: Nigel Russell (Abbey); George Barr (Alloa); Lyn Pengelly (Alverstoke); David Houston (Ardrossan); Gordon Neil (Ayr Indoor); Julie Colligan (Balornock); Brian Little (Banbury Chestnuts); Terry Humphrey (Barnes); David Smith (Berkeley Castle); Jane & Phil Saunders (Bewdley); Maurice Phillips, Patricia Theobald (Bishop's Castle); Ray Smith (Blackburn Subs); Chris Allason, John Anderson (Brampton); Colin Cooper, Mike Hewitt, Gerry Hindley (Cannock); Ray Moore (Carlisle Subs); Stan Smart, Martin Thacker, David Meakin (Chesterfield); Mary Poore (Christchurch), David Bryant, Pete Cornish, Vernon Perry (Clevedon); Maurice Young (Clun); Alan Porter (Cockermouth Castle); Debbie & Gary Wilson (Costessey); John Barnes (Crystal Palace Indoor); Bill Murphy (Dalkeith); Brian Taylor, Steve Sallnow (Dover); John Dickenson, David Cole (EBF); Bill Beveridge, John Kennerley (Ellesmere); Terry Gilder, Brian Stannard (Framlingham); Peter Dutton, Shirley Hughes (Gate Hangs High); Colin Everett, Alistair Scobie (Girvan); James Pratt, Ossie Ward (Gt Torrington); Mary Alexander (Guildford); Mike Woodman (Hadleigh); Mike Lovatt (Hadley Heath); Jonathan Thompson (Hartwell House); Robert Lyall (Hawick); Keith Taylor (Hillsborough Park); Len Hillier (Island Bohemian); Doug Macfarlane, Arnie Withers (Isle of Man); Derryck Corrighan, Vic Emmerson (Keswick); Bev Pritchard (King George V); Nigel Hind (Knott End Working Men's Club); Dennis Blair (Langdale); Colin Brent, John Farrant, Andy Gammon (Lewes); Maria-Louisa Raeburn (Maulds Meaburn); Peter Luckhurst (Milton Regis); John Ottaway (Norfolk EBA); David Blaxter, Brian Waring (Mitre); Rod Collins (Newbury); Peter Chapman, Brenda Whitehead (Norfolk); Tony Kerpel (North London); Roy Sanderson (Oakworth); David Bishop, Chris Clouting (Painswick Falcon); Harry Martin (Panel); Joe Barlow (Raikes Hotel); Janet & John Allen, Vic Waite (Reading); Richard Ashley (Royal Leamington Spa); John Kenyon (St Werburgh); Jim Scott (Sanquhar); John Sanders (Southampton); David Arnold (Spen Victoria); Steve Evans (Stile Inn); Shirley Lazarus (Temple Fortune); George James (Victoria, Norwich); Mark Audin, Alan Ward (Waterloo); Kevin McKay (Willowbank).

Finally, heartfelt thanks go to the countless librarians and archivists in so many of the national libraries, local studies libraries, county record offices, school libraries and local history societies across Britain, far too many to mention but all so obliging, friendly and knowledgeable. This book would not have been possible without them.

Index

▲ Viewed from the ruins of Clun Castle in Shropshire in June 2007, members of **Clun Bowling Club** step out onto their green, on what was once the castle's eastern bailey.

Since starting the research for this book in 2005, between myself, editor Simon Inglis and other members of the *Played in Britain* team, we have visited almost one thousand bowling clubs in every corner of the nation. Rarely have we wanted for tea or biscuits, beer or bonhomie. When you are at a bowling green, with turf under your feet and a jack in your sights, somehow the world seems a better place. Always we left with a smile.

'In order to form a just estimation of the character of any particular people...' wrote Joseph Strutt in 1801, it is 'necessary to investigate the sports and pastimes most generally prevalent among them'.

At the end of our journey, and looking down on this timeless scene, I can think of no better sport than bowls on which to base such an estimation.

There are over 7,460 bowling clubs in Britain today. This book is dedicated to them.

Hugh Hornby July 2015